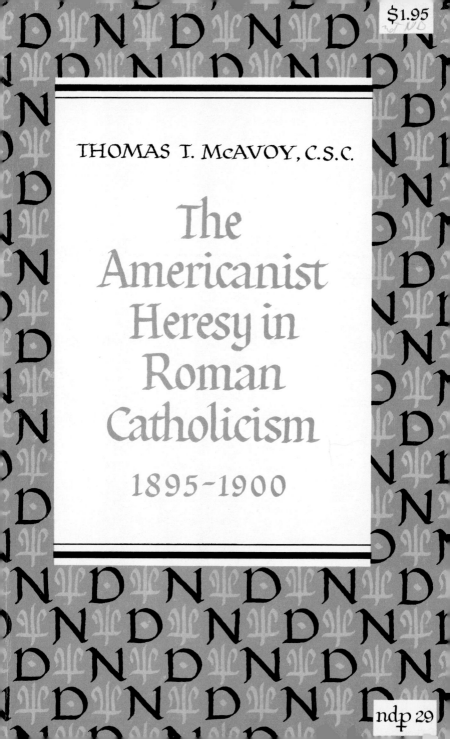

THOMAS T. McAVOY, C.S.C.

The Americanist Heresy in Roman Catholicism

1895-1900

ndp 29

The
Americanist Heresy
in
Roman Catholicism
1895-1900

The
Americanist Heresy
in
Roman Catholicism
1895-1900

1344

By

THOMAS T. McAVOY, C.S.C.

UNIVERSITY OF NOTRE DAME PRESS

1963

Nihil Obstat
Charles J. Corcoran, C.S.C.
Censor Deputatus

Imprimi Potest
Theodore Mehling, C.S.C.
Provincial

Imprimatur
Leo A. Pursley, D.D.
*Bishop of the
Diocese of Fort Wayne*

September 21, 1955

First Paperback Edition

First published in 1957 under the title, *The Great Crisis in American Catholic
History, 1895-1900,* by Henry Regnery Company, Chicago, Illinois

Manufactured in the United States of America

Table of Contents

Preface

To SPEAK of the controversy over the heresy of Americanism to the ordinary student of American history would not elicit much more than curiosity about the existence of such a heresy. Likewise to speak of a crisis in American Catholicism probably would produce expressions of incredulity, because the ordinary student of American history has come to regard the Catholic Church in the United States as a perfect organization in which all differences are minor and quickly settled. Even Catholic historians themselves, with their predominant interest in the growth of the Church organization in this country, especially in the lives of bishops, the increase in the number of churches and schools, and in the expansion of clerical and religious institutions, show little awareness of any real controversy within the Catholic ranks. Yet the descriptive phrase "The crisis of American Catholicism" was given to the controversy by a European observer who was at the same time an active partaker in the controversy, Abbé Georges Périès, onetime professor of Canon Law at the Catholic University of America in Washington, and at the time of his observation an active contributor to the French conservative Catholic newspaper *La Vérité*. He was personally aware of the critical nature of the differences then existing within the American hierarchy.

There are several reasons for the lack of writing on Catholic "Americanism." One easiest to understand is the desire of American Catholics generally to forget that the word "Americanism" was used in a deprecatory sense by the Pope. A second reason that held true for over a generation was that the participants in the controversy lived on for nearly three decades after the condemnation, and any discussion was likely to open old wounds or even renew the controversy. More important, however, was the fact that the Americanist controversy had been accidentally involved in racial and nationalistic feelings which, in an organization so conspicuously made up of newly arrived immigrants as the Catholic Church in the United States before World War I, could be quickly aroused to burning heat.

Another factor in the silence of American Catholic historians on the question was the condemnation of Modernism which followed within a decade after the papal intervention in the conflict and which caused a self-imposed suppression of theological discussion in American Catholic publications. The effects of the Modernistic controversy within the United States have not been estimated—and the history of that episode will be difficult to write—because most of the discussions were oral and were mostly in the formative stage when the encyclical *Pascendi Gregis* cast a paralyzing spell on American Catholic theological discussion. One might say that the late increase in theological activity of Catholicism in the United States was almost a new creation fostered by the wartime needs of Catholics in World War I; and that these new theological studies—with the exception of the studies in canon law—were mostly social and historical, with very little strictly dogmatic discussion. The new developments of Catholic historical study under Monsignor Peter Guilday stayed safely away from recent history. Consequently, when I began my exploration of the Americanist question, I received warnings from older men who remembered the bitterness of that age, that I might get into trouble; and from younger historians, that I would not be able to avoid renewing the controversy. I believe both predictions were erroneous. I am happy to say that in my investigations, with a few minor exceptions, I have received cooperation on all sides; so much so that my indebtedness to my fellow historians, to fellow archivists, and to librarians, as well as to other interested persons almost defies enumeration.

It is with regret that I mention the death on December 31, 1953, of Abbé Félix Klein with whom I had the privilege of discussing in 1951 the controversy in which he played an important part fifty-five years ago. I have had access, moreover, to what he saved of the papers dealing with the French phase of the battle. On the American phase, the papers of the late Bishop Denis

O'Connell, of Richmond, Virginia, discovered by Father John Tracy Ellis and made available to me by His Excellency Bishop Peter L. Ireton, and the papers of Archbishop John Ireland, preserved through the care of Monsignor Humphrey Moynihan and made available through his brother, Monsignor James Moynihan, the biographer of the Archbishop, were irreplaceable as source materials. The archives of the Cathedral of Baltimore, of the Archdiocese of New York, of the Diocese of Rochester, of the Diocese of Covington, of the Catholic University of America, and of the Paulist Fathers of New York have made the American phase of the controversy fairly decipherable. The great handicap to a complete story is the restriction on the use of the Roman Archives; but even this was minimized at the time by the consultation of the unpublished manuscript and especially the personal notes of Count Eduardo Soderini, which he had prepared on the Church in the United States in the pontificate of Pope Leo XIII, and in which he had consulted and copied letters dealing with the controversy in the Roman Archives of the day.

Aside from the official documents, the most important sources on the controversy were the organs of the Catholic and secular press in which so much of the public discussion was conducted. The collection of newspapers and clippings on the European controversy saved by Abbé Klein were indispensable. For the American side of the controversy, besides some Catholic newspapers in the University Library at Notre Dame, the great source of information is the invaluable collection of Catholic newspapers of the American Catholic Historical Society of Philadelphia, housed at Saint Charles Seminary at Overbrook. The secular newspapers are preserved in the public libraries of the cities in which they were published.

Perhaps it is important to state first what the crisis was about. Anyone familiar with the history of the Catholic Church in the United States during the last decade of the nineteenth century knows that there was serious friction between the Irish and the German bishops, and that there was a keen rivalry between Archbishop Michael Corrigan of New York and Archbishop John Ireland of Saint Paul to be the next cardinal from the United

States; but the decision in neither of these controversies could be called critical to the fate of the Catholic minority in the United States. Likewise there was a bitter controversy in France over the acceptance or rejection of the *ralliement*, the papal call for participation in the Republique Française, but that was not resolved in the Americanist controversy. The critical problem of the Catholic Church in the United States at the turn of the century was the extent of the adaptation of Catholic practices to the American milieu. Those favoring the adaptation were the Americanists—the Americanizing prelates, whether they were of American, Irish, French, or German birth. Those opposed felt that these adaptations were heretical. Whether that heresy was the condemned Catholic Liberalism of the *Syllabus of Errors*, or a new departure in radical criticisms later to be called Modernism, did not greatly matter to the conservative members of the hierarchy, clergy, and laity. These conservatives in many cases were foreign-born, but the essential battle was theological and cultural, not racial. That these distinctions were clearly seen at the time by many of the controversialists is apparently not so, because the earlier controversies over the rights of foreign languages in churches, over the parochial schools, and over Catholic membership in certain secret societies were dragged into the battle when occasion offered.

The greatness of the crisis does not stand out as clearly as that in the rites controversy in China during the seventeenth and eighteenth centuries, in which the perennial problem of East and West was involved. The Americanist affair concerned only Western culture. The differences were basically between democracy and monarchism—between the Catholic leaders of the young pragmatic United States, which was dominantly Protestant, and the churchmen of the old Catholic countries of southern Europe, who regarded republican governments as opposed to religion. On both sides of the ocean the issue was one of compromise and cooperation with political forces outside the Church. Furthermore, the importance of the controversy was dimmed for historians by the fact that the Apostolic Letter which ended the controversy did not award the victory either to the conservatives as in the Chinese rites controversy, or to those who advised adaptation to the American scene. The papal letter merely stopped the public discussion and allowed the forces in the controversy to work out quietly a series of practical solutions, some of which were unsatisfactory to the leaders of the controversy.

The purpose of this study is to tell as fully as space permits the story of this bitter battle as it arose and was fought. With the softening of the feelings between conflicting groups new studies have appeared, but none that has attempted to say what this "Americanism" really was. The author, by examining more thoroughly the sources used in these studies, by closer attention to non-religious factors in the controversy, and by the discovery of new materials, feels that he has brought into causal relations the elements of the controversy and the factors that brought it about. He feels that the story needs to be told today to clarify a confused picture of the position of the Catholic Church in the United States—to explain how something called "Americanism" could be condemned. At the same time he feels that from the story of the controversy much can be learned about the later developments of the Catholic Church in the United States, and about its present problems, and some neglected solutions to them which could be applied today.

The
Americanist Heresy
in
Roman Catholicism
1895-1900

CHAPTER 1 ❧ *The Emergence of John Ireland*

As HAS BEEN noted most historians of the United States in dealing generally with the period after the Civil War and Reconstruction find their subject matters too diverse to be gathered into one picture. While this is probably merely the result of a lack of perspective which the passage of time will supply, the manifold developments of the country during the latter part of the nineteenth century almost defy a unified treatment. So also the history of the Catholic minority during the period lacks any important unity once one goes beyond the essential dogmatic and sacramental principles and the disciplinary decrees of the Third Plenary Council. As a result there has been a tendency among writers of the Catholic history of the period to abandon any national, or even cultural history of Catholics, and to prepare histories either of particular institutions or of dioceses.[1] Such historical writings are useful for the preservation of church statistics, but they do not explain the growth of the Church in any area, or its decline, or describe the real life of the Catholic people. Other historians trying to escape this problem have tended to write biographical studies,[2] chiefly of the bishops, endeavoring to make their subjects into heroic figures who carried in their wake the life and death of the church of the regions in which they

[1] Typical of these institutional histories are those of J. T. Ellis and his students on the Catholic University of America, A. J. Hope's on the University of Notre Dame, Raphael Hamilton's on Marquette University, Sister Rosalita's on the Sisters Servants of the Immaculate Heart and Gilbert J. Garraghan's on the Jesuits of the Middle West. Recent diocesan histories include Reardon on Saint Paul, George Paré on Detroit, Michael Hynes on Cleveland, John K. Sharp on Brooklyn, and R. H. Lord, John Sexton, and E. T. Harrington on Boston.

[2] The chief biographical studies are Zwierlein's studies of McQuaid and Corrigan, J. T. Ellis and Allen Will on Gibbons, James Moynihan on Ireland, Patrick H. Ahern on John J. Keane, and Harrita Fox on Peter E. Dietz. John A. Ryan's autobiography *Social Doctrine in Action* (New York, 1941) belongs in this group.

worked. Unfortunately only a few of the hierarchy of the Catholic Church in the United States have been of such a strong personality as to be able to transcend the minority character of the flocks and to have any notable influence in the country generally. The few who have, have been for the most part clergymen who have realized the minority character of their flock and at the same time were aware of the dominant economic, social and political factors of the period as they affected the lives of the people over whom they presided. In general it can be said that the minority character of the Church in the United States not only was in itself a great problem for the leaders of the Church but that the most important factors governing the growth of the Church were the economic, secular and political factors in the non-Catholic majority among whom they lived.

In the period following the Third Plenary Council historians of American life have recognized such factors as the last frontier, urbanization, the rise of organized labor, the rise of the large corporations, the impact of Darwinism, and the beginning of a definite class struggle for the control of America's immense wealth. In the Catholic minority all of these major problems of the United States during the final decades of the nineteenth century had their effect, but not necessarily in the same way they affected the majority. The Catholics were not evenly distributed throughout the country and did not have the same characteristics of the majority groups in the regions where they lived. For instance, the Catholic body besides being mostly in the lower classes of society was inequally composed of the two chief distinctive types of people: the natives, including the converts among the natives, who entered more easily into the ordinary life of the region in which they settled, and the more numerous immigrants and to a great extent their children, who had first to become Americanized before they were to be accepted as members of the American community. Even within this two-fold distinction there were variations. The Catholic immigrants and the children of immigrants who lived together in compact communities were the most numerous in the Catholic body generally. The social unity among these immigrants limited the effects of current American social forces on such Catholic neighborhoods even though it did not seriously affect their essential religious faith and practice. Looking over the most distinguishable phases of American social life during the period it is notable that Catholics were not dominant in any of them. There was really no Catholic urbanization[3] movement, no Catholic labor[4] movement, certainly no Catholic corporation group, only a mild Catholic reaction to Darwinism and even less of a class struggle between Catholics.[5] Because of the large percentage of newly arrived immigrants among them, the great problem that cut across all other movements was Americanization and its accompanying problems, except in the later frontier regions of the Far West where the struggle for existence did not encourage foreign nationalism.

This "last" frontier, however, was in a sense a greater problem for the Church than for the country generally because while the American nation was multiplying its material wealth and resources for the conquest of the remaining West, the Catholic mission groups in contrast had scarcely the means or the missionaries to take care of the Church in the settled East and very little for the West. The bishops of the West had urged the calling of the Council because they wanted help in organizing the Church in their spacious but ill-supplied dioceses. The last western frontier had no great direct influence on the character of American Catholicism but the freedom of their western regions did allow for a stronger kind of Catholic leadership in some communities.

The 1880's can be considered the closing days of this last western frontier; this was to be officially announced during the following decade. Actually much of the frontier movement had ended before 1880, though smaller pioneer movements within the

---

[3] Aaron I. Abell is completing a study of the urban impact on Catholicism as a companion volume to his study of the *Urban Impact on American Protestantism, 1865-1900* (Cambridge, 1943). Some of his essays on this have appeared in the *Review of Politics*, VII, 464-495 and XI, 294-309.

[4] The chief study in this field is Henry J. Browne, *The Catholic Church and the Knights of Labor* (Washington, 1949). Cf. also Mary Harrita Fox, *Peter E. Dietz, Labor Priest* (Notre Dame, 1953).

[5] James V. Malin's efforts to estimate geopolitical theories as applied to the United States are worthy of study, especially *The Grasslands of North America* (Lawrence, Kansas, 1947).

country would continue even after the opening of the last Oklahoma regions in the second decade of the twentieth century. But the regions beyond Wisconsin and Iowa were still being filled by rail-borne immigrants from Scandinavia and by displaced "Yankees" from the East who had not yet learned that land in itself was not a source of wealth. The last mining frontiers were being opened and many an Irish name is found in the mining towns better known as scenes of bawdry and speculation. The Indian population in these western lands was being herded into reservations and placed under more honest supervision. Many a western town that had had hopes of being a metropolis began its gradual decline about this time. The meaning of this westward expansion was about to be considered and the spoils of its ruthless exploitation reckoned. Here again the Catholic history is only an accidental phase of the general story. Missionary bishops sent to organize the Church in these vast regions were trying to erect churches and to get priests to take care of the Catholic population, scattered in the mines or on the plains. Some bishops, such as Ireland and Spalding, were still trying to get Catholic slum dwellers to go into the newer dioceses of these western lands before it was too late. In some places along the railroads and in mining towns, there were enough Catholics to set up a church or a mission, but thousands who strayed too far from these communication centers became only nominal Catholics and lost the faith, unless they returned to the more urban centers in their later days. Few Catholics had the wealth to enter into the later phase of this western expansion, into large scale farming or mining. Some were able to maintain their farms, some stayed on to be workers in the mines for large corporations, some ran the stores in the villages; but in general the bishops who tried to tend these scattered flocks had insufficient priests and insufficient funds for churches to maintain the fervor of these wandering Catholics. The network of Catholic dioceses or vicariates spread over the region between the Missouri River and the Pacific Ocean, held together by scattered sees and more widely scattered missions cared for mostly by zealous but impoverished missionaries recruited from Europe. Catholicism did maintain proportionally its hold on the Catholics living in the midst of the mining regions, and the rugged careers of most of the western Catholics gave them a quality of leadership not found among many of the Catholic immigrants crowded in the slums of the eastern cities. Just as the later fight over the spoils of these western lands took place not in the mines but in the counting houses of the East, so also the more important struggles affecting the social and cultural progress of American Catholicism were taking place in the regions east of the Rockies. California was an exception to this trend, as it was an exception to most of the trends of the country. Catholics in California were important as long as the population remained chiefly pioneer, but as the transplanted "Yankee" from the Middle West began to move into Southern California that region became a new "Yankee" land and the Catholics became an unimportant minority.

Without subscribing entirely to the heartland argument of the geo-politicians one can maintain that culturally and socially the future of the American people in the later decades of the nineteenth century was to be the product of the great Mississippi Valley and its inhabitants. The more active Catholic bishops of the region tried to enable the Catholics of the area to obtain some share in this future, and it is significant that the outstanding Catholic leader of the hierarchy, Archbishop John Ireland, and the chief religious laymen of the period came from the Middle West. In 1881, the Middle West was already becoming financially tributary to New York, and the immigrant and urban trending population had made the eastern states most important in national politics; yet it can be said that that spirit which can be designated as most peculiarly American was being formed between the Appalachian Mountains and the Rockies. In the 1880's, this Middle West was the chief region of the small farm, of the small town, of the little red school house, the community churches, the country newspaper, and the scene of the first struggles of the poor boy who rose to wealth and influence. The Middle Westerner's school teachers, his doctors, his ministers, and lawyers came to a great extent from the East, and the literature upon which he formed the political and social ideas of his children likewise came from the

East. But despite this "Yankee" overcast the people of the Middle West were "on the march." They were religious people without either the dry theology or the dry decay of New England religion. Even the immigrants, whether Protestant—chiefly Lutheran—or Catholic, felt that religion was a sacred thing, a necessary element in an upright character. In this region there were occasional Catholic settlements, mainly German, but, for the most part, the Catholics—especially the Irishmen who moved about freely—erected their unpretentious brick church and went to Mass on Sunday. The Catholics did not get anywhere in politics, but they could buy small farms or could expect a general patronage if they opened stores; they could advance rapidly by zeal among the workers on the new railroads and in the new industries. Only the older, smaller Anglo-American Catholic group of families and some recent American converts could expect to have social equality or to advance readily in professional ranks. Socially speaking this was the age of the community fraternal society; and while Catholics knew they could not join Masonic societies, they were drawn toward the many other societies that provided the entertainment of the small communities where Catholics were not numerous enough to have their own parish social activities. The Middle Western bishops saw no harm in this, and the eventual prohibition of Catholic membership in these secret societies increased the social handicaps of Catholics in these communities. However, the chief cultural divisions between Catholic and Protestant, outside of some campaigns dominated by the A.P.A. or like agitators, were: in the Catholic's efforts to establish a parish school in which his children could receive instruction in religious truth, in his total abstinence from public interdenominational services, and in his occasional protest when the local public school became too Protestant for the Catholic children who had to attend it for want of a school of their own. The press of the region patiently tolerated the Catholics, admiring the industrious German Catholic farmer; but they regarded Irish Catholicism of the St. Patrick's Day parade as the chief example of Catholicism and told about Catholic public observances with the same misinformation they told about Oriental rites and ceremonies. The larger cities in the mill districts around the Great Lakes were really a part of the industrialized East and had many of the characteristics of it, since the later heavy Slavic immigrations of the region had not yet arrived and brought with them the problems of social reform. Nevertheless the railroads and the factories were attracting a type of worker—partly from the rural regions and partly from the immigrants—who resembled the inhabitant of the mill towns of the East. The larger cities of the Middle West were still rural metropolises, and there were many opportunities to advance in them because social classes were far from static. The bishops of the Middle West hampered by divisions arising from differing national origins and languages in these cities tried to build schools, perhaps a seminary and, if they had any extra priests, attempted to establish colleges. It was from these regions and from the towns and cities of the Middle West that the chief leadership of Catholics who entered into the realms of social and economic advancement was to come. In Middle Western America it was possible for a William J. Onahan of Chicago, a Henry Brownson of Detroit, a Peter L. Foy and Henry Spaunhorst of St. Louis, and others, to hope to achieve Catholic lay leadership and to receive the encouragement of such bishops as Ireland, Gilmour of Cleveland, Foley of Chicago, Kain of Wheeling, and Spalding of Peoria.

Despite the large number of Catholic immigrants into the Middle West, the numerical center of American Catholicism was in the eastern part of the United States. Eastern Catholicism formed a more or less inert mass, without notable leadership, without the financial means of moving or improving itself; and it was dominated by a continuing cultural and social non-Catholic majority that never intended to let go. Yet since American Catholicism of this period was judged chiefly in terms of Eastern Catholics, it is important to understand that they were in every way in a minority position at the end of the century. Religious leadership in the East was very weak, but insofar as it had expression in the press, in public celebrations, and in membership among the elite of the regions it was Protestant, with the Protestant Episcopalians, Presbyterians, and Congregationalists maintaining privileged positions contrasting with the large masses of Catholic immigrant workers in the large cities. Politically the region had been dominated by the Republicans, and only occasionally threatened since the Civil War by the minority Democrats, with whom the immigrant vote, especially Catholic, was identified. Socially and economically the "Yankee" hierarchy, noted by Henry Adams at the beginning of the century in New England, had been maintained with more or less success as those "Yankees" reached out into Wall Street and from New York into the industrial and mining regions of Pennsylvania and the Middle West. Even the railroads, with a few exceptions, by financial organization became the heritage of this same group.

Against such a background there were a few Catholics of prominence in these eastern States such as Charles Bonaparte, Alexander Herbermann, Andrew Shipman, Eugene Philbin, Hermann Ridder, and Thomas F. Ryan. Some families of wealth were accepted socially, but few Catholic bishops could meet the leaders of other religious groups on a social equality. Catholics generally were the hewers of wood and carriers of water, or whatever became the equivalent of that in the mills. They tended to join the Democratic party because that was the party of protest as well as the party most friendly to the immigrant. The type of Irish politician that achieved local leadership shed little lustre on his religious profession. Financially the Catholics had exchanged the peasantry of Europe for the status of the American laboring man. There were few farmers among the Irish Catholics because they associated farming with their peasantry and because they did not have the means to buy themselves a respectable farm. Because of their religious training and instruction Irish Catholic immigrants did not believe that the way to wealth or power was by revolution, but they soon felt the refreshing breath of American democratic movements and began to feel that they had rights to far more of this world's goods than they had. Along with other workers not of the Faith, they were ready to listen to the prophets of social reform who began to talk of new ways of getting out of the deserts and the wastelands of the panics of the 1870's and the 1880's. In so far as they had any religious self-consciousness, the

Catholic minority was made to feel that although the decrees of the Baltimore Council about infallibility and about ecclesiastical discipline were good and acceptable, these decrees were not the answer to the social and financial problems of the American Catholic in his new home. Even the Catholic school decreed by the Council, which Catholics wanted so much, would be impossible if the economic means to maintain it were denied. There was no defection in the faith of the Catholic worker when dominant problems were not religious dogmas, but the struggles for the means of making a living and the creation of his own future as an American citizen created a new problem for the Church. Frankly, unless the Catholic could join this struggle for existence as a Catholic there was danger that he would have to join it anyhow and perhaps without his religious faith. There were a few Catholic leaders who understood these problems; some of these clergymen and laymen were eloquent and literary. Among them might be mentioned: Terence V. Powderly of the Knights of Labor who later left the Church, Father Edward McGlynn, and Bishop John Lancaster Spalding of Peoria. Some were already beginning to seek solutions to these great problems in their own way, but not always with the blessings of their bishops. Some bishops were more anxious to maintain the Faith, even at the expense of the material welfare of their subjects, but other bishops not only saw no conflict but a glorification of both the Church and the future of the Catholic worker, if the Church would take the lead in the movement for improving the social welfare of the worker.

Unfortunately in the distress following the panics of the 1870's and the 1880's, the churches[6] were not very quick to take the lead in caring for the future worker, and if some Catholic bishops seemed more anxious than some other religious leaders to care for their own, their efforts were not sufficient to offset the lack of action on behalf of other bishops whose jurisdiction was over a Catholic population that was almost entirely made up of laborers. In the intellectual sphere of the eighties and nineties Catholics, having a religious faith dominated by intellectual ideas, tried to

[6] Abell, *op. cit.*, pp. 61-8, discusses the feelings of the labor leaders on this neglect by the churches.

do their share, but, lacking unified leadership and because of the poverty and the peasant backgrounds of so much of the Catholic population, they fell behind. In the new social and worker movements, the Catholics being mostly workers had to have a share or the Church would lose out entirely. There was some social welfare activity by Protestants among the worker class but not enough Protestant social reform to be of any great threat to the Catholic fidelity to the Church. The more important threat to the Catholic faith of the worker—aside from the accidental secret oaths of labor societies—was the appeal to violence by anarchistical elements and the newly arisen heresy of socialism.

As to the anarchical elements, although anarchists have always had a following in some of the nominally Catholic countries, American Catholicism has been relatively free of them. Among the Molly Maguires of the Pennsylvania coal mines, there was no doubt of the violence of the methods employed, but there is no clear proof of anarchical theory. Stern legal measures, backed by official Catholic disapproval of the Mollies, led to a sudden disappearance of this mysterious organization. Likewise the Fenian Movement, which was considered not so much anarchical as against the Church because of its oath, disappeared quickly once the condemnation of the Church was made clear. The Irish Land League was checked by the Church's stand on private property. Of the Carbonari, the number was never great in the United States, nor were they Catholic in anything but the country of their origin. Among the German Catholics, while socialism seems to have been a real threat among the German liberals who fled the new German government, most of the Catholic immigrants were farmers, and seemed to have brought with them an opposition to German Socialism. Even the German Catholics in such cities as Buffalo, Cincinnati, St. Louis, and Milwaukee did not manifest any great sympathy for socialism. American socialism was usually of a milder form than that of Europe and never had a very strong appeal to the worker in the United States while the country still had an expanding economy and possessed other remedies for its economic ills. The threat of socialism among the American workers was scarcely recognizable as such in the forms it took except by the conservative clergyman. There did develop in the German Catholic press in the United States a strange anomaly of admiration for the liberal programs of the German Center Party with an intense hatred of socialistic thought.[7]

When the Catholic worker in the mine, the factory, and the railroad began to feel the pressure of the industrial strife arising with the panics and depressions of the 1870's, he was naturally drawn to those organizations of his fellow workers which intended to defend his rights and to improve his economic standing. There were practically no Catholic workers' organizations, even where the Catholic population was concentrated; consequently Catholic workers tended to join organizations without religious affiliations just as they worked alongside other laborers of many religious affiliations. To the bishops and priests who were still building the churches or schools as best they could for these immigrant workers, these new labor organizations held a peril to the faith of the Catholic worker just as great as the public schools. There were generally three reasons for this fear. The first was the danger that an organization dominated by non-believers or Protestants, would tend to wean the Catholic worker from his faith. The second was the socialistic schemes proposed by some of these organizations. The third, which seems trivial in itself but which was the tool for accomplishing the other two evils in the eyes of the suspicious cleric, was the secrecy under oath which was notable in these societies, especially when these organizations had tried to copy the quasi-religious ceremonies and rituals of Masonic organizations. The problem became acute when the Knights of Labor, led by a Catholic, Terence V. Powderly, as Master General Workman, obtained a large Catholic membership and were challenged by some of the more conservative bishops.

Bishops McQuaid of Rochester, Gilmour of Cleveland, Chatard of Indianapolis,[8] and some others had pursued the Ancient Order of Hibernians as the real society of the Molly Maguires,

[7] This was quite noticeable in *The Review* published by Arthur Preuss in Chicago and later in St. Louis. Frederick Kenkel maintained to the author that the preservation of the German-American Catholics from socialism was a very important part of the activities of the American Central Verein.

[8] The correspondence of Bishop S. M. Chatard of Indianapolis, in the Archdiocesan Archives, contains much evidence of this fear. The decrees of the Second Plenary Council of Baltimore also warned against secret labor organiza-

and they were intolerant of all secret societies as breeders of anarchy, socialism and irreligion. They were impatient when the Council of Baltimore did not pronounce against all secret societies and were anxious to have the Council of Archbishops take such action. Nevertheless it is doubtful that the American Hierarchy would have ever taken any formal public action against labor organizations had not the Canadian Archbishop Cardinal Taschereau forced the issue by appealing to Rome for a decree making the Knights of Labor[9] come under the earlier Roman decrees against secret societies. The action of the Canadian Archbishop heartened the American opponents of the Knights. Luckily the Master General Workman, Terence V. Powderly, had taken away the secret oath which had been the most obvious obstacle to acceptance by Catholic authorities, and there was ground for evading the condemnation. The newly made Cardinal, Archbishop James Gibbons of Baltimore, as the primate and chief cleric of the Church in the United States, began at once to act to prevent a fateful Roman decision against the Knights. He took advantage of some indecisiveness about the answers the Canadian prelate had received from Rome and some contacts with Powderly through his suffragan, Bishop John J. Keane of Richmond, during the annual Assembly of the Knights in Richmond. Powderly visited Archbishop Gibbons in Baltimore on October 28, 1886, and Gibbons then obtained shortly after a vote of the majority of the archbishops against the condemnation of the Knights. He then pleaded with his fellow Cardinal, Henry Edward Manning of Westminster, England, to intercede for his petition in Rome. Going to Rome for the reception of his Cardinal's hat in 1887 and to take possession of his cardinalitial church he made a successful plea against the condemnation. In the formulation of the plea he had the assistance of Bishop John Ireland and Bishop John J. Keane who were in Rome on other business in connection with the Catholic University, and also of the rector of the North American College, Monsignor Denis O'Connell. These four prelates were to be joined in many another battle before the end of the century. The unintended publication of

[9] Henry J. Browne, *op. cit.*, pp. 203-15.

Gibbons' Roman plea in the *New York Herald* placed Cardinal Gibbons in the lead of Catholic friends of labor and saved the Church from any corporate loss of Catholic union workers. The Knights were not really approved by Rome and conservatives like Bishop McQuaid[10] tried to insist on a change in the Constitution of the Knights or the infliction of a papal condemnation. Gibbons and his co-workers, however, had saved the day and the decline of the Knights after the Haymarket Riots, which Gibbons had predicted to prevent the condemnation, removed the question from agitation. The action of Gibbons and Ireland in preventing the condemnation became famous throughout western Europe as the symbol of American Catholicism.

The threat of ideological socialism to the Catholic worker reached its peak in a rather confused story in New York, in which American politics, social reform, and personal ambitions are intertwined in such a way that no one has yet clearly related the story. There were few Catholic socialists in this country. Before Michael Augustine Corrigan had become Archbishop of New York in his own right, he had taken occasion to reprimand one of the most noted New York priests, Father Edward McGlynn,[11] for his political activities in favor of social reform. McGlynn, not an admirer of parochial schools, had been on the other hand a promoter of social reform, a fighter against poverty and suffering in the lower classes. He was an orator of considerable ability and had become a follower of the theories of Henry George who was regarded as a socialist by many. McGlynn had capable friends among the clergy of the New York area and in a test of popularity with his ecclesiastical superior would undoubtedly have won easily. But in his zeal to promote the cause of Henry George and in his refusal to accept what he considered an unfair limitation of his activities by Corrigan, he had spoken in a public political meeting contrary to the prohibition of Corrigan. He was suspended, and when he refused to go to Rome to report to the

[10] Cf. Zwierlein, Frederick J., *Life and Letters of Bishop McQuaid*, 3 vols., (Rome and Louvain, 1925-27) II, 436 ff.

[11] There is still no satisfactory history of the McGlynn episode. The most reliable source of information is still Zwierlein, *op. cit.*, III, 1-83, which is not very friendly to McGlynn.

Congregation of the Propaganda, was excommunicated. The resultant scandal split the faithful and the clergy in New York. But whatever may have been the justice of McGlynn's position in economic theory or the mistakes of his superior, his disobedience could not be supported even by his friends in the hierarchy. Henry George was defeated in his candidacy for mayor of New York and the importance of Father McGlynn declined. In 1893, Father McGlynn was reinstated by the new Apostolic Delegate on his open acceptance of the teachings of Pope Leo XIII, but he was appointed not to his old parish but to a suburban parish in the New York Archdiocese. Archbishop Corrigan, however, did not stop with this disavowal of heresy on the part of Father McGlynn. He insisted on a Roman condemnation of the teachings of Henry George. Cardinal Gibbons had refrained from taking any active part in the defense of Father McGlynn, although some other bishops, notably Bishop John Moore of St. Augustine, Florida, had helped the New York priest. But Gibbons without defending Georgism saw in the Roman condemnation of Henry George the same kind of restrictive action that he had been trying to prevent in the proposed condemnation of the Knights of Labor. Again he wrote to the Roman authorities and again he sought the intercession of his fellow prelate, Cardinal Manning.[12] But Corrigan, who had studied in Rome and had many friends in the Eternal City, was able to obtain a condemnation from the Cardinals on April 9, 1889. But through the intercession of Gibbons and Manning his victory was not complete. While the Roman Congregation ruled that the teachings of Henry George were to be condemned, they added to their condemnation that it was not to be proclaimed publicly, because, said the Cardinals, they were sure that the great pastoral vigilance of the American bishops would prevent Georgian theories from doing any great harm to their flocks.

But these battles against anarchism and socialism were only the

---

[12] Ellis, John Tracy, *The Life of James Cardinal Gibbons, Archbishop of Baltimore, 1834-1921*, 2 vols. (Milwaukee, 1952) I, 547-594, discusses Gibbons' activity in the McGlynn affair. A copy of the decree of the Holy Office against the doctrines of Henry George was found in the Archdiocesan Archives of New York.

negative side of the efforts necessary to promote the general welfare of the large body of lower class people of the United States whose religious faith was Roman Catholic. The positive side called for a tremendous effort to make these Catholics participants in all the privileges of American democracy, and to prepare them for full participation in the privileges of such citizenship. This positive side consisted for the most part of three major problems: Americanization, education—secondary and higher—and cooperation with other agencies in political, social, and industrial reform. All three of these processes had been going on among Catholics from the very beginning of the century and had centered primarily around the Anglo-American Catholic nucleus. In the latter decades of the nineteenth century the Anglo-American group which had been the nucleus in the movement for Americanization and education if not of social reform, while still providing the cultural nucleus of American Catholicism, was almost lost to view. In its place was the newer immigrant group who disagreed and divided on the approaches to these three problems. Some were anxious to hasten the Americanization of the Catholic minority. Among these Archbishop Ireland and Bishop Keane sought positive Catholic leadership in American life, such as Gibbons had shown in the Knights of Labor controversy. The more conservative clergymen, who had placed greater faith in old world solutions, felt that no good could come of hasty Americanization or too close association with non-Catholics; and for them greater reliance must be placed in the traditional conservatism of the Church in the face of modern liberalism. In this second group were the more conservative bishops of the East, chiefly Archbishop Corrigan, and the German bishops of the Middle West.

There had, of course, been faulty Americanization of the newly arrived immigrants under the auspices of political greed along the eastern seaboard; and that kind of Americanization had as its chief defect no solution of the other two problems, education and social reform. The decision of Cardinal Gibbons to defend the rights of Catholic workers to participate in movements for bettering the working classes, and the warding off of the public condemnation of the doctrines of Henry George were the chief examples of the activity of the progressive bishops in their effort to solve the third problem, social reform. In the solving of the second problem, education, there was involved a two-fold task. The first was the provision of Catholic education on the lower levels, and the second was the crowning of that effort by the establishment of a Catholic university from which the perfection of Catholic thought as well as a capable defense of Catholic positions in the American public could come. Unfortunately for the advance of Catholic education and social reform, the prior basic problem in dealing with hundreds of thousands of newly arrived immigrant Catholics lay in Americanization, because unless Catholics had first a basic Americanization in common with other Americans, there were bound to be serious differences with the non-Catholics both in educational programs and in any cooperation in social reform. Loyalties to old world traditions and customs were a great hindrance to Americanization even when there were no language difficulties. There was also the fact that the American dominant culture was Protestant or at least non-Catholic.

Where the Catholic immigrants lived in massed numbers these difficulties of Americanization arose early in the century. In the first instances no foreign language was involved, but the Irish had to learn that there was a difference between the culture of the poor immigrants from Ireland,[13] and the culture of the native English Americans even though these English were several generations away from the old Boston. And while the difference in national origin was complicated by religious prejudices, this cultural difference had to be recognized and overcome if the Irish Catholic was to achieve full Americanization. In the 1850's, Orestes A. Brownson called for the elimination of this cultural handicap of the Irish immigrant and was severely

---

[13] I have discussed this problem in "The Formation of the Catholic Minority," *Review of Politics*, X, 12-34, especially pp. 16-18. The pamphlet *L'Américanisme Jugé Par Un Prêtre Américain* (Lagny, 1900) in French and English which I discovered in the Bibliothèque Nationale is a very severe criticism of the role of the Irish—especially the Irish bishops—written by one well informed in the problems of the Catholic minority in the United States.

criticized by Archbishop John Hughes and the Irish leader, D'Arcy McGee, for his presumptions. Yet this handicap persisted in the East. In the Middle West and in the Far West where the Irish were scattered and could not set up their compact reproduction of Irish life, the Irish became quickly much like their fellow citizens except in matters of religion. These scattered Irish became often as puritan as their next door neighbor, although seldom as harsh in their business deals. The middle western and western Catholics could seldom get into the higher realms of capitalistic finance, but they did achieve a higher economic and social status than the Irish in the East in their positions on the railroad, in party politics, and in some minor businesses. Gradually the older Irish immigrant, joining forces with the Anglo-American group and the older generation of Irish immigrants, managed to conduct a few privately sustained Catholic academies and small colleges, but these were not sufficient to raise the Irish groups to a higher culture. The major exceptions to the lack of education among American Catholics were the clergy, who were taken from their farms or town homes into the seminary early in life and propelled through a classical program and a course in theology where insistence on orthodoxy had the saving grace that it made the young seminarian go much beyond his desires and cultural background. Some of the more favored of these clergymen were sent abroad for higher studies, to Rome, to Louvain, to Fribourg or to the seminaries of France. Some of these students of European universities became the teachers in the American seminaries, others became the bishops whose main task it was to bring this light of higher Catholic education to their flocks. Their coadjutors in the work were nuns and religious priests and Brothers, but again very few of these had the means for university education in the proper sense.

If one were to estimate the accomplishments of American Catholics of Irish abstraction in the United States, especially in the eastern states, outside of the clergy and a few successful entrepreneurs, it could be said that they had scarcely achieved more than primary education, had only the economic security of small wages, and found their chief social enjoyment in inexpensive parties at which the drink was cheap but potent, or in the meager social activities of their parishes. They were American in the sense that they had no real desire for anything else except their new country and were usually zealous in the defense of American liberties. What they lacked most was a wealthy middle class group who could finance the education and cultural leavening of the large masses of lower class people. Consequently, pleas of Archbishop and Bishop Spalding of the Anglo-American nucleus for a university fell on ears that had not yet had the benefit of secondary education. And there was no successor to Orestes A. Brownson of the fifties to carry on the unwelcome criticism of the cultural isolation and low ideals of these Irish immigrants. Their progress in Americanization was more or less by pulling at their own bootstraps. They were accepted as fellow workers by other laborers as long as they ceased to work for smaller wages, they spoke English with less and less brogue, and began to ascend the ladder of political success. To the Irish themselves, they were American, though Catholic. Their cultural differences with the "Yankee" neighbor they attributed to religious prejudice, not without some cause, and to them their differences with the German and Pole and Canadian French were caused by the lack of Americanism on the part of these "foreigners."

The German Catholic immigrants were never as poor economically or culturally as the persecuted Irishmen. Most of them could have remained in their old world homes, and they knew and loved their folk songs and folk lore in their native language. They were in so many cases successful farmers who prospered in the new and richer farm lands of the new world. And, like the Polish immigrants of later decades, they centered much of their social and cultural life around the parish church and the parish school. It is true that they did not bring with them too many Catholic intellectuals, but their German clergy were trained in European universities or higher seminaries and they could always look back or even send back to the Fatherland for capable leaders to keep alive their national traditions. They established a German language press and many German social and cultural societies to keep alive their traditions and to aid in the solution of mutual problems. In the Protestant German immigrant the persistence of these Germanic traits did not always bring about conflicts with co-religious groups because each Protestant group tended to be autonomous and could go its own way, whereas among Catholics the German groups, even when they extended over considerable regions, had by Church law to become part of the existing American Catholic organization which was very seldom even dominantly German. The international character of Catholicism was an interesting factor here, because the clergy attending the immigrants did not usually come from the American groups at first but from Europe and were chiefly Irish and German. The German clergy even when they were practically expelled from Germany during such controversies as the Kulturkampf did not lose their loyalty to the old cultural traditions; and the German speaking people (and later the French Canadians for the same reasons) demanded pastors of their own language traditions. Two important organizations which had fostered the German Catholic missions in America were the Leopoldinen Stiftung of Vienna and the Ludwigmissionsverein of Munich; and complaints were reported to the European headquarters of these organizations that the funds from these societies intended for the German immigrants were not always so distributed by the American bishops. The Germans also felt that the American higher clergy did not have proper respect for their national divisions and they felt that in the retention of these old world habits and languages in their churches and schools they were best preserving their religion. These German groups did not see why they should be subjected in the hierarchy to another foreign group, the Irish clergy, who in their minds had not yet become Americans. As a matter of fact to almost all those immigrant groups who thought of their own nationality in terms of a rich tradition and a language of Central and Western Europe, the Irish were cultural nobodies. Furthermore, to those fresh from Europe, the American nationality had not yet come into existence. Americanization to them under these conditions was not a desirable change.

There had been nationalist quarrels between the German and Irish Catholics from the early days of the nation, and the provincial and plenary councils had taken notice of the problem by insisting on a knowledge of German by the clergy attending the German parishes. Some bishops were more zealous in fulfilling these rules than others; but there were some clergymen—and some were Americans only by adoption—who felt that the persistence of these foreign languages, churches and schools was a blot on American Catholicism and a hindrance to the social progress of their flocks. Just how much the rise of German nationalism in the Fatherland after the victory in the Franco-Prussian war affected the German-Americans cannot be determined accurately, but German scholarship and German national pride were perceptible factors wherever Germans went in the latter quarter of the nineteenth century and raised obstacles to the process of Americanization. Three events particularly focused the Catholic attention on the problem of German nationalism in America, although there were many small local manifestations of this conflict.

The action of the German clergy against the dominant groups in the Church in the United States that first precipitated serious conflict was a petition presented in Rome by Father P. M. Abbelen, Vicar General of the Archdiocese of Milwaukee, in November, 1886.[14] The main complaint of this as well as an earlier petition of the German Priests' Union of Saint Louis[15] was against the inferior status accorded to the German parishes in the larger cities. A custom had grown up in some communities where there was more than one language group to have national churches in which foreign language sermons and other services were held. These foreign language churches were considered succursal churches and were not given the same rank as the English or main Church (called Irish by the Germans) of the city or part of the

---

[14] *Relatio de Questione Germanica in Statibus Foederatis a Rev. P. M. Abbelen, Sac. Milw. conscripta, a Rmo. et Illmo., M. Heiss, Archiep. Milwauk., approbata, et Sacrae Congr. de Propaganda Fide Mense Novembri 1886, submissa. Sequuntur objectiones plurimorum Rvmorum Praesulum eidem S. Congr. propositee, e lingua Gallica in Anglicam translatae.* This contains Abbelen's petition and the answer prepared by Ireland and Keane. This appeal is treated thoroughly by Colman Barry, *Catholic Church and German Americans*, pp. 62-69.

[15] This earlier petition is discussed in Daniel F. Reilly, O.P. *The School Controversy, 1891-1893* (Washington, 1943) pp. 59-60 and in Barry, *op. cit.*, pp. 52-56.

city. Abbelen and his fellow German clergymen wanted these national churches given full parochial status, and they went on to insist that all immigrants be assigned to the parish of their nationality and that the children of these immigrants be sent to the schools of those parishes, too. Abbelen on the way to Rome went with the approbation of Archbishop Heiss to Gibbons, and Gibbons, suspecting nothing, gave Abbelen a letter of introduction to Roman prelates. When Gibbons learned from Bishops Keane and Ireland and Monsignor O'Connell in Rome of the purpose of Abbelen's visit he immediately called a meeting of the archbishops in Philadelphia to prepare a protest. This protest was drawn by Archbishop Corrigan in the names of the archbishops of Boston, Philadelphia, New York, and Baltimore, and sent to Bishops Ireland and Keane in Rome. Bishops Keane and Ireland, who were on their way to Rome to take care of the preliminary work for obtaining papal approval of the proposed Catholic University of America when O'Connell notified them of the Abbelen petition, immediately published a refutation of Abbelen's petition and with the aid of Monsignor O'Connell took steps to present the side of the American bishops before Cardinal Simeoni and the other officials of the Roman Congregations. The Abbelen petition was rejected by the Sacred Congregation on June 7, 1887.

The second factor that aroused the feeling of the German bishops on Americanization was the enactment by the State Legislature of Wisconsin of the Bennett Law of 1889, which required that the chief subjects in the schools for children between nine and fourteen be taught in English, that the children be forced to attend the schools—public or private—within their district, and that only schools approved by the school board were to be recognized as fulfilling the law. Wisconsin probably was the chief center of German Catholicism in the United States and had German bishops in its episcopal sees. Since it was impossible for the Catholics to have a parochial school in every district and since the law invaded the liberties of the parochial school on the matter of language and textbooks, the bishops of the state united in a common pastoral on March 12, 1890, and voiced protests because they regarded the law not only as unnecessary, but also as of-fensive[16] and unjust. They said they thought it desirable that their children know an additional language such as German, although they accepted the fact that English must be the official language of the schools. In the campaign that followed the enactment of the law and in its ultimate repeal the German bishops of the state charged that they were not supported by Bishop Ireland, and that despite the fact that they were defending the parochial schools he even spoke privately against them for opposing the law. Ire-land, indeed, was a strong proponent of the Americanization of the Catholic immigrant and consequently his action in this and in the Abbelen petition aroused resentment against him in the minds of his neighboring German bishops. Nor was this feeling abated when Ireland and other non-German bishops of the Mid-dle West tried to have a non-German appointed to the Archi-episcopal See of Milwaukee in 1890 on the death of Archbishop Heiss. Rome, however, appointed Bishop Frederick X. Katzer of Green Bay.

The third factor in the German fight against Americanization had its origin in a very good proposal. One of the major problems of the Catholic Church in this country during the nineteenth century and even until the First World War, was the care of the newly arrived immigrants. During the first part of the nineteenth century when the Irish and Germans were fleeing from the famines, there was no agency in their country capable of taking care of them. Likewise, even in later times some supervision was necessary to prevent the defrauding of the newly arrived immi-grants or even worse evils. A German business man, Herr Peter Paul Cahensly,[17] while studying the export business in the ports of emigrant embarkation in Europe, especially Le Havre and

---

[16] This law and the controversy it aroused is discussed in Harry Hooper Heming, *The Catholic Church in Wisconsin* (Milwaukee, 1895-98), pp. 281-87. The bishops' protest is given on pp. 283-86.

[17] Father Barry's book is really a defense of Cahensly, in which he shows the very good intentions of this man. He gives the first Memorial in Ap-pendix IV, *op. cit.*, pp. 313-15. An earlier account of the controversy, based on the *Freeman's Journal* of Dec. 24 and 31, 1892 and Jan. 7, 1893, is contained in John T. Reily, *Collections in the Life and Times of J. Card. Gibbons* (Third Book, McSherrystown, Pa., 1895) Part III, 1-34.

Bremen, decided that something must be done in Europe for these emigrants. He even made a trip to the United States in 1883 to study the problem. The founding of the St. Raphael Society and the establishment of a hospice for German immigrants in New York were some of the effects of his efforts. In 1890, there took place in Lucerne, Switzerland, a meeting of representatives of the various European Catholic Emigration Societies, who were organizing help for the European emigrees. At the conclusion of the meeting a Memorial was prepared for the Holy Father concerning the sad condition of those emigrees once they arrived in the United States. The Memorial, signed by Herr Cahensly among others, began with a statement, quite exaggerated, of the great losses to the Faith among the immigrants in the United States. To overcome this evil it was proposed that greater recognition be given to the foreign groups in the Church organization in the United States, even to the point of allowing foreign representation in the hierarchy of the country. An account of the Memorial was carried in the American press. Among others, Archbishop Ireland attacked the Memorial publicly as a plot of the Germanizing American clergy. In June 1891, another Memorial for the same purpose was presented by Cahensly and other members of the Lucerne assembly and made public by the opponents of the petition. Again swift action by Archbishop Ireland and Cardinal Gibbons, aided by Monsignor O'Connell, checked any hope that the petition would bring about a national division of the hierarchy according to racial or nationalistic lines. Their action brought about a reply on June 28, 1891, from Pope Leo XIII through Cardinal Rampolla, that the Pope had rejected the petition. Ireland, however, was not content with releasing to the press copies of the Memorials of Cahensly, but arranged for a discussion of these proposals on the floor of the Congress in Washington, when Senator C. K. Davis charged the Germans with an attempt to interfere in the lives of American Catholics with the assistance and aid of the German Imperial Government.[18] The move for forcible divisions of the hierarchy

[18] Letter of Ireland to O'Connell, July 2, 1891 in Richmond Diocesan Archives. Barry discusses the controversy over the Memorials, *op. cit.*, pp. 134 ff.

on national lines was dead. But the feeling of the Germans against the Irish and especially against Archbishop John Ireland was quite strong, and was to cause the German Catholics to take sides against him in most of the later controversies of the decade. This was particularly true in the controversies over the school question in which they professed to regard him as an opponent of the parochial schools, in his efforts to force the German professors out of the Catholic University, and in the later controversy over Americanism. In this controversy over the Americanization of immigrants, non-German groups were not well represented. The large Polish immigration and that from other Slavic countries were not yet strong enough to have cause for national action. Neither were the Italians strong enough in the hierarchy or among the clergy to claim recognition. One other group which had a press in some sections of the country consisted of French Canadians. Their chief newspaper protector, *La Vérité* of Montreal, however, was published outside the country. But in certain regions of New England and in some localities in the Middle West, these Canadians felt that they too were being unjustly treated by the dominating Irish clergy; and when the Germans protested, they added their smaller voice against the Americanizing prelates. The question of Catholic education, particularly the school controversy of 1891 in which the foreign language groups played an important role, offered a new occasion for division.

The Catholic Church has always considered education as one of its chief pastoral functions. One manifestation of this was the monastic school that played its important role in the conversion and civilization of Western Europe in the early Middle Ages. This role of the Church as educator had since been challenged by the movements in the so-called Catholic countries designated as the Enlightenment. In those countries when the conflict between the Church and the State became bitter the State tended to deny the right of the Church to control education. Particularly in the Catholic countries of southern Europe the effort to wrest control of the school from the Church resulted in a lay or almost anti-religious state school. In Protestant countries, if Catholic schools existed at all, they were of necessity separatist schools and were supported generally by private subscription. In the United States the Catholic Church faced a new situation in which no religious group could be the established religion but in which education was provided by the state. In the generally religious atmosphere of nineteenth-century America no one could really say that the American schools were anti-religious in the sense of the later French anti-clerical schools of the twentieth century, but in the public schools of the United States, the Church could not carry out its professed obligation of Christian education. There were, when possible, Catholic academies and seminaries and in some communities Catholic grade schools attached to the parishes. The Germans were the chief leaders in this kind of school, because they more than other immigrants had the financial means to support such schools. Further, since so many of these schools were in totally German communities this was the important tool for keeping alive the national as well as the religious traditions. To provide Catholic schools for the mass of poor Irish immigrants who had fled starvation and persecution and lived in the larger communities along the eastern seaboard or in the settlements along the railroads or about the mills and mines, was a financial impossibility for the American hierarchy. In the 1840's such aggressive leaders as Bishops John Hughes of New York and Francis Kenrick of Philadelphia had brought down wrath upon their heads by attempting to force public recognition—in the form of financial aid to Catholic schools—of the right of their Catholic children to have only Catholic education. The First Plenary Council of Baltimore in 1852 recognized the difficulty of the situation, and the Second Council in 1886 recommended the establishment wherever possible of a Catholic school in each parish. But Rome was not satisfied. Unless the children were instructed in the Faith the future of the Church in the United States seemed dim. In 1875 the Roman prelates first had sent out an interrogatory to the American bishops about the public and the Catholic schools and later in the same year issued an instruction calling for the building of Catholic schools in each parish. In 1884, this ruling was made mandatory within two years by the Third Plenary Council of Baltimore.

No bishops really objected to this decree about parochial schools. To the German bishops in the Middle West this was a confirmation of their own position. In many communities, however, such a school was manifestly impossible either because of the fewness of the faithful or their lack of financial means. In the larger cities the building of some schools was easier but the number required was usually far beyond the financial means available. Some dioceses could report within a few decades a remarkable organization of parochial schools, with diocesan supervision, and a fairly successful attainment of the Council's decree that these schools must be the equal if not the superior of the public schools in the quality of their education, while teaching at the same time the necessary religious elements. Had the American Catholics been a wealthier group the financial burden of a separate school system would have been a heavy burden, but not being wealthy they felt the burden even more and recognized that it was too heavy. Hundreds of thousands of Catholic children could not expect even Catholic grade school education. The maintenance of the schools where the means did exist, the building of supplementary buildings, and the hiring of the necessary teachers were severe financial handicaps on the desire of the Catholic immigrant to raise his social and economic position in other matters. The actual picture was very complex, depending upon the compactness of the Catholics in any community, their desire for education, and also upon the zeal of the bishops or priests of the locality in undertaking the stupendous task of providing schools and teachers. The controversy over the Bennett Law in Wisconsin had set in relief the activity of the German bishops of the Middle West in their fight for parochial schools. In the East, leadership for Catholic schools was manifested by Bishop Bernard McQuaid of Rochester. In some local communities in the country compromises had been worked out in which at least part of the financial support of the Catholic schools was supplied by municipal or county funds. As the Church in the

United States grew in numbers the financial problem became more acute. Such was in general the status of Catholic parochial education in the United States when Bishop John Ireland was invited to speak before the convention of the National Educational Association in St. Paul in 1890.[19]

Most of Ireland's audience on this occasion were not Catholics and nearly all of them were teachers in public schools. Ireland expressed the usual need of public education, and the obligation of the state to provide it and praised the efforts of the American people to fulfill this obligation. He likewise regretted the need of a separate school system in order to provide religious education for Catholic children. He did not recommend any specific solution to this second problem. He mentioned some existing plans in which the buildings were provided and the teachers supplied by religious organizations but the maintenance and the salaries were paid by the state. In such schools the religious education took place after the school hours. But Ireland shocked Catholic supporters of Catholic education by granting the right and obligation of the State to educate and suggesting that the parochial school was an unnecessary burden and should be abolished. For his Catholic critics Ireland had conceded too much. The general Catholic criticism of the public schools were that they were irreligious if not godless, and that the right of education remained with the parents who were obliged to see that the children received Christian education. Chief among his critics were those who had been offended by his supposed activity in the controversy over the Bennett Law. Just at this time Ireland also tried an experiment in two schools in Faribault and Stillwater, Minnesota. The principles of the agreement drawn up in 1891 between the local school boards and the Catholic schools of these two towns called for the use of the Catholic school buildings, the hiring of nuns or Catholic teachers and the restriction of religious teaching to hours after the regular school periods. There was to be only a nominal fee for the use of the school buildings and the teachers were to be approved by the public school board. Similar agreements had existed in Poughkeepsie, New York, and in other

[19] Reilly, *op. cit.*, pp. 46-55, is friendly to Ireland in the controversy.

parts of the country, but this agreement suddenly received un-expected publicity both in the Catholic and non-Catholic press. The Minnesota Baptist organization made a formal protest. Cath-olics criticized the agreement and within a year the whole agree-ment was abolished by the school boards of the two cities.

Because of the charges made by Catholics against the agree-ments Archbishop Ireland felt constrained to explain his stand at the annual Council of the Archbishops in November, in 1891, held at St. Louis when the hierarchy gathered to celebrate Archbishop Kenrick's jubilee. Father Thomas Bouquillon, pro-fessor of theology and canon law at the Catholic University, had published at this time a pamphlet *Education to Whom Does It Belong?*, which was erroneously supposed to have been prepared at the instigation of Archbishop Ireland. In it he recognized the right of the State over education. Archbishop Corrigan arranged for Father Rene Holaind, S.J. to publish an answer. Another at-tack on Ireland's position appeared in the *Civiltà Cattolica* pub-lished by the Jesuits in Rome. The German theologians Joseph Pohle and Joseph Schroeder at the Catholic University threw their weight back of Holaind in the controversy. It was then that Archbishop Ireland went to Rome to explain his position and to defend himself against the complaints of his opponents.

In this controversy over parochial schools, the Catholic Uni-versity of America at Washington, D. C. became involved by the action of some of its professors, chiefly Father Thomas Bouquil-lon on Ireland's side and Father Joseph Schroeder on the German and conservative side. The Catholic University had been almost from its inception a project of the more progressive groups of the hierarchy, and had had the special protection of John Ireland who had gone to Rome with Bishop John Keane to get Roman approval for their plans. Similarly at the time his counterpart among the conservatives, Archbishop Corrigan, withdrew from the trustees of the proposed University. The thinker whose ideas were most directly involved in the proposed University was Bishop John Lancaster Spalding, the most broadly educated member of the hierarchy and one of the most philosophical among the prelates. Further, through Spalding's agency, the donation of $300,000 from the Caldwell sisters which helped to make the University a reality was obtained. Spalding however refused to be the first rector and instead Bishop John J. Keane of Richmond, a close friend of Ireland, was nominated and appointed the first rector by Pope Leo XIII. Keane with the papal approval went about the Catholic universities of Europe gathering a faculty. The University which began chiefly as a higher theological school did not have the support of the Jesuits, partly because there had been a proposal of a Catholic University under their direction in New York by Corrigan and partly because the new University was situated actually only a few miles from the Jesuit college of Georgetown. The Catholic University during its formative years[20] had not had the full approval of Archbishop Corrigan who wanted the Catholic University situated in his part of the country, nor of his suffragan Bernard McQuaid who regarded it as a rival for his newly established theological Seminary of St. Bernard. The life of the new theological school was constantly disturbed by internal bickering, partly because the first professors had no real unity, having been drawn from many nations, and partly because of ideological differences between members of the faculty. Two very prominent German university professors secured by Bishop Keane for the new Theology school were Joseph Pohle and Joseph Schroeder. Another was a French student of canon law Georges Périès. When the controversy over Cahenslyism and the school question became bitter the faculty took sides. Dr. Thomas Bouquillon by reason of his pamphlet became the chief defender of Ireland's viewpoint, especially after these opinions were attacked by Father Rene Holaind, S.J. and other Jesuit writers. In the Faribault controversy the two German theologians were on the side of the Germans. Most of the American members of the faculty quite naturally also took the side of Ireland in the controversy. The opinions of the two groups were echoed by the Catholic press of the day. As a result of the bitterness aroused in the controversy Monsignor Pohle returned to

[20] The controversies about the Catholic University are treated by Ellis in his *The Formative Years of the Catholic University of America* (Washington, 1946) and *Gibbons*, I, 389-438.

Germany in 1894, but Monsignor Schroeder continued and was an outspoken critic of the Ireland policies in the German press. But so long as Keane was the Rector, the University was officially on the side of Ireland in the discussions. Thus from parochial schools to the University the problem of Catholic education became involved in the growing controversy between the progressives and conservatives in the hierarchy.

Closely connected with the problems of Americanization and especially with the establishment of the University were the efforts by the progressive members of the Catholic clergy to demonstrate the Americanism of the American Catholic by their participation in movements for civic and social reform. In the question of civic reform the progressives, especially Archbishop Ireland and Bishop Keane, were outspoken advocates of the temperance movement which in the United States had been predominantly Protestant. The German bishops were unsympathetic to the movement, indicating that their flocks had no need for the reform. In social reform the concept of social justice developed in later encyclicals had scarcely been discussed in the United States when Cardinal Gibbons made his intercession for the Knights of Labor, and the chief point of contact between Catholics and non-Catholics in public welfare works was in political and civic life. While there were various interpretations of the American separation of Church and State practically no one held to absolute separation. The more conservative Catholic clergymen felt that since the State was at best neutral, the Church should avoid entangling alliances with it. Others, especially those who had some acquaintance with the so-called "neutral" states of Europe not only insisted on avoiding alliances with them, they even had doubts that fulsome patriotism towards such a state was desirable. On the other hand, the Anglo-American members of the hierarchy and clergy found no good reason for failing in patriotic devotion to the American state. Likewise the Irish-American bishops, even when they felt great sympathy towards suffering Ireland, were outspoken in their devotion to the American government and American public life. There were several manifestations of this public mindedness. The first was the desire by some public churchmen to avoid linking the Church to any political group—specifically the Democratic party which was for the most part the party of the immigrant along the eastern seaboard. Another one was the cooperation manifested by such men as Archbishop John Ireland and Bishop John Keane in the promotion of the temperance movements. Other activities of these Americanizers which excited the criticism of the conservative groups were the praise of public education and the participation in public social enterprises. As a result of the Church's traditional opposition to Masonic organizations, conservatives opposed Catholic membership in any non-Catholic societies. In the controversy over the Knights of Labor the main point at issue was the membership of Catholics in a secret, oath-bound society in obvious imitation of Masonic oaths and ceremonies. There was also the fear generated by the Mollie Maguires and the Carbonari. This question of Catholic membership in secret societies soon came to another crisis, when the Catholic membership in the Knights of Pythias, the Odd Fellows and the Modern Woodmen was discussed at the time of the Baltimore Council. To the Germans and to the conservatives who had in mind the activities of European secret societies against the Church, Catholic membership in these societies was a dangerous situation. To Ireland, Gibbons, and some of the western bishops, these organizations were less Masonic and more purely social and insurance organizations; and to prohibit them to Catholics would merely hinder the social and civil progress of Catholic citizens. In this matter and in the discussion of public schools and cooperation in social matters with the government, the conservatives claimed to detect a theological minimism in Americanization, and even an evidence of that false liberalism condemned by the *Syllabus of Errors*. It was indeed true that there had been some questionable incidents in which Catholics had associated themselves in public enterprises with members of other organizations. Bishop Keane had worn his episcopal robes in the chapel at Harvard. The incident of Bishop Scanlan praying at the site of the Brigham Young monument in Salt Lake City had even aroused derision among his more conservative critics, although the Bishop did answer that he had merely participated in a civic ceremony and had not blessed the monument as some had charged. In the newspaper and pamphlet war over Cahenslyism and Americanization the Germans and French Canadians had pointed to the increase in the frequency of divorce, the increase in American crimes, and other public evils as an indication that American civilization was beneath that of Europe and therefore should not be accepted too readily by Catholics. Thus, in the fight between the progressives and the conservatives this field of social and civil relationships offered the most opportune circumstance, when coupled with an accusation of opposition to parochial schools, to raise the charge of heresy against the Americanizers. Probably the most direct charge of liberalism appeared in the *Catholic Quarterly Review* in April 1891, under the name of Father Thomas Preston, the Vicar General of Archbishop Corrigan. Father Preston, with the consent and perhaps the urging of Archbishop Corrigan whom he quoted, intended his article to give a definition of true American Catholicity and at the same time to charge Archbishop Ireland, Cardinal Gibbons, and Bishop Keane, without mentioning their names, with the liberalism condemned by the *Syllabus of Errors* of Pius IX. He insisted that he yielded to no one in patriotism and love of country. Nevertheless he pointed out certain errors called American Catholicity which he regarded as incorrect. The chief characteristic of this "peculiar kind of Catholicity" he described as "less hostile to those who differ from us in faith or morals."

We have heard it said, as a mark of the peculiarities of American Catholicity, that we do not pretend to judge between error and falsehood as far as others are concerned; that we embrace them all, no matter what they believe or profess, as really *one* with us in the profession of a conservative Christianity. It is also said that our differences are not as great as has been supposed; that we are willing to meet all our fellow citizens on an open platform of wide Christian belief; that we are willing to yield to the majority, or even to the State, the education of our children, provided we are allowed the liberty of teaching them privately the principles of our faith. It is also maintained that the rights of the Sovereign Pontiff, especially in his temporal principality, may in this country be waived, and that those Catholics are more truly American in their sympathies who look upon the temporal power of the Supreme Pontiff as a thing of the past; who are willing to let it die, and feel no obligation to do anything in their power to restore it.[21]

[21] *Catholic Quarterly Review* (April, 1891) XVI, 396-408. The death of Preston shortly after writing the article removed an important critic of the liberal group.

Among the peculiarities of this American Catholicity Father Preston rejected was the teaching that the American government is "the best possible and most suited to our religion." Another was a doctrine of progress that holds "that we better understand the truths of our revelation than the ages before us." Other doctrines he attacked were those which: "destroy the rights of property;" holds the form of government as best in which the "Church is entirely separated from the State;" and "the error that religion and education can be separated without vital injury to the Commonwealth."

The death of Father Preston shortly after this removed him from the controversy, and further attacks on the progressive group were made by the pens of others.

To Archbishop Ireland and his friends, on the other hand, the American scene was witnessing the greatest actual progress of the Catholic Church in modern times, and they thought that in the American republic and in the American people the whole Church could learn a valuable lesson. Perhaps the most notable statement of this opinion had been made by Father Isaac Hecker in the *Catholic World* and in his book *The Church and the Age*. Speaking of the relations between Church and State in America, Hecker said:

> Socially and politically Catholics are slowly taking the rank to which education, virtue, wealth and numbers entitle them among the prominent forces of the republic, and the light which their religion throws upon its vital principles and its Constitution will make them conspicuous as intelligent and patriotic citizens.
>
> The future of the United States belongs, under God, to that religion which, by its conscious possession of truth and by its indwelling Spirit of Divine love, shall succeed in bringing the American people to unity in their religious belief and action, as they are actually one in the political sense. . . .[22]

So also in his speech at the Baltimore Council Bishop John Ireland had said, "To Americans, then, who love this Republic, I fearlessly say: Your hope is in the Catholic Church, because she is today the mighty power to resist vice and unbelief."[23]

[22] *The Church and the Age: An Exposition of the Catholic Church in View of the Needs and Aspirations of the Present Age* (New York, 1887), pp. 91-92.
[23] "The Church—the Support of Just Government," *Memorial Volume of the Third Plenary Council*, pp. 31-32.

Bishop John Lancaster Spalding, Father Hecker, Bishops Ireland and Keane and Cardinal Gibbons were making determined efforts in speeches and articles in such magazines as the *North American Review* and the *Catholic World* to show the American people that American Catholics were united with them in their efforts to improve the civic and social welfare of the country. In this country the progressives had their followers as well as their critics in their program of cooperation between the "Church and the age," but in Europe even friendly observers of American Catholic progress were not so sure of their orthodoxy. Possibly the existence of the A.P.A. movement is sufficient evidence that the optimism of Ireland, Keane, and Gibbons was not soundly based, since the majority of the American people had not been much affected by the numerical growth of the Church. Nevertheless, the ease with which these progressive clergymen moved in public political and social affairs was something real. But there were other factors besides those outside the Church working at cross purposes to the roseate hopes of these Catholic Americanizers. Among these were the defeated leaders of the foreign national Catholic groups in this country who did not feel either affection or admiration for these Americanizing policies. These lined up readily with the conservatives and echoed the charges of "minimism" and "liberalism." Also, to these two groups were joined those individuals who opposed Archbishop Ireland and his friends on matters of Church policy and matters of personal ambition.

On the question of the growth of the Church in the West and the Indian missions there was no real basis for controversy within the American Church, nor on any other really missionary project. But in those regions where the Catholic body was numerous enough to organize itself and to offer a Catholic program in public affairs, the division of the hierarchy and their clergy and laity on the questions of Americanization, education, social and political reform became quite definite not only to the Catholics of the country but in some degree to the general American public and the American press.

Thus within the first few years after the Third Plenary Council the hierarchy of the Catholic church in the United States seemed divided into two groups, backed in most cases by their clergy. The division was only partly on geographical lines. The conservatives were headed by the conservative bishops of the East, and chiefly Archbishop Corrigan, Bishop McQuaid, and Bishop Ignatius Horstmann, and aided by the German bishops of Wisconsin. In Rome they were aided by Father Salvatore Brandi, S.J., editor of the *Civiltà Cattolica*, and Cardinal Camillo Mazzella, S.J., both of whom had lived for some time in the United States. The Archbishops Williams of Boston, Ryan of Philadelphia, Feehan of Chicago, and Elder of Cincinnati seemed to remain mostly neutral in the controversy, with Williams and Ryan more inclined to take the Corrigan side of any argument and Elder and Feehan siding more with Ireland. In St. Louis the dying Kenrick was replaced by Archbishop John J. Kain who sided generally with the Ireland group and on the west coast the new Archbishop, Patrick Riordan, formerly of Chicago, definitely was of the Ireland school. Feehan of Chicago seemed to take little part in any of the controversies, although he had opposed any action against secret societies or against labor unions. Cardinal Gibbons was usually on the side of Ireland and his friend Bishop Keane, the rector of the University. In Rome their representative was Monsignor Denis O'Connell who had likewise the friendship of the two Cardinals Vannutelli.

The Catholic press of the time was deeply divided over the controversy of the day. Indeed, the character of the American controversies from the Third Plenary Council to the end of the century cannot be understood without a careful scrutiny of the American press of the period, especially the Catholic press. The reading public of Catholic America had little use for technical theological journals since there were practically no speculative theological schools. The decrees of the Baltimore Councils were not translated into the vernacular nor were there more than a dozen special theological documents dealing with American Catholicism. The *Catholic University Bulletin* had high aims but like the University faculty which edited it, it suffered strangulation because of national differences. The chief quarterly was the

Catholic Quarterly Review in which the best Catholic thought was published but the journal was as conservative and as non-partisan as its ecclesiastical supervisor, Archbishop Patrick Ryan. The *Catholic World* was the chief monthly magazine and followed the ideals of its founder Father Hecker who was a cultural and literary partisan for Americanization and for Catholic participation in social reform. The Jesuit *Sacred Heart Messenger* while mostly devotional was the chief organ for American Jesuits and tended to be conservative and critical of the liberal tendencies of the Americanizers. The chief theological publication was the *American Ecclesiastical Review*, founded in 1886, edited by Father Herman Heuser in Philadelphia. Besides publishing Roman documents affecting the United States and discussions of liturgical and pastoral problems, the *Ecclesiastical Review* became one of the chief conservative organs in the social and cultural controversies of the period. Heuser was of German origin but was not necessarily anti-Irish. His sympathy with Monsignor Joseph Schroeder and Father Salvatore Brandi, S.J., stemmed mostly from his opposition to the liberal tendencies which these men were attacking.

The *Ave Maria* published each week at Notre Dame, Indiana, was devotional and literary but independent under its editor Father Daniel Hudson, who, although he had friends among both progressives and conservatives, seemed closest to the progressives.

The chief organs of Catholic expression on matters of public discussion were the weekly newspapers which in the day of cheap newsprint had multiplied easily. The Catholic weekly newspaper shared somewhat the sensationalism and the personal journalism of the age of Pulitzer and Hearst although it never had the reading public of the secular daily. Most of the newspapers were edited by the publishers, in most cases literate and devoted Catholics who were partisans of the bishops who tolerated them. The stronger papers edited in the centers of population frequently were unofficial partisans of the local bishop in times of controversy. An editor's criticism of bishops was possible because his paper was privately owned and because several of the bishops themselves were publicity minded. Among the Catholic papers which did not give immediate support to the local bishop were the *Freeman's Journal* of New York which under Father Louis Lambert did not side with Archbishop Corrigan, and the *Review* of St. Louis (formerly of Chicago) which did not support Archbishop John J. Kain of St. Louis. The editor of the *Review*, Arthur Preuss, was well informed on theological matters, and was a trenchant defender of the German-Americans and the conservative bishops, —and criticized the Americanizers. Also in St. Louis was his chief critic Father David Phelan, whose *Western Watchman* was the outspoken organ of his unruly personality. For him Archbishop Ireland could do no wrong but Bishop Keane could do little good. To him any action favorable to Protestantism was at least semi-Pelagian. Otherwise Phelan seems to have had little affection for the German Americans. Also in St. Louis was Condé B. Pallen's *Church Progress*, quite conservative, but not as trenchant as Preuss' *Review*. Pallen was expected to speak the opinions of conservatives but he was American in his general outlook. The *North-Western Chronicle* of St. Paul was privately owned but close to Archbishop Ireland who frequently wrote editorials for it. The *Milwaukee Catholic Citizen* and the *Monitor* of San Francisco were generally liberal but not quite as vitriolic as Father Malone's *Colorado Catholic*. The New York *Catholic Herald* varied its stand with its editor, Michael Walsh. The Baltimore *Catholic Mirror* represented the general impartiality of Cardinal Gibbons with a friendliness towards the progressives. So also the Boston *Pilot* represented the mildness of Archbishop Williams. *The Buffalo Catholic Union and Times* edited by Father Patrick Cronin was in general sympathetic to the progressive bishops. The other papers were generally less outspoken in controversial matters. The German language papers in New York, St. Louis, Pittsburgh, Milwaukee, Buffalo, Columbus, and St. Paul were definitely partisan but their influence was generally limited to the local German Catholics. The *Ohio Waisenfreund* of the Josephinum in Columbus, the *Die Amerika* of Edward Preuss in St. Louis and the *Buffalo Volksfreund* were outstanding journals. The chief outlet for the opinions of the Germans in English was Preuss' *Review* in St. Louis.

The American secular press also had an important part in these Catholic controversies of the 1890's. Archbishops Ireland and Corrigan were front page characters, partly because of their personalities and partly because of their controversies. The newspapers of that period were molders of public opinion and well-placed stories on the Church in Europe or America were used by the controversialists with telling effect. The Roman correspondents of the *New York Sun, Herald, Tribune* or *Times*, the *Washington Star*, or the *Baltimore Sun* were under the direction of the Roman agents of these parties. Occasionally a well-placed article in a New York or Baltimore paper supported one side or the other claiming that one side or the other was in favor in Rome. Thus when the German bishops attacked Archbishop Ireland in the Faribault and Stillwater agreements and denied the State's right in education, a special article in the *Baltimore Sun* pointed out that the Catholic schools of Germany were State supported and not separated as in this country. The chief Roman correspondent for the progressives was Monsignor Eugene Boeglin, later expelled from Rome by Count Crispi, whose chief pen name in the *New York Sun* was "Innominato." His articles usually in praise of Archbishop Ireland or the Americanizers appearing in the very city of Archbishop Corrigan were a constant source of irritation to the Archbishop and his followers. In this connection should also be mentioned a lady correspondent, Ella B. Edes, "la signorina" to the progressives, who had almost unlimited access to ecclesiastical information in Rome and who used to supply information to the conservative Catholic leaders. She nursed a definite grudge against the progressives whom she designated as "the clique."

How much the lower clergy and the laity participated in these controversies is not easy to determine. The Irish clergy in the Middle West and West generally supported Ireland and opposed the Germans and other foreign language clergy. In the East there was a division among the Irish with the majority following the leadership of their bishops of Irish descent, except where some of the Irish were led by such popular orators as Father Edward

McGlynn. The laity generally followed the clergy and the Catholic journalists, but there were few ways in which they, outside of the lay editors of the Catholic newspapers, could express an opinion. On the Irish question except for temporary disagreement on the Fenians or the Land League, there was a unanimity against England that was used successfully by unscrupulous politicians. While these controversies on Catholic questions were popular in the sense of dealing with popular and everyday issues, insofar as they were basically religious and theological the chief actors in them were the bishops and some of the clergy who were the best educated and the chief leaders of the Catholic population.

It is not difficult to see that the chief protagonists of these controversies were Archbishops John Ireland and Michael Corrigan, and it was of great importance that each of these men aspired to be the next American Cardinal. While interests in the controversies were real, the victory of either one was expected by their friends to culminate in the conferring of the red hat on the victor. Between them the gentle Cardinal Archbishop of Baltimore tried to maintain a certain superiority and impartiality, although he could not help being drawn to the more magnetic personality of the Bishop and later Archbishop of Saint Paul. Bishop Ireland did not need to have a popular subject for high sounding oratory. A born orator, with all the necessary natural gifts that make for power in public speaking—a large physique, readiness in speech, a smiling tolerance of lesser men—he had an ability to act quickly and strongly. His voice was not musical, but the power of his utterance and the clarity of his thought made him the best orator in the hierarchy of his day. Beginning in his own locality, he was a popular priest who had served as chaplain in the Civil War, as a fighter for temperance and for the social and civic betterment of his people; and he had the affection and admiration of his superior, Bishop Grace. He never lost an opportunity to make friends or to urge what had become the great passion of his life—his desire to see Catholics and Catholicism take advantage of the great opportunities that lay before them in this grand country. He had the tolerance and freedom that abounded on the

American western frontier—whether because of it or accidentally we may never know. As a youth he had witnessed the settling of his adopted state and had obtained a respect for the daring and the democracy of the western American. His French seminary training had given his quick mind a vision of old world education and at the same time a chance to develop himself above the opportunities of American frontier education. It seems that he also came into contact at the seminary in Meximieux with some of the Liberal Catholicism of De Lamennais. Be that as it may, there seems to be little of the French piety in this rugged young priest who attended the Vatican Council as the representative of Bishop Grace and who became one of the orators of the Third Plenary Council. As a matter of fact, he seemed quite critical of the French clergy, and of all the European clergy who hung back from democracy and modern social reform.

Strangely, it seems as if Archbishop John Ireland appeared full grown in the American Catholic scene at the Third Council, and the Catholics in the United States who had lacked strong leadership since the death of Archbishop John Hughes had to accept him as the chief exponent of American Catholicism. He had allies in Baltimore, in Rome, in Washington and in other parts of the country, but the leadership came from Saint Paul. His speech at the Baltimore Council, especially his plea for a reconciliation between the Church and the modern age at the celebration of the centenary of the hierarchy in 1889, were stirring appeals to the glowing loyalty of the Irish Americans. In that 1889 speech he had called for aggressiveness, for the acceptance of democracy, and for lay leadership. His Civil War service, and his activities among Civil War Veterans and in public welfare generally, gave him an army of friends throughout the country. His speeches had been published in part in the French liberal press and gave him already an international standing.

In his battles he had drawn to his side two other clergymen, one in Washington and one in Rome. Whether this trio were friends before Ireland and Keane went to Rome in 1886 to settle problems concerning the Catholic University is not clear, but Keane had been O'Connell's bishop in the diocese of Richmond for a short time. But in these problems and especially in the defeat of Abbelen and Cahensly, they began to act together. Of Bishop John J. Keane,[24] even his opponents had few harsh words. He was tall and stately, and the smile that shone from his broad countenance disarmed many of his opponents even if it did not earn their respect. When Bishop John Lancaster Spalding refused to be considered for the rectorship of the new Catholic University, Keane, then the Bishop of Richmond, was the choice of Gibbons and the other friends of the University and was appointed the first rector by Pope Leo XIII. He was not a deep thinker, but had definitely clear notions of what the new center of Catholic learning should be. With the blessing of the Holy Father, Pope Leo XIII, and the assistance of Bishop Ireland, he planned to draw to the University the best available minds of Europe and at the same time to obtain fraternal acceptance from the American universities of the day. More than anyone else he bore the burden of trying rather unsuccessfully to raise the money required to finance his grand plans. To some, particularly the sharp-penned Father David Phelan, he was too liberal, too ready to join in non-sectarian activities, even though all admitted that he did this for the furtherance of the Church. As the rector of the University he had to bear the brunt of the criticism from its opponents, and as a close friend of Archbishop Ireland he was a more vulnerable target and a less dangerous opponent than the vigorous Archbishop when the feelings against Ireland became bitter.

When Keane and Ireland went to Rome after the Third Plenary Council they came into direct contact with Monsignor Denis O'Connell, rector at the North American College where they

[24] Patrick Henry Ahern's, *The Life of John J. Keane, Educator and Archbishop, 1839-1918* (Milwaukee, 1954) is an interesting and forceful study of this great prelate. Father Ahern is very just in his appreciation for Keane and does not try to build him up above Ireland or Gibbons. He brings much information to his study, but does not seem able to resolve the question of Keane's acceptance of any of the doctrines reprobated in the papal letter, *Testem Benevolentiae*. He was handicapped by the destruction of Keane's own papers. It is worth noting here that Ireland tried to induce his friends to destroy their papers under the promise of destroying his. Ireland and O'Connell did not carry out their part of this understanding, but apparently Keane and Father John A. Zahm, C.S.C., did.

stayed. O'Connell[25] was a native of Ireland who had become as American as his friend Archbishop Ireland. As a seminarian of the Vicariate of North Carolina and a priest of the diocese of Richmond he had been a close friend of Archbishop Gibbons, both while Gibbons was Vicar Apostolic and later Bishop of Richmond; and he had helped Gibbons as a kind of secretary when Gibbons became Archbishop of Baltimore and Apostolic Delegate at the Third Plenary Council. He was sent to Rome by Gibbons and through Gibbons' efforts was made the rector of the North American College in 1885. Partly because he had studied in Rome and partly because he had a great facility in making friends, Monsignor O'Connell became the chief agency for the American bishops in Rome after his appointment. He was particularly loyal to Cardinal Gibbons, keeping him informed on Roman affairs and guiding the Cardinal as much as distance and time would permit. His cooperation with Keane and Ireland in the Cahensly affair, the school controversy, the discussions of the condemnation of the Knights of Labor, and the Henry George condemnation was proper by reason of his position and his sympathies. At times he seemed the most determined of this triangle. But Monsignor O'Connell was even more vulnerable than Keane, because he was not only not a bishop but was definitely desirous of being one. Nevertheless it would be unfair to imply that he would have sacrificed his principles to attain that position.

If there was a theologian of the progressive group it was Denis O'Connell. Unfortunately O'Connell's activities were in an advisory capacity, and there are not enough of his writings to enable one to say what his full theological opinions were. He was not the giant leader that Ireland showed himself to be, yet the correspondence between the two showed that many of Ireland's ideas were urged upon him by O'Connell. He was an adviser to Gibbons, and to Keane. Later when he became rector of the Catholic University, the university had declined and had become involved in

[25] A full length biography of Bishop Denis O'Connell has not been written, although the discovery of his papers in great number will undoubtedly make a full length study possible. Colman J. Barry, O.S.B., *The Catholic University of America, 1903-1909, The Rectorship of Denis J. O'Connell* (Washington, 1950) is devoted almost entirely to O'Connell's rectorship.

financial disaster and internal trouble, and he had no chance to become a great educator. Nor was his later appointment to Richmond made until after he had passed his prime. Therefore the lacklustre of these later years should not lessen his brilliance in his earlier career. As the Roman agent of the Archbishop of Baltimore, and the partisan of Ireland and Keane in the years after 1886, he, too, was soon to feel the sharp attacks of the opposition.

Cardinal James Gibbons, the Archbishop of Baltimore, whose stately yet ascetical figure became a symbol of Catholic participation in public affairs, tried to use his position as holder of the primatial see to keep peace between the warring parties of the hierarchy. He was very sympathetic to Archbishop Ireland because he was thoroughly American, yet he tried not to offend Archbishop Corrigan and the conservatives. These conservatives, Archbishop Corrigan and his suffragan Bishop McQuaid, were a bit resentful of the dignity of Gibbons and opposed any move to centralize the government of the Church in the United States, such as the establishment of the Catholic University. Gibbons' attempt to mediate between the two groups tended to limit his effectiveness and led to Roman intervention and the setting up of the Apostolic Delegation.

Archbishop Michael Corrigan[26] had been raised to his important office without the wide public experiences of either Ireland or Gibbons. He was a good student but had never been a parish priest. He was the special protégé of Bishop McQuaid whom he succeeded at Seton Hall and was suggested by McQuaid for the see of Newark and the coadjutorship of New York. His photographs show him as a pleasant cleric with large features and a round face. He was not a great speaker but was active in correspondence and in conferences. His friends were mostly conservative and his political interests were with the conservatives of New York City. Archbishop Corrigan had allies but none who were

[26] *Memorial of the Most Reverend Michael Augustine Corrigan, D.D., Third Archbishop of New York*, compiled and edited by authority (New York, 1902) is not a biography. Archbishop Corrigan left much correspondence and a diary. The papers include many carbon copies of his letters, but in some collections there are frequently other letters written by hand of which copies were not kept. Archbishop Corrigan defended the less popular side of most of the controversies of the day and his biographer will have a difficult task, but a biography is needed.

drawn to him by similarity of ideals such as drew together the three leaders of the progressive group. Of the Germans, Archbishop F. X. Katzer of Milwaukee, Bishop Ignatius Horstmann of Cleveland and even Bishop Michael Wigger of Newark were opposed to Ireland chiefly because of his opposition to their efforts to protect their German language schools and his support of rapid Americanization. They gave some support to the charge of liberalism against Ireland. Of Archbishop Patrick Ryan of Philadelphia and Archbishop John Williams of Boston, while they seemed to be sympathetic to Corrigan in his opposition to Ireland, they do not seem to have had much positive interest in the controversies of the day.

Bishop Bernard McQuaid, a stout Irishman of high intellectual ability and uncompromising orthodoxy, remained the chief protagonist of Corrigan. Had the controversy been solely over the parochial schools or social reform, undoubtedly McQuaid would have been a foeman worthy of the Archbishop of St. Paul. Actually he and Ireland found later that their differences were minor. But to the militant Bishop of Rochester, Archbishop Corrigan, even though his superior in rank, was his pupil; and when Corrigan complained to McQuaid that Ireland had unreasonably invaded the New York province and attacked him on his own grounds, McQuaid was quick to spring to the defense of Corrigan, daring even to attack Ireland from the pulpit after Ireland had participated in a New York State political campaign. From that action it was a simple matter for him to see in Ireland a serious opponent in his support of the Apostolic Delegation, in Ireland's founding and fostering of the Catholic University in Washington, in his opposition to the condemnation of Henry Georgism, and in the controversy over the parochial schools. McQuaid was a great pastor to his flock, although he did not allow opposition within his diocese. He built churches and schools. He established a first class seminary which trained young men for many other dioceses as well as for Rochester. His jealous interest in this seminary and his desire to see the Catholic University centered at Seton Hall, his old college which was having financial difficulties, made him an opponent of the Catholic University in Washington and of the group that fostered it in its early years. McQuaid's activities were entirely on the surface. As a public spirited man he would not stoop to attack his opponents secretly, but he was undoubtedly led into traps by friends and opponents who were not so open and direct.

These were the leaders of the opposition when Archbishop Ireland came under fire in the school controversy. Here again Gibbons tried to act as intermediary. After the meeting in St. Louis in November 1891, Gibbons had written to Rome in explanation of the position of Ireland, stating clearly that the archbishops in their St. Louis meeting had accepted as satisfactory Ireland's Faribault and Stillwater agreements. Likewise when Cardinal Simeoni requested an explanation of Ireland's views from Bishop John J. Kain of Wheeling, that prelate, a close friend of the progressive groups, had likewise defended the position of Ireland. Nevertheless the attacks of some of the American Catholic press, particularly *Church Progress* of Condé Pallen of St. Louis, had found support in Rome in the editorials of the *Civiltà Cattolica* under the editorial guidance of Father Salvatore Brandi, S.J., formerly of Woodstock, Maryland. Ireland decided to go to Rome to defend his position. First, however, in December 1891, when in New York, he answered Pallen and defended Bouquillon in an interview with the *New York Herald* on December 12. A month later he sailed from New York on his way to Rome.

No matter how well Archbishop Ireland maintained his position amidst his fellow bishops, his eyes regularly looked to Rome and the good will of the Supreme Pontiff. There were practical as well as dogmatic reasons for listening to every word that came from the Eternal City. Rome was the seat of Catholic orthodoxy and the source of guidance and of jurisdiction. Rome was also the power that would decide which of the two factions would dominate the American Church, and incidentally which of the leaders might become the next American Cardinal. The Holy Father himself, and his Secretary of State, Cardinal Rampolla, did not really favor either faction but hoped that the two groups would unite in the service of the Church. Count Soderini,[27] who was a member of the papal household and who had access to the papers of the Secretary of State, said that the real reason why Leo XIII wanted an Apostolic Delegate in America, and later appointed Archbishop Francesco Satolli, was to bring the two parties together and to promote the desired unity. Cardinal Gibbons likewise seemed to have hoped to play the mediator between the two groups, although he seemed to feel that in most matters Archbishop Ireland was in the right, especially in his insistence on Americanization and higher education. Gibbons wanted to see a strong Catholic Church in the United States with friendly relations with the government and close Catholic participation in civic affairs; he wanted to see the Catholic University prosper as the head of the Catholic educational system in the United States. In all this, however, he moderated his friendship for Ireland lest he antagonize the opponents of the St. Paul prelate, so much so that Ireland sometimes doubted his support.

When he arrived in Rome Archbishop Ireland obtained an interview with Pope Leo XIII and explained his position. He found that the Roman prelates who were opposed to the newly formed Triple Alliance of Italy, Austria and Germany were sympathetic to the prelate who had attacked the Germans for their apparent interference in American church affairs. He found also that Cardinal Rampolla, the Papal Secretary of State, was a friend of Dr. Thomas Bouquillon. Gibbons' letters and Kain's explanations were supplemented by the activities of Monsignor O'Connell. Ireland's agreement with the Holy Father on social and political matters, particularly on the subjects of the two recent papal documents, the *Rerum Novarum* and *Au Milieu des*

[27] Count Eduardo Soderini (1853-1934), prepared a seven volume history of the pontificate of Leo XIII, of which only three were published. The manuscript of the fourth volume is in the possession of his widow, from whom a microfilm copy and the notes upon which it was based were obtained. The title of the manuscript is "Leone XIII e gli Stati Uniti di America." The first three volumes in Italian are entitled *Il pontificato di Leone XIII* (Milan, 1932). An abbreviated translation of the first two volumes has been prepared by Barbara Barclay Carter and published as *The Pontificate of Leo XIII* (London, 1934), and *Leo XIII, Italy and France* (London, 1935).

Sollicitudes, aided Ireland in obtaining a friendly hearing. In the meantime, however, Archbishop Corrigan had obtained by subterfuge the signatures of seven archbishops to a letter to Rome denying that Cardinal Gibbons had properly interpreted their opinions in the St. Louis meeting. Archbishop Corrigan's letter implied that Cardinal Gibbons had erroneously represented that the archbishops yielded to Ireland because of a fear of a state persecution similar to the Kulturkampf in Germany. When Cardinal Gibbons learned of this action of Corrigan he was seriously offended. Cardinal Ledochowski, the new prefect of the Sacred Congregation, however, did not seem to be affected by the letter. Incidentally, also Archbishop Francesco Satolli, then a member of the Vatican court wrote a letter to Archbishop Ireland at this time denying charges of the St. Louis German newspaper *Amerika* that he had attacked Ireland, and expressing his own high opinion of the St. Paul prelate. Again Corrigan obtained the consent of his suffragan bishops of New York State to a new protest against Ireland's use of a threat of force. This time he received from Pope Leo a rather sharp rebuke denying that such a threat had been used either by Cardinal Gibbons or by Ireland.[28] The unauthorized publication of this correspondence in secular newspapers increased the bitterness between the two groups. Meanwhile, the Sacred Congregation in an assembly of April 21 decided that the Faribault—Stillwater plan could be allowed as long as the decrees of the Council of Baltimore were preserved.

This decision had quick effects in the United States. Misled by a cablegram from Rome, Archbishop Corrigan had boasted at a dinner in Albany, on May 5, 1892, that Ireland had been condemned. To his chagrin later messages from Rome brought the actual decision and the news of the victory of Ireland. To Gibbons, Keane, and their friends the victory of Ireland was very precious. Gibbons, who had just completed his second defense of the St. Paul prelate, summed up his opinion of the expected victory in this fashion: "God bless the Pope. Yesterday I prayed at Mass that the Lord might inspire him, and that right and justice should prevail. It is not the Faribault School that is on trial, but

28 Reilly gives the Pope's answer, *op. cit.,* pp. 180-83.

the question to be decided is whether the Church is to be governed here by men or by children,—by justice and truth, or by diplomacy and intrigue,—whether the Church is to be honored as a bulwark of liberty and order or to be despised and suspected as an enemy of our institutions."[29]

Ireland left Rome later in June after making the *Civiltà* publish Gibbons' first letter to O'Connell defending his actions at St. Louis. He left with a consciousness of victory. But as he himself said, he was also a bit saddened, chiefly by the letter signed by the seven archbishops. He could not understand how Corrigan had obtained the signatures of the other archbishops, especially of his friend Archbishop Patrick Riordan of San Francisco. As he wrote to Keane[30] he felt very much alone. He must have known, however, that his friends, Austin Ford and Richard Kerens and Father Alphonse Magnien, S.S., were trying to seal his victory by securing for him the Cardinal's hat. At the request of Kerens, a prominent St. Louis Republican, they almost secured a letter asking for the red hat for Ireland from the President of the United States, Benjamin Harrison.

There was a mild controversy in the Catholic press over the meaning of the *Tolerari Potest*. Some tried to minimize Ireland's victory but in general, even though the decisions of the Baltimore Council were renewed, the plans of Ireland had been approved and his orthodoxy certified. Later Ireland was further disturbed when he discovered that his long Memorial to the Sacred Congregation, in which he defended himself against the Germans, the Jesuits, and the conservative bishops, had been obtained by Corrigan, apparently through Miss Edes. It was published in part in some American newspapers.

But Ireland had broader visions than the American controversy. He did not go directly home. Part of his conversations with the Pontiff had been about French politics, and when he went to France to speak he went—as it were—with the blessing of the

---

[29] Gibbons to O'Connell, March 1, 1892, from the O'Connell papers in Richmond Diocesan Archives.

[30] Ireland to Keane July 3, 1892 in the O'Connell Correspondence, Richmond Diocesan Archives. Writing to O'Connell on July 7, 1892 Ireland expressed the same sentiments, Richmond Diocesan Archives.

Pope himself, and was not an ordinary visitor to France. Furthermore, through the maze of charge and countercharge and because of his undeviating defense of American ways, John Ireland had emerged in western Europe as the chief Catholic of the United States and it was really in this role that he spoke to France in June, 1892. And coming directly from the Pope who had written the letter *Au Milieu des Sollicitudes* in February, 1892, he seemed to be also a kind of papal messenger.

IRELAND'S VISIT to France in 1892 had elements of the dramatic, partly because of his own new prominence and partly because of a new European interest in American Catholicism. Several aspects of Catholic life in the United States had attracted the attention of European Catholics in the late 1800's. The heavy emigration from Europe to the United States in the latter part of the nineteenth century had forcefully drawn the attention of the nations from which these people came to the welfare of these migrants both enroute and in the United States. A very heavy percentage of the later immigration was Catholic. In the case of the Irish, persecuted and English-dominated Ireland had influenced the Irish immigrants only in so far as it asked the exiled Irish to continue the struggle for Irish liberation from English rule. Instead of the Irish helping the Americans, in this instance the Americans were expected to help the Irish. This situation had involved American Irish in the Fenian movement and the Irish Land League, and lost for these Irish leaders the support of the more conservative American bishops, despite the Irish sufferings from recurrent famines. In the case of the Germans, the creation of emigrant aid societies and the activity of Herr Cahensly, together with the ascendant German nationalism following the Franco-Prussian War had involved some of the German immigrants in an American manifestation of German nationalism in the United States in the decade following the Plenary Council. This nationalism fostered a notion of German superiority and a diffidence about American culture among the recent immigrants. The Italians, Poles, and other immigrants were just beginning to be numerous in this country but the governments of their fatherlands were neither capable nor interested in protecting them. The French Canadians, although speaking French, were of no great interest to France, and the agitation to protect these Canadian immigrants came from Montreal and Quebec. For the French in France the interest in America lay primarily in the fact that the United States was the sister republic of the west. Some of the French saw in the American situation a possible solution to their own problem of a Catholic organization in a democratic atmosphere. France and the United States are traditional allies, yet there has never been an adequate study of the cultural exchange between French Catholicism and the Church in the United States.[1] The first great French Catholic contribution to America in the 1790's came with the exiles of the Revolution, especially the priests of Saint Sulpice, who took over under John Carroll and his successors the administration of the small Catholic minority in cooperation with the few native and other French clergy. Later the Association of the Propagation, founded in Lyons in 1822, provided a high percentage of the European funds made available for the American missions. The influence on the character of the American priesthood of the French Sulpicians through their seminaries in Maryland, Kentucky, New York, and Boston was very great. To that source of spiritual formation can be added many French communities of priests, Sisters and Brothers who gave to the Catholic system of education in the United States a definite touch of French asceticism. There were not many French Catholic immigrants in the nineteenth century, however, and the dominance of the Irish in the clergy and laity has tended to obscure this French influence. These facts surely are worth remembering when liberal Catholic writers of France began in the 1890's to praise the growth of the Church in the United States. It was not the traces of French asceticism or the influence of the French religious that attracted such writers as Count Guillaume de Chabrol,[2] Paul Bourget,[3]

[1] A satisfactory study of the French cultural influence on the United States remains to be done. Howard Mumford Jones, *American and French Culture, 1750-1848* (Chapel Hill, 1927) is very inadequate on the Catholic phase. Frances S. Childs, *French Refugee Life in the United States, 1790-1860* (Baltimore, 1940) and Leo Francis Ruskowski, *French Émigré Priests in the United States, 1791-1815* (Washington, 1940) are better on this phase but as their titles indicate they are very limited.

[2] Count Guillaume de Chabrol contributed his articles to *Le Correspondant* in 1867 and 1868, "Les partis politiques aux États Unis," LXXII, 397-446.

[3] *Outre Mer: Notes sur l'Amérique*, 2 vols. (Paris, 1895).

Claudio Jannet,[4] Max Leclerc,[5] and Vicomte De Meaux;[6] they were interested in the new world phenomena of Catholicism reconciled with democracy and the liberal spirit of the age. For them John Ireland's praise of the American Republic in the Third Plenary Council of Baltimore, and his and Gibbons' defense of the Knights of Labor were traits they hoped to see imitated in the French clergy. But the French Catholic story was vastly different from that of the Church in America.

Both countries were republics and had been allied during the revolutionary period in which these republics were formed. There are also other similarities between French Catholicism and Catholicism in the United States which are not so apparent to the casual observer. France has been known as the eldest daughter of the Church, a Catholic country even when its government was one of the severest persecutors of the Church in the nineteenth century, while the United States—although not officially of any religion—was dominantly a Protestant country. But there is one point of similarity between Catholicism in the two countries which can be the source of interesting speculation. The percentage of practicing Catholics in France during the last decades of the nineteenth and early twentieth century has a close similarity to the percentage of actual Catholics in the United States. The large percentage of practicing Protestants in the United States corresponds quite closely to the percentage of baptized but non-practicing French Catholics. There was, however, in the 1890's a very striking difference between the relationships of the Catholics of the United States and their non-Catholic government, and between the French Catholics and the anti-clerical and republican government of France. In the United States, despite flurries of anti-Catholicism in public life, the loyalty of the Catholics to the American government and their acceptance of American democracy had been loudly demonstrated. In France, because of

[4] *Les États Unis Contemporaine ou, Les Moeurs, les Institutions, et les Idées depuis la Guerre de la Sécession* (Paris, 1875).

[5] *Choses d'Amérique: Les Crises économique et religieuse aux États Unis* (Paris, 1895), although some of the essays were printed before that date.

[6] De Meaux wrote essays on the United States in *Le Correspondant* which were subsequently published under the title, *L'Église Catholique et la Liberté aux États Unis* (2 ed., 1893).

the conflict between the Church and the Revolution and certain accidents of the Empire of Napoleon III, the Church had become traditionally an ally of legitimists and royalists and uncooperative with the republican government. Even the return of the bourgeoisie to Catholicism left the mass of the people unresponsive to Catholic teaching. The want of cooperation with the Third Republic had serious results in the internal life of French Catholicism. With the exception of the attempted rise of Catholic liberalism in the first half of the century under the leadership of Lamennais, Chateaubriand, and Montalembert, and the early years of the Empire, the churchmen's decline from power had given rise in French Catholicism to a spirit of retreat and reaction from the more democratic and scientific spirit of the nineteenth century. This spirit of resistance to the Republic characterized French official Catholicism at least until the death of its chief spokesman, Louis Veuillot, the editor of the *Univers*, and the election of the new Pope, Leo XIII. The dominant democratic and liberal movements in western Europe in the nineteenth century found little correspondence in the life of Catholicism of so-called Catholic France. In politics, the Catholics were usually considered royalists and anti-democratic; in the realm of intellectual interests they were considered as opposed to the scientism of the nineteenth century which had indeed become not merely neutral on religious matters but anti-religious chiefly because of the absence of Catholicism from the great universities now government controlled or non-Catholic. Along with their conservatism in politics and university studies, the Catholics were usually considered out of touch with the social and economic reforms of the age, which tended to be socialistic. Theologically the growth of the higher criticism and the worship of science in the secular universities had given rise there to a liberalism in religion and to an extremely critical attitude towards the Scriptures in which the lack of Catholic participation was further damaging to the popular position of the Church in France and Italy.

The loss of the universities and the lack of government support for Catholic universities planned to replace them—together with the irreligious tone of so much scientific and scholarly writing of the nineteenth century—had made the retreat of Catholicism even more emphatic. As a result the enlightening encyclicals of Pope Leo XIII on labor and on reconciliation with the French Republic met with shock and even resistance by the majority of the French clergy.[7]

There had always been a minority in the Catholic groups in the countries of southern Europe and in the Catholic Rhineland which had not gone along with these retreatist policies of the dominant leaders of Catholicism. There were always some followers of Montalembert and Lacordaire. Almost simultaneously with the election of Gioacchino Pecci as Pope Leo XIII, new programs for intellectual revival and social reform began to flourish in France and to a lesser degree in Italy. While all these movements had something in common—a kind of progressivism which led their opponents to accuse them of the condemned liberalism of the *Syllabus of Errors*—the revival of progressive Catholic thought in France did not seem able to unite the various leaders of these progressive programs, except in an occasional person. Yet those who were opposed to royalism, and those who were advocating social and economic reform, seem to have had more in common than some of the other groups; and those who were turning against the worship of science, and those who were adapting the philosophy of St. Thomas Aquinas to the modern battle, seemed to have been rather closely associated. In general, however, the various groups participating in the resurgence of Catholicism and Catholic thought in France during the last two decades of the nineteenth century all seem to have something in common—chiefly the inspiration of Pope Leo and the desire to show that the Church was not in conflict with the progress of the Modern World. The interest of the French liberal Catholic in the growth of Catholicism in the United States stemmed mostly from the desire to find a solution to these conflicts in France similar to that manifested by the leaders of the Church in the

[7] This situation is treated by Adrien Dansette in his *Histoire Religieuse de la France Contemporaine sous la Troisième République* (Paris, 1951), pp. 13-124; also in J. Brugerette, *Le Prêtre Français et Société Contemporaine*, 3 vols. (Paris, 1935) II, 24-65. To get some idea of the distance between French religious thought of the nineteenth century and that of American Catholicism one can examine the account of Georges Fonsegrive, *L'Évolution des idées dans la France Contemporaine* (Paris, 1921).

United States, especially by Gibbons, Ireland, Keane, Hecker, and Zahm.

It was remarkable coincidence that in the Third Plenary Council of Baltimore the prelate chosen to speak on the relations between the Church and the civil authorities in the United States was the eloquent Bishop of Saint Paul who was well informed on the French Catholic situation. The basic problem in the adaptation of Catholic ideals to the American scene lay in the field of citizenship and social and economic reform. And in these early years of his episcopate, John Ireland had shown a remarkable sensitiveness to American ideals. He had tangled with the civil authorities in his own state in seeking the elimination of intolerance and prejudice in state charitable and penal institutions, and in his working for temperance and for the welfare of the immigrants he had manifested a sense of American tolerance. Further his clear grasp of theology and his oratorical ability made him the natural choice to express for the assembled bishops the proper relationship between the Catholic Church, absolute in the field of revealed religion, and the young American democracy which rejected with a strong jealousy anything that savored of tyranny.

In his sermon at the Baltimore Council[8] Bishop Ireland had spent most of his time establishing the Catholic doctrine of authority and rejecting the various kinds of tyranny whether of state absolutism of monarchical regimes or of state absolutism based upon the false doctrine of Rousseauistic or Hobbesian theory. Then he had proceeded to show that the Catholic Church was not concerned with the form of government as long as authority and the essential human liberty were preserved. In the United States he found the greatest aid to the Church was the liberties she enjoyed. From this fact Ireland went on in his sermon of 1889, on the centenary of the hierarchy, to give to American Catholicism the duty of reconciling the Church and the age, "to maintain in the world the supremacy of the supernatural, and to save the age to the Church."[9] He admitted that not all the modern ideas and movements were in all respects deserving of ap-

---

[8] The speech was reprinted in his *The Church and Modern Society*, 2 vols. (New York, 1903) I, 27-65.

[9] *Ibid.*, I, 71-101, "The Mission of Catholics in America."

proval, as had been shown by Pope Pius IX in his *Syllabus*, but there was much good in the age and Catholics must distinguish between the bad and the good. Thus he praised as the watchwords of the age, "knowledge," "the amelioration of the masses," "material comfort"; "socialism" in so far as it is an aspiration "towards a perfect civilization, towards the enjoyment of God's gift in full measure, and by the largest number of God's children." "This is an intellectual age," Ireland said and also "ours is essentially the age of democracy." Further he called for an aggressive Catholicism which would seek men out and urge them to come into the Church, especially among the masses.

The French press, besides reporting these speeches, had given Archbishop Ireland an important part in the defense of the Knights of Labor because he was in Rome at the time and probably helped compose the plea for the Knights presented by Gibbons to the Cardinals. Likewise, his public resistance to the Cahenslyites struck a responsive cord in the French hearts who still smarted from the German victories of the Franco-Prussian War.

John Ireland when he left Rome to go to Paris realized that he was far from an unknown in France, at least among the supporters of the *ralliement*. As he himself had written to Monsignor O'Connell on March 8, 1891,[10] "The *Journal des Débats* has made it almost impossible to go to France. I am sure a mere sight of me will take me down from the pedestal on which I am placed. The 'Figaro' and the 'Petit Journal' and numerous others continue to give extracts of that Baltimore sermon." Indeed, that sermon at the centenary of the American hierarchy in 1889, in which he not only praised the Church in America but also praised democracy, progress, and lay leadership in the Church, was the very kind of message that certain French laymen who were actively supporting the new policy of Pope Leo XIII were anxious to hear. Not being able to get a reply directly from Ireland himself, Henri Lorin and his associates had turned to Monsignor O'Connell[11] to

[10] Archbishop Ireland to Denis O'Connell, March 8, 1891 in Richmond Diocesan Archives.

[11] O'Connell to Ireland, Jan. 12, 1891, in which O'Connell tells of his correspondence with Lorin, Archives of the Archdiocese of Saint Paul.

solicit his intercession in obtaining a visit and a lecture at Paris from Ireland when he came to Europe. If Archbishop Ireland saw a great future for Catholicism in the American republic, he would undoubtedly have some encouraging message for Catholics in the French Republic.

Most of the French literature about the United States written in the second half of the century took a liberal and friendly view of the democracy beyond the sea. But it was not to be expected that the more numerous monarchists—clerics or laymen—of the French Church would find much to admire in a democratic America. The *réfractaires* against the liberal policies of Pope Leo XIII felt that the French Revolution was essentially evil, and that the existing Republic was so tainted with the same anti-religious philosophy that there could be no cooperation between the Church and the Republic. This rejection of republicanism greatly influenced the attitude of these conservatives toward the advancement of science and even toward social reform. Nevertheless, even among some conservatives there were many who felt the need of improvement in the condition of the workers in the factories. This Catholic Social Action in France[12] was for the most part independent of the Monarchist-Republican division, yet found its greatest allies in democratic clergymen and laymen who hoped to bring about some kind of reconciliation between democracy and the Church. Under the leadership of Pope Leo XIII, French Catholic Social Action became a real force in French Catholic life. At first the reform movements had tried to stay within the existing social and traditional political order. Most notable of the leaders of Catholic social reform were Du Pin, Harmel and Count de Mun. But two actions of Pope Leo XIII changed the status of Catholic social and political reform in France. The first was the *Rerum Novarum* of May 15, 1891, in favor of the workers, which canonized the social reform of Count de Mun and advocated state intervention when necessary to protect the rights of the workers. Strangely this encyclical, by its ac-

[12] Henri Rollet, *L'Action Sociale des Catholiques en France, 1871-1901* (Paris, 1951) is a very fine treatment of this Catholic social action movement but it carefully abstains from other phases of French Catholic life.

ceptance of the rights of workers and the need of social legisla-
tion, seemed to eliminate the milder reforms and the *cercles*
advocated by some of the Catholic bourgeoisie. The second was
preceded by the famous toast of Cardinal Lavigerie at Algiers on
November 12, 1890, in which with the apparent blessing of the
Pope he called for closer union between the Church and the Republic. Amid the sharp disagreements with the Cardinal's speech,
Leo wrote his encyclical *Au Milieu des Sollicitudes* of February
10, 1892, which called for the French Catholics to accept the Republic. The papal inspired movement to accept the Republic
was called the *ralliement*. Neither papal document had received
complete support among the Catholics in France, although the
circles of workers of Leon Harmel, Du Pin, and Lorin seemed to
be encouraged somewhat by the first encyclical until the issue
became confused with the political problems. Some French leaders, and a few bishops did accept the encyclical on the Republic,
but for the most part the bishops and the clergy, especially the
religious orders, held back from the *ralliement*. It was under such
conditions that the French progressives—whether democrats or
legitimists—began to look more continuously to Catholicism in
America, if not for leadership, at least for examples which could
be studied with profit, or imitated in France. To these, the
speeches of Archbishop John Ireland were very attractive. The
first of his sermons to receive notable attention in France was the
sermon at the Third Plenary Council on the relations of Church
and State. They noted with quickened interest his remarkable
peroration, "Republic of America, receive from me the tribute of
my love and of my loyalty. I am proud to do thee homage, and I
pray from my heart that thy glory may never be dimmed—*Esto
Perpetua*."[13] To those who were advocating social Catholicism
in France, Ireland's speech at the centenary of the American hierarchy was even more attractive, for in that he called for the
Church to enter into the social and political movements of the
day and win them for the Church. In that oration he had said
"We should speak to our age of things which it feels and in
language it understands. We should be in it, and of it, if we

[13] Ireland, *op. cit.*, I, 62.

would have it to listen to us."[14] He further demanded a sympathy with America and that American Catholics should be the greatest patriots of the land. He said the age was an intellectual age and the Catholic schools, particularly the new Catholic University, should be the best. "The strength of the Church today in all countries, particularly in America, is the people. Ours is essentially the age of democracy."[15] In the meantime some of these progressive French leaders had visited the United States. Chief of these probably was the Vicomte De Meaux who heard Ireland and interviewed him. His articles in the *Le Correspondant* later published under the title *Liberté Religieuse aux États Unis* praised highly the progress of the Church in the United States under the liberties of the American constitution. The second edition of this in 1893 was prefaced by a laudatory letter of Cardinal Gibbons.

Although Henri Lorin, a rich manufacturer with liberal interests, had been most active in securing the visit of Ireland the committee that took charge of his visit and especially his public lecture included MM. Eugene Melchior de Vogüé, Georges Picot, Anatole Leroy-Beaulieu, Albert de Mun, and Max Leclerc. The committee arranged the lecture for Saturday evening, June 18, in the hall of the Société de Géographie. The hall was filled for the occasion chiefly with men notable for their progressive ideas, although prominent conservatives also attended. *Le Moniteur Universel* of June 20 estimated the audience at six hundred people and mentioned many of the people by name, such as A. Leroy-Beaulieu, General Annehoff, Boutmy, Paul Deschanel and others. Ireland took advantage of the occasion. Dressed in a simple cassock, with manners appropriately quite simple, he apparently wanted to convey to his audience the simplicity of the leaders of the Church in the United States. He gave a glowing account of the progress of Catholicism in the United States, laying particular stress on the statements that in America the Church was the church of the people, that there the bishops lived among the people and were regarded as the people's protectors. He continued,

14 *Ibid.*, I, 90-91.
15 *Ibid.*, I, 93.

that while the clergy gave much time to their religious functions, they did not remain in the sanctuaries and sacristies but went much into public life. He told them that he himself spoke publicly on industry, agriculture, railroads, and social questions. He told them that the Catholic people themselves though formerly poor immigrants had acquired wealth, and that they were accepted as loyal sons of the Republic—this he noted had been proved in their rejection of Cahenslyism. Alluding to the recent encyclicals of the Pope he mentioned that the Church was willing to try living under the French Republic. In America the solution to the social questions was easier because of the fundamental recognition of the dignity of man, the same principle that "underlies Christian sociology." His audience was enthusiastic and the speech was carried at great length in *Le Figaro* and in many other papers of France.[16]

On Saturday, June 25, Ireland was the guest at the annual dinner of the students of the Cercle Catholique du Luxembourg in Paris. Ireland presided at the banquet having at the table with him, the chaplain of the Cercle, Abbé Fonsagrives, Monsignor D'Hulst, the rector of the Institut Catholique, and Monsignor O'Connell who had accompanied him from Rome. He took as his subject "The Social Action of the French Youth."[17] In his address he recalled his own youth and spoke of the friendship between the Republic of France and the United States. He spoke of the great mission of the French youth, of the necessity to be modern

[16] Volume XXII of the clippings in the Archdiocesan Archives of Saint Paul contains many excerpts from the French newspapers on this speech. Most notable of these are from *Le Figaro*, June 19, 1892; *France Nouvelle*, June 19; *Le Petit Journal*, June 19; *La Libre Parole*, June 19; *Le Moniteur Universel*, June 20; *Le République Français*, June 20; *Observateur Français*, June 21; *Salus Public* of Lyons, June 21; *Phare de la Loire* of Nantes, June 21; *Le Temps*, June 21; and many others. The discourse, the personality of Ireland, and the liberty of the Church in the United States were widely discussed in the French press for several days following the discourse. Henri Berenger, in *L'Aristocratie intellectuelle* (Paris, 1895) describes vividly the impression made on him by Ireland. The speech is given in English by Ireland, *op. cit.*, I, 365-95.

[17] Ireland's speech to the students is quoted at length in *Le Monde*, June 28, 1892, although *Le Journal des Débats*, *Le Gaulois*, *Le Temps* and *Le Figaro*, among others, gave accounts of the meeting on June 26 and June 27. *Le Figaro* opened its account of this speech with the statement that Ireland was at that moment the lion of the Christians of Paris.

and to be for the people. "It is better," he said, "to try to do things and fail than not to try to do them." "Catholics," he added, "should be the most ardent defenders of the people." Apparently a few days later[18] he spoke privately to a group of about 150 priests at La Maison de la Bonne Presse, including a rather large number of the curates of the parishes of the city. "The Gospel," he said, "is the best manual for priests." He told the priests to go out and meet their parishioners, to make themselves known and loved by the people. They must be interested in the welfare of the faithful on earth as well as in their happiness in heaven. Finally he told them to go out of their sanctuaries and sacristies. The younger clergy received his words with great enthusiasm. There were some muffled criticisms from those who did not agree, but since he apparently came directly with the approval of Rome, they dared not openly attack him. This third discourse was also carried in some of the newspapers.

The effects of Ireland's visit and speeches on French Catholicism is difficult to estimate. It is quite evident that he was not received openly by many of the hierarchy. His hosts were for the most part laymen active in Catholic social action and young clergy who had reacted favorably to the *ralliement* of Leo XIII, but there is no question that Archbishop Ireland became to friend and foe a symbol of American democracy in the field of religion. This was to become especially true when Abbé Félix Klein, a young writer and editor, translated and edited the speeches of Ireland in 1894, under the title *L'Église et le Siècle*, the title of his speech at the silver jubilee of Cardinal Gibbons. All who were interested in the religious revival that was affecting France during this last decade of the nineteenth century manifested an interest in this American bishop who had spoken so directly and with so much apparent freedom from traditional restrictions. His actions were hailed notably by the Néo-Chrétien movement headed by MM. Melchior de Vogüé, Henri Berenger,[19] and Paul

[18] *Le Temps*, June 28 has a notable account of this speech. It was also summarized in *Le Grenoblais* of Grenoble, June 29, 1892.

[19] Cf. Berenger, *op. cit.*, for a statement of the position of the *néo-chrétien* movement. His reaction toward later developments is contained in his *La Conscience Nationale* (Paris, 1898).

Desjardins.[20] These Néo-Chrétiens, called by Berenger an intellectual elite, constituted basically a revolt from the materialism of the cult of science which had held sway in France during the nineteenth century. They were blindly turning back towards the traditional faith of the French nation, but for the most part they were unwilling to accept the definite faith or the dogmas of Catholicism. The movement of Desjardins called for a "Christian moralism" in much the same spirit, even though Berenger disagreed with him on this moralism. These movements were in many ways related to all the revivals of Christian religion and culture that could be felt in France at the beginning of the last decade of the nineteenth century. Berenger and Desjardins admired the action of Cardinal Gibbons and Archbishop Ireland in preventing the condemnation of the Knights of Labor, and they welcomed the speeches of Ireland. Writing of Ireland, Henri Berenger could say that Ireland gave them a concept of a new clergy, a new race and of the renewed religion.[21] Paul Desjardins said that Ireland had given proof that religion should be the best support of democracy. This episode of Ireland's speeches in Paris was but an interlude in the Archbishop's American battles, but it did have a startling effect on the new religious movement of France. Ireland with the backing of Pope Leo could not be attacked by the conservatives. But the conservatives accepted Ireland's notion of the reconciliation of the Church and the age even less than they accepted Pope Leo's suggestion of reconciliation between the Church and the Republic. The conservative press was waiting for the opportunity to discredit him and his *Américanisme*. But the Archbishop himself during the next few months had so many problems of his own in America that he had little time to think more of France. Within a few years the books and articles praising democracy and Catholicism in the United States became very numerous in France. Besides assembling the chief orations of Ireland into a single volume,[22] the young Abbé Klein published in

[20] Desjardins' moralism as mentioned by Berenger is well exemplified in Desjardins' *The Present Duty*, translated from the French by E. N. (Philadelphia, 1893).

[21] Berenger, *op. cit.*, p. 92.

[22] Klein, Abbé, ed., *L'Église et le Siècle* (Paris, 1894).

1894, his own *Nouvelles Tendences en Religion et en Littérature* praising the new spirit. And to add to the fervor of the admiration for American Catholicism and the urging for imitation in France, Cardinal Gibbons had given, in 1895, in an interview[23] to the press in Paris while returning from Rome, his own criticism of the French clergy. They stay too much in their sacristies, he said.

There were two developments on the campaign between the Ireland and Corrigan factions while he was returning home. Archbishop Corrigan had obtained from Rome a copy of Ireland's *Memorial* presented in defense of his educational theories and, on June 26, had portions of it appear in the *New York World*.[24] Corrigan wanted to strengthen the charge that Ireland had won his *tolerari potest* by threatening an American Kulturkampf. At about the same time Ireland's lay friends, especially Austin Ford[25] and Richard Kerens, continued their efforts to get a letter from the President or the Secretary of State to Cardinal Rampolla urging the naming of Ireland as Cardinal. Actually the Secretary of State, James G. Blaine, did write a letter which was directly acknowledged by Cardinal Rampolla. Ireland was aware of these political moves although he seems to have had little confidence in them. He was more disturbed with the publication of parts of his *Memorial*.

When Archbishop Ireland arrived in New York on July 8, 1892,[26] he found that a meeting between himself and Archbishop Corrigan had been arranged at the New York Protectory by persons hopeful of healing the breach between the two prelates. However Ireland did not attend the dinner. Instead, he did receive a visit in his hotel room from Father Edward McGlynn, the

[23] *La Vérité* (Paris) July 30, 1895 quotes from *La Gaulois*. In *La Vérité* of August 21, a writer warned Gibbons about the *Syllabus of Errors*.

[24] There were bitter charges made against Miss Ella B. Edes, a Roman correspondent for the conservatives and friend of Corrigan, that a copy of the Memorial had been stolen. Ireland did have a phrase referring to the Kulturkampf in the Memorial. The Memorial is printed in the appendix of Daniel F. Reilly, *The School Controversy, 1891-1893,* (Washington, 1943) pp. 250-266.

[25] This story is told in the letters of Austin Ford to Ireland, Gibbons and O'Connell contained in the O'Connell papers in the Richmond Diocesan Archives.

[26] Ireland to O'Connell, July 7, July 9, July 11, and August 3, 1892.

New York priest then in trouble with Archbishop Corrigan, although he gave no encouragement to his visitor. In a few days he went to Baltimore for a visit with Cardinal Gibbons and to Washington before going home to his archdiocese. But he was soon actively corresponding in a new development in this burning controversy, the proposed appointment of an Apostolic Delegate.

The American hierarchy had been aware for many years that Pope Leo XIII desired to establish a nuntio or resident delegate in Washington to receive information and to act as his representative on special occasions. The establishment of a nuntio had not appeared feasible. To the American hierarchy, almost to a man, the appointment of a resident delegate was not desirable because the bishops feared that it would lead to interference by him in the government of their dioceses. Pope Leo, however, had not given up the idea, and in his conversations with Monsignor O'Connell the Pope had again brought up the question, as O'Connell[27] subsequently warned Gibbons. Nevertheless, available correspondence indicates that Ireland had no reason to expect the imminence of such an appointment when he left Rome in May. But events were happening in the United States that gave the Pope his desired occasion to carry out his plans to appoint a delegate whose chief function should be to check the growing rift in the American hierarchy.

In preparation for the celebration of the 400th anniversary of the landing of Columbus in the New World, Chicago planned a World's Fair, later called the Columbian Exposition, to be formally opened on May 1, 1893. In connection with the Exposition it was suggested that certain maps and charts of the fifteenth century in the possession of the Vatican be exhibited. After some discussion, Secretary of State John W. Foster wrote to Gibbons to arrange the loan of the desired maps and charts. After some conferences among Foster, Richard W. Kerens—a Republican Cath-

[27] O'Connell to Ireland July 1, 1891. Ellis, John Tracy, *The Life of James Cardinal Gibbons, Archbishop of Baltimore, 1834-1921*, 2 vols. (Milwaukee, 1952) I, 595-652 has the best account of the establishment of the Apostolic Delegation. Soderini in his unpublished manuscript maintains that Pope Leo XIII wanted a resident delegate to heal the breach between Ireland and Corrigan and their followers.

olic from Missouri—and Gibbons, it was arranged that Foster would write to Cardinal Rampolla asking for the loan of the documents. Foster wrote on September 15, Rampolla answered promptly on September 28, not only promising the maps and charts but announcing that the Pope was appointing a personal representative to accompany them and to represent the Pope as ablegate at the Exposition. Since the dedication of the Fair building was to take place in October, it was imperative that the appointment be made immediately. But the one chosen, Archbishop Francesco Satolli, had not only been the Papal Ablegate at the celebration of the Centenary of the hierarchy in Baltimore in 1889, but had defended Archbishop Ireland when the German newspaper *Amerika* attacked him in 1891. Just how much Monsignor Denis O'Connell had to do with the Pope's choice for delegate is not clear, but it seems that he and Archbishop Ireland had promoted his appointment in case any delegate was sent. Certainly Archbishop Ireland had cultivated Satolli's friendship in Rome, and felt that in him the Pope had appointed a friend. He immediately wrote to his friend Monsignor O'Connell to make sure that Satolli should remain in his care when he came to this country, even suggesting that the Pope or the papal Secretary of State should commit Satolli to his care once he got to this country.[28]

The circumstances of Satolli's appointment are rather complicated. Soderini who had access to the office and papers of the papal Secretary of State maintained that the chief reason that Pope Leo appointed Satolli was to get a representative into this country who could mediate between the two factions and to prevent a wider division. Soderini believed, however, that Satolli was not so informed by the Papal court, and that, in his ignorance of the English language, Satolli made many errors. If the purpose of the appointment was to heal the breach between the two factions, the circumstances of the coming could not have been arranged

---

[28] Ireland to O'Connell, August 20, 1893 Richmond Diocesan Archives and O'Connell to Ireland, September 16, 1893. O'Connell in his letters to Ireland before they left Rome indicated that the appointment of Satolli as legate to the Exposition was a temporary cover and that the permanent appointment would be announced before Satolli returned to Rome.

worse. Accompanying Satolli and writing ahead to make the plans for the visit was Monsignor Denis O'Connell. Between O'Connell and Ireland, and with the unwitting cooperation of Cardinal Gibbons, a revenue cutter had been secured to meet the *Majestic* and the Ablegate in the New York harbor, and a special train secured on the B & O Railroad to rush him from New York to Baltimore. Archbishop Corrigan received just enough information to feel that the Ablegate was entirely aligned with Ireland and decided to stay in his residence awaiting the visit of the Ablegate. Apparently the Ablegate could not understand why the Archbishop was not at the docks to meet him. In a letter to Bishop McQuaid, Corrigan admitted that he showed Archbishop Satolli scant courtesy.[29] Without much ceremony the Ablegate was hurried into the special train to Baltimore, thence after a visit to Washington, and to Chicago to assist at the dedication of the main Fair building in Chicago on October 21. After that he went to St. Paul where he was the guest of Archbishop Ireland. Up until that time there had been no manifest purpose in his visit except to represent the Pope at the Columbian Exposition. That he had other purposes soon became apparent. From St. Paul he went to New York to attend the annual meeting of the archbishops on November 16. To the consternation of Archbishop Corrigan and Bishop McQuaid and the other conservatives, he made to the archbishops two proposals. First, he offered a solution to the public parochial school question in fourteen points which seemed to carry out the principles set forth by Archbishop Ireland, insisting that Catholic schools be as good as public schools in subject matter, allowing Catholic children to attend public schools when other plans could not be carried out, forbidding pastors to refuse the sacraments to parents who did not send their children to Catholic schools, and allowing compromises such as Ireland had used, while insisting on education in the Catholic religion according to the Third Plenary Council of Baltimore. In the second proposal he suggested that there be a permanent resident Apostolic

[29] Frederick J. Zwierlein, *Letters of Archbishop Corrigan to Bishop McQuaid and Allied Documents*, (Rochester, 1946) pp. 151-52. The accounts of the arrival of Satolli and his meeting with Corrigan are not too clear as to whether there was any real contact between them.

Delegate in the United States. Satolli then retired from the arch-bishops' meeting, and both proposals were rejected by the arch-bishops, although Satolli was apparently not fully informed of this fact. On the first point, the reaction of the conservatives, especially Bishop McQuaid, was bitter. They were more than ever convinced that Satolli was the tool of Archbishop Ireland. They rejected the fourteen points of Satolli by a vote reported to have been unanimous with the exception of Ireland, and voted a four point solution reaffirming the decrees of the Third Plenary Baltimore Council. The Satolli suggestion later got into the public press and occasioned a bitter controversy between the Catholic newspapers supporting the progressive and conservative parties. Later that spring the Pope asked the opinion of the individual bishops. Of the letters of the bishops to Rome on Satolli's proposals that of Bishop McQuaid was very forceful. He argued that instead of upholding the decrees of the Baltimore Council, certain of Satolli's propositions, especially the proposition forbidding the refusal of the sacraments to parents who did not send their children to Catholic schools, went contrary to the decrees of the Council. After receiving these letters, on May 31, the Pope wrote a letter to the American hierarchy stating that one of the prime objects of Satolli's appointment as Delegate was to settle the school controversy and that unless the latter propositions of the Delegate were to be interpreted in a sense contradictory to the first proposition, the bishops should have understood that the decrees of the Baltimore Council and whatever else had been prescribed by the Roman pontiffs "are to be steadfastly observed."[30]

On the second point, the question of the proposed delegate, Cardinal Gibbons was instructed by the archbishops to gather the opinions of the bishops and while thanking the Pope for sending such a wise and gracious representative to the Fair, to inform the Pope that the bishops felt that the appointment of a permanent delegate was now inopportune. He sent off this letter to the Pope through Monsignor O'Connell on January 3.

In the meantime Archbishop Satolli went on to Washington to

[30] Cf. Reilly, *op. cit.*, pp. 226-230, which gives the Pope's letter; the passage referred to is on p. 229.

take up his residence at the Catholic University. Apparently he was to stay there for a year and to represent the Holy Father at the Columbian Exposition proper, which would open the following May. In the meantime, he startled the American bishops by announcing December 3, that he had received extraordinary powers to handle certain problems concerning American ecclesiastics. This grant of powers did not seem too important, except that under it he arranged for Father McGlynn, the New York priest suspended since 1886 by Archbishop Corrigan, to subscribe to the Leonine doctrines on private property and socialism. On December 23, Satolli reinstated him as a priest in good standing after an examination by a committee of Catholic University professors. McGlynn promised to go to Rome as he had been commanded before his suspension. Archbishop Corrigan had to receive him back into the archdiocese. He did not restore McGlynn to his large urban parish of St. Stephen, but after a time made him a pastor at Newburgh.

Suddenly, while Cardinal Gibbons' letter to the Holy Father announcing the rejection of the suggestion that there be an Apostolic Delegate was on its way to Rome, Archbishop Satolli, on January 14, announced that he had been appointed the first resident Apostolic Delegate to the United States. Gibbons had time to have O'Connell stop his letter, but some mischievous individual obtained a copy of the Cardinal's letter of January 19 to the archbishops and bishops—asking what to do and implying that they were all opposed to the delegation—and gave it to the press on February 5, to afford an amusing contradiction to Gibbons' second letter of January 30, on the pleasure of Gibbons and the other bishops at the appointment of the delegate. In the meantime in some secular papers appeared some rather scurrilous attacks upon the delegate with implications that he had failed. Another incident in this connection that added bitterness to the controversy was the appearance in the *Chicago Sunday Post* on January 8, 1893, of an article entitled "The Catholic World Shaken by a Scandalous Plot Against Papal Authority," accusing Archbishop Corrigan, Father Michael Lavelle, and Father Gerardo Ferrante, the Archbishop's secretary, of being the author of the articles that had appeared in American newspapers attacking Archbishop

Satolli. Archbishop Corrigan in turn accused Ireland of being responsible for the *Chicago Post* story. Nevertheless the Delegate began to exercise some of his powers in the settling of disputes particularly between certain bishops and their priests in various parts of the country. There was no friendly exchange between him and Archbishop Corrigan during the spring of 1893.

On June 16, 1893, Archbishop Satolli left Washington for an extensive visit to the west, visiting Chicago, St. Paul, and certain sees west of the Mississippi, devoting some of his time to the difficulties of Bishop Bonacum of Lincoln, Nebraska. While visiting St. Paul he gave to the public a statement in strong praise of Archbishop Ireland, mentioning the fact that he had received from the Pope when he came the previous year a special letter and commendation to the care of the archbishop. Since the attacks on the Delegate were continuing and the source was being attributed to the archbishop of New York, the Delegate also expressed to Ireland a regret that he had ever had any dealings with Corrigan.[31] He had apparently reported this antagonism between himself and the New York archbishop to Rome because Cardinal Gibbons received a letter dated June 15 from Cardinal Rampolla asking Gibbons to try to heal the breach between Satolli and Corrigan. In the meantime Archbishop Corrigan had learned how the coming of Satolli had been maneuvered by Ireland and O'Connell, and so informed Gibbons who professed not to have been a party to the scheme. Then, through Gibbons, Corrigan gave a formal invitation to Satolli to visit him. At a public reception in Saint Patrick's Cathedral in New York on August 15, 1893, Corrigan was allowed to make amends. On the way back to Washington Satolli was also the guest of Archbishop Patrick Ryan, a friend of Corrigan's, and thus the apparent rift between Satolli and the conservatives came to an end.

Satolli continued to live on the grounds of the Catholic University and seemed to belong to the party of Keane.[32] In the meantime, Satolli had also become acquainted with Monsignor Joseph

[31] Ireland to Gibbons, June 13, 1893, Baltimore Archdiocesan Archives.

[32] The account of "Spectator" (apparently Dr. F. X. Kraus) in his letters in *Beilage zur Allgemeinen Zeitung* of Munich in 1897 indicates the influence of Satolli's stay on the campus of the Catholic University. Cf. "Kirchenpolitische Briefe XXIII," p. 5; *Beilage zur Allgemeinen Zeitung*, May 1, 1897.

Schroeder, the leader of the German faction at the Catholic University of America, and Abbé Georges Périès, the canon law teacher, both of whom were opposed to the policies of the Rector, Bishop Keane, and to the minimism or liberalism—as they called it—of the "Irish" party. Nevertheless, until the Delegate moved to the house on the Washington property purchased by the hierarchy for him, there was no apparent change in his attitude towards the Ireland party.

The Catholic Columbian Congress of September 4-9, 1893, in Chicago was a lay Congress patterned after the Baltimore Congress of 1889 and was addressed by bishops as well as laymen. Of this Catholic lay Congress no satisfactory history has yet been written. Its outstanding characteristic was the opportunity it offered to Catholic laymen to speak on Catholic aspects of the problems of the day. While the Congress had been planned by such laymen as Henry Brownson and William J. Onahan, the inspiration and assistance of Archbishop Ireland were never wanting and the general tone could be said to have been progressive rather than conservative. At the time Satolli was just finishing a tour of the western and middle western dioceses, and his appearance before the Congress on the second day was one of the important incidents of the festivities, especially as he came in the company of Archbishop Ireland. As a matter of fact Satolli's speech at the Columbian Congress[33] in Chicago on September 5 expressed ideas much like those of Ireland. Standing alongside Archbishop Ireland, who later translated his Italian into English, Satolli gave a very spirited address to the Congress in which he praised the American Catholics and their devotion to Pope Leo. It was in the peroration of this speech that he said "Go forward, in one hand bearing the book of Christian truth and in the other the Constitution of the United States."[34] There is, however, no evidence that he had any influence on the annual meeting of the archbishops which took

[33] There is a brief account of this in Sister M. Sevina Pahorezki, O.S.F., *The Social and Political Activities of William James Onahan* (Washington, 1942), pp. 136-159.

[34] *Loyalty to Church and State, The Mind of His Eminence, Francis Cardinal Satolli* (Baltimore, 1895), p. 150.

place that week in Chicago and which he apparently attended. At the meeting a resolution was passed deprecating the attacks on members of the hierarchy then appearing in the Catholic press.

Two other events, however, of this first year of the Apostolic Delegate attracted wide attention. The first was the Parliament of Religions,[35] held in Chicago, September 11 to 28, in which several Catholic prelates appeared on the platform with representatives of other religions. The decision to participate in the Parliament had been made at the archbishops' meeting in New York in 1892, and Bishop Keane had been placed in charge of the Catholic representation. The participation of the Catholic hierarchy was given prominent publicity, and was noticeable throughout the Parliament. On the first day Archbishop Feehan gave an address of welcome. Cardinal Gibbons was not well and while he was present his speech was read by Bishop Keane. Keane gave two papers during the Parliament: one on the "Incarnation Idea in History and in Jesus Christ" and one on "The Ultimate Religion." Several other Catholic clergymen and laymen read papers on phases of religious social activity. For the most part great care was taken by the Catholic speakers not to imply any derogation of Catholic claims to supremacy in the gatherings, although the Anglican version of the Pater Noster was used in the public prayers. Gibbons and Keane and the other Catholic speakers insisted on Catholic supremacy, but they were meeting on an equality with numbers of sects and pagan religions. Subsequently Keane's final address on the "Ultimate Religion" was criticized severely by conservative Catholics.[36] Satolli himself seems to have been unwilling to participate and to have withheld his approval of the Catholic participation, but the participating bishops felt that a real service had been done to the Church by allowing those

[35] Rev. John Henry Barrows, ed. *The World's Parliament of Religions*, 2 vols. (Chicago, 1893) is the most complete account of this assembly and contains almost all the papers read at the Congress.

[36] Keane had written to O'Connell as early as Oct. 10, 1893 that he had participated only at the insistence of Archbishop Ireland and the other Archbishops. He also noted that Archbishop Satolli apparently did not approve the Catholic participation, although he himself thought that much good had been accomplished by their participation. Keane to O'Connell, Oct. 10, 1893, Richmond Diocesan Archives.

who would otherwise not have listened to them hear the truths of Catholicism expounded. But there was a rather strong chorus of criticism in the Catholic press, and in the correspondence of some of the more conservative bishops. The climax of this criticism came later when the *Civiltà Cattolica*[37] wrote an editorial accusing the American prelates of a neo-Pelagianism.

In the meantime Cardinal Gibbons celebrated in Baltimore his silver jubilee as a bishop on October 18, 1893. For the Mass the Cardinal invited the archbishop of New York to preach and Archbishop Corrigan's praise of the Cardinal, while not eloquent, removed any evidence that the two were not close friends. That evening at the solemn pontifical vespers, the sermon was preached by Archbishop Ireland. He expressed the great theme of the Cardinal's episcopate under the title "The Church and the Age."[38] In this sermon Ireland expressed his own rejection of mediocrity and of conservatism, and proclaimed the greatness of the times and the necessity that the Church should accept the age and make it her own. He called for a new crusade in which the Church and the age would unite, in which the Church would accept democracy under the leadership of Pope Leo XIII, the people's Pope. One passage which must have sounded strange to many European ecclesiastics when they read it in the European press said: "The Church is at home under all forms of government. The one condition of the legitimacy of a form of government, in the eyes of the Lord, is that it be accepted by the people. The Church has never said that she prefers one form of government above another. But, so far as I may from my own thoughts interpret the principles of the Church, I say that government of the people, by the people, and for the people is, more than any other, the polity under which the Catholic Church, the Church of the people, breathes air most congenial to her mind and heart."[39] As one observer

---

[37] Father David S. Phelan—in The *Western Watchman*, Feb. 27, 1896—who had been a constant critic of Bishop Keane claimed to have been the first one to raise the charge of neo-Pelagianism. The important charge in the *Civiltà Cattolica* came in the wake of the Pope's prohibition against further Catholic participation in such Parliaments or Congresses and was printed in January, 1896, "Cronaca Contemporanea: Stati Uniti," XLVIII (4 Gennaio, 1896) 118-124.

[38] Ireland, *op. cit.*, I, 105-34.

[39] *Op. cit.*, pp. 117-18.

noted, the sermon was even greater than the jubilee itself. It was rushed into print in this country and was copied and quoted abroad. It found a noteworthy echo among the French followers who had listened so rapturously to his speeches the previous year.

But there were other echoes of Ireland's activities in Europe which were to cause less praise and some embarrassment. Paris was looking forward to the celebration of the next world fair in the centennial year 1900. The liberal thinkers, particularly those who had heard the praise of the Parliament of Religions in Chicago, had begun to agitate for a similar Congress in Paris. In the United States, meanwhile, other problems were arising.

The papal letter of May 31, 1893, on the school question with its praise of Archbishop Satolli and its insistence that his propositions were to be interpreted as insisting on the decrees of the Baltimore Council, apparently brought to an end the controversy over the schools. That fall the Faribault and Stillwater arrangements were dissolved by mutual consent of the parties concerned. Neither side could be said to have won, and the Pope had achieved his expressed purpose in stilling controversy. The Catholic newspapers of the day—especially those privately owned and published—continued to belabor each other on this and related questions. Most outspoken for the Ireland side of the controversy was the *Western Watchman*, whose editor, Father David S. Phelan, of St. Louis, Missouri, became a severe critic of Keane, particularly because of his friendliness to Protestants. Phelan admitted that he could see no good in Protestantism and felt that Catholics could not cooperate in any measure—even a proposal to divide governmental aid to denominational schools—with Protestants. Nevertheless Phelan was an uncritical admirer of Archbishop Ireland. On the whole the exchanges between the Catholic editors were rough and perhaps undignified at times. At the annual meeting of the archbishops in Chicago in September, the archbishops had suggested the observance of the decrees of the Baltimore Council restricting the criticism of the bishops by the lay editors, but there was little restraint shown. Some papers such as the Cincinnati *Catholic Telegraph*,[40] which was for the most part

40 *Catholic Telegraph* (Cincinnati), July 20, 1893.

neutral with a leaning towards the conservatives and Archbishop Corrigan—possibly because its editor Schoenenberger was German—pleaded with the editors and the hierarchy to stop attacking each other in the public press. With the coming of the winter months of 1893, there seemed to be some prospect for peace between the two factions, although there had been no peaceful exchange between the two groups.

On November 16, 1893, the Apostolic Delegate with his household, including Monsignor Donatus Sbarretti as auditor and Father Hector Papi as secretary, moved to the new home of the delegation, the old Bradley House in Washington. From this independent position the Delegate continued his activities in settling disputes between priests and laymen and their bishops, and to represent the Pope on various occasions. The move from the Catholic University grounds, and the table of Bishop John J. Keane, of itself may not have been of great importance, but from the perspective of time it can be noted that the real independence of Satolli begins almost from this date. Father F. X. Kraus in his account[41] claims that Satolli also came under the influence at this time of an additional secretary, Father A. Minckenberg, a former student of Satolli in Rome and now a follower of Monsignor Schroeder. He had by his New York visit removed the public disagreement between himself and Archbishop Corrigan. The papal letter supporting his stand on the school question had really not supported either side fully. Archbishop Ireland felt sure that the Delegate was still his friend, despite the New York reconciliation. The public attacks on the Delegate—if we discount the A.P.A. scurrilities—had died down. There were disturbances and differences in various parts of the country but for the most part they were local.

Archbishop Ireland, however, called this the lull before the battle,[42] apparently feeling that he was in possession of the field and that he could expect further attacks upon his position from the opposing faction. Although he felt that the Delegate was still on his side, he also knew that his friends in the University and

---

[41] *Op. cit.*, p. 5.
[42] Ireland to O'Connell, Oct. 2, 1893, Richmond Diocesan Archives.

his policies were under criticism both in this country and in Rome. The lull was really on the surface. In the *New York Herald* of October 13, 1893, appeared an interview with an unnamed Jesuit in Rome in which the Jesuit approved the appointment of the Apostolic Delegate but attacked Ireland and the Catholic University. In the Catholic newspapers, chiefly under the leadership of Father Phelan, there was continued criticism of the bishops' participation in the Parliament of Religions and of the "liberalism" of Bishop Keane. Strangely, while Phelan seemed to accept everything that Ireland did, he was very critical of Ireland's friend Keane, and Keane himself was sensitive to this criticism. Nevertheless Cardinal Gibbons[43] had sent a favorable report on the Congress to Rome, and received a noncommittal acknowledgement from Cardinal Rampolla. At the jubilee celebration of Bishop Stephen Ryan at Buffalo on November 8, all the contestants were present and gave an outward appearance of harmony. The line of division outside of the rivalry between the two candidates for the red hat—who seemed to have cancelled each other out—seems to have remained the charge of liberalism or minimism against the progressives, the question of the support of the Catholic University, and the attitude towards secret societies. For the time being the school question seemed to have been decided by papal action, although as Soderini indicated neither of the parties involved in the controversy had achieved its aim.

The calm continued on into the spring of 1894, with Bishop Keane offering explanations for the shortcomings of the University at the April meeting of the trustees.[44] Doctor Joseph Pohle gave up the fight and went back to Muenster, but Doctor Schroeder insisted on remaining, although he was opposed by most of the American members of the University. In the summer Bishop Keane and Father Thomas Gorman went to Rome to defend the University. Both were well received and the Holy Father gave

[43] Gibbons to Rampolla, Oct. 28, 1893 (French draft of the letter in the Baltimore Archdiocesan Archives).

[44] Cf. Patrick Henry Ahern, *The Catholic University of America, 1887-1896: The Rectorship of John J. Keane* (Washington, 1948) pp. 143-4; letter of Keane to O'Connell, April 13, 1894, Richmond Diocesan Archives.

them evidence that he was determined to support the University and that he was offended by the opposition of Archbishop Corrigan and other critics of the Delegate and the University.

That fall the peace achieved by the settling of the school controversy ended abruptly when Archbishop Ireland went to New York in October to borrow some money.[45] While on this financial business Archbishop Ireland counselled and otherwise publicly aided the Republicans in their campaign for the control of the city and state. In the previous winter because of the death of Bishop Francis McNeirny of Albany, there had been a vacancy on the Board of Regents of the University of New York State. The conservative bishops wished to nominate Bishop McQuaid for the vacancy. Their opponents, led by Fathers L. A. Lambert and Sylvester Malone and aided by Bishop Stephen Ryan of Buffalo, sponsored Father Malone. Archbishop Ireland was accused of writing letters to the Republicans of New York favoring Father Malone who received the nomination of the Republican caucus and was elected to the vacancy in the spring of 1894. Thus, when Archbishop Ireland openly participated in the 1894 campaign in favor of the Republicans, he aroused the wrath of his critics. After the election, on November 25, Bishop McQuaid mounted his pulpit in full pontificals and denounced the action of Ireland in the regency question, and for coming into another province and diocese and engaging in politics against the local ordinary, and for associating with disgruntled priests in the New York Archdiocese. Ireland's defense of his political activities was his claim that the Catholic Church was being harmed by being identified with one political party, especially a party so seriously accused of corruption as the Democratic party in New York. That he was deliberately offsetting the friendliness of Corrigan for the other side is not clear. The German bishops of Wisconsin and McQuaid insisted that he was paid for his activities by the Republicans. Ireland insisted that he was in New York to borrow money to pay some bills and that his political activity was just incidental. Archbishop Satolli immediately reprimanded McQuaid

[45] Frederick J. Zwierlein, *Life and Letters of Bishop McQuaid*, 3 vols., (Rome & Louvain, 1925-27), III, 203-210.

and sent a report on the incident to Rome. Rome in turn reprimanded McQuaid. In answering the reprimand McQuaid had the desired opportunity to tell his side of the fracas and to defend the actions of those opposed to Ireland.

In the meantime there was an echo of the renewed controversy in France when the speech of Ireland at the jubilee of Cardinal Gibbons was published in the *Univers* and later in the *Moniteur* of Rome. It was also reprinted in whole or in part throughout the country and raised up a partisan discussion with the liberals and conservatives taking side approximately along the same lines as in the United States. In his visit to France and Belgium in 1893, Father Thomas Bouquillon[46] had found the divisions between the progressives and conservatives to be about the same as in the United States.

On June 20, 1894, the Sacred Congregation of the Holy Office had issued a new decree against Catholic membership in secret societies naming specifically the Odd Fellows, the Sons of Temperance, and the Knights of Pythias. Ireland was at once disturbed and together with Cardinal Gibbons tried to prevent its application to the American dioceses. In the discussion of these secret societies, McQuaid of Rochester, Chatard of Indianapolis and Corrigan, as well as the German Bishops—Archbishop F. X. Katzer of Milwaukee had written an article in the *American Ecclesiastical Review* in April, 1892,[47] showing that most of these secret societies were already condemned—lined up against Ireland, Keane and Gibbons with O'Connell trying to aid the latter group in Rome but being opposed particularly by Father Salvatore Brandi. The Ireland group wanted to prevent the decree from going into effect and their opponents insisted that it was already in effect. At the annual meeting of the archbishops in Philadelphia[48] in October, 1894, the decree was discussed and the opinion of the archbishops was that the decision of the Sacred Congregation should not be given immediately to the suffragans. Although

[46] Bouquillon to Monseigneur Keane, July, 1893 Archives of the Catholic University of America.

[47] VI, (April, 1892), 241-247.

[48] Ellis, *op. cit.*, I, 465-468. The minutes of the meeting are in the O'Connell papers, Richmond Diocesan Archives.

the decree had been sent to Satolli to be distributed, no real action was being taken and Satolli still seemed to be taking his cue from Ireland. On November 24, 1894,[49] however, Rampolla through Satolli told the archbishops by letter that it was the Pope's wish that the decree be published. Some bishops immediately complied but Ireland and Gibbons continued to protest in the hope of getting a modification of the decree. Their efforts were in vain but their opposition shown by the non-publication of the decree gave their critics another handle for charging them with minimism and liberalism.

The American bishops figured in the discussion in the French press of any religiously progressive movement. Ireland's speech on "The Church and the Age" at the Gibbons jubilee had been translated and published first in the *Univers* and then in the volume of his speeches edited by Abbé Félix Klein. These and his earlier address of 1892 formed part of the background for the European discussion of the Parliament of Religions. In 1894, there had been something like a debate in Europe between Father Tappert of Louisville on the one side at Cologne and Bishop Keane at the International Scientific Congress of Brussels on the other, on the value of the Parliament. Tappert condemned the Congress as a sample of condemned liberalism.[50] Keane felt called upon to defend the participation of the Catholic clergy in the Congress, and went even farther in pointing out the good that had been accomplished by preaching the Christian religion before those who otherwise would never have heard such truths.[51] To the charge that the participants had minimized the Catholic doctrine the bishop gave a definite denial. He even claimed that in the United States there was room for such a meeting because in the United States the old national and racial lines that divided Europe were being erased. Keane indicated that the meeting gave the Catholics

[49] Soderini, *op. cit.*, Chapter VII discusses the controversy over the secret societies and summarizes the correspondence between Satolli and Rampolla.

[50] The passage is quoted in George Zurcher, *Foreign Ideas in the Catholic Church in America* (Roycroft Quarterly, East Aurora, N.Y., 1896), pp. 52-53. The whole speech was printed in the *Waisenfreund* of Columbus, September 26 and October 3, 1894.

[51] *Compte Rendu du Troisième Congrès Scientifique internationale des Catholiques tenu à Bruxelles du 3 au 8 Septembre, 1894*, 9 vols. (Brussels, 1895) I, 67-74.

a chance to show to the divided and scattered children of God that they had nothing to fear from the Church, so that Catholics could more easily teach them the true Faith. It is necessary, he said, to prove to them that the truth of these false religions is to be found in its fullness in the Church. Keane decried the scandal of some Catholics at the presence of Catholics in the Parliament, saying that the pagans and members of false religions were not really enemies but brothers to be led back to the fold. In the meantime in France the *néo-chrétien* movement was flourishing under Henri Berenger, and a proposal was advanced by certain writers in *Le Monde*, including Abbé Klein, Georges Goyau and Georges Fonsegrive, that a similar Congress of Religions should be held during the proposed World's Exposition in Paris in 1900. Vicomte de Meaux had published his account of the Parliament in *Le Correspondant* of January 10, 1894, and M. Bonet-Maury another in the August 15, 1894, *Revue des Deux Mondes*. Klein published Keane's speech at Brussels on the Parliament in the *Bulletin de l'Institut Catholique*. Meanwhile Abbé Victor Charbonnel, a young writer and priest of Paris, assumed the leadership of the movement and published in the September 1, 1895, *Revue de Paris*, an article favoring the holding of a Paris Parliament of Religions at the World's Exposition in 1900. His article patently made all religions equal and compromised the movement. Klein then withdrew an article he had written supporting the movement and Cardinal Richard of Paris definitely disapproved of the plan.

In January, 1895, there appeared the long awaited papal encyclical of Leo XIII, *Longinqua Oceani*, to the Church in America. Although the general tone of the letter was one of praise for the great growth of the Church in America and a plea for unity of all under the delegate, there was one passage in which the Holy Father, while praising the growth of the Church in the United States, warned the Americans not to say that this was the ideal relationship.

> . . . for the Church amongst you, unopposed by the Constitution and Government of your nation, fettered by no hostile legislation, protected against violence by the common laws and the impartiality of the tribunals is free to live and act without hindrance. Yet, though all this is

true, it would be erroneous to draw the conclusion that in America is to be sought the type of the most desirable state of the church, or that it would be universally lawful or expedient for State and Church to be as in America dissevered and divorced. . . .[52]

This passage did not seem to mean much to many readers but to Ireland this was so disappointing that he turned down a request of the *North American Review* for an article on the encyclical. Some of his critics, however, noted the passage, especially Monsignor Joseph Schroeder in the *Catholic Quarterly Review*. Nevertheless despite this passage this encyclical probably marked the high water mark in the influence of the progressive clergy of that period over the Church in America.

One element in the change was not immediately apparent. In February, 1895, Bishop McQuaid in answer to the Roman reprimand for his attack on Archbishop Ireland prepared a detailed answer.[53] As McQuaid noted, the reprimand was not without its value to him since it gave him a chance to state the conservatives' side of the battle headlined by Ireland and Corrigan. In his preparatory remarks McQuaid told Cardinal Ledochowski, to whom he addressed the letter, that he had been fearful that the health of the archbishop of New York would break down completely under the strain of the attacks of Ireland and Ireland's friends. Then McQuaid proceeded to charge Ireland with two direct interferences with the politics of the State of New York. In the first case, that of the election to the regency, he emphasized the importance of the regency of the University of the State of New York and of the Catholic member on it for the protection of Catholic school interests. In the second case of interference McQuaid placed the odium of Ireland's action in the New York election on the fact that the Republicans whom Ireland supported had refused to condemn the A.P.A. movement.

In the second part of his letter McQuaid accused Ireland of carrying on for over two years a steady persecution of Archbishop Corrigan, accusing Ireland of preparing the attack in the *Chicago Post* of January 8, 1893, in which Corrigan was accused

---

[52] Quoted in the *Catholic Quarterly Review* (1895), XX, 359.
[53] Zwierlein, *Life of McQuaid*, III, 216-225 gives the whole letter.

of a plot to thwart the Delegate. He accused him of associating in New York with priests who were in opposition to Corrigan. Then he also accused Ireland of being the chief cause of the confusion that existed in the United States on the status of the condemned secret societies. This he said was an indication of "a spirit of false liberalism" springing up under the leadership of Ireland and Keane "that, if not checked in time, will bring disaster on the Church."

The extant papers of Archbishop Ireland do not show any evidence that he was aware of this document, but, with the prior existence in Rome of a critical attitude towards American Catholicism, the document probably played an important part in the gradual shift of Roman sentiment away from the progressive prelates in America.

For many months the progressives, Keane and Ireland, had been aware that important decisions about the American Church were being made in Rome. Ireland had urged upon Keane his visit to Rome in the summer of 1894, to look after the interests of the University. During the same summer Dr. O'Gorman had also gone there for interviews with the Cardinals, especially Cardinal Rampolla, and the Pope. They were all anxious for Cardinal Gibbons to go to Rome, feeling as they did that his position would give greater weight to his words in defense of American institutions. Gibbons finally sailed on May 18, 1895. The progressive bishops and their friends were aware that charges were being made against Monsignor O'Connell. Ireland had warned O'Connell not to be absent so much from the North American College and to abandon a proposed trip to the Holy Land. But apparently the criticisms of O'Connell's opponents had their effect, because on June 7, 1895, O'Connell wrote Gibbons that he would have to resign. The resignation given for reasons of health did not fool anyone.[54] There was some rejoicing among the conservatives and it was generally noised about that O'Connell had been removed

[54] Salvatore Brandi, S.J. to Archbishop M. A. Corrigan, July 8, 1895, in the New York Archdiocesan Archives. "Dr. O'Connell's resignation has surprised nobody in Rome. It was given *spinte* and not *sponte* at the demand of the Holy Father, to whom complaints against the Rector had been made by the Cardinals of the Propaganda."

because of his partisan activities for the progressive Americanist group. Gibbons then made O'Connell the vicar of his cardinalitial church of Santa Maria in Travestere, and O'Connell continued to act for Gibbons through his friends in Rome, although his influence must have suffered from the change.

At about the same time the first definite change in the position of the two groups in the hierarchy in relation to the Apostolic Delegate became manifest. Although it has been maintained that Archbishop Satolli had been influenced by his former student in Rome, Father H. A. Minckenberg,[55] there is the better evidence that he had come under the influence of Father Joseph Schroeder and perhaps of Father Georges Périès, who was professor of canon law at the University while Satolli was residing on the University grounds. The rift between Schroeder, Pèriés, and the other professors at the Catholic University became intense in the spring of 1895, on the appearance of the first number of *Catholic University Bulletin* in which nothing appeared from the pen of Schroeder or Périès, apparently as a result of the feud. The conflict over this matter was aired in the newspapers and carried to the Chancellor of the University, Cardinal Gibbons. Satolli seems to have been sympathetic to Périès and Schroeder. Nevertheless, the first notable manifestation of Satolli's friendship for the Germans came at the laying of the cornerstone of St. John the Baptist School at Pottsville, Pennsylvania, on April 25, 1895, where Satolli had gone in the company of Monsignor Schroeder. On that occasion first Schroeder had spoken in defense of the Germans and their ideals, and Satolli followed with a speech in which he made a declaration of the virtues of the German position especially of their adherence to their language and traditions. Just what had caused the Delegate to lean towards the Germans is not clear but aside from the influence of Minckenberg and Schroeder it is most likely that the constant charges of liberalism and minimism which the conservatives and Schroeder and Périès were making had begun to make their mark on the thinking of the

---

[55] Minckenberg is mentioned not only by F. X. Kraus in his "Spectator" letters mentioned above but also by the *Review* (St. Louis) Oct. 15, 1896. Minckenberg later returned to the archdiocese of Cologne where he died as pastor.

Delegate. In the meantime the Parliament of Religions of 1893, which never had the full approval of Satolli and which had drawn the attacks of Father David Phelan and other critics of Ireland and Keane, was also being discussed in France in connection with the 1900 World's Fair in Paris.

On August 12, 1895, Satolli—whether he was prompted by the American or the French discussion is not clear—had written to Rome suggesting that the Holy Father write a letter to the American hierarchy condemning in a mild way the holding of such interdenominational congresses. At the same time Satolli urged the Holy Father to praise the activities of the Paulists in giving missions to non-Catholics.[56] The papal letter of September 15, 1895, followed closely the recommendations of Satolli, specifically telling Catholics to "hold their assemblies apart." Archbishop Ireland at first denied that the letter would prevent congresses of religion. Perhaps he meant that Catholics could participate in the assembly but hold separate meetings but certainly no one else so interpreted the papal letter.[57] In France where the prohibition had a more definite application the movement for the Parliament of Religions at the Paris Exposition of 1900 was dead. In 1896, Charbonnel tried to call upon his friends to support him in his plan but Abbé Klein rushed into print not only to defend his own name but that of his American friends against the charges that they were urging the prohibited congress.[58] Victor Charbonnel eventually left the Church professing, however, to be a follower of the American progressive group.

Cardinal Gibbons in the meantime had finished his visit in Rome. His visit was marked by none of the fiery exchanges which accompanied the tours of Archbishop Ireland, or of the innocent mistakes of Keane. But when interviewed in Paris[59] he did say that the trouble with the French clergy was that they stayed too much in their sacristies and did not go often enough among the

[56] Soderini manuscript quotes the letter in part.
[57] Cf. *Northwestern Chronicle*, Oct. 18, 1895, for an editorial along the lines of Ireland's explanation. Also *Freeman's Journal*, October 26, 1895.
[58] *La Nouvelliste de Lyon*, October 28, 1896, also *La Vérité*, (Paris), same date.
[59] Quoted in *Northwestern Chronicle*, June 7, 1895.

people. In Germany he spoke against his German critics in the United States.[60] In France he also paid a special visit to the chateau of Vicomte de Meaux at Ecotay, but did not give any public speeches in the manner of Archbishop Ireland. Gibbons, however, could not speak French like his confrere of Saint Paul.

The first problem that faced Gibbons on his return, besides writing consoling messages to O'Connell, his saddened friend in Rome, was to enforce the decree on secret societies. Despite the efforts of Ireland and Gibbons to keep the decree from being enforced openly, some of the bishops, when they had received it, announced the decree publicly. At best, Gibbons and Ireland could obtain only permission that those who could not leave these forbidden societies without loss could retain passive membership for the sake of insurance and similar benefits with the permission of the local ordinary. In the meantime Satolli was named a cardinal in November and Cardinal Gibbons conferred the red biretta on him on January 5, 1896, in the Cathedral at Baltimore.

If there was doubt about the meaning of the prohibition of congresses of religion, a chronicle of events in the United States that appeared in the *Civiltà Cattolica* of January 4, 1896, was sufficient warning that the triumph of the progressives had been short lived and that with the shift of Satolli the conservatives were beginning to regain lost ground. This chronicle of the year 1895 in the United States claimed that the end of that year had ended a period of confusion, thanks to the action of Satolli. The evil tendency in the United States which the chronicle says was checked by the Delegate was Pelagianism, jokingly called neo-Pelagianism (apparently a tribute to Father David Phelan who claimed first rights to the word); and this had been checked by two actions, the condemnation of the secret societies and the action against the Congress of Religions. It is the second of these that the chronicle emphasized, since the Chicago Congress had already resulted in a similar Congress in Toronto and led to the planning of one in Paris in 1900. Continuing, the chronicle said that a third element in the American scene, which had grown up from a wrong inter-

[60] *Northwestern Chronicle,* August 2, 1895, quoting *Frankfurter Zeitung.*

pretation of American political traditions, was a kind of Gallicanism, a lack of sympathy for the Pope in his efforts to regain his temporal power. But under the leadership of Satolli the American Catholics had clearly demonstrated their loyalty to the Pontiff in a series of public demonstrations of loyalty on September 20, 1895. Fourthly the chronicle called attention to the existence of a kind of separatism which brands people according to race or nationality and accuses them of anti-Americanism, which has also been charged against some religious orders. In the non-Catholic world this had been manifested in the growth of an A.P.A. attitude, which the chronicle proceeded to condemn. The article was not signed and was really an editorial rather than a chronicle. It was the charge of "neo-Pelagianism" that offended the progressive bishops and their followers.

The attention of the United States at large, however, was beginning to concentrate on the approaching election of 1896 and the discussion of the demonetization of silver. Ireland, partly because he was a Republican and partly because he had no great sympathy for the silverites, gave public utterance of his opposition to the silverites prefacing his remarks that he spoke only for himself and not as an archbishop. On international problems the Catholic papers also expressed their backing for any government policy that would be opposed to that of the traditional enemy of the Irish and Germans, the British.

The external peace noted by the *Civiltà Cattolica* that covered the Church in the United States at the beginning of 1896, was again only a lull before the storm. Now that the Apostolic Delegate had achieved his major purpose in the settling of the school question and had achieved a certain balance between the two contesting factions, it seemed evident that he would soon return to Rome and receive the reward of a place in the Curia. From Rome itself there were reports that Satolli had changed over to the camp of Archbishop Corrigan and the conservatives. Such a statement was probably unfair to the Italian Archbishop. Soderini[61] has indicated that when he came to the country Satolli was so ignorant of English and of American ways that he was dependent

61 Unpublished manuscript.

upon the friends around him, in this case, Ireland, Keane, and Gibbons. But as he became better acquainted with the language and the people in the country who spoke it he also began to form his own judgments or at least to receive contradicting information from Germans and conservatives. Then came the forced truce between himself and Archbishop Corrigan. On this we have available only the letters to Gibbons from Cardinal Rampolla. Undoubtedly Satolli also received definite directions from Rome to extend a more friendly hand to the Corrigan faction. On the question of personalities Ireland and Corrigan had really killed each other's chances of becoming cardinal. Corrigan at the time was accused of being the instigator of the attacks on Satolli in the New York press. In turn Bishop McQuaid in explaining his own conduct had laid down bitter charges against Archbishop Ireland in defense of his friend Archbishop Corrigan. There remained then two questions about which the two factions disagreed. The first one of nationalities and languages was really a dead issue, settled by the decrees sent in answer to the Memorials of Abbelen and Cahensly, but because of the bitterness that remained, was very much alive in the results of those answers within the field of the manner of Americanization. It is quite clear that the German and other language groups no longer—if ever—had any notion of setting up foreign enclaves of Catholicism in the United States; but at the same time, partly because of the animus aroused by the previous controversy and partly because the foreign language groups felt that they were being too roughly treated, they retained a resentment against Ireland and Keane among the embers of old angers. These embers were fanned by *The Review* of Arthur Preuss published in Chicago and later in St. Louis, by the German language papers generally, and by Professor Joseph Schroeder at the University. But these Germans were not charging national or racial prejudice now. Joining the other conservatives they were raising a second question against the orthodoxy of the progressive group, a charge of liberalism.

On April 19, 1896, Thomas O'Gorman was consecrated bishop of Sioux Falls by Cardinal Satolli in Washington. The sermon was given by Archbishop Ireland and, after praising Satolli and

O'Gorman, Ireland gave a thinly veiled attack on religious orders. He blamed the Jesuits for the loss to Catholicism of Japan and England. He further praised the diocesan clergy. The bishop he said could not depend on the religious clergy because he could not control their formation but must rely on the "underestimated and neglected diocesan clergy." Another passage of this sermon was significant:

> The Church recognizes as her own sphere faith and morals. She possesses and claims no mission in civil and political matters, and assumes no authority in the domain of faith and morals. There is no room for conflict between Church and State; both move in separate and distinct spheres; separation of Church and State, most assuredly.[62]

The portion of the sermon that attacked religious orders was answered by Father Joseph Havens Richards of Georgetown at a reception for Satolli and was widely discussed in the Catholic press but the general charge of liberalism was of greater concern.

There is perhaps no more tricky word in modern English than liberalism. One can distinguish economic liberalism—a coat of many colors of its own—political liberalism, and religious liberalism. Each of these has a very definite meaning and they are seldom found in the same individual. However, in the last decades of the nineteenth century political liberalism and religious liberalism had much more in common in south European countries whereas religious liberalism and economic liberalism had more in common in the Anglo-Saxon world. The democratic countries in political thinking were for the most part also liberal at least on the relations between Church and State. But while political liberalism had found a friend in Pope Leo XIII, especially in his policy in France and in his opposition to the Triple Alliance, religious liberalism was clearly condemned by the *Syllabus of Errors*, to which Pope Leo XIII also gave adherence. On the question of the relations between Church and State the liberals seemed to follow Montalembert's "free church in a free state" which in its absolute meaning

[62] *Freeman's Journal*, April 25, 1896. Rev. Thomas Crumley, C.S.C. to Rev. John W. Cavanaugh, C.S.C. Washington, D.C., April 24, 1896 said of the sermon and the attack on the Jesuits, "It can do no good and I am positive it will do much harm. It has done a great deal already. . . ." University of Notre Dame Archives.

was rejected by the *Syllabus*. To complicate matters in the Anglo-Saxon world the question was involved with political relations with those outside the Church. Liberalism also involved the Church's approach to modern science and the association with non-Catholics in the solution of social and economic problems in the industrialized state.

Whether Satolli ever really believed that Ireland and his friends were tainted with the condemned kind of religious liberalism is hard to determine. His statement at the Columbian Congress of 1893 was as strongly democratic as any of Ireland's perfervid orations on the Church and democracy or the Church and the age. But there is nothing in his writings that can be classed as liberalism in the strictly religious field. Keane, the planner of the Catholic participation in the Parliament of Religions, admitted that Satolli had never really approved that participation. In the school question, while Satolli seemed to follow the Ireland lead, he was dealing with concrete compromises in fact not in theory, and insisted that he always adhered to the decrees of the Baltimore Council. When he took occasion to praise the Germans at Pottsville, and in St. Louis later, he praised the Germans for their loyalty to their religious practices. But it soon became clear that the steady anvil chorus of German and conservative papers from St. Louis to Rome was beginning to create doubts about the progressives in the mind of the Apostolic Delegate. The one problem that seemed to turn the tide was the question of Catholic membership in secret societies, although the definite change in Satolli's attitude had begun in the question of the Parliament of Religions.

The background of the opposition of the conservatives and most of the Germans to secret societies is rather confused. Certainly none of the American bishops had any desire to remove the prohibition against Masonic societies which had been repeated so many times in the two previous centuries. Neither was there any desire to raise the prohibitions against the anarchical societies, such as the Carbonari, the Fenians, or the nihilists or communistic societies. The question arose about the societies to which good Catholics might be drawn for social advancement or comfort which were regarded as dangerous for Catholics, because they observed secrecy about their practices, and took oaths of secrecy which hindered the practices of their religion. To this might be added the trend in most of them to Masonic rites which were quasi-religious in character. The most prominent of these, especially in the Middle West, were the Odd Fellows, the Sons of Temperance and the Knights of Pythias. In so far as they were for the most part social and insurance societies and were the social meeting ground of many western communities, the question of secret societies offered a good test of the religious validity of the program of Americanization and of any trend towards minimism.

It is doubtful that any American bishops wanted Catholics to join these secret societies, but those who were anxious for their flocks to attain leadership in the community did not like to see their flocks locked out of these occasions of social importance by a hard and fast decree. The membership in these societies had none of the necessity of the public schools which Catholics in some localities found their only source of education. Nor was there a clear *communicatio in sacris* of which some of the progressives were accused because of their attendance at interdenominational religious functions of public character, and funerals of public persons. The societies held social functions, and outside of the money invested in insurance, offered only social advantages. To the conservatives the societies were a source of danger to faith, since they were undoubtedly outside any Catholic influence. Even the Ancient Order of Hibernians had been attacked by conservative bishops such as Chatard and McQuaid,[63] particularly because of their supposed relations to the Molly Maguires and to the violence in the Irish land quarrels. The Knights of Labor had been attacked on the same grounds, until Gibbons' actions gave them protection. One might say that the defense of Catholic membership in these societies was about the same as that in the question

[63] The correspondence between Chatard and Corrigan in the Chatard Correspondence in the Indianapolis Archdiocesan Archives is of interest on this point.

of the Knights of Labor and in the proposed condemnation of the doctrines of Henry George. Both Ireland and Gibbons felt that by placing the Church on record against these social phenomena, the Church would merely bring down upon itself criticism and drive away from its doors those friendly to Catholicism. But this time Rome was adamant and continued clearly the policies it had stated in regard to the Masonic societies. Finding that they could not undo the action of the Sacred Congregation, Ireland and Gibbons then tried to have the enforcement of the decree left to the individual bishops. Here they met two kinds of opposition. The conservative bishops such as Corrigan and McDonnell of Brooklyn immediately announced the decrees. Secondly, Satolli refused to consent to such an interpretation. Probably after receiving instructions from Rome, he definitely announced that the decrees had to be enforced. The action of the progressive bishops in this question gave substance to the anvil chorus charge of liberalism that was pouring out from the German press and especially from the conservative writers in the other Catholic press. The conservatives coupled to the charge that the progressives were not enforcing the papal decree against secret societies, the charge that the progressives were opposed to the Catholic parochial school and were engaging in minimizing the Faith in such instances as the Parliament of Religions, Keane's appearances in episcopal garb at Harvard, and at the funerals of non-Catholics, and the like. Preuss's *Review* of January 30, 1896, quoting the Baltimore *Volkszeitung*, answered the question "What is a liberal" as it concerned the American Catholic citizen as follows: "In a religious sense we use the word to designate a Christian who does not feel himself bound to certain principles which are considered orthodox in the denomination to which he professes to belong; who is willing to make concessions incompatible with these principles. That there are 'liberals' of this stripe in the Catholic Church in this country no one will, we know, venture to deny."

The editor of the *Northwestern Chronicle*, in the November 6, 1896 issue, in summing up the attacks of the conservatives gave a cynical definition of liberalism.

So far as we have been able to observe experts in "liberalism" would find microbes of the disease in the following classes: The advocates of temperance and especially the believer in teetotalism; those who hold that baptism administered by a non-Catholic confers grace; that it is lawful to inculcate patriotism; that the state as constituted in our country has some rights; that obedience to the just laws of the state is permissible; that intelligent interest in public affairs is incompatible with the spirit of religion; that it is right to be truthful even in dealing with an opponent; that it would not be wrong for the Church to make converts even in this country; that sobriety is better than drunkenness; that purity in public life is to be preferred to corruption; that the Christianity of non-Catholics is not worse than paganism; that an educational arrangement like the public parochial plan carried on by the Jesuit Fathers in St. Louis and elsewhere and by many bishops of the country, providing for the teaching of religion in the schools, is as good as the out and out public school; that to make an end of the catalogue, the Council of Jerusalem made no mistake in refusing to exaggerate details of discipline and declining to make the path of God's Church as difficult of access as possible.

Since Archbishop Ireland wrote the better essays in the *Chronicle* there is some suspicion that he may have written this editorial. There were many discussions of the charge of liberalism in the Catholic press of the day.

Father David Phelan in the *Western Watchman*, although generally friendly to Ireland and critical of Keane, had rather rigid notions about permissible cooperation with non-Catholics. He did not believe that Keane could advocate support of Protestant schools just because Catholic schools would receive aid under the same circumstances. He was quick to attack the participation of the hierarchy in the Parliament of Religions. Phelan, however, would scarcely use the word liberalism. He charged the prelates at the Parliament, especially Keane, with neo-Pelagianism. Whether the author of the Chronicle in the *Civiltà Cattolica* received his inspiration from Phelan or not, the phrase reappeared in that journal which had a better reputation for orthodoxy than the *Western Watchman* and had definite influence in Rome. The *Civiltà* article of January 4, 1896, was later taken up by Monsignor Schroeder in the *Review* where he claimed that Father Brandi of the *Civiltà* wrote in defense of two papal actions, the decree against secret societies and the letter to Satolli against

Parliaments of Religion. Much of the other captious writing in the *Review* during 1895-96, however, was devoted to the new friendship between Satolli and the Germans, especially to speeches of Satolli to the Germans in Washington in January and in St. Louis at Easter time.

The ebullient editor of the *Western Watchman* claimed prior authorship of the charge of Pelagianism but distinguished between his friend Archbishop Ireland and Bishop Keane, and pointed out that Father Brandi should know that Pelagianism was not condemned for praising virtues in those outside the Church but for saying that "their virtues were independent of grace." Phelan spoke approvingly of Archbishop Ireland's strictures against religious orders made in the sermon on the occasion of the consecration of Bishop O'Gorman in April 19, 1896, and of his insistence on separation of Church and State but with definite limitations on godlessness. When Father Havens Richards, S.J., of Georgetown, spoke in defense of religious orders, Phelan felt called upon to disagree with him in his editorial of May 21, 1896. Earlier on January 30, 1896, Phelan had admitted that "word had reached the Holy Father that there is in this country a disposition towards corporate cooperation with Protestants on grounds of common religious interests, and one that is dangerous to the faith and menaces the morals of our Catholic people. The Holy Father was greatly displeased."[64] On Ireland however, Phelan adds "When it comes down to a religious question pure and simple, Archbishop Ireland is as stubbornly uncompromising as the Pope himself." Phelan admitted that some prelates did speak incautiously but did not name them. He continued however to criticize Bishop Keane and the basis of his criticism of Keane is noted in this sentence on March 19, 1896, "We have had to differ with Bishop Keane in some views which we regard as extremely liberal. We don't know of any good in Protestantism."

The conservative *Church Progress* and the German papers such as the *Herold des Glaubens* of St. Louis and the *Review* did not stop at Phelan's criticism of Keane. The editor of *Church Progress*, Condé B. Pallen, who was later to espouse the extreme anti-

[64] These quotations are from the *Western Watchman*.

liberal views of the Spaniard Don Felix Sarda Y Salvany in his small volume *What is Liberalism?* (St. Louis, 1899), quoting the speech of Father Michael Rickardt, O.S.F., to the Deutsche Katholische Vereinsbund of the State of Illinois, pointed out the defects of American civilization such as its divorce laws, the compulsory schools, marriage problems and the like. He condemned the liberalism that would accept these American errors too readily. "They have in America especially recommended a yielding and accommodation. They wish to win the Protestants, the 'Americans,' by appearing less Catholic, although the Church in her infancy when she had all still to win, stood forth apart."[65]

A new field of disagreement was found in the relations between science and religion. Father John A. Zahm, C.S.C., a friend of Ireland and Keane and an "Americanist," had published his *Evolution and Dogma* in 1895, in which he found evidences of evolutionism even in St. Augustine and St. Thomas and in general professed to find no contradition between biological evolutionism and the scriptures. Zahm who had previously written to deny any great conflict between science and religion was generally attacked in the *Freeman's Journal* by Father De Concilio, in the *Ecclesiastical Review*, and later by Father Salvatore Brandi in the *Civiltà Cattolica*. Far more important than the discussion of evolution was the answer in several American Catholic papers to the charge of American neo-Pelagianism raised by Father Brandi in the *Civiltà*. Further, the *Freeman's Journal* pointed out that in the controversy over the schools, Cardinal Rampolla had written to Archbishop Ireland that the *Civiltá* was not an official organ of the Pope or even of the Jesuits. But the conservatives hailed the Brandi article as a correct statement of the evils of American Catholic liberalism. Monsignor Schroeder of the Catholic University, writing in the *Review* on May 7 and 14, 1896, had said that Brandi was merely writing in defense of the recent papal decrees. In Europe that summer Schroeder spent some time in Rome. During the spring, however, his friend Father Georges Périès, the professor of canon law who had been outspoken in his criticism of Keane, had been notified by the officials of the Catho-

[65] *Church Progress*, May 30, 1896.

lic University that his contract would not be renewed for the next year. He at first protested that he had a permanent appointment but when that was denied by the trustees and his contract renewed for only one year, he left the University with a promise that he would have his revenge.[66]

As the summer months of 1896 approached it was rumored that the Apostolic Delegate would soon end his stay and be replaced. After Archbishop Satolli had been named a cardinal in the previous November and had received his red hat in January, he was really a pro-delegate acting in the place of his successor but there was no indication given then as to when he would return to Rome. In February he made a trip to New Orleans, and in April he made a trip to St. Louis. The Germans had begun to claim his friendship. In the first place they manifested resentment when Satolli's Pottsville speech was printed in the collected speeches of the Delegate with the complimentary passage on the Germans left out. This they blamed on Father Frederick Rooker, Satolli's secretary, and claimed that the Delegate was incensed at the omission. Then during his visit to St. Louis in the spring he was given a reception by the Germans at which Father F. S. Goller[67] gave his special praise to the Germans, while criticizing carefully the liberalism the Germans had avoided. The German press began to claim now that Satolli would return to Rome a friend of the Germans, but there was no clear indication that he had definitely turned against the progressive groups. The speakers in the summer conventions of the German societies as usual were outspoken in their criticisms of the Americanizers, and the progressive and conservative Catholic journals continued their sniping at each other; but on the whole one might think that Satolli was about to end his visit to the United States by achieving a precarious balance between the contending forces in the Catholic Church in the United States. Both sides were claiming him as a friend.

Looking back over the years from 1892 to 1896, it can be seen that Cardinal Satolli had been gradually shifting from his friend-

[66] Patrick Henry Ahern, *The Rectorhip of John J. Keane*, pp. 152-56.
[67] *The Review*, April 16, 1896.

ship towards the progressives to a more reserved attitude towards them. It is clear now that he had begun to listen more attentively to the complaints against Ireland and Keane on the part of the conservatives. One might add that his Italian background, despite his reputation as a student of Leo XIII, would tend to make him less sympathetic to American institutions and the American way of life than his speech at the Columbian Congress might have indicated. He made it clear to Keane that he did not favor the hierarchy's participation in the Parliament of Religions. Only the failure of Corrigan to be friendly, the tendency of the conservative press during the first year to attack him and his administration as the tools of Ireland and the progressives, made for him an impartial position impossible. His complaints to Rome about Corrigan and the subsequent rapprochement with the New York prelate through Gibbons, and the forced recognition in the country of the Delegate by the papal letters made friendly relations between Satolli and the conservatives possible. Then had come the political activities of Ireland in New York in 1894, and the public attack on Ireland by Bishop McQuaid. When McQuaid was reprimanded by the Delegate, McQuaid had made a rather strong case in his answer to Rome against the progressives. As Father Brandi noted to Archbishop Corrigan, McQuaid's speech was a *felix culpa* as far as the conservatives were concerned. In the meantime there is definite evidence that Satolli was influenced by Monsignor Schroeder, the University leader of the conservatives, and perhaps by his private secretary, Father A. H. Minckenberg. Nevertheless, neither Ireland or Keane, nor even Gibbons or O'Connell, apparently was prepared for the blow struck by Satolli when he arranged for the removal of Keane from the rectorship of the University.

The letter of Pope Leo to Gibbons dated September 15[68] indicated that the reason for the removal was the custom in pontifical universities to set a limit to the terms of office of rector. There had of course been exceptions to the rule but it was true that such a term for the office would be expected. Probably it was upon

[68] Ahern, *The Rectorship of John J. Keane*, pp. 162-80 quotes the official records of the removal of Keane from the Rectorship.

such an assumption that Ireland, when he first heard the news, indicated that Keane might be reappointed. There is also a reasonable assumption that the Holy Father and Cardinal Rampolla did not in any way anticipate the tremendous reaction to this move which would take place in the United States and in interested centers in Europe. Gibbons called Keane to him in Baltimore on September 28 and gave him the enclosure from Rome which announced his removal, and promised that he could either stay in this country as an archbishop or go to Rome where he would be assigned to aid in the Sacred Congregations of the Propaganda and Studies.

Bishop Keane had spent the summer in western Europe resting and planning for the new year. The letter was a severe shock. Nevertheless he immediately sent to the Holy Father his complete submission to the Pope's request, choosing however to remain in this country without any ecclesiastical title or "official position whatsoever." Ireland, Gibbons, Keane and their friends were stunned. Their opponents were likewise surprised but they soon recovered from their astonishment to begin to boast. The news became public on October 4 when Keane read to the assembled students and faculty the letter from the Pope and his answer. Soon after that he departed for the West Coast for a retreat and a rest. The students immediately drew up statements of regret, and in Washington on October 8, a public mass meeting was held in Carroll Institute at which prominent educators and civic officials drew up public resolutions of regret. Some papers began to hint that the forced resignation was the first blow in a general reaction against the American or progressive party. Monsignor Joseph Schroeder was interviewed and denied that he had spoken against Keane during his interview with the Holy Father the previous summer. Father David Phelan and some of the less cautious Catholic writers were quite frank in their interpretation of the papal action. Phelan probably was not entirely correct but the explanation he gave was probably indicative of the type of the discussion that swept the ecclesiastical circles of the country. He pointed out in his editorial of October 8, first, that Keane was not liked by the Germans who had become a power in the American church; secondly, that the Germans did not like the total abstinence advocated by the bishop, and further that the Germans did not like his advocacy of woman enfranchisement. "Bishop Keane," he said, "has advocated the cause of Protestantism in our schools, penal institutions and asylums where it was impossible to introduce Catholicism. His motto was: if not the creed of Trent, then the creed of Geneva, Canterbury, or Wittenberg. This brought him into sharp antagonism with Catholics of all nationalities and cost him the support and confidence of the Apostolic Delegate." The papers of the East blamed Cahenslyism but Phelan denied this saying that Schroeder was working with the rest of the faculty by this time. Phelan was wrong on this last point as he was inexact in most of his opinions. Certainly it seems that Cardinal Satolli had been the one who arranged for the removal of Keane. That he had any intention of producing the defeat of the progressives that it was made out to be, is doubtful. Nevertheless his public conduct after the removal of Keane indicated that his sympathies had shifted to the conservatives. Satolli visited New York in August, calling the New York diocese the greatest in the country on one occasion. When he departed for Rome later in October it was after a formal reception and party tendered him by the archbishop of New York, although Ireland had a separate conference with him in New York at about the same time.

In the meantime Archbishop Martinelli, the new delegate, had arrived and been installed as his successor. Martinelli was very cautious about making any statement, and for all intents and purposes remained neutral in the controversy. One point could be noted, however, Martinelli was a religious of the Order of St. Augustine, and this was interpreted as in itself a rebuke to Ireland who had attacked religious orders and had insisted that the new delegate would not be an order man.

But Ireland was already busy about other things. The great and noisy campaign of 1896 was in full swing and the fiery archbishop of St. Paul in his tense loyalty to the Republican party could not restrain his tongue, giving forth a strong denunciation of the silverites in October. The Catholic press generally either reprimanded him for speaking on political matters or brushed aside his partisanship because most of the Catholic editors favored in a quiet way the cause of Bryan and the silverites. Further, the Democrats had taken a stand against the A.P.A. in their platform, and the Republicans had refused to do so. Nevertheless the American Catholics as usual were divided in their political loyalty.

In his private and ecclesiastical circles, however, Ireland had much to worry about. In this country he and his party were declared to have suffered defeat. In the *Sacred Heart Messenger* there appeared a summary of the battle by "The Reader," in which the progressives were said to have suffered a whole series of defeats. The *Messenger* said:

> It is still fresh in our memory how, some years ago, a liberal crusade was opened against our Catholic parochial schools. They were to be secularized or reduced to mixed schools, with religion only a side-show. Their defenders were blackguarded and ridiculed, and threatened with the vengeance of Rome. The Pope and his representative were loudly quoted in favor of mixed or public schools. A great revolution was to be effected in the domain of Catholic education. What was the upshot? Rome, with admirable forbearance, upheld the decrees of Baltimore in their entirety; and now, within the last few days, the illustrious prelate who, of all others, was supposed to have led the liberal movement, to his honor be it said, comes out publicly in the strongest and most unmistakable language in favor and defense of the parochial school.
>
> In like manner, we heard it loudly asserted by the same liberal agency, that the ban was to be raised from secret societies in this country, even from the Free Masons. What happened in reality: Leo XIII's teaching on Free Masonry was enforced anew, and three other secret orders were put on the list of the forbidden.
>
> Much capital was made by the liberal party of the Parliament of Religions, as a new departure that broke down the barriers which separated the Church from the sects, and thus prevented free interchange of thought. The result was the explicit prohibition to Catholics to take further part in such gatherings.
>
> Bishops, religious orders, and other "laggards" were to be coerced into the liberal movement by the Pope and his representative; the Church was to be Americanized (whatever that means). And yet not a bishop has been unseated, not a religious order has been disciplined, and the Church is where it stood—loyal, but not officious or subservient to any political influence.[69]

The article concluded with a discussion of the noted corres-

[69] *Sacred Heart Messenger* (November, 1896) "The Reader," XXXI, 950-51.

pondent "Innominato" of the *New York Sun*. "Innominato" was the correspondent in the *Sun* who gave out stories from Rome in support of the progressives. Among his reports was a story that the new Apostolic Delegate would not be a religious and therefore not Archbishop Falconio, a Franciscan. The "Reader" did not seem to know that Monsignor Boeglin was the person, but he knew that he was formerly connected with the *Moniteur de Rome*, and said that he was the mouthpiece of the progressive group. "In short," he says, "Innominato's letters are models of liberal style and liberal tactics." The "Reader" then proceeded to make fun of both Innominato's prediction that Falconio would not be the delegate because he was a monk and his predictions about reform in the delegation curia. Finally he took him to task for predicting a move to modernize the Church in France, quoting a rather strong paragraph of the *Correspondant* in which he listed most of the changes that the progressive clergy were proposing in France.

Suddenly in November, particularly by writers in the *New York Herald* and the *New York Journal*, the removal of Keane began to be interpreted as not only a defeat for the progressives, but as the beginning of wholesale destruction of the party. Rumors printed chiefly in New York newspapers in November 1896, but copied widely in the Catholic papers, began to spread that Archbishop Ireland was to be called to Rome or removed, and that Cardinal Gibbons was to be removed or at least to be given a conservative coadjutor. Further the story had been given out in the *New York Journal* of November 12 and 13,[70] that when Satolli had returned to Rome he had given an unfavorable report on the progressives, and that he had recommended the dismissal of three of the more liberal professors of the Catholic University, Fathers Bouquillon, Shahan, and Pace. In the French Catholic conservative paper *La Vérité*,[71] there appeared a letter by Saint

[70] The *New York Journal* of November 12, 1896 headed its first column with the phrase "Ireland lashed by Satolli," and on November 13, "Satolli's Report Means New Men." Various other newspapers not only in New York but also in Washington carried similar stories.

[71] *La Vérité*, October 21, 1896. Périès uses at first the name Saint Clement and quotes from Périès as if he were a third person in some of the early articles.

Clement outlining the disaster that had befallen the progressives, showing how they had failed and predicting that the removals would follow. It was apparently written by the dismissed canon law professor of the Catholic University, Dr. Georges Périès, now living in Paris. The denials by Archbishop Ireland and Cardinal Gibbons could not stem the wave of rumors. On November 26, 1896, Father Phelan in the *Western Watchman* quipped: "Not a cardinal nor an archbishop nor a university professor has been deposed in this country for a week. Even a sense of relief can become monotonous." Finally Ireland wrote to Rampolla and Rampolla felt compelled to send a cablegram on December 3 to the new Apostolic Delegate, Archbishop Martinelli, denying the rumors.

In the meantime Bishop Keane, after a short visit to the West Coast and a rest, decided on the advice of his friends to go to Rome where he could be of service to his friends.[72] As his friends soon realized, the suggestion that he go to Rome might have been made by the Pope from friendly motives. He sailed for Rome on December 5. When Keane arrived in Rome he found a growing opposition to Americanism in all forms and he reported this back to Ireland and Gibbons. Monsignor O'Connell, in the meantime, was sending from Rome urgent letters to Archbishop Ireland. In a letter of January 7, 1897, he begged him to make it clear that he was not opposed to the Germans as Germans, but to those Germans who were opposing progress. "On a suitable occasion, and that very near, you must seek an opportunity of publishing your real program to the world, i.e. not war of race on race but idea on idea, of progress on stagnation. Do it and in consistency you can do it, and in duty you ought to do it and you will lead the world. . . ." Again on January 28, he wrote "We are to have no name at all, we are the same thing all the time. We are no party at all. We are the Church. All the other fellows, the opposition are a party, a party in the Church, as there always was and they are Refractaires." And again on February 1 he warned Ireland about his proposed speech. "Don't make the Refractaires

---

[72] The best account of these trying days in the life of Keane is told by Ahern, *Life of John J. Keane*, pp. 191-98.

simple kickers against the Pope's political policy in France. Enlarge the idea by assuming the Pope is laboring for the advancement of civilization and science, to put the Church at the head of the Age and that, oh, so unfortunately those fellows named by the Pope Refractaires are opposing him . . ."[73]

Some of the conservative journals gave a peculiar interpretation to the rumors about Ireland's removal, implying that Ireland had planted or permitted the rumors in order to strengthen himself by the denial of them by Rome. But there were other conservatives who did not hesitate to continue the battle. In the *American Ecclesiastical Review* of February 1897,[74] under the pen name "Tharseus" appeared an article, "Elements of American Liberalism." Under the guise of discussing the Chapter "De Fide" of the decrees of the Baltimore Plenary Council the author launched into a bitter attack on the American liberals. The article listed four characteristics of the false liberalism threatening the Catholics in the United States.

> The first is, if we mistake not, an effort being made to nationalize the Church by robbing its children of the Catholic feeling and the Catholic instinct, which qualities have never been a detriment to the development of most ardent patriotism and civic loyalty.
>
> A second symptom of false liberalism is found in the impatience with which we look upon the tried ways of attaining true knowledge. . . .
>
> A third symptom of liberalism is recognizable in the growth everywhere of disrespect for authority, both in matters of doctrine and discipline. . . . It is the constant appeal to the judgment of the American people which, however flattering to our National self love is at the same time inconsistent with the divine plan of governing the Church. It is such appeals without necessity which in reality weaken the bases of authority. . . .
>
> The fourth and final sequel of danger to all true religion is the freedom with which we allow ourselves occasionally to identify Protestantism, such as it is, with the only true religion. . . .

Ireland made up his mind that, once the inauguration of McKinley had taken place and his position in regard to the new admin-

[73] Letter of Monsignor Denis O'Connell to Archbishop Ireland in the Archdiocesan Archives of Saint Paul.

[74] "The Chapter 'De Fide Catholica' in the Third Plenary Council of Baltimore," pp. 147-154. This was attacked in the *Freeman's Journal* of February 13, 1897.

istration had been made secure, he would have to go to Rome to defend his good name and the interests of his friends. In the meantime on a Sunday, March 28, from the pulpit of St. Patrick's Church in Washington, taking his cue from O'Connell in a sermon which he called "The New Age," he struck back at his critics in an effort to turn the tide. By representing himself and the progressives as defenders of the ideas of Pope Leo XIII and denying that either nationality or race had anything to do with his position, Ireland tried to make his critics appear as working contrary to the intentions of the Pope.

He asked his audience: "Where should Catholics stand in regard to all the questions that press themselves today upon the minds of men, in regard to all the movements with which humanity today palpitates?" In his answer he was very blunt.

... Thus, in France, despite Leo's repeated invitation to all Catholics to see in the Republican form of government which the people of that country have adopted the representative of law and order, and the legitimate government according to the necessities of the age, despite his repeated invitation to rally around the Government and work loyally and earnestly under it for the welfare of the country and of Mother Church, certain Catholics dream of reconstituting dead empires and monarchies, and are, as Leo himself has lately characterized them, "refractaires" to his commands. Such Catholics are in rebellion against their chieftain.

"Refractaires," rebels against Leo, are found outside of France. They are found where we should least expect to find them—in America. There are, unfortunately, divisions among Catholics in America; not, indeed, in strict matters of faith and morals, but in tendencies and movements, and in adaptations of actions to modern circumstances and surroundings. There should be for us but one tendency, one movement, one mode of adaptation—those indicated by Leo. Separation from Leo, opposition to his direction, however much it clothes itself in America as it does, with the specious titles of conservatism and traditional Catholicity, a religious fear of novelties is nothing but rebellion. Those in America who resist the direction given by Leo are rebels and refractaires, however much they dare push themselves forward as the only true and trustworthy Catholics. Names are of small moment. Realities are the things that count. Loyal Catholics have but one name—Catholics. They have but one rule of action, Leo's will and example. It is thought sometimes that Catholics in America are divided sometimes on lines of race and language. It is not so. So far as they may be divided, the line of division is that the great majority follow Leo's direction and some hold themselves aloof from him. The loyal Catholics and the refractaires are confined to no one language. I speak now for myself, but in what I say, I know I speak for all the loyal Catholics in America. There is for me no race, no language, no color. I rise above all such accidentals. In seeking out my brethren, I wish to find those who work for God and for truth, those who work with Leo. When I move away from Catholics, I move away from the refractaires and from none other. When the French Catholics are with the Pope, I am with the French Catholics; when they are against him, I am against them. When the German Catholics are with the Pope, I am with them; when they are against the Pope, I am against them. I would scorn to draw distinctions among Catholics because of race or language. I am— I must be—as Catholic as is God's Church. I differ from men—I war with men on account of ideas, not on account of race. And so it is with Leo. And so it is with all loyal Catholics. It is well that this be understood and proclaimed aloud, far and wide. Efforts are being made to identify certain refractaire tendencies with whole races of Catholics. This is wrong. This is an injustice to those races, the great number among which are most loyal to the Pope, most ardent to follow his directions, most earnest in working with him. Self-constituted leaders, in order to advance their own ideas, are often too ready to call around them a whole race of men and blinding them to the real issues, lead them under the banner of nationalism, to follow where true Catholics should not go.[75]

Ireland knew full well the position of the *réfractaires* of France, having done his share in the battle against them in his speeches in France in 1892. To find a parallel in the opposition of the conservatives of the United States required all the oratorical ability of the St. Paul prelate. Probably he had no basic national prejudice, but the Germans were loath to believe it. But if we accept his plea for cooperation with the spirit of the age and progressiveness generally, there was some basis for his charge that his opponents were not following the leadership of Leo XIII in their conservatism.

O'Connell and Keane in Rome were delighted with this thrust and urged Ireland to continue his effort to win the favor of the liberals in Germany in order to make it appear that the opposition to the Germans in America was not on national lines but on lines of policy. But in this country the Germans denied that they were opposed to Ireland as *réfractaires*. They insisted, and Monsignor Schroeder and Preuss were loudest in such statements, that they

[75] *New York Freeman's Journal*, April 3, 1897.

were opposed to Ireland because of his liberalism and that this was shown primarily in their devotion to the Holy See, in their devotion to the parochial school, and in their opposition to Catholic membership in secret societies. Preuss reprinted the article from the *Ecclesiastical Review* on liberalism. The battle between the groups continued. This time the new Apostolic Delegate took no part. Cardinal Gibbons inclined towards his friend of St. Paul. Archbishop Corrigan gave his friendship to the conservatives and Schroeder.

There was no danger of the revival of the Germans' plea for national churches and national bishops but the Germans were very strong in their efforts to attach to the progressive group the charge of liberalism. This charge was based partly upon national feeling but, of course, had the usual basis in the facts. In English the chief exponent of this charge of liberalism against Ireland was Arthur Preuss and his *Review*, although the *American Ecclesiastical Review* under the editorship of Herman Heuser was also against the views of Ireland, although at the same time Heuser was printing articles by modernists Loisy and Tyrell. The actual leader of this battle against Ireland was Monsignor Joseph Schroeder of the Catholic University. He had published without using his name, in the Pittsburgh German Catholic paper *Katholisches Familienblatt*, articles attacking the liberalism of the Ireland party. Preuss translated and published the articles under the name of Schroeder as the author. Although Schroeder could deny that he had authorized Preuss to use his name, for all intents and purpose they were generally known to be from Schroeder's pen. Thus for the first few months of 1897, the attack upon Ireland began to look like a German attack against the Irish American clergy. With the removal of O'Connell and Keane accomplished, and the rumored removal of Ireland and Gibbons, the Germans seemed about to achieve revenge if not victory. It is true that after Ireland wrote to Rome, Rampolla had written to the Apostolic Delegate, Archbishop Martinelli denying the truth of the rumors; but this was offset by the reports sent back from Rome by Archbishop Keane who had with difficulty obtained the appointment promised him by the Holy Father, and had found the opposition to the Americanist group very strong.

The nomination and appointment in November, 1896, of Father Thomas Conaty of Worcester, Massachusetts as rector of the Catholic University to succeed Bishop Keane did not cause much excitement. He was a much less capable man than Keane, but was generally considered to be of the progressive party. His chief activities in the years before his appointment were as president of the Catholic Summer School of Plattsburgh. On January 19 he was installed as rector of the University. But he was not to have an easy term of office. The University faculty was deeply involved in the controversy, because the accusation was made in the press that Monsignor Schroeder had made the charges against Keane in Rome in the summer of 1896 which had led to Keane's removal. Schroeder made light of the accusation but he did not cease his attacks on Ireland and the progressives, who in turn were determined to drive him from the University.

As the articles by Saint Clement (Périès) in *La Vérité* showed, there was more than an accidental connection between the progressives in France referred to by Innominato and those in the United States. Through Boeglin and his friend Monsignor Denis O'Connell, there was a definite common bond between the progressives in the two countries. Part of this had its origin in the fact that both groups advocated cooperation with their respective republican governments. Also important was the fact that both groups were anxious to promote cooperation between the Church and the spirit of the modern world, in government and the sciences, and in social and economic reform. Apparently the French group found its best ammunition in the doings and writings of Archbishop Ireland and Cardinal Gibbons. The two prelates had both added their bit when they visited Paris and France in 1892 and 1895.

On the other hand, Abbé Périès had not been long back in France when he received the news of the removal of Bishop Keane, towards whom he felt little affection. Using the pen name Saint Clement he wrote in *La Vérité* on October 21, 1896, that Keane had really been dismissed in disgrace because the alternative offered to him by the Holy Father was not real. Saint Clement gave two reasons for this: because Keane did not have enough friends in the American hierarchy from whom to obtain a nomination to an American see; and second because for Keane to return to Rome like a worn-out missionary would be unbearable. He exulted in the deposition of Keane because Keane had been pointed out to the French for admiration by Klein, Charbonnel and the *néo-chrétiens*. Formerly "the Gibbonses, the Keanes and the Irelands" were the giants and the prophets, and the Pope had been patient. Now the Pope had not hesitated to strike at the very "fortress of American liberalism," the Catholic University. Saint Clement pointed out that Keane was known in France for his invention of the Religious Parliament of Chicago and his plan for the Congress of All Religions in Paris which had been urged by Charbonnel and Klein. The Pope had already condemned the congress and now had put a check on Keane.

In the October 24 *La Vérité*, Saint Clement, quoting New York and Washington papers, claimed that the Church in the United States was divided and that the internal wars had been renewed. The one responsible for the change of status was Cardinal Satolli. In this, he said, Archbishop Corrigan had remained faithful to his duties. As a source for this statement he professed to quote an interview with himself. The Holy Father, Périès said, had not acted too soon.

On October 28, *La Vérité* published a letter from Klein in which he denied that he took part in the planning of the proposed Congress of Religions in the 1900 Paris World Fair. He further insisted that in his article on the *néo-chrétiens*, he had insisted that the *néo-chrétiens* were in error in their effort to separate morals from dogma. Further, he said that there was no connection between the moralist movement of M. Desjardins and the resignation of Keane. Nevertheless, he added that he was happy to be mentioned with Keane, Ireland and Gibbons, and added a postscript warning against those who try to impose their own opinions as those of the Holy Father.

Saint Clement returned to the battle on October 30, rejecting the claim that Klein was not associated with the proposal to hold a Congress of Religions in Paris in 1900 since he was part of the group that edited *Le Monde* which had advocated the congress. Further he pointed out that Klein had said in his preface to the translation of Ireland's speeches that he thought as Ireland did. On November 5, he discussed the rumor that Keane was to head the new archdiocese of Buffalo and rejected the rumor. Saint Clement further quoted various American newspapers on November 7, under the title of "Les Libéraux Américains," to show that Ireland had called down upon himself criticism because of his mixing in politics and pointed out that now Archbishop Corrigan was avenged. For the rest Saint Clement gathered up the various rumors about the controversy in the United States and denied the statements made in defense of Keane and Ireland. On November 24, he repeated the stories from the *New York Journal* of November 12, that Satolli had arrived in Rome and given an adverse report and that certain professors at the Catholic University would be removed and Ireland would be called to Rome. Adding to these reports, on November 26, Saint Clement indicated that since Gibbons had been mixed up in these affairs he would receive a coadjutor. The professors to be removed were Fathers Bouquillon, Grannan, Pace and Shahan. In his article of November 28, he dropped the name of Grannan, but added that the other three were definitely compromised. On December 4, after *L'Univers-Monde* had denied the story about the depositions, Saint Clement quoted the German *Amerika* of Saint Louis in support of the story that Satolli had turned against Ireland after going to Rome. But on December 18, Saint Clement quoted from *L'Univers-Monde* the cablegram received by Archbishop Martinelli from Rampolla denying the story about Satolli and the removal of Ireland. But he did not keep quiet long.

On December 28, Saint Clement again took up the cudgels against the liberals under the title "Catholiques Romains ou Libéraux?" He gave a laudatory description of the conservatives saying that they were timid men, not like Keane who participated in the Congress of Religions and then dared to boast about it at Brussels and Paris. Now the Pope had made Keane give up his job, and yet Ireland claimed that Keane would be made a cardinal, because the Pope had said that Keane had "a bright future in Rome." Satolli had made his report on Ireland and it was not favorable to Ireland, and the cablegram of Martinelli to Rampolla was necessary to save the Catholic University. Saint Clement said the liberals claimed that the whole question was one of patriotism and race, just as they raised that question in the school controversy and won with the aid of the Associated Press and other journals working as tools, but they could not win again. The progressives were for secret societies, Protestant ideas of religious congresses, and non-confessional schools, but they were opposed by the French, the Germans, and the majority of the American episcopate. These "Irish," of birth or attachment, he said, were ultra-liberals, the others were traditional Catholics. Saint Clement said that he wanted to clear the air and to show why these liberals were praised by such men as Charbonnel. He quoted from Father Joseph Jessing of the Josephinum's *Waisenfreund* that there was danger that the American Church would separate from Rome if the liberals had their way, but he said also that these liberals were in the minority and that the majority of American Catholics would not follow them. The next day *L'Univers-Monde* ridiculed Saint Clement's statements, claiming that he did not properly quote the American newspapers from which he got his information. In answer Saint Clement quoted the Washington *Herald* as speaking of the two parties, one led by Keane and the other by Monsignor Schroeder. As to the future, Saint Clement claimed that the future of the Church in America rested with the majority of American Catholics and not with the liberals who followed Ireland and who were but a small coterie.

Ireland in far off Saint Paul heard of these articles in the French Catholic press, and he attributed them to Périès; but while he was disturbed by them he was also much more disturbed by the rumors of his own removal. He could scarcely have understood how much he and his ideas were to figure in the internal religious controversies of France during the next few years. In France in the meantime Abbé Charbonnel had rejected the papal letter to Archbishop Satolli of September 15, 1895, against the religious congresses and had decided to leave the Church. Nevertheless, he professed himself a follower of the Americanists and expressed himself unkindly towards Abbé Klein for his denial of his part in planning the congress. At the same time the *néo-chré-*

tien movement in the person of Henri Berenger also turned against Catholicism because of the papal letter to Satolli on the religious congresses and disapproval of Klein's denial that he had worked for the proposed Paris Congress. The lines between the progressives and the conservatives within the French church were just as sharply drawn as the lines between the two groups in America. And by the articles of Périès and his followers, the readers of the French Catholic press were alerted to any attempt to introduce American Catholic ideas into French life.

CHAPTER 3 ❧ *The French Controversy*

THE COUNTER-ATTACK by Ireland on Sunday, March 28, 1897, against the *réfractaires* had aroused only resentment among his opponents in the United States. In Europe, however, the words found friendly echoes in those who were fighting reaction in the Church. In Germany the speech had the effect of appealing to the progressive as distinct from the conservative Germans, and winning the support of the progressives, Hermann Schell of Wurzburg, and Franz Xavier Kraus of Freiburg. O'Connell wrote to Ireland on July 24, 1897, "Your sermon against the *réfractaires* has cleared the atmosphere for us here, and rendered all explanation about opposition to Germans superfluous. The active element in Germany is with you now. But mind, you must proceed cautiously regarding Kraus. Never let anyone suspect any kind of understanding existing between you. He is the antithesis of the policy of the Pope in Europe. . . . We intend to go on spreading the movement in Europe. . . ."[1]

In Rome Ireland's speeches had little effect, although O'Connell suggested to Countess Sabina di Parravicino[2] of Milan, the Italian translator of Ireland speeches, that the latest speech be included in the Italian translation of *L'Église et le Siècle*. Nevertheless, early in the spring of 1897, O'Connell[3] reported to Ireland that Cardinals Mazzella and Satolli had begun a campaign against the Americans. On May 2, 1897,[4] the American correspondent of the *Civiltà Cattolica* renewed the attack on the progressives by raising the question of whether the United States was

[1] Monsignor Denis O'Connell papers, Richmond Diocesan Archives. The "Spectator" letters in the *Beilage zur Allgemeinen Zeitung*, especially that of May 1, 1897, criticized the German-Americans for their opposition.
[2] Monsignor Denis O'Connell to Countess Sabina di Parravicino di Revel, May 14, 1897. Microfilm copy in the Archives of the University of Notre Dame.
[3] Letters of O'Connell to Ireland, February 5, March 1, 1897.
[4] *Civiltà Cattolica*, Series XVI, pp. 506-10.

a Christian nation, implying that Ireland and Gibbons were in error when they said they would not change one iota of the Constitution if they had the power. The implication of this comment was that "Americanism" was not Christian. This the writer supported by statistics on church membership showing that nearly forty million Americans did not profess membership in any church. Among these, he indicated, were from five to ten million pagans. On this basis, the article then proceeded to attack the great interest of some American Catholics in Protestants, their minimizing of differences between Catholics and Protestants, their praising of the separation of church and state, their tolerance of secret societies, their repression of foreign languages, their sacrificing the Catholic schools, and their desire to conform the Church to the spirit of the day. Finally the writer made light of the preference expressed in some papers, in the aftermath of Ireland's attack on the religious clergy at O'Gorman's consecration, for the word diocesan instead of secular for the non-religious clergy. In answer to this article, Ireland, Keane and O'Connell insisted that "Americanism" was not racial or national but was simply the progressive ideas of Pope Leo and the Church itself. In France Ireland's speech made little change even though his friends there continued to report all his utterances with the respect due to an oracle of progress. It is doubtful that the *ralliement* and the progressive ideas of Pope Leo XIII had made much progress by the spring of 1897, when Count Guillaume de Chabrol made final arrangements for the publication of the French version of the life of Father Hecker by Father Walter Elliott.

Father Isaac Hecker (1819-1888),[5] a convert, was the first American founder of an American community, the Congregation of St. Paul the Apostle, called the Paulists. Isaac Hecker was the son of German immigrants. After receiving very little formal education he had spent his early youth working with his brothers

---

[5] The Reverend Vincent Holden, C.S.P., is now at work on the long overdue biography of Father Hecker. Father Holden's earlier study *The Early Years of Isaac Thomas Hecker, 1819-1844* (Washington, 1939) indicates his qualifications for the task. The controversial *Life* was that by Father Walter Elliott (New York, 1891). Father Joseph McSorley of the same community has published *Father Hecker and His Friends, Studies and Reminiscences* (St. Louis, 1952).

in a bakery in New York. Despite his meager schooling he read rather widely and (in his late teens) he became active in workers' organizations. As a result of this association he came in contact with Orestes A. Brownson in 1841. Through Brownson he spent some time in socialistic enterprises such as Brook Farm and Bronson Alcott's Fruitlands before deciding to enter the Catholic Church in 1844. After his baptism he decided to become a Redemptorist, going to that community's novitiate in Saint Trond in Belgium. There he experienced difficulties in learning but was professed and was eventually ordained in 1849. He worked as a priest in England for a brief time before returning to the American province of the Redemptorists in 1851.

The American province of the Redemptorists had been especially active among the German immigrants in the United States. With the increase in the number of American-born members in the province, the Redemptorists began to give missions also to English-speaking Catholics. In this Father Hecker and several other converts were very active. Since they were stationed in different houses of the congregation when not on missions and since these houses were predominantly German in character, Hecker and the other American missionaries felt that their special work would be improved if they had a separate English-speaking house. Several members of the American hierarchy, especially Archbishop John Hughes of New York, Archbishop John B. Purcell of Cincinnati, Archbishop Francis Kenrick of Baltimore, Bishop Martin J. Spalding of Louisville and Bishop James R. Bayley of Newark, were in favor of this project. To obtain this permission Father Hecker went to Rome in 1857. Not only was the petition rejected but because he had gone to Rome contrary to a directive issued by the General of the Redemptorists he was summarily expelled from the community without a hearing. He appealed to the Holy See against the action of the congregation. Through the intervention of American bishops and Cardinal Barnabo he and his fellow petitioners were released from their Redemptorist vows by the Pope. With the blessing of the Pope, Hecker and his fellow converts decided to form their own community, to work for the conversion of America. They called their community the Congregation of Saint Paul the Apostle but did not take religious vows. Their headquarters were established at the Church of St. Paul the Apostle in New York and, besides engaging in preaching missions, they advocated social welfare work, promoted temperance, and fostered the apostolate of the press, particularly by founding the *Catholic World* in 1865, and the Catholic Publication Society in 1866. Father Hecker became an influential adviser of American bishops, especially of Archbishops Spalding and Purcell, Bishops John J. Keane and J. L. Spalding, and in a lesser degree of Cardinal Gibbons and Archbishop Ireland. At one time Bishop Keane,[6] as a young priest, sought permission to become a Paulist, but did not receive the permission of his superior, Archbishop Bayley. Hecker, especially in his later years, urged the compatibility of American political institutions with the Church,[7] placing considerable stress on adapting the approach of the Church to modern conditions, advocated in the spiritual life of the people a greater and more personal devotion to the Holy Ghost and the necessity of making known to the American people that Catholicism was the only religion that would satisfy their aspirations and longings. Worn out by his labors he died in 1888. Shortly after Father Hecker's death, Father Walter Elliott, who had joined the Paulist community after the Civil War, prepared a biography of his superior which began to run serially in the *Catholic World* in April, 1890, and was published in book form the following year.

In his brief preface to the published book Father Elliott called attention to the fact that in the biography the words of Hecker were three times as numerous as his own. To do this Elliott used the diaries of Hecker, especially those made before his conversion to Catholicism and his essays published toward the end of his life. Nevertheless, the arrangement of the biography and occasional comments by the author pointed to Elliott's conviction that Isaac Hecker was a specially chosen person who could have had

---

[6] Ahern, *Life of John J. Keane*, pp. 28-30.

[7] Isaac Hecker, *The Church and the Age: An Exposition of the Catholic Church in View of the Needs and Aspirations of the Present Age* (New York, 1887) contains Father Hecker's final views on this question.

wealth and a comfortable life but was led by a supernatural guide to leave this business opportunity and family affection in search of something higher. Even when Hecker went to Brook Farm and Bronson Alcott's Fruitlands, Elliott indicated that there was the possibility of marriage which he rejected in his search for this higher good. Eventually Hecker found the answer to his search in the Catholic Church.

After a year of meditation on his future career, yet finally with unusual haste, he rushed to join three other converts who were entering the Congregation of the Most Holy Redeemer and sailed for that community's novitiate at St. Trond in Belgium. Elliott brought out that Hecker, during the novitiate and seminary studies, because of spiritual influences was incapable of serious concentration in philosophy and theology, but this did not prevent his promotion to Holy Orders and ordination to priesthood. While his inability to study rendered him subject to ridicule by some of his confreres, his superiors and his director had the necessary confidence in his interior life and his gifts of prayer. Elliott indicated that his mortifications during this time were severe and his prayer was of mystical quality. Before his ordination he was sent to England for a year of study at Clapham. After his ordination on October 23, 1849, he worked in England until January 23, 1851, when he sailed for America. Elliott indicated that on the missions Hecker was not considered capable of the main sermons but was assigned to give the less formal instructions and to hear confessions, but that he developed a technique for instructions which made them a most important part of the missions. According to Hecker's own words he had felt for years the call to share with non-Catholics the fruit of his long trials in coming into the Church. He now tried to do this in a special way in his earlier books, *Aspirations of Nature*, and *Questions of the Soul*, as well as later in his essays and sermons. Elliott explained that a disagreement between the American Redemptorists and their superiors in Rome about the establishment of a separate English-speaking house where their activity would be centered led to the decision of these Americans to send him to Rome to explain to the Rector Major their intentions and secure the necessary permissions. In

Rome he was expelled from the Redemptorists for this action. Elliott made it quite clear that Hecker acted with a clear conscience, was dismayed by his expulsion from the congregation, and that he was received in friendly fashion by the Redemptorist superiors despite his expulsion. His release from his vows and the foundation of the new Congregation of Saint Paul took place with the blessing of Pope Pius IX. With the exception of the account of the long illness of Hecker before his death which led to travels in Europe and Africa, and which for a long time prevented his living in the community and from saying Mass, the remaining chapters of the book were devoted to Hecker's notion of the religious community of the modern day and his ideas about the role of the Church in modern times.

Elliott pointed out that in his plans for the new community, Father Hecker felt that God raised up different kinds of religious societies to meet different problems and situations. In the modern world he felt that the religious leaders should be able to direct their followers to a correspondence with the action of the Holy Spirit which raises the natural virtues to the supernatural. The modern age was characterized by widespread education and greater liberty. This widespread intelligence and liberty he regarded as invitations "to the apostolate of the Holy Spirit." They demanded a greater independence of action under the direction of the Holy Spirit, although these inspirations must always be under the direction of the external discipline and guidance of the Holy Spirit in the Church. This spirit of independence was to characterize his community along with personal perfection and zeal for souls. The new religious would not take vows but would be willing to take them if necessity called for them. The individuality of the new religious would enable him to show the modern man how to use his new freedom and individuality to attain perfection and salvation. Elliott repeated in this connection a statement found in the diary of Hecker before his conversion: "The Eternal-Absolute is ever creating new forms of expressing himself." He added a paragraph which was not from Hecker and which contained words that could be construed as erroneous theology.

With regard to stability, men of stable character need no vow to guarantee adherence to a divine vocation, and men of feeble character may indeed vow themselves into an outward stability, but it is of little fruit to themselves personally, and their irremovability is often of infinite distress to their superiors and brethren. The episcopate is the one religious order founded by our Lord and its members are in the highest state of evangelical perfection; yet they are neither required nor advised to take the oaths or vows of religious orders.

Elliott added, however, that neither Hecker nor his associates had any aversion to vows but had merely decided that a condition without vows better suited their purposes.

Elliott added a chapter on Father Hecker's "Spiritual Doctrine." Culling certain quotations from the letters and writings of Father Hecker, Elliott maintained that Father Hecker had no really new doctrine but a view of the Catholic doctrine of Divine Grace suited to the aspirations of our times. Essentially this doctrine called for an elevation by grace of the natural faculties of understanding and will to a union with God beyond their natural powers. This elevation was to be brought about by a greater union with the Holy Spirit, and in seeking this union even the role of the Spiritual Director must not be allowed to stand in the way of the inspirations of the Holy Spirit. Hecker thought that the great need of the day was to remove the obstacles to this greater cooperation with the gifts and inspirations of the Holy Spirit. He even felt that there was to be an increase of the action of the Holy Spirit to meet the conditions of modern times. According to Father Elliott, Father Hecker believed that a large number of persons could be led to perfection in this way. Hecker wrote that the modern age was not an age of martyrs or a monastic age, but that the saints of the modern age were to be found enduring the toils and duties of modern daily life. To attain this elevation, the natural powers were perfected by the use of the sacraments and prayer, but the ultimate direction of the souls would come from the Holy Spirit.

Discussing Father Hecker's missions and public lectures Elliott stressed the informality of Hecker's presentation, and that he took for granted the correctness of the Catholic doctrine and the fact that this teaching answered the aspirations of the soul. His appeal to Protestants was based on his own experiences and he emphasized the fact that only Catholicism answered their search for truth and perfection. "To say that he Americanized in the narrow sense would be to do him injustice," said Elliott. "The American ideas to which he appealed he knew to be God's will for all civilized peoples of our time." To his lectures Hecker had added the apostolate of the press, not only in his books and pamphlets but in the establishment of the *Catholic World* and *The Young Catholic*, and of the Catholic Publications Society.

Father Hecker attended the international Catholic Congress of Malines in 1867, and was a proxy for Bishop Sylvester Rosecrans of Columbus at the Vatican Council. That Council, Hecker said, had settled for all time the external authority of the Church. During the three previous centuries, in order to preserve this authority, the Church had insisted on the less active virtues; now that this authority was established, attention could now be centered on the more active virtues.

Elliott devoted a whole chapter to an essay that Hecker composed in 1875, during his last illness, and which he published first anonymously in England: *An Exposition of the Church in View of the Recent Difficulties and Controversies and the Present Needs of the Age*. The essay was prompted by the subservient condition of the Church in western Europe which he had observed during his travels. In general, Hecker's explanation for this unfortunate situation of the Church in western Europe, whereby an unfriendly minority was able to dominate the Catholic countries, was the continuance in the Church of the defensive tactics she had been forced to use during the period of the Reformation and the rebellion of the Protestants. Hecker had said that the virtues developed under this situation were "more passive than active." Elliott pushed this figure further and spoke of the "passive virtues" of that age which must now yield to the "active virtues" necessary for the modern age. Hecker expected a greater effusion of the Holy Spirit to enable the faithful to meet the new situation of modern liberty and independence. Hecker coupled the rising power of the Saxon races and the decline of the Latin races with this new development, and found this new development of the Church to correspond to the demands of these Saxon races for greater interior spirituality and greater independence. And in this development he foretold a return of the Saxon races to the Church.

Elliott finished his biography with passages about the interior life of Father Hecker and a peroration in which he praised Hecker's fidelity to his interior voice and his higher vocation. He invited others to join in greater devotion to the Holy Ghost and to the practice of Hecker's principles and methods as the best guides to success.

Archbishop John Ireland had promised an introduction for Elliott's biography but sent it in too late for publication with the first chapter in the April, 1890, *Catholic World*, and it appeared in the July issue. In it he credited to Father Hecker his "most salutary impressions," for which he was "glad to have the opportunity to profess publicly" his gratitude to him. He called Father Hecker "the typical American priest" having not only the qualities universally expected of a good priest but qualities specially suited for America. Ireland expressed his admiration for the Catholic immigrants but said they did little "to make the church in America throb with American life." Ireland said that Hecker looked to America "as the fairest conquest for divine truth," and added that "the American current, so plain for the last quarter of a century in the flow of Catholic affairs, is, largely at least, to be traced back to Father Hecker and his early co-workers." Ireland praised Hecker's devotion to the Constitution of the United States and the American Republic. Without in any way minimizing the supernatural the Archbishop called attention to Hecker's "stress on the natural and social virtues." Ireland reviewed briefly Father Hecker's many activities and his enthusiasm. Further, Ireland said Hecker's profound conviction was that "the order of the day should be individual action—every man doing his full duty, and waiting for no one else to prompt him." There was a time, Ireland said, when the Church had to put the brakes on individual activity but now "the need of repression had passed away." His final sentences called Hecker "the flower of our American priesthood," the great lines of whose personality should be guarded "in the formation of the future priestly characters of America."

The book, when published in 1891, bore the imprimatur of Archbishop Michael Corrigan of New York. It is significant that there appeared in the *American Ecclesiastical Review* at that particular time the article of Father Thomas Preston, Corrigan's Vicar General, which was a sharp attack on the liberal tendencies in the American Church. Nevertheless, since the tone of the book was consistent with the general patriotism of the day it occasioned no controversy. It had run serially in the *Catholic World*, and there were several American editions of the book, but the Catholic reading public was comparatively small. Hecker by his long life had outlived his contemporaries and this type of book published by the press of the Catholic minority was not of great interest to the cultural majority in the United States. There was also a certain quality of the book which made it lack popular appeal in the United States. Elliott, himself a writer and preacher on spiritual and ascetical matters, did not emphasize the points in the character of Hecker which would appeal to the secular non-Catholic majority.

While the "Life of Hecker" was being published in the *Catholic World*, the author, Father Elliott, wrote[8] to Vicomte de Meaux of Ecotay, France, who had recently published his book on the liberties of the Church in the United States, proposing the publication of a French translation of the biography. De Meaux in turn consulted with his friend Count Guillaume de Chabrol, who had become acquainted with Hecker during his own visit to the United States and was an admirer of the Paulist founder. Chabrol secured the aid of his cousin, Countess de Ravilliax,[9] who

[8] Count Guillaume de Chabrol to Father Walter Elliott, July 14, 1891. Chabrol tells Elliott that he had heard from De Meaux about Elliott's request that De Meaux translate the biography. Apparently De Meaux consulted Chabrol who secured the services of his cousin, the Countess de Ravilliax. The letters dealing with these arrangements with the Countess de Ravilliax in the Paulist archives are: Chabrol to Elliott, July 12, 1893, July 13, 1897, and July 21, 1897, and Countess de Ravilliax to Elliott, June 11, 1894.

[9] The confusion about the translator of the biography arises from the fact that the name was never given to the public. Edouard Lecanuet *La Vie de L'Église sous Léon XIII* (Paris, 1930), p. 569, and Félix Klein in the fourth volume of his *Souvenirs, Américanisme* (Paris, 1949) p. 10, had said that the trans-

prepared the translation; but, in its full-length version no publisher would accept it. Since Father Elliott had stipulated that the translator's name would not appear on the volume and since the Countess de Ravilliax had really wished to remain an anonymous translator, she offered to revise the book, if Elliott agreed, to suit the publisher and still to remain anonymous. Count de Chabrol in the meantime approached several publishers with the translation and all insisted that the translation would have to be adapted for French readers. Elliott agreed to this adaptation but domestic affairs together with the delays incident to this revision prevented Count de Chabrol from pushing the publication for a few years. Finally at the suggestion of Lecoffre, the Paris publisher, he consulted young Abbé Félix Klein,[10] the translator of the speeches of Archbishop Ireland and a rising teacher in the Institut Catholique of Paris. Abbé Klein read the translation and agreed with Chabrol that it deserved to be published but indicated that it needed to be adapted further to the French audience both as to length and as to choice of incidents. Chabrol then urged Klein to make the necessary changes and to write the preface for the translation. Klein was busy with lectures and writings and refused on the ground that he lacked the time for the work. Chabrol was not one to be defeated so easily, and so, he enlisted the aid of his friends, especially M. Thureau-Dangin, and they persuaded Klein that he should do the work of editing and smoothing out the translation.

In its new form with its preface, the editing of Abbé Klein, and the backing by a group of progressive French writers, the life of

lator was Mlle de Guerines, a known translator of spiritual books, who had given considerable notice of the translation in the press. The correspondence in the Paulist Fathers' Archives shows that the translator was Countess de Ravilliax whom De Chabrol named as his cousin. She did not want her name to appear and Elliott did not want a translator's name to appear in the translation. Later in a letter to Father Joseph McSorley, Klein indicated that he did not remember who the translator was. It seems from the Klein papers and the correspondence of Father Elliott that Klein had no real dealings with the translator and hence can be excused for not knowing who she was. He dealt directly with Count de Chabrol, Elliott, and the publisher.

[10] Klein, *Souvenirs*, IV, 10-11. Klein tells with irony of the accidents which brought about his connection with the French life.

Father Hecker[11] became a new factor in the life of French Catholicism. Count de Chabrol and Klein did not see in the life of Hecker the biography of a spiritual leader of a new religious community, although it seems that Father Elliott really had such a biography in mind. To Chabrol who had known Hecker in America and in Europe, Hecker was a symbol of a new type of clergyman which he had experienced in the new world and which he thought would check the decay of religion in France. The *néo-chrétien* leaders' admiration for the simply dressed and informal Archbishop of Saint Paul; the admiration of De Meaux, Leclerc, Bourget, Duval for the growing and thriving Catholicism in free United States; the reaction among the younger clergy and writers against both tradition-bound European Catholicism and materialistic science; all these suddenly found in the subject of Father Elliott's biography, a new hero, a model about whom they could preach a new crusade. That Abbé Dufresne thought Hecker was a subject for canonization, and that Elliott thought of him as the leader in a new kind of asceticism merely added to the picture.

The Elliott life as translated by Countess de Ravilliax was a fairly faithful transcription of the biography by Elliott. The introduction by Archbishop Ireland added much to the biography for those who had been following in translation with breathless impatience the speeches of the Saint Paul prelate, for really Archbishop Ireland had pointed out that in Hecker he had found a man who had exemplified his theory of the reconciliation of the Church and the age. One might even wonder that the appearance of the book with that kind of introduction, in 1890-1, at the very time that Ireland was engaged in his first bitter controversy over nationalism and the schools, had not brought down upon the biography in the United States a torrent of attack. But when Klein in a sense "gilded the lily" and, building on the biography and on Ireland's preface, pointed up even more in his preface the novel-

---

[11] *Le Père Hecker Fondateur des "Paulistes" Américains, 1819-1888* par le Père W. Elliott, de la même Compagnie. Traduit et adapté de l'anglais avec autorization de l'auteur. Introduction par Mgr. Ireland. Préface par l'Abbé Félix Klein, (Paris, 1897).

ties of the life of Hecker as they appeared to the eyes of the French progressives, there was bound to be a reaction from the sullen conservatives who were so strongly fighting the trend towards reconciliation with the *République*.

In his preface Klein told the French that he was bringing to them an American priest of whom they knew very little, and was introducing them to a book which cast such a bright light on human affairs that no book like it had appeared for more than fifty years.

He assured his readers that he had only to tell them about Hecker, of whom Pius IX, Archbishop Ireland, and Cardinal Newman had spoken such grand things, and their desire to know more of him would do the rest. Klein compared him to Benjamin Franklin and Lincoln as a self-made man who had elevated himself by his own intelligence and work (iii). That is the reason why the Americans recognized him as one of their own; and Klein quoted briefly the tributes to this Americanness from James Parton in the *Atlantic Monthly* and from Lockhart. Klein even compared him to Saint Augustine arising from Manicheism in his passing from the Yankee prejudices to Catholicism, even comparing the passages from Hecker's journal to the passages from Augustine's *Confessions* (v). Like Saint Theresa, Hecker had become conscious of a special mission for which he had been chosen by God (vi). Klein said that among pioneers there are two kinds, those who pave the way but do not know what they accomplish and those who at the same time are conscious and write of their experiences. Hecker he said belonged to this second kind. Although the perfect type of the hard-working American priest, Hecker was at the same time a doctor (vii) who had formulated the principles for the training of the priests of the future (viii), although his *mystique* would also apply in a way to all Christians. Klein here quoted in a footnote Abbé Dufresne who called Hecker not only a type of the ideal American priest but the ideal type of the modern priest who could overcome modern Protestantism and incredulity. Hecker he said was universal in space and time.

Noting particular qualities of Hecker, Klein quoted the passages from the biography in which Hecker explained the formation of his new community as (x) a result of the fact that as man continued to march irresistibly towards freedom and personal independence so also the eternal absolute did not cease to manifest itself in new forms. Thus Hecker was manifesting the complete harmony of the new conditions of the human mind with real Christianity. The scientific changes of the previous thirty years had demanded in human moral conditions more teaching, more energy, more independence, more initiative, more aptitude to change, to change work, to follow discoveries, to renew methods and even ideas(xi).

The particular care of Hecker to recognize these natural tendencies was indicated, according to Klein, in the way he proved that Protestantism could not answer human needs and that Catholicism did answer these needs, particularly the modern need of self-government. Catholicism had been misrepresented to these Protestants as a hierarchical conspiracy to enslave, whereas it was actually the source of real liberty.

Turning to Hecker's mystical theories Klein pointed out that Hecker insisted on a more direct approach of the soul to God in order to make the union with God more intimate. The priest, he quoted Hecker as saying, was the guide of the faithful soul and in this he persuades the soul that God lives in it and makes the soul act under the direction of the Holy Ghost. There are two kinds of direction, that without and that within, and there can be no conflict between the two. During the past three centuries the Church had, in its reaction to Protestantism and Protestantism's exaggerated individualism, insisted on the external direction and submission, but in the new age greater emphasis must now be placed on the interior direction. In this interior direction, according to Klein, Hecker had insisted that no two souls were exactly alike and that each would receive its own proper grace. In Catholicity, instead of a restraint badly advised, the soul would find real liberty in which the only rule was to avoid what is false (xix). Hecker, taking as his model Saint Joseph, had insisted on the intense development of business and industry, which activities he found not at all inconsistent with Christian perfection. In all this the Christian soul wants to obey the will of God and it is the work of the priest to enable him to know God's will. Likewise this individuality of spiritual life was to be the principal characteristic of the members of his community, the Paulists (xxi). Thus as Klein summarized the Hecker principles, they consisted first of the direct action (xxii) of God on the soul and secondly on the fact that the life of man marches irresistibly towards personal liberty and independence.

Quoting Hecker, Klein said that in the sixteenth century the Church thought it necessary to accentuate obedience to overcome the attack of the Protestants, but that a free kind of spirituality was necessary for today with greater insistence on faith, hope, charity, and the action of the Holy Spirit (xxix). The (xxxi) passive virtues which produced such great victories in the periods of the attack on the Church must give way now to the active virtues in a time that demands initiative and personal effort. The present century was not to be an age of martyrs, of hermits, of monks. It would indeed have its martyrs, recluses, its monastic communities, but they would not be the best type of Christian perfection. Present day Catholics live and work in their market places, their banks, their factories, their shops, in all situations common to human life; and here sanctity is introduced. In these situations will be found the stylites of the new day. These ideas are the same as those of the great saints such as St. Francis, St. Dominic and St. Catherine of Siena. Further, the very life of man in the secular and natural order marches irresistibly towards freedom and personal independence (xxiii). This insistence on an enlargement of the interior life of the individual will in no way conflict with the external authority of the Church but lead to a better understanding of that authority (xxi). The Latins are attached to exterior institutions and the Saxons to interior forces, but the future belongs rather to the Saxons. Hecker wanted to lead to the Church his fellow countrymen, the non-believers and the rationalists. He would abolish the customs house (xxvii) and facilitate the entry into the Church.

With these thoughts as an opening view, Klein quoted some strong passages from the writings of Hecker and called him not only the priest of the present but the priest of the future, the genius of the new age.

But Chabrol and Klein did not leave to chance the reception of this book. Count de Chabrol had intended to write the preface for the translation but instead he wrote two articles for *Le Correspondant*, May 25 and June 10, 1897,[12] in which he spoke of meeting Hecker when he visited the United States in 1866 to witness the Second Plenary Council. Hecker he had met and admired but, as he noted, he did not then know of the great interior life of the priest as he did now. Hecker's close follower and intimate, Elliott, who also had possession of his journal and writings, could describe his great interior life. Chabrol had wanted to publish the translation immediately after its appearance in English but had been delayed by counsels from Father Elliott who was not sure that it would be well received in France. Elliott thought he was a hero only for America; Chabrol said that he was a personality who could not be kept isolated in one country. Hecker, according to Chabrol, was formed by three influences, his mother, his labors, and the interior guidance of the Holy Ghost. Chabrol told of Hecker's experiences at Brook Farm with the transcendentalists and of Brownson, whom he himself had interviewed in 1867. Chabrol in his article departed from the story as told in the biography to discuss the Yankee inheritance from the Puritans and Jonathan Edwards, of the great revival, and of the America in which Hecker grew up. In the second article he related the story of Hecker's experiences with the Redemptorists as a missionary and the founding of the Paulists. Speaking of Hecker's experiences at the Vatican Council Chabrol compared him favorably with the disposition of the Abbé Lamennais when they faced their crises. He compared the *Catholic World* in the United States to *Le Correspondant* in France and gave a brief account of Hecker's work in Catholic journalism, quoting his rules for Catholic journalists. Further Chabrol discussed the interior desolation of Hecker during the last years, saying that this is the common experience of great souls. Finally he claimed that the

---

[12] *Le Correspondant* May 25, 1897, "Un Prêtre Américain, Le Réverend Père Hecker," pp. 664-683; June 10, pp. 893-912.

great message of Hecker was the necessity for the reconciliation of the authority of the Church with individual initiative of the day as in times past the Church reconciled the authoritarianism of the Latins with the principles of authority.

Klein printed his own preface in *La Revue du Clergé Français*. The introduction of Archbishop Ireland, with a two page notice, was printed in *La Quinzaine* of June 1. Klein's friend Abbé Tourville printed a review with notable quotations from the biography in *Science Sociale* for June. Either he or his publishers had made sure that the *Semaine Religieuse* of the French dioceses received a brief notice of book. Most of the weekly journals[13] received at the same time a prepared review in which the question was first asked "Who is Father Hecker?" Taking for granted that the people did not know, the article then proceeded to tell them about the articles in *Le Correspondant*, *La Quinzaine* and *La Revue du Clergé Français*, and to give a brief eulogy of the priest. By the middle of the summer this campaign had been most successful. The volume which went quickly into three printings was known throughout the country and was beginning to be read, not only by reviewers for the journals, but by friends and critics of Abbé Klein and Archbishop Ireland. In the meantime Father Elliott, having received Chabrol's articles, advised the Count[14] that he should watch carefully for a reaction and that he should especially watch Rome because he would not be surprised if an attempt were made to place the book on the Index.[15]

Throughout June and July the notes and reviews continued to appear in the various French weeklies. Most of them were prepared reviews sent out by the publishers but occasionally there

[13] The Klein papers in the Archives of the University of Notre Dame contain clippings of many of these reviews and notices.

[14] Elliott to Chabrol, June 18, 1897 (copy) in the Klein papers in the University of Notre Dame.

[15] Letter of Elliott to Klein, New York, July 28, 1897, "[As to the Jesuits], of course they cannot see Frenchmen taking to the free ways of the Holy Spirit without a protest—Frenchmen especially, whose Christianity is supposed to be either a high order of external discipline or a grand and universal absorbant, or nothing. But there are Jesuits and Jesuits, and the spirit of dear Father Lallement [sic] is by no means dead among the members of that Great Society . . . Rome . . . I should not be at all surprised if an attempt were made there to put the French life under censure. . . ."

were some comments. Thus *La Vérité* of June 25 printed a favorable review by P. Ragey, Mariste, but the editor added a brief note of reservation about the Ireland introduction. The *Revue Bibliographique Belge* of June 30, printed a friendly review but added that Hecker was a self-made man and that there was the possibility that if his ideas were adopted too completely, a dangerous tendency to independence would be developed. *Le Peuple Français* in a review by J. Delaporte of July 6, thanked Klein for introducing Hecker to the French and claimed that Hecker's ideas were a paraphrase of the ideas of Pope Leo XIII. A review by Eugene Tavernier in the July 7 *L'Univers* said that Hecker was concerned with the French as he was with the whole world new and old. The *Semaine Religieuse* of July 17, of the Diocese of Belley, praised the book but added a reservation about the introduction by Archbishop Ireland. The number and friendly character of most of the reviews constituted a regular publicity campaign among the French Catholics.

A rather notable study of the book appeared in *La Justice Sociale* of July 31, by P. Dunnan. Dunnan called the phrase about "the eternal absolute" an American idea in Hegelian words. He said that in Europe one can become a democrat but in America one is born one. Americans, he said, reject not only monarchy but also bureaucracy and worship of the state. Dunnan praised the note about the eminence of the Anglo-Saxon. A week later in a continuance of the article Dunnan praised Hecker's insistence on internal inspiration but added that the internal inspiration would lead to external submission. Society had become more free and we must accept this situation as a manifestation of divine will. According to Hecker democracy is more favorable to the growth of the Church. On August 1, Georges Fonsegrive in *La Quinzaine* wrote an editorial praising Hecker and the Paulists, adding that he was arguing for individuality not individualism. Perhaps it is not without significance that an article in *La France Libre* of Lyons on August 18, 1897, signed by "un Diplomate," warned that some have not read the book solely for edification but that some propose the mystique, the historical theory of Hecker, for imitation. That, he warned, is contrary to the Council of Trent and to the

Church's doctrine on the Holy Ghost. He claimed that Hegelianism had led Hecker to his doctrine about the Anglo-Saxons and the exterior life. This writer asked where were the Anglo-Saxon saints? He did not want French democracy to suffer from these excesses.

In Rome, Monsignor O'Connell read with interest the accounts in the French press of the French translation of the life of Father Hecker and the excitement that the book aroused. It is quite apparent that O'Connell himself was not greatly interested in Father Hecker, and only when Hecker's name began to be coupled with the European concept of American Catholicism that he became interested. Up to the spring of 1897, the chief occasion for the spread of Americanism in Rome was the French translation of the speeches of Archbishop Ireland for which O'Connell was arranging an Italian translation by his friend, Countess di Parravicino di Revel, an important contributor to the Milan *Rassegna Nationale*. Now O'Connell began immediately to estimate the effect of the publication of the life of Father Hecker on his campaign in Rome.

The struggle between Archbishop Ireland and his opponents in America had definitely tended to have echoes in Rome and in Europe, and O'Connell and Keane had warned Ireland that the real battle for their ideas would be fought in Rome. The removal of Keane and the subsequent rumors that Ireland and the Catholic University professors were to be removed were clear indications that if effective action was to be taken against Ireland and the progressives it would be taken in Rome. It was in this connection that O'Connell, writing to Ireland, noted that their enemies had made a mistake in having Keane[16] sent to Rome because there he could be more powerful for the cause of the Americanists. It seems that their opponents were not entirely unaware of this because they delayed as long as possible the appointment of Keane to any position of importance in Rome. In return it was under the direction of Keane and O'Connell writing from Rome that Ireland had made his speech against the *réfractaires*, hoping only to obtain support from the liberal Germans, and to change the argu-

16 O'Connell to Ireland, July 21, 1897.

ments against them from one of race to one of ideas. Thereby they hoped also to bring about their shoulders the protective mantle of Pope Leo XIII. The conservatives in the United States, however, were not idle. Condé B. Pallen and Preuss, and several of the German newspapers continued to harp upon the false liberalism and minimism of Ireland. An article in the *Independent* of January 14, 1897, by Dr. Edwin Randall Knowles, had served to bring to the general public some awareness of the conflict that still existed between the Germans and the Ireland group. Against this article Preuss and other German writers began to publish editorials to prove that here was no question of nationalism involved but merely one of doctrine, and to reiterate the charge of liberalism against Ireland and the progressives.

In the meantime the quarrel at the Catholic University over Schroeder had become common property of the Catholic press and the secular press in Washington. The *Washington Post* again republished the Schroeder articles from the *Review* and published them under Schroeder's name. Then Ireland, Gibbons, and their friends on the staff of the University began to concentrate on Schroeder and to demand that he be ousted. That Schroeder was guilty of some social errors of conduct could not be denied but it is quite evident that they alone were not sufficient for removal. Schroeder had been to Rome in the summer of 1896, and had made friends among the cardinals, particularly with Cardinal Steinhüber, S. J. who became active in Rome in his defense. It was in connection with this visit that Monsignor Schroeder was credited by some with the removal of Bishop Keane. Thus, at the time of the publication of the *Vie du Père Hecker*, a new development in the battle came about that brought together these various progressive movements.

During the summer months of 1897, a meeting of the progressive professors of the University was arranged for the International Catholic Scientific Congress at Fribourg, Switzerland, in August. Besides Father Zahm, who was a close friend of Ireland, Keane and O'Connell were to meet with Fathers Edward A. Pace and Grannan of the Washington University at the Congress. Zahm was to give a paper on evolution. O'Connell prepared a

paper entitled "A New Idea in the Life of Father Isaac Hecker."
As he wrote to Ireland, Hecker was doing for them what they
had failed to accomplish by all their efforts and he proposed to
take advantage of the favorable publicity of the Hecker biography to better the position of Americanism.

> It is surprising how circumstances are combining in favor of the new
> idea. Hecker's life gives a tremendous impulse. You can hardly imagine
> it. Klein wrote a masterly preface that is a tour de force of itself and
> has received a stupendous welcome. Klein is a noble fellow, body and
> soul in your idea and ready he writes me, to sacrifice everything to the
> cause. I shall write to Father Elliott asking permission to have his
> Father Hecker translated into Italian. Klein has already placed his pref-
> ace at my disposal. Father Hecker's life is regarded as the supernatural
> philosophy of the whole movement—given out by a saint.[17]

In the section of the Fribourg Congress devoted to *sciences
juridiques et économiques et sociales*, Monsignor O'Connell presented his paper. He was assigned originally to be the third
speaker, but by special arrangement O'Connell gave his paper
first in the morning session. O'Connell was not directly interested
in Father Hecker and apparently had not read Elliott's biography.[18] But since the French translation with Klein's preface
had aroused such great interest in American Catholicism, O'Connell wanted to make sure that the interest in the life was harnessed
to the spirit of the "movement" as he had begun to designate his
own and Ireland's ideas. The paper can be considered as a continuation of the program outlined in Archbishop Ireland's *réfractaire* paper and a defense of Americanism as attacked by the
conservatives in the United States and Europe. In general his paper[19] had little to do with Hecker. He was explaining the ideas
of "Americanism" currently discussed in Europe, especially in
France as the result of the study of Hecker's life and writings.
O'Connell distinguished between political and ecclesiastical

[17] O'Connell to Ireland, Milan, August 12, 1897.

[18] O'Connell to Countess Sabina di Parravicino di Revel, December 1, 1897.
O'Connell admits that he had not read the life.

[19] Denis O'Connell, *A New Idea in the Life of Father Hecker* (Freiburg im
Breisgau, 1897). The French version which appeared in *La Quinzaine* on October 15, was also published in Paris by Lecoffre under the title *L'Américanisme
d'Après le P. Hecker: Ce qu'il est et ce qu'il n'est pas* (1897).

Americanism. The first part of the paper was a glowing account of American democracy or "political Americanism," based chiefly on the Declaration of Independence and the Constitution—showing how consonant the political ideas in them were with the Catholic faith, by recognizing the dignity of man and the equality of persons, and guarantying liberty and dignity. This was the kind of "Americanism" Hecker held. This he contrasted with the ancient Roman law, with the supreme power of the emperor, and the absolute right of the ancient state. Then he examined a second meaning of "Americanism," the ecclesiastical. He admitted that the ideal situation in the relation between Church and State would be the acceptance of the Church either as the religion of the state or in a special relationship to be secured by concordats, but neither of these conditions were possible in the United States because of the first article of the Constitution. That ideal situation, he said, was the "thesis," but the "hypothesis," the practical solution offered in the United States, allowed the Church full freedom which it would not have if there were an established church which in the United States would undoubtedly be Protestant. Further O'Connell pointed out that the Pope had blessed the United States Constitution when he had received a copy of it and that his delegate, Archbishop Satolli, had praised the condition of the Church under the Constitution. "Nowhere is the action of the Church more free, and the exercise of Pontifical authority more untrammelled. The Church lives entirely under her own freely made laws; the relations of the bishops with the Holy See are direct and unhampered, and the exercise of the authority of the Pope is immediate and uncontrolled." Finally O'Connell insisted that Hecker accepted both Americanisms. He accepted the political as good if not better than any other existing system; further, because he felt that the Roman political law was destined to pass away and be replaced by democratic power—the American idea—he also accepted ecclesiastical Americanism since he could find nothing that served the Church better in America. Finally, he assured his listeners that this was no new form of "heresy of liberalism or separatism, and that fairly considered Americanism is nothing else than that loyal devotion that Catholics in

America bear to the principles on which their government is founded, and their conscientious conviction that these principles afford Catholics favorable opportunities for promoting the glory of God, the growth of the Church, and the salvation of souls in America."

Bishop Charles Turinaz of Nancy, one of the more conservative bishops of France, had understood that the paper of O'Connell was to be third and arrived late for the meeting, missing O'Connell's paper. When he discovered this he insisted on being allowed to read his criticisms of the life of Hecker in which he accused Hecker of having left Catholicism and of introducing the Protestant notion of internal guidance. O'Connell and his friends had departed and those present were not prepared to defend Hecker against this attack. When O'Connell and his friends learned of Turinaz's attack they prepared to demand an opportunity to answer the bishop. In the meantime Abbé Klein had arrived and at lunch they talked over the problem. After lunch Abbé Klein asked for the floor of the section and proceeded to defend Hecker quoting from the biography to show that Bishop Turinaz had misinterpreted the writings of Hecker. Later the directors of the Congress decided to erase the account of Bishop Turinaz's speech from the records.[20] Thus through this incident at the end of the summer and the biography of Hecker, the European phase of the Americanist movement which had prospered through the publication of the French translation was apparently still triumphant but beginning to suffer attack. The close of the summer vacation, however, was to witness the renewal of hostilities.

During the summer there was also an interlude in the press controversy; as has been noted a few paragraphs had appeared in the chronicle section of the May 2, 1897, *Civiltà Cattolica*, questioning whether the United States was a Christian nation. The *Free-*

[20] Accounts of this exchange between O'Connell and Klein on one side and Turinaz on the other are told by O'Connell in a letter to Father Walter Elliott, October 12, 1897, and by Klein in his autobiography, IV, 75-87. The incident was omitted from the official account, *Compte rendu du quatrième Congrès scientifique international des Catholiques tenu à Fribourg (Suisse) du 16 au 20 août, 1897* (Fribourg, 1909), pp. 34-36.

man's Journal of June 19, 1897, took special cognizance of the *Civiltà* article, calling it an attack on Gibbons, Ireland, and Keane and insisting that it constituted a breaking of the peace that had existed since the removal of Keane. The *Freeman's* editor pointed out that these prelates were not trying to conciliate Protestants, and that the question of languages in the churches had been decided by Rome. Further, he denied that any large American group wanted to abolish the Catholic schools. On secret societies American Catholics, he said, accepted whatever Rome decided. As to religious liberty they spoke only of what the Constitution really granted. Finally the author chided the *Civiltà* for being taken in by Diana Vaughan,[21] the fake medium, created by Leo Taxil to deceive the European Catholics who were so violently opposed to Masonry. Subsequent issues during the summer of the *Freeman's Journal* carried protests against the *Civiltà* and the *Sacred Heart Messenger*.[22] In several issues the *Freeman's Journal* also answered attacks of the Antigonish *Casket* which had charged Americans with liberalism and minimism.

With the opening of the autumn session there was renewed activity in the Americanist movement on both the European and American fronts. The point at issue was not the same in each case, despite the attempts of O'Connell to make the issue everywhere the cooperation of the Church with democracy. After the Fribourg Congress, while arranging for the publication of his speech in a French journal, he warned his friend Klein that they should insist on the political aspect of "Americanism" because that would be in line with the program of Pope Leo XIII and because as such it would not be attacked in the United States. The spiritual side of "Americanism" would come later. In the American Catholic press, however, the issue was the attack on Ireland and his friends by the *Civiltà*, and the continuation of the charge of liberalism

[21] J. St. Clair Etheridge in his article "The Genesis of 'Americanism'" *North American Review*, CLXX, 679-693 gives a succinct account of this mythical character (p. 686) who figured very much in the French religious literature of this same period. A certain Leo Taxil, a pretended convert from Masonry, gave out the revelations from this mythical person supposedly also a convert from Masonry. Some of the more conservative journals, among them the *Civiltà Cattolica*, accepted these "revelations" until Taxil admitted the deception.

[22] *Freeman's Journal*, July 17, 1897.

in *Church Progress* by Pallen, and by *La Vérité* of Quebec and the Antigonish *Casket*. The *Catholic Citizen* of Milwaukee, the *Western Watchman*, the *Freeman's Journal* and the *Northwestern Chronicle* were probably the chief defenders of the Americanists, trying to show that the liberalism which they were advocating was not that condemned by Pope Leo in his encyclical "Libertas" but the kind which he accepted, the progress which the Pope himself advocated.

In that encyclical of June 20, 1888, Pope Leo XIII had condemned various forms of liberalism which tried to apply the principles of naturalism or radicalism in the domain of morality and politics. He had condemned those liberalisms which either reject the supreme authority of God in public or private affairs, or accepting the authority of God, reject all laws of faith and morals which are above natural reason or at least assert that no regard should be paid to these higher laws by the state. Thus Pope Leo also rejected the doctrine of the entire separation of Church and State, those doctrines which denied to the Church the right of a perfect society, and those which insisted that the Church should conform to the modern system of government by changes in her practices or doctrine. Pope Leo further rejected unconditional freedom of thought, of speech, of writing and of worship. He did allow freedom in these things for a just cause. Pope Leo added: "Again it is not wrong to prefer a democratic form of government, if only the Catholic doctrine be maintained as to the origin and exercise of power. . . ." "And the Church approves of every one devoting his services to the common good, and doing all that he can for the defense, preservation, and prosperity of his country."[23]

As the 1897-98 school year approached the practical problem of the progressive battle was the elimination of Professor Joseph Schroeder from the faculty of the Catholic University.[24] The

---

[23] *The Pope and the People, Select Letters and Addresses on Social Questions* by Pope Leo XIII, Pope Pius X, Pope Benedict XV and Pope Pius XI, (London, 1950). The encyclical "Libertas Praestantissimum" is given in translation, pp. 70-94.

[24] Colman Barry, *The Catholic Church and German Americans*, p. 235 and Hogan, *The Catholic University of America, 1896-1903*, p. 158 contain the best accounts of the forced resignation of Schroeder. On June 4, 1891 Father John

charge that he had been observed drinking beer in public might concern public propriety, but was scarcely a basis for dismissal. The line of division when the University trustees met in October was on the question of forcing the resignation of Schroeder because of his attacks on Ireland in the press. Word having reached Rome that Schroeder's resignation was to be demanded, Cardinal Steinhüber in Rome became active in his defense and Cardinal Rampolla finally sent a letter to Cardinal Gibbons suggesting that his resignation not be demanded. Nevertheless, the majority of the episcopal committee was determined to force the resignation and so voted ten to four, and Gibbons was instructed to send their decision to Rome demanding Schroeder's resignation. Rome then acquiesced provided Schroeder could save his good name. Schroeder agreed to resign if he could do so without damage, and the Cardinals agreed to this procedure. However, the decision was permitted to leak out to the secular press and caused a bitter furore.[25] As agreed, on December 20 Schroeder sent his resignation to be effective at the end of the year and it was accepted by Cardinal Gibbons. Schroeder in the meantime had obtained a position at the University of Muenster where he also came under attack from the pens of Kraus and Schell. With the departure of Schroeder that spring, the Americanists were in control of the University but German support for the University had been alienated.

In the meantime the reviews of the French life of Hecker continued to appear in the various European periodicals. Most notable of these was the review of Father A. de La Barre, S.J. in *Études* of September 20, 1897. De La Barre wrote in a personal

Hogan, S.S., had written to Father Herman Heuser, the Editor of the *American Ecclesiastical Review* about Schroeder and his criticism of Canon Bartolo's book. . . . "They take different views of things but nobody sees anything personal in that except perhaps Dr. Schroeder who is rather disposed to consider as reflecting on himself any exception taken to his opinions. Of course we are all anxious he should be a success here, both for the sake of the University and of the man, who is really gifted and good. But he has so far no following to speak of and this I believe owing to the unpopular and sometimes extreme views he takes and his lack of endurance of what runs counter to them. . . ."

[25] *The Review* (St. Louis) from November 4 to December 16, 1897, had some discussion of the Schroeder case in each issue and quoted comments from other newspapers on the matter.

letter to Klein that he regretted that he could not be more friendly. In this review while indicating the contents of the biography he merely asked some questions about the loose theological terminology of the book, and said that the insistence on a too great contrast between the past and the present was dangerous. He added a disagreement on the question of the value of religious orders. Klein, however, in the *Revue Française d'Edimbourg* for September-October, 1897, "Catholicisme Américain— Le P. Hecker, fondateur des Paulistes de New York," called the book one that would exercise a profound influence on the elite of the Catholic clergy. This interest of the clergy in Hecker, he said, came not from Ireland's introduction but from the nature of the life which was unrolled for the reader of the book. After summarizing the life of Hecker, Klein added some fervent sentences on the adaptation of the Church to the needs of the day— not in doctrine but adaptation to meet the external changes of the times. He praised the new ideas of independence, the notion of finding the inspiration of God within. For the rest, he urged his readers to consult the life of Hecker. There were many other reviews some of which indicated a possibility of later critical estimates, but the attack by Bishop Turinaz was the only important criticism before November. On November 29, according to his letter to Father George Deshon, Archbishop Keane[26] presented a copy of the French translation to Pope Leo XIII who manifested interest in the work of the Paulists. In the meantime Klein was notified that he would be proposed for an assistant professorship at the Institut Catholique. There was some opposition to his election but he received the affirmative vote of the bishops on November 24, with the exception of one, whom Klein suspected to be Turinaz.[27] In the meantime he became aware of a new counter campaign.

In his memoirs Klein says that on November 6, his friend M. Ollé-Laprune told him that there would be an important sermon the next day at Saint Sulpice at vespers, by Père Coubé, S.J., and

---

[26] Archbishop John J. Keane to Father George Deshon, November 29, 1897, in the Paulist Fathers Archives.
[27] Klein, *Souvenirs*, IV, 156.

suggested that Klein attend the services. Klein sat in the sanctuary of Saint Sulpice. The first part of Coubé's sermon was a panegyric about St. Charles Borromeo whose feast had been celebrated a few days before. The second half without mentioning names was a picture of the evils that now threatened the Church. Chiefly they were four: The Parliament of Religions; Brunetière's recent article in the *Revue des Deux Mondes* on the "Bankruptcy of Science"; Maurice Blondel's philosophy; and Father Hecker's Americanism. *Le Peuple Français* reprinted the summary of the sermon adding for their readers the names of the persons attacked. On November 11, *La Vérité Française* reprinted that article. Père Coubé then denied that he had attacked any one in particular. The following Saturday, November 12, Ollé-Laprune informed Klein[28] that the next day a similar attack could be expected at St. Clothilde from Père Gaudeau, S.J., after the three o'clock vespers. Since Klein was on good terms with the rector of that Church he went with him to hear the sermon. After a short talk about the dedication of church the preacher launched on a similar attack on the four great evils that threatened the Church. Later a similar sermon was preached by a third Jesuit at Sacré Coeur. It seemed that the Jesuits were making a concerted attack on these four evils. Abbé Alphonse Magnien, S.S., of St. Mary's seminary, Baltimore, who was in Paris at the time, indicated that only the intervention of the council of the archbishop of Paris prevented the continuance of the campaign.[29]

In *La Revue Générale de Bruxelles*, Edouard Trogan's "Lettres de Paris" dated 22 November, 1897, followed a sad note on the defection of Charbonnel with an account of the attack in the pulpits on Americanism. He noted the speech of O'Connell at Fribourg and Bishop Turinaz's attack, the dismissal of Keane and his

[28] Klein preserved the personal card of M. Ollé-Laprune containing a written note inviting him to accompany him to Père Gaudreau's sermon. It is in the Klein papers in the Archives of the University of Notre Dame.

[29] A. Magnien, S.S., to Archbishop Ireland, December 16, 1897, Archives of the Archdiocese of Saint Paul. Charles Maignen in his letters to Father J. F. Meifuss January 12, 1904 says that Coubé and Gaudeau were intimate friends. Letter in the Central Office of the Central Verein, Saint Louis. This might be a better explanation for the supposed action of the Order or even of a group of the Order.

replacement by Conaty, who he said held the same ideas as Keane and had demanded the resignation of Schroeder. He even noted the details of the Roman intervention and the eventual resignation of Schroeder. Trogan also noted that Père Delattre had attacked a previous speech of Abbé Klein made at the Congrès d'Intellectuels at Gand, and had accused Klein of wanting to move Rome to Minnesota and to replace Pope Leo XIII by Archbishop Ireland. He wondered if they were going to see a quarrel between the Paulists and the Jesuits like that between the Thomists and Molinists of old. To clear up the situation he quoted the speech of O'Connell as to the real meaning of Americanism. Trogan suggested that these ideas had already existed in France but that they were recognized only after they had gone to America and returned as American.

A similar article in *L'Italie* of Rome was reported by O'Connell in a letter of December 1, to Countess Sabina di Parravicino. O'Connell added that in Rome the movement was now called Americanism. He was urging the Countess to prepare an Italian translation of the life of Hecker. He added that there was no danger that the book would be put on the Index. He agreed with her that the original life was too long, and that he should have Father Elliott prepare a briefer life which she could then translate into Italian. An Italian translation of Monsignor O'Connell's Fribourg speech had been published early in 1898, in Naples, and was being praised by several reviewers. The translation had been made by Lorenzo Salazar-Sarsfield and an enthusiastic preface by Alfredo Capice Minutolo di Bargnaro had been added.

The incident at Fribourg apparently brought together in O'Connell's mind the two controversies. On September 3 from Freiburg im Breisgau he wrote to Abbé Klein:

> ... After some deliberation it was deemed best to send out my paper on "Americanism," and, in the public mind, to transfer the combat from the theological to the political issue, and only after the political side of the life of Father Hecker had been well placed before the American public, to make them acquainted with the intention of "our Fathers." Of course every American in America must endorse Father Hecker's Americanism, because it is defined as nothing else than that devotion to America and to its Constitution. To put that on the Index

would be to condemn our government and that would create too great a controversy. In that case, too, the theological question would fall to the second rank. We have had here the Professor of the Washington University and have printed the article. We will send in a few days a copy to every Bishop in America and to all the Catholic papers. I will expect you to look after the French press, to have the article appear first in the "Correspondant" and afterwards to be reviewed favorably in the Catholic papers of France and Belgium. In your review you might show how Americanism, in its political phase, is nothing else than the policy the Pope recommends for France. In America I don't see how the "Fathers" could safely attack Hecker's politics. And in the public mind, the two questions will be merged into one. I hope to send you the brochure in a few days. To get it into the "Correspondant" you might add the sub-heading "Americanism true and false." We will work to engage everybody in the work. Then I expect to call attention of our friends in America to the danger of the Index and have representations made to Rome that the condemnation of Hecker would mean in the mind of the public, the condemnation of America. That would prevent any serious quarrel.

A friend of mine coming from Fribourg after the close of the Congress informed me that there was a general understanding to write against the life of Hecker, and that after our dinner, it was agreed to let it pass. They say the Dominicans were in it.

Then our program is to place first the political side of Hecker's life well before the public, especially in America. Then to make known the designs of "our Fathers," and to arrange all American and democratic sentiment against it, and so save the day. You look out for France. We are sure the Jesuits cannot do anything in America. They would incur universal odium.[30]

In the meantime, while the arguments were being multiplied and the *Vie* continued to receive additional notices in the press, Abbé Klein was invited to give an address in the Institut Catholique on March 22, on "True and False Americanism." When Klein accepted the invitation he immediately wrote to his American friends for advice. Keane, whom O'Connell called "Father Hecker's spiritual child in everything"[31] was pleased to give Klein a few definite suggestions. In the first place he advised him to follow closely the text of Monsignor O'Connell's Fribourg address, repeating O'Connell's formula "It is no new form of heresy, of liberalism, or separatism."[32] Keane went on to discuss the three main charges made against the Americanists as he saw them.

[30] O'Connell to Klein, September 3, 1897, in the Paulist Fathers Archives.
[31] O'Connell to Klein, October 27, 1897, Paulist Fathers Archives.
[32] Keane to Klein, January 18, 1898, Paulist Fathers Archives.

No. I—Not heresy.—Our enemies in America have accused us lately of being Neo-Pelagians. The charge is absurdly false and calumnious. There is no country in the world where the supernatural and the channels of Grace are so insisted upon and are so appreciated by the people as in the United States. Our clergy work as hard as any priests in the world and I think it will be readily admitted that our people flock to the Sacraments as frequently as any other people. The devotions to the Holy Eucharist and to the Sacred Heart are universal.

Again Monsignor O'Connell says expressly that Father Hecker recognized in the social principles of the United States a broad basis whereon to begin among men the work of the supernatural.

Our adversaries cannot cite a single utterance of any prelate of the United States to the contrary. We insist of course upon the natural virtues, and we are glad that these are very strong in the American character, but never for a moment do we forget that these are only the bases of the supernatural virtues. To assert it is a calumny.

No. II—Not liberalism.—Liberalism is rejection in various degrees of the authority of God, or of the Church, or of the Pope. I defy our enemies to show a single instance of this among the Bishops or people of the United States. There is no country in the world where the authority of the Church and of the Pope is as free and as lovingly honored as in the United States. It is the only country in the world today where the Pope can exercise his authority without limit, and where it is always bowed to most lovingly. Only in one instance did it seem as if a papal decision was not welcomed as heartily as it ought to be. This was in regard to the fourteen propositions on the question of the schools presented to the Bishops by the Apostolic Delegate, Monsignor Satolli.

The partial and temporal want of agreement then manifested did not at all arise from any tendency towards liberalism on the part of the Bishops, but on the contrary was owing to their belief that these propositions were too liberal and could not represent the mind of the Pope. For it must be known that at that time Monsignor Satolli had not presented any credentials to show that he had been sent as Delegate to America by the Pope. As soon as the Pope made clear that these propositions were his own, there was no more opposition either to them or to Monsignor Satolli.

In his encyclical "Libertas" the Holy Father had defined the various degrees of Liberalism which the Church condemns and the one degree of Liberalism which the Church approves. I defy any man to show a single instance in which the teaching or action of the church in America transcends the limits of the Liberalism here approved by the Holy Father.

No. III—Not Separatism.—No American could be such a fool as to have any desire for a separate national church. They see too plainly that the idea of National and Catholic are contradictory. Even were they free to choose they would infinitely rather be a portion of the

Universal Church than be a church to themselves. It would be atrocious calumny to assert the contrary.

Finally, Americanism does not mean a Propaganda, aiming at imposing American conditions on the rest of the world. We mind our own business and only assert and defend what concerns our own country. What fits our circumstances would of course not fit countries where the circumstances are different. We are not foolish doctrinaires [sic]. We agree absolutely with the wisdom of Leo XIII in saying that our conditions are not to be regarded as a rule for the rest of the world.

Whether O'Connell would have agreed to these limitations can be doubted. Certainly the "movement" of which O'Connell and Ireland spoke wanted the rest of the Catholic world to adopt some of the American approach to modern problems, although both these Americanists probably would have agreed with Keane that they intended to keep within the dictates of Pope Leo XIII, regarding themselves not at all as separatists but as upholders of the papal program.

To Father Elliott[33] who was preparing the new and briefer version of the life of Hecker, Keane also gave some additional warnings. They are important since they come from one who could be regarded as a veritable son of the Paulists' founder. He told Elliott to profit by the criticisms that were being made of the French version to avert misunderstandings. He continued:

You know that in the first place, they accuse Father Hecker's doctrine concerning the Holy Ghost as incorrect being substantially that of Petavius, who, though not explicitly condemned, is looked upon with great disfavor; that is to say they think that he makes the action of the Holy Ghost too separate and distinct from the actions of the Holy Trinity. Of course, it is very easy to guard against this imputation without at all modifying Father Hecker's doctrine. He, of course, held the Catholic doctrine about the absolute unity of the action of God, but this being presupposed, even though not explicitly mentioned, he contented himself with developing what all theologians admit, namely the action specially "attributed" to God the Holy Ghost.

In the next place they accuse Father Hecker of unfairness and error in his comparison of the Anglo-Saxon and Latin races. We know that in this he is substantially correct, but we must bear in mind the sensibilities of our judges and also the amount of arguments which they can advance on their side.

Thirdly, they accuse Father Hecker, and still more Father Klein in

[33] Keane to Elliott, December 13, 1897, Paulist Fathers Archives.

his preface of wishing to make the condition of things in the United States a norma for the Church in general, and they remind us that the Holy Father in his Encyclical to the Bishops of the United States explicitly warned us against this very thing. . . .

On December 2, 1897, O'Connell wrote to Ireland to congratulate him on the forced resignation of Monsignor Schroeder from the Catholic University. He was exultant over this victory and the effects of his Fribourg encounter. He added:

> The whole atmosphere of Europe is redolent of Americanism. Your conferences, Hecker's life and my little brochure. It is now three months that the French press has been occupying itself with that little paper. And the subject assumes greater proportions the more they handle it. Americanism now means no longer provincialism but modern society. Modern Law in contrast with Ancient Law. In France the movement only needs watching. In England some of the best writers have placed themselves at my service. And I hope to avail myself of their offer. Klein writes me that a new edition of your "Église et siècle" will appear in Flemish. There is more Americanism here than in the church in America. And when you arrive you will everywhere be regarded as a colossus. The question is really the conflict of two civilizations as Archbishop Keane puts it.[34]

Had nothing further happened to acerbate the controversy, the conference of Abbé Klein on Americanism might have been the most important document in the controversy. But two things intervened. In the first place beginning with the March 3 issue of La Vérité, there appeared a series of articles signed "Martel" attacking Americanism. Secondly the health of Abbé Klein, never too strong, weakened to such an extent that he had to give up his work, including his proposed conference on Americanism and to leave the country temporarily in search of renewed health. In the meantime other publications had added to the background of this French controversy. Archbishop Keane had published in the Catholic World[35] for March, 1898, an article "America as seen from Abroad" which drew upon him criticism from the conservatives, especially in the German Catholic press. Keane noted that in Europe those who were facing the social problems ran to ex-

[34] O'Connell to Ireland, December 2, 1897, in the Archdiocesan Archives of Saint Paul.

[35] Catholic World, LXVI (March, 1898) 721-30.

tremes and did not understand the way that Americans representing opposite views worked together. They could not understand how Americans coming from so many nationalities were being formed into a unified people. Further they could not understand the American relations between Church and State, a separation of Church and State "which means simply that each leaves, and is bound to leave, the other free and independent in the management of its own affairs; each, however, respecting the other, and giving the other moral encouragement and even substantial aid when circumstances require or permit." Neither could they understand the friendly relations between Catholics and non-Catholics. In this, says Keane, they regarded the Parliament of Religions as something "treasonable." In both matters, however, the Holy Father had warned that the American situation was not suitable for other countries. This difference of the two continents reached its climax in the sympathy of the Americans with the "age, its ideas, and its civilization," as contrasted with the European Catholics feeling that the age was hopelessly Voltairian, infidel, and anti-Christian. Keane noted that the Americans subscribed readily to the encyclicals of Pope Leo XIII, but his passage on liberalism became a source of irritation to his critics. It was entitled "Leo's Encyclicals."

When Leo XIII came to the Chair of Peter, the intestine strife among Catholics was so scandalous that, in his Encyclical *Immortale Dei*, he uttered against it words both of paternal pleading and of authoritative denunciation, especially against the newspapers that were ringleaders of dissension. But with little result. The attacks on Liberalism continued as before, and all the blame was thrown on it. Then the Holy Father, in his Encyclical *Libertas*, in June, 1888, clearly defined the several kinds of liberalism which the church condemns, as the abuse and corruption of liberty. These are: first, the repudiation of all divine law and authority; second, the repudiation of the supernatural law; third, the repudiation of ecclesiastical law and authority, either by the total rejection of the church or by the denial that it is a perfect society; fourth, the notion that the church ought to so far accommodate herself to times and circumstances as "to accept what is false or unjust, or to connive at what is pernicious to religion." Then he takes care to state plainly that the opinion is commendable (honesta) which holds that the church should accommodate herself to times and circumstances, "when by this is meant a reasonable line of action, consistent with truth and justice; when, that is, in view of greater good, the church shows herself indulgent, and grants to the times whatever she can grant consistently with the holiness of her office."

It was hoped that this would end the assaults of Catholics on fellow-Catholics; for surely none who cared or dared to profess themselves Catholics would be found outside of the very liberal limits here granted by the Holy Father; and surely none would be so fanatical as to brand Catholics with an epithet which, in its theological signification as defined by the Pope himself, was so evidently inapplicable to them. But narrowness and fanaticism have shown themselves capable of even that.

So much allowance must be made for European traditionalism, that we can very well have patience with the quixotic onslaughts on the bugbear of Liberalism by men and journals that legitimately inherit the mania. We can even make some allowance for the virus of European periodicals making such erroneous and calumnious statements concerning American conditions and personages. But reasonable people can have no patience with the wretched thing when imported into America, or at least into the United States, where its exaggerations and injustice cannot plead the palliating circumstances of loyalty to old notions and lingering impressions. They can feel nothing but unmitigated condemnation for a periodical which accuses American Catholics of fostering the Liberalism which has antagonized and is still antagonizing religion in France! And they can feel little short of disgust for petty journalists who bring discredit on religion and scandalize multitudes by spreading abroad insinuations of heterodoxy against prelates from whom they ought to be learning their catechism.[36]

Finally Keane noted the wide acclaim given to the life of Hecker in its French translation, how this had brought American conditions to the knowledge of Europe, and how this had been intensified by the publication of Monsignor O'Connell's pamphlet. He admitted that there had been attacks on both but claimed that they had been mild and indicated a future better understanding of the Americans in Europe.

Letters of another tone in the meantime were appearing in the German press. Ireland's and O'Connell's appeal to the liberal Germans had produced a series of "*Spectator*" letters from Dr. Franz X. Kraus, while visiting the United States, in the *Allgemeinen Zeitung* of Munich. While Ireland and O'Connell might not agree with everything that was said in these letters, they found that Kraus was a definite partisan against Monsignor Schroeder and that he undertook to show that the main battle

[36] *Ibid.*, pp. 728-9.

between the progressives and conservatives in the United States was not one of race or nationalism. These letters were attacked, particularly in *Germania*, but O'Connell could boast that Schroeder's claim to be a victim of German nationalism had been discredited by Kraus and his friends. But the main battle over Americanism was to be fought not in Germany or in America but in France and Rome and the first gun in the main struggle was the article in *La Vérité* of March 3.

In *La Vérité* of Thursday, March 3, there appeared the first of a series of articles under the heading "L'Américanisme Mystique" over the pen name of "Martel." "Martel" was Charles Maignen, a priest of the Society of the Brothers of Saint Vincent De Paul and a nephew of Father Maurice Maignen who had distinguished himself in the French social Catholicism of the previous generation. Charles Maignen, however, had acquired some notoriety by attacking Count de Mun for accepting the *ralliement*, and had as a result lost his chaplaincy to the Workers' Circle of Mont Parnasse. Maignen had asked the editors of *La Vérité* to send him a copy of *La Vie du Père Hecker* for review. After he began to prepare his articles on the book he became acquainted for the first time with Abbé Georges Périès whom he consulted about the Catholic University of America and the Paulists. The two apparently collaborated in the later articles, although they were apparently written by Maignen who was Martel as Périès was Saint Clement.[37] The first article, a column and a half long, said that the *Life* of Hecker had aroused great interest and was bound to have great effect. Quoting the preface of Klein to the effect that this book was the most important book to appear within the past fifty years, that it cast light upon the religious evolution of the world and on the new relations that were to exist between God and the modern mind, Martel asked if the relations between God and the human soul had really changed. Since Archbishop Ireland had called Hecker in his introduction the priest of the future and the model of the new priest, Martel promised in subsequent articles to discuss the "*mystique*" of Father Hecker.

[37] Charles Maignen to Father J. F. Meifuss, January 12, 1904 in the Archives of the Central Verein, Saint Louis, Missouri.

The next day, March 4, the second article had the sub-heading "Le P. Hecker.—Conduit par l'esprit. Le Fiancé de l'Avenir." Dividing the life of Hecker into three periods, 1819-1844, 1845-1857, and 1858-1888, Martel further subdivided the last period into the periods 1858-1872 and 1872-1888. He asked if Hecker was a saint or a fool and claimed that he was neither, indicating that he had virtues and also illusions. Admitting that Hecker had a special grace before his conversion, he claimed that he spoke like a Methodist at the time of his conversion. Quoting at length from the biography and especially from the diary as quoted in the book, Martel indicated that Hecker was directed by an interior guidance but indicated that this guidance was a mixture of grace and illusions and suggested that Hecker was suffering from his extreme penance while at Brook Farm. On March 5, under the title "Le P. Hecker, témon de sa propre sainteté," he quoted from Hecker about his inability to learn during his period of studies and said that lack of theological study is an irreparable defect in the life of a priest, especially in a director of others. Against suggestions of L'Ami du Clergé that he was like the Curé d'Ars, Martel claimed that Hecker unlike the curé did not prepare his sermons. Martel, however, mockingly said that Hecker admitted that he had no other director than the Holy Ghost. Yet Martel added this man tried to tell the Pope how to govern the Church, suggesting that he make the Propaganda the right arm of the Church, that he choose cardinals from all nations and adopt modern methods in the offices of the Church. Martel said this man could not for a long time say Mass or receive Communion, and suggested that a priest should be able to go to the altar if he is to be raised to the altar.

In the fourth article of March 6, using information he claimed to have received from the Sacred Congregation of Religious and Regulars and from the Procurator General of the Redemptorists, he explained the circumstances of Hecker's leaving the Redemptorists, claiming that Hecker was entirely in the wrong. Because Hecker and his companions were converts and Americans, while the other Redemptorists were German and Europeans, they wanted to devote themselves to the Protestants and not to Catholics. Despite the fact that they were working contrary to their rule these Americans thought they had a special mission for humanity and civilization—the same mission that is claimed by the Americanizers in France—and to carry that out they went to Rome contrary to their rule.

In the next issue, Monday, March 7, under the title "L'Exode du P. Hecker" Martel showed how this trip to Rome was against the rules of St. Alphonsus and particularly the decrees of the Redemptorist General Chapter of 1855, and could be only a grave sin of disobedience. Further it was a sin against poverty because Hecker was spending money for the trip without permission. Under the circumstances he and his associates could not be received back into the Redemptorists and the Holy Father then released them from their vows. In the March 8 issue, Martel then proceeded to attack Hecker as the "religious of the future," pointing out that in all these things Hecker had merely followed his own impulses. Martel said that the Paulist Society was not a new form of community simply because it did not have vows. The Oratorians and others did not have vows but these other communities did not set out to change the Church. The Paulists, however, tended to have confidence in themselves, persuaded of the superiority of their system. Martel found in this a similarity between the subjectivism of Hecker and that of Kant. Further he indicated that the slow growth of the Paulists compared to the notable growth of the Redemptorists in the United States cast doubt on the quality of their inspiration.

On March 9 in the seventh article, Martel proceeded to attack the new apologetics of Hecker, especially his desire to make the approach to the Church for the rationalists easy. Hecker he said would abolish the customs house, break down the barriers between the Church and the rationalists. Martel indicated that this was what Hecker meant when he spoke of the personal direction of the Holy Ghost and of the interior life. He criticized Hecker's notion of human dignity and the evolution of grace in the soul. Hecker he found to be an immanentist and a kind of semi-Pelagian who held that grace must necessarily correspond to human needs. He called Hecker's joyous confidence a Protestant notion and accused him of minimism. On March 10, Martel discussed Hecker's teaching regarding the passive virtues, quoting Abbé Naudet as being led by the Hecker biography to teach the excellence of the cardinal virtues and to say that the *Imitation of Christ* belonged to another age. Thus according to this new teaching the passive virtues are for monarchists but the active virtues are for republicans and those who live under constitutional governments where individual initiative and personal efforts are needed. Hecker, he said, insisted on both the natural and the supernatural but gave a large place to the interior direction of the Holy Ghost. Martel claimed that Hecker did not have this notion when he was a Redemptorist but developed it later. Martel admitted that Hecker pointed out that this interior guidance would lead to external submission but questioned what Hecker meant by that external authority, especially since Hecker claimed that the director must never take the place of the Holy Ghost. Summing up, Martel said what was good in Hecker was not new, and what was new was not good.

On March 13, Martel turned his attack more upon the democratic notions surrounding the Americanists. He attacked the article of Abbé Dufresne in the *Revue du Clergé Français* of March, 1898, in which Dufresne compared Hecker to Saint Francis de Sales and made fun of the suggestion that Hecker was a candidate for beatification. Martel claimed that the purpose of this campaign was to propagate under the cover of an eminently saintly person, such as Hecker, the doctrines of Christian democracy. He criticized also the speech of Monsignor O'Connell at the Congress of Fribourg. Martel ended this article with a vehement claim that what the Americanists were trying to sell under the appearance of religion and sanctity was not a priest or a saint, but their errors and illusions.

On March 15 he returned to the attack, charging Hecker with holding that those who defended the Church were in the wrong, and indicated that this was what Hecker really meant by his desire to abolish the customs house. Hecker, he said, spoke of the Church's activity in the counter-reformation as if it were detrimental to the natural virtues. Thus, he said, according to Hecker the Council of the Vatican and the Jesuits had done fine work but now a new era was opening up for the Church in which new methods were to be used. Continuing in the next issue, March 16, Martel attacked particularly Hecker's attitude towards religious orders. Quoting Ireland's statement that this was not the age of martyrs, hermits, and monks, Martel answered that the religious orders were of the very essence of the Church. Those communities without vows, Martel said, may increase but those with vows will remain typical of the Church. Further he claimed that Hecker's teaching about the Holy Ghost was contrary to the encyclical of Pope Leo XIII of May 9, 1897, on devotion to the Holy Ghost; and that it was contrary to the teachings of the doctors of the mystical life, especially those of Saint John of the Cross. Finally Martel said that Hecker was not really a saint. Martel found no trace of devotion to the Blessed Virgin in Hecker's writings or of devotion to the Sacred Heart. Hecker had reproached the young priests who wanted to give more time to prayer. Further he had separated the Holy Ghost from the Holy Trinity, and Martel added that the name of Jesus was not mentioned five times in the biography. On March 17, Martel attacked Hecker and the Americanists because of their theory of the superiority of the Saxon races. He claimed that Hecker would end the utility of Latins with the Jesuits at the Vatican Council; that Hecker held that the Latins take naturally to the supernatural, the Saxons take supernaturally to the natural; that the Latins' religion is external, that of the Saxons is interior. Martel answered that the Saxons have produced no saints since the sixteenth century and no missionaries. The English have money and the Americans are consumed in making physical progress. Actually Hecker and the Americanists had failed to distinguish between the interior life and the subjectivism of Kant. Further, referring to the Parliament Congress of Religions, Martel said the Americanists regarded the Catholic Church as a middle ground between the Protestants and the Greek Orthodox Church.

On March 18, Martel turned on Hecker as a republican democrat and sneered at American civilization. De Maistre had said

America was an infant, but Martel said America had not yet been born. He listed the two parties of the controversy in the hierarchy of the United States, including among the progressives, Ireland, Keane, and O'Connell as liberal and democratic, and in the other the Germans and the conservatives. He called it a war between races in which the progressives wanted to set up a democratic and separate Church. Martel said that philosophy had proved that monarchy was the better form of government, and when America had grown and developed then a judgment could be made about the perfection of American republicanism.

In the article of March 19, Martel took as his subject the motto of the liberals under Montalembert, "A Free Church in a Free State," and discussed O'Connell's speech at Fribourg. O'Connell, he said, had revived the old doctrines of the Congress of Malines at which Hecker had assisted. He compared O'Connell's reasoning to tricks of photographers. O'Connell, he said, was saying that the old doctrine is true but that better results are obtained by using false theories. Against O'Connell he quoted the propositions of the *Syllabus of Errors* and the *Quanta Cura*. The Church cannot permit corruption of morals, perversity of the mind, or the pestilence of indifferentism, yet these evils are found in Americanism. The Constitution in the United States can be praised in the interpretation given by O'Connell but such a Constitution could not be permitted in France, and Martel quoted Leo XIII against separationism in France. The American idea was the old liberalism condemned by the Proposition LXXX of the *Syllabus*.

On March 23, Martel inserted a note in *La Vérité* that Abbé Klein had failed to give his lectures on the true Americanism, indicating with a tone of sarcasm that he was much disappointed. In the same issue, continuing his attacks, Martel examined the article of Archbishop Keane in the *Catholic World* of March, 1898. He quoted Keane as saying that nothing had served better to explain to Europeans what Americanism is than the life of Father Hecker. In answer Martel denied that Ireland, Keane, and the Americanists represented the majority of American Catholics, and said that there were many other American bishops and many other American Catholics who thought otherwise. He insisted that when

Keane had called Protestants fellow-Christians he was sustaining the doctrine condemned by Proposition XVIII of the *Syllabus of Errors*. Further he maintained that the Congress of Religions was condemned by the condemnation of Proposition LXXVII, which denied that there is only one true religion and of Proposition LXXIX, which called for a reconciliation with liberalism.

On March 27, *La Vérité* announced that the essays of Martel would appear in book form. On April 2, Martel again attacked Keane's article in the March *Catholic World*, especially the passage in which Keane had implied that Dupanloup had received praise from the Pope for his liberal teachings whereas, according to Martel, Dupanloup had received papal approval only for his defense of the temporal power.

On April 3, Martel published the fifteenth essay on the life of Hecker under the title "Father Hecker, Chief of the American School." In this Martel pointed out that the *Vie* was not just an ordinary book with intrinsic importance. It was a symbol, a flag of a party, a machine of war, a sort of Trojan horse bearing in its flanks the entire phalanx of the leaders of Americanism. To support this claim he pointed out that although the book did not appear until June, and had a preface dated June 5, the articles on it had begun to appear on May 25 in *Le Correspondant*. On June 10, Count de Chabrol had published his article calling Hecker the precursor of Ireland and Keane. All the reviews in the various other periodicals had appeared simultaneously and this was not a mere coincidence. Further *La Quinzaine* had published the introduction by Ireland before it had been published in book form. Thus Martel claimed this entire series was the action of the whole school of Americanists. Martel then proceeded to quote the article of Chabrol to show that Hecker had influence on the Pope and on Rome. Martel himself as he read the biography was more and more struck by the influence of Hecker. Hecker was in reality the founder and the beginner of the school—an enlightened subjectivist who gave in his writings the germ of all the ideas of the Americanist prelates. Further, Keane was a long time under the direction of Hecker as was Bishop O'Gorman, and Archbishop Ireland in his introduction admits Hecker's influence on himself.

Martel added that first, the disciples had surpassed the master, and secondly, that they had not changed the opinions of Hecker, unless to minimize his influence.

In the April 4 issue, Martel began to discuss the plot of the Americanists against the Church. Their first campaign he called the Parliament of Religions in Chicago. There, just as the Americans pointed to the discovery of America as the beginning of a new era in the world in which America had arrived at new heights, so the disciples of Hecker wanted to show the attainment of new intellectual and religious heights in the new world. Quoting the statements of Keane, at the Brussels Congress of 1894, to the effect that just as in America the old barriers of race and nationality had been broken down, and so also in the Parliament of Religions the barriers of religions were broken down, Keane, Martel said, did not understand the old divisions of Europe, and added that there were other divisions and quarrels in America. However, in applying this theory to religion Keane had said that it was not necessary to live at war with those who understand the faith in a way other than one's self. This, Martel said, is the same idea of Hecker—that the barriers between churches should be lowered and the customs house abolished. Martel further denied Charbonnel's claim that the whole American episcopate approved of the Congress, and claimed that only the Ireland group approved. Martel further criticized Keane's story about the dominance of the Catholics in the Parliament. The two published volumes about it show otherwise, he maintained. He mentioned, for example, the fact that these books showed that at the common prayer the Protestant version of the "Our Father" was used. Further, the Catholic members of the Parliament were followers of Hecker. Finally Martel made fun of Keane's comparing himself in his last discourse at the Congress to Saint Paul. Saint Paul, he said, was rejected by the rationalists because he refused to minimize. Martel showed that Keane in his article in the *Catholic World* admitted that the European Catholics could not understand American Catholic participation in the Parliament of Religions. As further evidence of this Americanist campaign against the Church, he quoted the letter of Archbishop John J. Kain of Saint Louis accepting a vice-presidency on the committee to welcome General Booth of the Salvation Army to Saint Louis, and quoted Charbonnel's article in the *Revue de Paris* on the purpose of the Parliament of Religions.

On April 5, Martel described the second campaign against the Church—the movement for a Congress of Religions at the Paris Exposition and the checking of Charbonnel. He quoted Charbonnel's article in the *Revue de Paris* of September 1895. In it Charbonnel used Ireland's ideas of the Church coming out of winter quarters, and out of the sacristies and sanctuaries. Then Charbonnel claimed that the Church had so much to offer to the crowd and spoke in praise of the activities of Ireland and Gibbons, especially in defending the Knights of Labor. Charbonnel further mentioned how he had helped translate the speeches of Ireland for publication. He had claimed further that the intellectual clergy accepted the idea of a Paris Congress of Religions in 1900. Among them were those who were active in social action, such clergy as those at the Congress of Rheims, Fathers Didon, Lemire and Naudet and such laymen as Georges Fonsegrive and Georges Goyau. They were supported by the paper *Le Monde*. M. André Hallays in the *Journal des Débats* analyzed the movement correctly when he claimed that for them theology was the translation of religious experience into the scientific language of the metaphysics of humanity. Again quoting Charbonnel, Martel maintained that subjectivism was the essence of Hecker's theories, the greatest error of the day. Charbonnel foresaw not a unity of religions, but a pact of silence on the points of difference by a pact of common action of hearts on the moralizing and consoling ideas which are in every faith. Other articles supporting the proposed Congress had been published by M. Anatole Leroy-Beaulieu in the *Revue de Paris* and by Leon Gregoire in *Le Monde*. Gregoire called for a lowering of the drawbridges which, said Martel, is a typical idea of Hecker. Martel then quoted the whole letter of Leo XIII of September 15, 1895, forbidding such Congresses of Religions. The words of praise by the Pope for the Paulists, he said, was not really praise but a softening of the blow, and would hardly have been included if the ideas of Hecker were known then as they are now. Charbonnel left the Church. This defection Martel blamed on Americanism.

On April 9, Martel proceeded to describe the Americanists' third campaign against the church—an attempt to conquer the Old World. The failure of the plans for the holding of a Congress of Religions at the Paris World Fair in 1900 stopped the movement for a while. They now needed a saint and for this purpose Father Hecker was "invented." Their success exceeded their hopes, as Keane admitted in his article in the *Catholic World*. Keane had spoken of plans for an Italian translation of the *Life* but Martel warned that that would be a tactical error because there were too many theologians in Rome who would put the book on the Index of forbidden books. Keane said that Europe would soon understand America better. Martel pointed out that Keane admitted that Americans were not interested in theology and did not understand the religious quarrels of Europe, yet Martel noted that Keane felicitated himself on this ignorance. Martel admitted that he could not follow Keane in this, especially when Keane called this religious controversy a kind of quixotism. But Keane's attack on those who charged the Americanists with liberalism proved to Martel that there was another Americanism, a real Americanism of those who did not hold these ideas of Keane. The Americanists made a loud noise but they did not have much influence. In support he quoted the attack of Bishop McQuaid on Archbishop Ireland in 1894, as reported in *La Vérité*.

On April 11-12, in answer to a letter from the diocese of Quimper, the editor of *La Vérité* promised that the articles of Martel would appear in book form. On April 22, after the beginning of the Spanish American War, *La Vérité* wrote an appeal for a new crusade of Europe to save the old Europe from the barbarous Americans, pleading "for Spain, for France, for the civilization of Christian Europe, for the future of the world." The early daily commentary in *La Vérité* on the Spanish American War was very sympathetic for Spain and full of alarm for the old civilization. On May 2, "XXX" implied that the war could have been prevented if the business interests had taken action when they saw the war approaching. A few days later *La Vérité* quoted from the Washington *Times* Rampolla's denial to Martinelli that the Vatican had taken part in the war, indicating that the Vatican was interested only in peace. In this *La Vérité* seemed to express the feelings of the Latins generally about the rising power of the United States; and it is of interest that at the very time these articles appeared, Archbishop Ireland was insisting in his letters to his friends that the Church recognize this rising power of the United States and see that the future lay with the Anglo-Saxon powers.

In the meantime Klein, who had been forced to cancel his lectures on Americanism by ill health, did not answer these charges. As a matter of fact some of his friends were fearful that he would answer them after he recovered his health, and begged him not to give this recognition to what they considered a base attack. But a short time later another charge did bring forth an answer from the convalescent priest. On April 11, in *L'Éclair*, there appeared an article about the defection of some French clergy. The article claimed that between twenty and twenty-five priests had left the Church since Abbé Charbonnel had announced his defection from the Church. The article quoted at length the letter of Abbé E. Bourdery of Marolles to Bishop Fuzet of Beauvais of April 7, 1898, announcing his defection. The article attributed the defection of these priests partly to the influence of Americanism introduced by Abbé Felix Klein and M. Victor Charbonnel, and partly to the book of August Sabatier on the philosophy of Religion. This article had been copied by other papers in the country and Klein felt that he had to make some disclaimer. In his letter to *L'Éclair*, he said that in so far as the paper credited him with making known the ideas of Hecker and Ireland he was proud to accept credit, but he asserted there was no connection whatever between these ideas and the defection of the priests mentioned in the article. Gibbons, Ireland, and their friends, he said, had been outspoken in their complete submission to the Holy Father.

In the meantime, however, the word of the attack on the life of Hecker had become known in the United States and at the urging of Abbé Alphonse Magnien, Cardinal Gibbons wrote two letters, one to Elliott praising the Paulists and Father Hecker, and another on May 20[38] to Abbé Dufresne, complimenting him on his praise of Hecker. Elliott sent Gibbons' letter to Klein to be published in the sixth edition of the *Life*. Cardinal Gibbons in his letter to Father Elliott dated April 14, 1898, said of Father Hecker:

> He was undoubtedly a providential agent for the spread of the Catholic faith in our country, and did immense good by drawing non-Catholics nearer to us, allaying prejudice, obtaining a fair hearing for our holy religion, besides directly and indirectly making a multitude of converts. His spirit was that of a faithful child of Holy Church, every way Catholic in the fullest meaning of the term, and his life adorned with fruits of personal piety, but especially he was inspired with a zeal for souls of the true Apostolic order, aggressive and yet prudent, attracting Protestants and yet entirely orthodox.

After praising the Paulists, Gibbons added,

> I am pleased to learn that Father Hecker's apostolic career is every-day more and more appreciated in Europe by reason of the publication and circulation of his life and writings.[39]

In the meantime Klein sent his own answer to *L'Éclair* to *L'Univers* for publication. Besides publishing Klein's letter on May 5, the editors of *L'Univers* added a paragraph of criticism of Abbé Maignen for his unscrupulous attack on the life of Father Hecker, and another paragraph which referred to articles attacking the Catholic University in *La Vérité* signed by Saint Clement. In naming Abbé Georges Périès as "Saint Clement," the article said he was a former professor discharged from the Catholic University. The next day, May 6, August Roussel, editor-in-chief of *La Vérité*, answered under the heading "Explosion d'Américanisme." First, Roussel printed the letter of Gibbons and the comments of the editors of *L'Univers et le Monde* but defended Maignen, saying that Gibbons was not impartial and that they had letters of praise of Martel's articles from many other eminent clergymen. As

---

[38] Gibbons to Dufresne May 20, 1898, in Klein Papers, University of Notre Dame Archives.

[39] Cardinal Gibbons to Father Walter Elliott, April 14, 1898, printed copy in Klein papers and in the sixth edition of *La Vie* in French.

to "Saint Clement" Roussel indicated that he could take care of himself. As if to prove that, the next article in the paper was by Périès, in which he claimed that the life of Hecker was a forbidden book because it did not follow the recent decrees of Roman Constitution *Officiorum* on the Index by obtaining an imprimatur from the archbishop of Paris.

On May 10 Maignen sent a letter to the editors of *L'Univers et le Monde* in answer to the charges of that paper on May 5, 7, 9, in which, while printing the letter of Cardinal Gibbons, it had made reference to Maignen's previous attack on De Mun, and to his uncle Father Maurice Maignen. Maignen charged: 1, the *Life* had been published without an imprimatur contrary to the law of the Index; 2, that it maintained that Hecker was a saint and a kind of father of the Church; 3, that he had shown in his articles that Hecker was not a saint; and 4, that the man who boasts of never having a spiritual director nor of having studied theology is not a model for clergymen. He mentioned then that the title of his own book—which had not yet appeared—was *Le P. Hecker est-il un saint?* He claimed that not he but the defenders of Hecker had attempted to preview the decisions of the Church on Hecker's sanctity; 5, he maintained that he had fortified his articles by documents from the constitutions of the Redemptorists; 6, he maintained that the letter of Gibbons had not taken away the facts of the limited growth of the Paulists as compared to the Redemptorists. He then listed the chief errors of Hecker. These were: 1, a system of apologetics which tended to conclude *a priori* the existence of natural aspiration to the necessary existence of a supernatural good; this he said would destroy the integrity of nature and the liberal munificence of God; 2, Hecker taught the distinction between the active and passive virtues which does not exist in theology; 3, Hecker had wrong notions about the direction of the Holy Ghost; 4, Hecker accused the Church of wrong actions, especially in regard to its reception of converts, and that is why he wanted to abandon the customs house; 5, Hecker ignored the distinction between the precepts and the counsels and opposed the religious orders as not necessary in modern times; 6, Hecker was in error about the new diffusion of the Holy Spirit in the souls as was shown by the encyclical of Leo XIII, the *Divinum* of May 8, 1897; 7, his comparison of the Latins and Saxons was based on a wrong notion of the interior life; 8, and that Ireland and his partisans were *réfractaires* to the papal decrees by seeking to subject the Church to a form of government and in upholding the separation of Church and State as applied in the United States.

To this, Pierre Veuillot, who kept *L'Univers* faithful to the *ralliement* after the departure of the editors of *La Vérité*, accused *La Vérité* of permitting Maignen to resume his attack on Hecker despite the fact that Maignen was known for his intemperate attacks. He claimed that Maignen taught that universal suffrage is wrong and that to vote is a sin. This was denied in time by *La Vérité*. He quoted the attack of Maignen against De Mun. *La Vérité*[40] reprinted the article from *L'Univers* and merely regretted the change in *L'Univers* of Louis Veuillot.

In the meantime Father A. Poulain,[41] the Jesuit mathematician who was also an authority on mystical prayer, wrote a friendly letter to Klein on May 16, suggesting that Hecker was not a mystic but rather an ascetic although he had read the writings of St. Theresa and other mystics. Poulain also called Klein's attention to certain phrases against the vows which he said expressed the ideas of Elliott and not those of Hecker. The vows are not just for the weak. So also Poulain mentioned that Elliott had erred in speaking of the superior virtue of the bishop over the priest, the sacerdotal perfection has nothing to do with mortal sin.

In the meantime on May 28, *La Vérité* announced the publication in Rome of the articles of Martel, to which other essays had been added, under the title *Le P. Hecker est-il un saint?* and printed the preface of the book.

In this preface, in which the author now admits his identity, Maignen explained that in the confused times it was necessary to clarify the confusion that seemed to cover everything. For this purpose, in presenting his evaluation of Father Hecker and his

[40] Published in *La Vérité*, May 14, 1898, under the title "Deux Façons de Controverse."

[41] A. Poulain, S. J., to Klein, May 16, 1898. In Klein papers, Archives of the University of Notre Dame.

followers, he has tried to use as much as possible the original statements of their ideas. He admitted that he had not followed any chronological order, but that was not important since Father Hecker never denied that the spirit that guided him in his early career was the same that guided him in his later years. The French version of the life of Hecker, launched in a period when the French were upset, called for a special remedy which he has tried to give. If he has used biting words they were drawn from his pen by the language of those he was writing about. Is Father Hecker a saint? He will be attacked for bringing up the question. He does not know if he is a saint. A man can be a man of Christian virtue and not be a saint, but certainly it is not permitted to anticipate the decision of the Church that a man is a saint and a Father of the Church. He has sought justification for these titles in the life of Hecker and has not found them. This same attitude is retained in his discussion of the Paulists as the religious of the future. The third part of his book attacks Americanism. These Americanist ideas are not those of a dreamer in good faith but of people who are still alive and they can answer him. Finally he gave an emotional defense of his book claiming he was only interested in preserving the truth.

CHAPTER 4 ❧ *The Battle Crosses the Alps*

THE EVENTS AFFECTING American Catholicism in that spring of
1898 are almost too complicated to unravel. There was always
a certain parallel between the political developments of the United
States and her religious experiences, but only those Americans
who were trying to bring the Church into direct influence on the
American people show this parallel. The Americanists or progressives not only were very much concerned with the growing social
and economic problems of the country but they were also very
much aware of the growing importance of the United States in
world politics. And there is a further possible parallel between the
attitude of Europeans towards the United States as a political
power and the feeling of European Catholic leaders towards the
attempt of the Church in this country to have influence in European Catholicism. Maignen had expressed the extreme of this unfriendly European opinion when he had said that the United
States had not yet been born. Only the European "Americanists"
seemed to have any admiration for things of the United States.
With the general friendliness between the United States and England during the latter half of the nineteenth century there was
only one country geographically close enough to come into conflict with the United States and that was Spain, the mother country of Cuba, and Cuba was a very troublesome child which Spain
seemed unable to control.

American journals had been loud in their demands that the
United States intervene in the Cuban insurrection and these demands became much louder when the American battleship
"Maine" was sunk on February 15 in Havana harbor. When war
threatened, the intervention of the European powers and the Pope
had caused Spain to promise to make amends and to change her
policy. President McKinley seemed himself desirous of avoiding

war. In these circumstances Pope Leo, through Rampolla, asked
Keane[1] on March 27, to have Archbishop Ireland go to Washington to see what he could do to prevent the impending war. Keane
passed the word on to Ireland and on April 6,[2] Ireland informed his
friend Cardinal Gibbons that he was in Washington endeavoring
to obtain from the Spanish a promise of an armistice during which
he hoped to solve the problems and preserve the peace. Spain delayed. The President wanted to address Congress on the subject
on April 7, but Spain did not answer. Finally, on April 9, the
Spanish government gave way and promised to grant an armistice. But the President's letter to Congress did not stress too
much the Spanish concessions. Yet Ireland thought that peace
was assured. Nevertheless Congress urged on by the press and
popular excitement demanded Cuban independence and decreed
that the American military forces should carry out these decrees. Finally on April 25, the Congress declared that a state of
war had existed since April 2. An important factor in the decision
was the coming election and the fear of the Republicans that unless they went to war the Democrats under Bryan would drive
them out of power.

Ireland wrote ruefully to the Pope that the Catholic senators
had voted against the war and that even the Protestant clergymen
had lauded the efforts he had made in the name of the Pope to prevent the war. His only complaint was the effort had not been
started soon enough[3] and that Spain had delayed too long the dec-

[1] Rampolla to Keane, March 27, 1898, No. 43158, quoted by Soderini in his
manuscript (see n. 27, ch. II). "The danger of a conflict between the United
States and Spain has caused His Holiness as well as all Catholics great anxiety.
Therefore, knowing how effective the words of Monsignor Ireland could be in
many respects with the President of the United States, the Pope has expressed his
desire that the Archbishop of Saint Paul, Minnesota, take all possible steps
towards a peaceful solution of the conflict. I am referring the desire of His
Holiness to you, knowing that you have direct connections of friendship with
Monsignor Ireland. I am adding my own most sincere good wishes." Keane
cabled to Ireland the same day No. 43164 and so notified Rampolla, according to
Soderini, adding that Spain would be warned to change her stand on the sinking
of the Maine. Soderini also claims that Keane mistakingly asserted that the
President was not planning intervention.

[2] Ireland to Cardinal Gibbons, April 6, 1898, Archdiocesan Archives of Baltimore.

[3] Ireland to O'Connell, May 2, 1898, Richmond Diocesan Archives. Cf. James
Moynihan, *The Life of Archbishop John Ireland*, (New York, 1953), pp. 162-76.

laration of the armistice. Ireland felt that had the armistice been declared even two or three days earlier so that the President's advisers could have changed his address, the war might have been avoided. It was generally acknowledged that the efforts of the Pope were highly regarded and praised in all the capitals of the world. But Ireland had failed and, as he remarked sorrowfully to his friend, success in such matters was all that counted at Rome.[4] The Pope himself preserved neutrality in the short conflict although Spain was before the world the Catholic country in the conflict. But to many of the European ecclesiastics American aggression was not admired, and in the ecclesiastical conflict into which the American bishops were drawn, the Spanish-American war did not improve the feeling towards any Americanizing tendencies in religion.

Ireland and O'Connell knew that the failure of Ireland to prevent the war was something that would inevitably count against Ireland in Rome. Both prelates felt sympathy for Spain in the war despite their loyalty to the American government, but to them the outcome was never in doubt. They hoped, however, that the Church officials in Rome would understand the significance of the American victory even though they knew that the French and Italian presses were unfavorable to the victorious United States. To these prelates the victory was but a symbol of the future importance of the Anglo-Saxon world and particularly of American ideas in the coming world struggles. They were probably too optimistic and in a sense even premature in their claims for American diplomacy and influence, but at least it is in this connection that the meaning of Americanism for O'Connell and Hecker was delineated. Answering Ireland's note on his failure to prevent the war, O'Connell seemed to brush past that event to discuss the future of America and of Archbishop Ireland in the post-war world. His letter is a very important contribution to a definition of the Americanism as conceived by the Americanists.

May 24, '98

My dear Friend:

I read your letters with intensest interest and I thank you cordially for them.

---

[4] Ireland to O'Connell, May 11, 1898, Richmond Diocesan Archives.

It seems to me that you have now reached the providential period of your life;—it seems to me the culminating point—where all your dreams are to be realized and all your poetic visions are to be turned into prophecies. Now is a moment in which it will be utterly impossible for you to expand your power or your personality too much: "[sic] for this were you born for this you came into the world: to realize the dreams of your youth for America and to be the instrument in the hands of Providence for spreading the benefits of a new civilization over the world. To this point has really tended even without your knowing it, everything you have hitherto done in all the period of your activity, and now from this point you are to radiate your influence as far and as intensely as you can all the world over. You have now the whole field free and you are a citizen in America, and a Bishop in the Church without a rival. All the former little questions of local content in the Church in America are now for you as nothing, and henceforth you are to consider yourself as a figure in history with no Corrigan beside you. Your dreams were for the Church but you were born for the country and it will be through your direct labors for the country that you will later prepare greater benefits for the church. At the Vatican of course they did not reap all they hoped from your intervention. It was to be expected, and the fault is their own. They never asked you nor any American until they reached the moment of despair and then you were employed more as an instrument of their wishes than as a partner in their counsels [sic]. From the beginning I trembled for you and I thank God that you have escaped a terrible danger with universal triumph, in an awful pass, where some were ready to sacrifice you, and many would have laughed in joy to see you fall. You have put John Ireland to the front in America & Europe as no other American Bishop was ever put before. You have compelled the Vatican to publicly and solemnly recognize him and the cause he represents. And instead of hurting yourself in the eyes of the public in working for the odious cause of Spain you have only increased & confirmed & sanctified the confidence reposed in you by your fellow citizens. I congratulate you and thank God for you. And now only one word more: all doubts & hesitation to the wind and on with the banner of Americanism which is the banner of God & humanity. Now realize all the dreams you ever dreamed, and force upon the Curia by the great triumph of Americanism that recognition of English speaking peoples that you know is needed.

For me this is not simply a question of Cuba. If it were, it were no question or a poor question. Then let the "greasers" eat one another up and save the lives of our dear boys. But for me it is a question of much more moment:—it is the question of two civilizations. It is the question of all that is old & vile & mean & rotten & cruel & false in Europe against all this [sic] is free & noble & open & true & humane in America. When Spain is swept of [sic] the seas much of the meanness & narrowness of old Europe goes with it to be replaced by the freedom and openness of America. This is God's way of developing the world. And all continental Europe feels the war is against itself, and that is why they are all against us, and Rome more than all because when the prestige of Spain & Italy will have passed away, and when the pivot of the world's political action will no longer be confined within the limits of the continent; then the nonsense of trying to govern the universal church from a purely European standpoint—and according to exclusively Spanish and Italian methods, will be glaringly evident even to a child. "Now the axe is laid to the root of the tree." Let the wealth of Convents & Communities in Cuba & the Philippines go; it did nothing for the advancement of religion. No more patching of new pieces on old garments; it serves neither one nor the other. And the foundation of religion need be laid anew "in spirit and in truth." Begin there anew with the Gospel and with such accessories & canon law as the Gospel requires without making paramount the interests of comfortable-living personages or communities.

After having reflected on this matter a long time and after long interviews with European diplomats, especially with attachés of the English Embassy I am convinced that the material progress of America lies likewise on the lines I have indicated above.

It is the impression over here that the prosperity and internal peace of America depend upon her finding advantageous markets for her agricultural products: for her grain & cattle. They hold that if the Western farmers can find no advantageous market for their farm products, discontent & disorder will follow. They say that a large proportion of the population in America is still unamalgamated, and that from discontent arising in the West Bryanism, class-war and confusion could likely follow with so many of the masses against the Government in a serious position. To effect that, and to save themselves from the invasion of American influences is now the aim of the Continent. The plan is, I have been told, to build a Chinese wall against American products and to depend upon Russia and India to supply the deficit of their own production. Now it seems to me the only way America has of thwarting that combination is by making herself a great maritime power. Make herself as great maritimely as England or Russia and then no continent will be strong enough to conspire against her. When that is done and the power of retaliation and of hostile alliance is in her hands, no power dare close her markets against her while today she is at their mercy. America must do for her products what England has done for her manufactures and that implies navies, and that implies coaling stations and that means ports of her own at every favorable point all over the world, where she can find them. The time is gone by when America can live in a state of domestic isolation. It was all very well at the beginning when in the world America did not count, but now the idea of a country of 75,000,000 with its wonderful power of production, its tremendous output of wealth, the idea of that power thinking that it can peaceably fence of [sic] a piece of the world in which to live all quietly by itself without taking into account its relations to the rest of the world whose financial, commercial & industrial harmony it is continually and almost unconsciously disturbing, that seems to be the idea of a child. We are too provincial even few of our statesmen know anything of the movement of the world at large and in your advantages, you are ahead of the best of them. The more possessions you have, the better and the more you can get possession of your own markets or of your own sources of every kind of supplies independently of every other power, the more, it seems to me, the better.

Again it seems to me that above all nations, moving them on along the path of civilization to better, higher, happier modes of existences it is the constant action of a tender divine Providence, and that the convergent action of all great powers is towards that common & destined end; to more brotherhood, to more kindness, to more mutual respect for every man, to more practical and living recognition of the rule of God. At one time one nation in the world now another, took the lead, but now it seems to me that the old governments of Europe will lead no more and that neither Italy, nor Spain will ever furnish the principles of the civilization of the future. Now God passes the banner to the hands of America, to bear it:—in the cause of humanity and it is your office to make its destiny known to America and become its grand chaplain. Over all America there is certainly a duty higher than the interest of the individual states—even of the national government. The duty to humanity is certainly a real duty, and America cannot certainly with honor, or fortune, evade its great share in it. Go to America and say, thus saith the Lord! Then you will live in history as God's Apostle in modern times to Church & to Society. Hence I am a partisan of the Anglo-American alliance, together they are invincible and they will impose a new civilization. Now is your opportunity—and at the end of the war as the Vatican always goes after a strong man you will likewise become her intermediary.

I write this letter after much thought and much hesitation fearing sometimes you would suspect my modesty or again my common sense. And I assure you however rapidly I may have written I have long pondered these thoughts and if you have had the patience to plow through them I shall be greatly flattered and rewarded if you say you agree with them. I believe you will say they are right and that our destiny was not thrown together for nothing. War is often God's way of moving things onward. The whole realm of life of every kind lay under the operation of one law: struggle. In that way all the plans of nature are worked out and the name for struggle between nations is sometimes "war." The "horrors of war" often a sentimental phrase is often better "the glories of war" the triumph of Providence, see the war of secession & negro emancipation. The whole history of Providence is the history of war; survival of the fittest. There is not room in this little world for anything else and bad as the world is today how much worse it certainly would be if by war & struggle the worse elements had not to go to the wall.

Then build navies & give your men employment, enroll an army picking up for it as England does fellows fit for nothing else. Take the place God has destined for America and leave John Ireland's name imperishable among those achievements. You are the only man in America lay or cleric who can properly take in and give the right initiative to this design.

The history of every good nation has been a history of expansion, Rome, Greece, Venice, England.

So build your navies and give employment to your laborers. Create your armies and like England enroll in its ranks all those idle fellows hanging 'round the towns that are good for nothing else. You will now have a work that will enlist all your strongest sympathies.

Please let me hear from you what you think of it.

> Ever Sincerely yours
> D. J. O'Connell[5]

Had the religious controversy over Americanism remained merely a newspaper conflict in France the discussion might not have spread to Rome. When the editors of *La Vérité* announced that the essays by Martel, admittedly now Maignen, were to be published in book form they probably thought the book would appear in Paris. In the meantime, however, it seems that Abbé Alphonse Magnien, the leader of the Sulpicians in the United States and a close adviser of Cardinal Gibbons, had arrived in France and was influential in determining the attitude of the Paris Sulpicians and at least indirectly of Cardinal Richard of Paris in refusing an imprimatur to the book. In this Cardinal Richard was influenced not so much by the Americanists but by the fact that the book contained an attack on several prominent members of the American hierarchy and more probably because of his desire to avoid public conflict within the Church, since he had previously summoned Klein[6] and asked him not to continue publishing new editions of the *Vie*. Thus the new laws of the Index which Périès had quoted against the publishers of the *Vie* now hindered his confreres in their desire to publish their own book. To get around this situation they added a Roman publisher Desclée, Lefébvre et cie., and sought the imprimatur from the Master of the Sacred Palace, who at that time had the right to give it. The master of the Sacred Palace was Father Albert Lepidi, O.P., who seems to have been a man sympathetic with those who were having trouble getting

---

[5] O'Connell to Ireland, May 24, 1898, Archives of the Archdiocese of Saint Paul.

[6] Klein to O'Connell, May 14, 1898, Richmond Diocesan Archives.

their opinions before the public. Since Cardinal Richard had informed the Roman authorities that he had refused the imprimatur to Maignen's book, there must have been some general knowledge in Vatican circles that Lepidi was giving the permission. Whether the papal authorities had any real knowledge of the book and its contents or not, the fact that it had received the approval from the Vatican gave the book an authority before the world that it probably did not deserve and set the stage for the final battle over Americanism.

The book, *Études sur L'Americanisme Le Père Hecker est-il un Saint?* by Charles Maignen, was dedicated to the Most Holy Hearts of Jesus and Mary and was approved by A. Leclerc, Superior General of the Brothers of Saint Vincent de Paul.

The first two parts of the book were essentially the essays that had appeared in March in the columns of *La Vérité* but to these were added some rather important footnotes from *La Vérité* of Quebec and *Church Progress* of Saint Louis. The thirteenth essay was composed mostly of the thirteenth and fourteenth essays of the original articles with additional statistics on the growth of secret societies in the United States.

The third part of the book was entitled "Les Campagnes de l'Américanisme" and the first essay was "Le P. Hecker, Chef de l'École Américaine" which had been published in the April 3 *La Vérité*. In the second chapter Maignen reprinted the essay of April 4, "Première Campagne-Le Parliament des Religions à Chicago."

The third essay was that published April 5 on the efforts of Charbonnel to arrange for a second Parliament of Religions at the Paris World's Fair of 1900.

The fourth essay was taken from *La Vérité* of April 9 on the carrying of the campaign into the old world and finding of a saint in Father Hecker. The rest of the book had not been published in *La Vérité*.

The fifth essay (pp. 271-293) was entitled the "Fourth Campaign—under the Walls of Rome" and treated of recent happenings at Rome. Maignen recalled the enforced resignation of Keane and Keane's unwelcomed going to Rome where he joined the deposed rector of the American College, Monsignor O'Connell. Maignen then reported how in Rome O'Connell and Keane who had been cultivating the nobles of Rome, offered a banquet to Cardinal Vincenzo Vannutelli, Archbishop Kain, and others at which M. Brunetière, the new editor of the *Revue des Deux Mondes*, offered a fervent toast of praise to the United States, to which Keane added a speech of praise for American accomplishments. Maignen noted that the *Washington Herald* in its account of the banquet indicated that Keane would soon be made a cardinal. The same day that paper mentioned the long visit of Monsignor Martinelli, the Apostolic Delegate, with Archbishop Ireland in Saint Paul. All these activities Maignen summed up into a campaign to add to the three Romes of Monsignor Gaume, a fourth Rome—the American Rome. Maignen then mentioned the press accounts of the intervention of the Pope through Monsignor Ireland to prevent the Spanish-American War. Yet, Maignen said, Ireland accomplished nothing. He claimed that it was the Queen Regent of Spain who had sought the papal intervention to prevent the war. America was led by commercial and financial reasons alone to go into the war incited also by the secret societies of Cuba. This, he said, is an example of how the Americans use the Church for their own ends. Next in the campaign was that Keane had planned an Italian translation of the *Life* of Hecker, probably to prepare the way for Anglo-Saxons to enter into the Roman hierarchy, and here he quoted a statement of Abbé Dufresne about the end of the period of Latin domination of the Church. Further Maignen quoted a letter of a Frenchman in the United States who feared that Archbishop Ireland was about to create a schism—an American Church. Hecker, when he left Rome, said he returned to his country more American and a better Catholic. Maignen added here a quotation from "Tiber" writing in *Le Journal de Roubaix* of February 7, 1898, that Cardinal Gibbons as a possible next pope could be considered a symbol, a bearer of the new civilization that America was bringing to Europe. Since Gibbons cannot be elected, "politics" would solve the Italian problem by an Italian pope favorable to Americanism, who would modernize and Americanize the Church. Maignen added a quotation from the article in *La Revue du Clergé Français* of March, 1898, in which Dufresne said that the new spirit in the Church prepared the way for the conversion of Protestants and free thinkers into the Church by removing prejudices, and another quotation from Dufresne in the *Vie* that the Church is protected from error by the new dogma of infallibility, to statements from an article by "Romanus" in *The Contemporary Review* of London in December, 1897, entitled "Liberal Catholicism." "Romanus," as a liberal Catholic, said Maignen, was the representative of a party which had announced a program from which the party can retreat if attacked. This article in *The Contemporary Review*, he claimed, expressed the integral doctrine of Americanism. Since the Americanists had not repudiated these doctrines they can be imputed to them. Maignen hinted that the anonymous translator of the life of Hecker, the "Tiber" of *Le Journal de Roubaix*, and the anonymous writer "Romanus" of *The Contemporary Review* were of the same school.

In the sixth essay (pp. 294-310) Maignen rejected Keane's denial that the Americanists were liberals. "Romanus," he said, held the opposite opinion, since he accepted the name for the party. "Romanus" in his article admitted that liberalism was not a thing of the past. "Romanus's" argument that in the Anglican Church there was approaching a movement towards Catholicism was very similar to the ideas of Hecker. "Romanus" praised the great good which the Church was doing and recognized the Church as the only institution capable of uniting in God all the people. To accomplish this, however, the Church must abolish the customs house. The means for doing this is the "evolutionism" of which M. André Hallays had spoken. This evolutionism, "Romanus" indicated, prepared the way for the advance of Christianity in the second century. A similar evolution was now preparing the way for the Church, such as had been mentioned in England. "Romanus" indicated that the Church adapted itself to each period of its history and that therefore it must do likewise today, adapting itself to scientific advances. Further "Romanus" said that so as not to shock the faithful by a too sudden revelation of the new discoveries in science and in the study of the scriptures the doctrine of evolution considered with a theist doctrine should be advanced.

In the seventh essay (pp. 311-327) also on this "Evolutionism," Maignen explained why he united the discourses of Keane on "The Ultimate Religion" and on "The Idea of the Incarnation in the History of Jesus Christ" at the Chicago Parliament of Religions and the article of "Romanus." Despite differences of style he maintained they were the same in ideas and doctrines. He mentioned that Keane in Chicago had pointed out how Christ had answered the aspirations of humanity and that the Christian religion is the only one that answers the universal aspirations of mankind. Keane, he said, preached the idea not the fact of the Incarnation. This he said appeared in Keane's beginning in which he showed that the idea of redemption was implicit in all the pagan traditions, distinguishing between the Eastern and Western concepts of redemption. Maignen found similar passages in the article of "Romanus." As Keane had added in his speech at Brussels, the old technique of telling these pagans that the founders of their religions were devils is false. Rather God has given to all of them some part of the truth. Thus the Incarnation is the answer to these aspirations of all the peoples. Keane, said Maignen, found the acceptance of the fact of the Incarnation one of inescapable logic, but that actually he had proved not the fact of the Incarnation but the evidence of it. Keane's argument was subjective and in that he followed the method of Hecker in his books. It was parallel, said Maignen, to the evolutionism of "Romanus."

Pursuing this same "Evolutionism" in his eighth essay (pp. 328-347), Maignen found the ideas of Keane's speech on the "Ultimate Religion" quite the same as those of Abbé Charbonnel in the *Revue de Paris* in which Charbonnel argued for the Congress of Religions in Paris in 1900. Keane argued for the recognition of ancient truth in all these forms of religion. Keane said that all religions are systems for arriving at the grand end, the union of the soul with God. The Christian command to teach all people is a lesson to each individual, the greatest individualism the world has ever known. In his Brussels speech, Maignen added, Keane spoke of the necessity of irenics instead of polemics to bring all the branches of the heavenly vine to the love of Jesus. To this Maignen added a definition given elsewhere by Keane of the nature of the Church in which he speaks of it as an organic unity. This he compared to the argument of "Romanus" that one must not separate oneself from the Church but take over the Church. Again he added another quotation of Keane's speech on the "Ultimate Religion" in which he said that it is wrong to separate these men of good faith from the Church. Keane's words about the changes in this organic unity of the Church he found a perfect expression of ecclesiastical evolutionism. Keane said at the meeting in Brussels he did not reject this idea of evolution but distinguished two kinds of philosophy, the evolutionary naturalistic philosophy which he rejected, and the other philosophy which teaches that all things come from the love and power of God and work for an eternity of happiness. This evolutionism, Maignen claimed, was the process which Keane used to explain the progress from the erroneous ideas to the truth. And at Brussels he deplored the failure of the Church to carry on this work of teaching those who were seeking the full truth. And Maignen added this was just the complaint of "Romanus," that the Church failed to understand the ardent desires of all men for unity. The "Ultimate Religion" then will be the synthesis of all religions. Maignen then turned to the essay of "Romanus" for his explanation of the evolution of the Church and the papacy.

He pointed out that the theory of evolution would insist that it inspires one to be in communion with the future. This he pointed out was what the author (Dufresne) of the article in the *Revue du Clergé Français* speaks of in saying that the Church demands a perpetual search for deeper meanings in truths already known. "Romanus" called this an adaptation of old ideas to new truths, especially in scientific truths. This Maignen applied to a passage in the life of Hecker which speaks of adapting the Church to the new phases and to the scientific changes in the modern world. All these doctrines of Americanism, he added, are contained at least in principle in the life and the writings of Father Hecker.

In the ninth essay (pp. 348-370) entitled "Strongholds to be captured" Maignen asked, if, as Keane said, the Church teaches this grand message, why is she so silent? How explain this contradiction? The answer is that the Church did not speak the language of the day. This question, Maignen said, was also answered by "Romanus" when he claimed that the failure of the Church lies in its opposition to science. This answer had been given timidly at the International Scientific Congresses where O'Connell and Keane had spoken. That which hinders the Church, according to "Romanus," from speaking the language that the world understands is an encumbrance of old theological terms. These writers, said Maignen, imply that the stories of the Gospel have been proven to be legends. Maignen said he did not impute these theological enormities to any one person but Americanism is so widely spread that they need not be attributed to one person. "Romanus" admitted that some doctrines should be retained, and tried to apply this to the recent decrees, even to the *Syllabus of Errors*, and to present biblical decrees. These men, said Maignen, and those who deny certain doctrines of the Church are already out of the Church and they should be exposed. For this he quoted a passage from the encyclical *Providentissimus Deus* of Leo XIII in which the Pope condemned those who had attacked the authenticity of the Sacred Scriptures. Since "Romanus" had attacked the recent decree of the Holy See on the Johannine comma, Maignen also quoted the attack of "Romanus" on the recent decrees about the Roman Index, and added that it was in virtue of a false interpretation of this decree that the translation of the *Life* of Hecker had been published. "Romanus" had spoken of some foreseeing people who occupy important places in the Church. Maignen said it would benefit the Church if such people would leave it.

In his concluding essay (pp. 371-391), Maignen summed up his argument by stating that the ultimatum given to the Church by the liberal Catholic is to submit to the teachings of science and accommodate the teaching of the Church to the findings of science. Against this idea Maignen in the *Review* quoted a confession of Brownson contained in the *Ave Maria*[7] in 1871, of his having held liberal ideas and of having turned from them. Brownson admitted that during the time of his error he tried to make as

[7] In Orestes Brownson's articles "On the Religious Orders," *Ave Maria* VII, 66.

short as possible the distance between Catholicism and Protestantism, but he discovered that this policy would have led him out of
the Church. Maignen said this has been the effect of like tendencies among certain priests who had left the Church, and he cited
the recent apostasies including the letter of E. Bourdery. He added
also a quotation from the *Literary Digest* of March 26, 1898,
about this movement of priests out of the Church, and another
article from Preuss' *Review* of January 27, 1898, about a Protestant mission for Catholics in Washington.

In such times of peril Maignen said that instead of lowering the
draw bridges and abolishing the customs houses it is necessary to
raise the draw bridges higher and increase the scrutiny of those
who try to enter the Church. He then summed up his book with
a brief statement in which he said that Hecker was a good man
who might have become a saint if he had been more humble. The
life of Hecker lacked biographers who knew theology. As to the
disciples of Hecker, he had nothing to say to the Paulists in New
York; as to the Americanists they deserved the consequences of
their master's principles. As to Americanism, he had used the
freedom to speak and write, of which the Americans boast, to
check as far as possible the errors of Americanism.

Just when the book actually was made available is not clear. *La
Vérité* announced it on May 24. Since the book gave great of-
fense to Archbishop Keane, it was he who made the first official[8]
protest not only against the book but chiefly against the granting
of the imprimatur by the Master of the Sacred Palace.

In the meantime, although there is evidence that Abbé Maignen
had been in touch with Archbishop Corrigan,[9] and Bishop Sebastian Messmer[10] had been in Rome, there does not seem to be

[8] Soderini in his manuscript refers to a letter of Keane to Rampolla of June 2,
1898.

[9] The letter of Maignen to Corrigan of March 31, 1899, in the New York
Archdiocesan Archives, speaks of this earlier letter and indicates that had the
papal letter of condemnation been delayed Maignen intended to ask Corrigan's
permission to publish this earlier letter. Maignen sent Corrigan a copy of his
book on June 12, 1899. Cf. Maignen to Corrigan, June 12, 1899, in the New York
Archdiocesan Archives in which Maignen also says that the book has been read
by many bishops and cardinals both in Rome and in France.

[10] O'Connell to Ireland, July 20, 1898, O'Connell blames Messmer for the
trouble he has had with Lepidi.

any direct relations between the other opponents of Archbishop Ireland and the Paris writers Maignen and Périès. The "Spectator" letters of the spring of 1897, in the *Allgemeinen Zeitung* of Munich, attacking Monsignor Schroeder and describing the conflict between the Germans and Archbishop Ireland, had drawn a heavy attack not only in Germany—especially from the *Germania* of Berlin where Dr. Pohle had gone to the defense of his confrere—but also in the German-American Catholic papers. The American writers, particularly Father J. F. Meifuss[11] in the *Review*, were quick to point out that Kraus, the "Spectator," was not impartial since his book on Reform Catholicism had been reviewed hostilely by Schroeder. Further they ascribed to his informers in this country other motives of unfriendliness to Schroeder. The answers of Dr. Pohle to the "Spectator" letters were translated and reprinted in the columns of the *Review*.[12] In the meantime a writer in the *Review*[13] attacked the suggestion that the Germans were a faction in the Church in the United States; and in the same issue Father Meifuss began to compare the characters of Father Hecker and Bishop Neumann of Philadelphia. These attacks were so violent that the editor of the *Church Progress*,[14] not at all friendly to the Americanists, noted on July 16, 1898, that they were excessive.

In the meantime, also, the article of Archbishop Keane in the March *Catholic World* on "America as seen from Abroad" with its denial of the charge of liberalism brought forth a regular barrage from the conservative editors renewing the charge of liberalism. Although some American editors were aware of the French controversy over the life of Hecker, it can be asserted that there was little of that controversy proper in the American Catholic press during the spring and summer months of 1898.

Even before he had a chance to read Maignen's book, Monsignor O'Connell had written a letter to Cardinal Gibbons in which he was pessimistic about the future of Americanism.[15] The

---

[11] *The Review*, (St. Louis) Feb. 17, 1898. *Ibid.*, March 10, Meifuss claims that the "Spectator" letters failed.

[12] *The Review*, December 9, 1898.

[13] In *The Review* of March 17, 1898.

[14] July 16, 1898.

[15] O'Connell to Gibbons, May 15, 1898, in the Baltimore Cathedral Archives.

feeling in France and in Rome about the Spanish-American War was one of hostility towards the United States. For Ireland and O'Connell, despite their sympathy for Spain in the war, the facts were that Americanism, as a result of the evident American victory, would be in the ascendance and that it would be foolish for the Holy See not to recognize this point. In the meantime Abbé Klein[16] had notified O'Connell that he had visited Cardinal Richard, and that while Richard had been inclined to ask Klein not to publish any more of the life of Hecker he had not done so. Richard had consulted with the Jesuits and Sulpicians[17] about the imprimatur for Maignen's book when it had been requested by Father Leclerc, the Superior General of the Brothers of Saint Vincent de Paul, and when LeClerc spoke of going to Rome to get it the Cardinal had readily assented.

O'Connell's[18] first reaction to the book was rather one of confidence. He seemed to think that the book was so extreme that it would be its own best refutation and that, further, the American bishops by protesting against the Lepidi imprimatur would merely enhance the Americanist cause.

For Archbishop Keane the reaction to the book was one of indignation. The way in which Maignen had intertwined his writings with those of "Romanus" of the *Contemporary Review* and of "Tiber" in *Le Journal de Roubaix* and had pieced together stray quotations from his speeches, had made the Archbishop out to be a rationalist, and if the term had been then in vogue, a rank modernist. As Keane[19] himself put it, if the charges were true he should no longer continue in his office or even in the Church. Keane then took the lead in protesting the imprimatur of Lepidi. He wrote to Lepidi and to Rampolla. Rampolla[20] told him that the imprimatur was regrettable and indicated that neither he nor the Pope were aware of the granting of the imprimatur by Lepidi. This according to some was not entirely correct since Richard had given some notice to Rome that he had refused

16 Klein to O'Connell, June 14, 1898, in the Richmond Diocesan Archives.

17 Klein to O'Connell, May 14, 1898, in the Richmond Diocesan Archives.

18 O'Connell to Ireland, June 3, 1898, also O'Connell to Klein, June 2, 1898 in which O'Connell implies that the book furnished them with ammunition for fighting back.

19 June 2, 1898 Keane to Rampolla, quoted in Soderini's manuscript.

20 Keane to Ireland, June 4, 1898 in the Archdiocesan Archives of Saint Paul.

the imprimatur. Keane also wrote to Cardinal Gibbons and especially to Ireland[21] insisting that they write strong letters of protest against the granting of the imprimatur. While it was true that the imprimatur did not imply that the contents of the book were true, it did in some way indicate popularly a kind of Vatican approval. The American prelates were concerned even by this approval because, as Keane pointed out, while Gibbons was accused in the book merely of giving a kind of tacit approval of the rationalistic doctrines, Ireland was directly accused of leading an intended schism.

To Keane's dismay Lepidi[22] did not indicate any sorrow for his action. In the first place Lepidi merely indicated that his imprimatur meant only that there was no doctrinal error in Maignen's book. Lepidi in defense of his action had maintained that it was his policy to tolerate vividness of language in controversy because he tried to maintain a uniform policy and that it was a principle of his to act with charity wherever there was a doubt in his mind. It was, moreover, his opinion that the book on Americanism could really do some good insofar as it would bring out in controversy the real nature of Americanism. Americanism was not welcome to everybody. Some people, he said, regarded it as too impetuous, too much inclined to disregard the past as well as the present of the Church. It was accused of being inspired with innovative and democratic ideas and of claiming a mission within the Church to replace old influences by new ones. Such exalted doctrines, he said, if announced in a too lofty and indeterminate way, were apt to cause erroneous and dangerous interpretations.

Keane rejected Lepidi's answer[23] and indicated that the book was offensive to the American bishops as well as false. In his letter to Rampolla,[24] Keane pointed out that the refractory elements in the United States would claim that the approval of Lepidi represented the attitude of the Holy See. Apparently referring to the fact that Lepidi was a Dominican, he further indi-

[21] Keane to Ireland, June 4, 1898, in the Archdiocesan Archives of Saint Paul. Although Keane mentions writing to Gibbons his letter is not preserved in the Baltimore Archives.

[22] Lepidi to Keane, June 12, 1898, quoted in the Soderini manuscript and notes.

[23] Keane to Lepidi, June 13, 1898, summarized in Soderini.

[24] Keane to Rampolla, June 13, 1898, quoted in Soderini.

cated that Père Berthier—the Master General of the Dominicans—
had been against the United States in the Spanish-American War
with bitter hostility. Americanism, he said, is nothing but the
sentiment the American Catholics have towards their country, a
feeling of satisfaction, of gratitude, of devotion, which was first
expressed by the great Archbishop John Carroll. The definition
of Americanism as presented in the book of Maignen was an
infamy, whereas the one given by Lepidi in his letter was a dis-
torted and an unjust one.

The only satisfaction that Keane had received in Rome was
the assertion of Rampolla that the imprimatur was regrettable and
that neither Rampolla nor the Holy Father had been consulted.
But this satisfaction was shaken when "Don Abbondio," who was
really Périès, published in a supplement of *La Croix* on June 14, a
statement that both Rampolla and the Pope had been consulted
and had agreed with the granting of the imprimatur. Keane was
preparing to leave Rome for his summer vacation at the end of
June, as he had planned, but did so with the feeling that the protests of Gibbons and Ireland would undo the harm of the book.
Keane as usual was too much the trusting soul. Nor did he answer
the request of Klein for a letter on the statement of Rampolla that
he had not known of the imprimatur, which Klein could print in
answer to the article by "Don Abbondio."

From far off Minnesota came the strongest protest as Ireland
wrote to Rampolla[25] on July 11, 1898. Ireland mentioned that
there were wild rumors spreading in the American journals already as a result of Maignen's book, some indicating that a war
existed between America and Rome. The book, he said, had little
intrinsic value if it did not bear the Roman imprimatur. Further,
he noted that the very names of Maignen and Périès, the authors,
and their previous histories should have been sufficient to prevent
the granting of the Roman imprimatur. The Paulists, he said, can
defend themselves. The original life of Hecker had the imprimatur of Archbishop Corrigan and the sixth edition of the translation
had a letter of approval from Cardinal Gibbons.

[25] Ireland to Rampolla, July 11, 1898, quoted in Soderini manuscript and notes.
The original probably was in French.

An announcement on the part of Rome that says that the Paulists no longer enjoy the full confidence of the Holy See and that their orthodoxy is under suspicion would be a terrible blow to the American people, be they Protestants or Catholics. It is said that I am the head of a movement, which is being described as one of the greatest dangers of our time. The courteous visit paid to me by Monsignor Martinelli last December is thus turned into an official inquiry. Sinister motives are attributed to the steps taken at the advice of Your Eminence with the President of the United States in the interest of peace between this country and Spain.

I am the terrible Bishop who is at the point of provoking schism. That is what I, among others am accused of. That is what is involved in "Americanism," a dreadful menace to the Church and to the Supreme Pontiff. And such assertions are covered by the "imprimatur" of Rome! Here I am, before the eyes of the members of my diocese and my fellow-citizens, proclaimed to be a heretic and a schismatic, deserving of "official inquiry," and an enemy of the Church and of the Pope! May your Eminence think of the great damage such a book can do.

To the American people the word Americanism is, in a certain way, sacred, a symbol of what they consider the dearest thing they have, their civil and political institutions. And it is "Americanism" that is publicly condemned by such an "imprimatur." If Maignen intended to irritate the whole American people as well as to strengthen their prejudice against the Church, he could not have found any better way to realize such intention than by this book of his. And in order to quite evidently demonstrate that it were the American institutions that he is making a target of his attacks, he selected as typical representative of Americanism, which he condemns, Cardinal Gibbons and other prelates whom the American people respect and esteem for their loyalty and attachment to the United States.

Therefore the Americans will say, our institutions have been condemned by Rome, and therefore, Rome is opposed to America. Those prelates who have engaged their forces in an effort to demonstrate that the Catholic faith is compatible with the civil duties of an American citizen are being censured. Consequently, the Church and America cannot live together in concord. Is it wise, is it prudent, to thus provoke the American people, to render the position of the Catholics in the United States more difficult than it should be, to raise the anger of the American people, all this at a time, when, under the conditions of war, America will soon have to decide the fate of 12 millions of Catholics in the Spanish colonies? This is certainly a most inopportune moment. This book attacks a large portion of the American Episcopate. Is it not reasonable if those concerned appeal to the judgment and to the justice of the Holy See?

We are accused of invading Rome and conquering the government of the Church with our ideas. Only a sick brain could have come upon such a thought. The prelates who are being thus attacked, have only one system; that of the Holy See. They will obey nothing but the orders coming from the Holy See. They are willing to respond to the least movement made by Rome. When the sovereign Pontiff dispatched his Delegate to the United States were not those prelates the ones who surrounded him with zealous attention and let him benefit from their public influence? Where is the instance in which we have not followed the desires of the Pope? And here are P. Lepidi and Msgr. Cassetta claiming that these prelates want to dominate the Holy See, that they are at the point of becoming heretics and schismatics, or even have become such already.

Moreover, "Americanism" is being defined on the basis of the statements of those French apostates, as well as on that of an anonymous article in an English Review, which gives a completely false and ridiculous picture of our opinions. Maignen may resist such errors, but why should he charge the American Bishops with them? For several years certain books, pamphlets, journals, etc. have been attempting to slander the American prelates. We have tolerated all with much patience in order to keep the peace of the Church of God. Now, however, our situation has become much more difficult. The attacks against us are coming from the Vatican, and we are at a loss what to do. If P. Lepidi and Msgr. Cassetta do represent the Vatican we are ready for an act of deep submission. In such a case we have nothing else to do but to request the Vatican to point out our faults and to make a promise of absolute obedience. If, however, and this we believe, the "imprimatur" was not made in the name of the Vatican, is it too bold a demand, if we request that a statement be issued to clarify the situation and to enlighten the public, and thus to extract us from the depth of desolation into which we have been cast?

On August 6, Cardinal Rampolla answered this letter telling Ireland that the Pope had received the letter and asking Ireland to keep calm—that the Pope would make a just decision in the matter. Keane in the meantime had protested again to Rampolla, sending him clippings from *La Croix* summing up the story of Maignen's book. Again he wrote to Cardinal Rampolla on June 18,[26] asking the Holy See to stop these malicious attacks. Again before leaving Rome he wrote again to the Cardinal pointing to a statement in the bibliography of *La Voce della Verità* which outlined chapters of Maignen's book and repeated the substance of the attack. Keane complained that the Americanists were accused of trying to found a new church. Such attacks he said could not do good for the Church.

On July 10, 1898, O'Connell wrote to Klein about the develop-

26 Keane to Rampolla, July 25, 1898, quoted in Soderini manuscript and notes.

ments in Rome. Here is his account of his dealings with Father Lepidi, an account that he related substantially the same to Ireland a few weeks later.

July 10, 1898

My Dear Friend

I am very sorry to have to inform you that all negotiations have failed and that there seems danger ahead.

In the mind of Lepidi, Master of S. Palace, Americanism is what is found in the article signed by Romanus, in the articles of Desjardins & c. and the results are found in the priests in France that threw off their soutanes. I showed him my discourse and talked at length. He then admitted he had fallen into a confusion confounding "American" with "European Americanism" but "how could he know?" Even in Hecker's life there was nothing against faith or morals, but many dangerous expressions capable of mis-interpretation. Then we agreed that a) he would correct Hecker's life as freely as he pleased and it would have a new edition made on the corrections. b) that he would write down all he found wrong in Americanism, and that I would have them all authoritatively denied. But he wanted a few days' time to prepare them and to *consult upstairs*. It was my intention after having received those notes to go on and see you and prepare an edition of the Life with Lepidi's imprimatur. On my return at the appointed time all was changed. The Pope had reserved the matter to himself. He, the Pope, would write to Gibbons and Ireland, but would give the imprimatur to the new edition of Maignen. That is what we particularly objected to. He could not make any corrections in Hecker's life. "They were the very words of Hecker." I asked "If you will not correct the book, do you mean to condemn it?" "Oh no," he answered. All will be done for peace and charity. I said there would be no peace if they published, as they said, a revised edition of Maignen.

. . . .

Lepidi says Americanism is invading Europe, and that every man that wants to work against the Church puts on that armour. . . .[27]

O'Connell did not mention then the notes rejecting "religious Americanism" he gave to Lepidi and which were to be published later. The attacks on the Americanists continued. About June 16 there had appeared from the pen of A.-J. Delattre of Namur, who had previously attacked Klein for a pro-American speech he had made at Gand in February, a small brochure of 184 pages under

[27] O'Connell to Klein, July 10, 1898, in the Paulist Fathers Archives. Also O'Connell to Ireland, August 28, 1898, to Keane, July 12, 1898, apparently sent on to Ireland by Keane, and preserved in the Archdiocesan Archives of Saint Paul.

the title of *Un Catholicisme Américain*.[28] The title of the book was taken from the article by Klein published in the *Revue Français d'Edimbourg* in September-October, 1897. In its preface Delattre announced his purpose not only to answer Klein's article, but, since he did believe that Hecker was responsible for the ideas in that article, also to examine the views of Hecker about asceticism and the religious vows and of course to reject them. He quoted Maignen and the French translation of Elliott's life, although he professed to be acquainted with the English original of the latter. Delattre answered Klein's praise of the Americans with a quotation from the travel book of Max Leclerc on the United States in which Leclerc painted the Americans as very materialistic, devoted entirely to the acquisition of riches and honors and filled with pride. The proper cure of these views Delattre found in the rule of the Exercises of Saint Ignatius. Further, he attacked Hecker's notion of the world as a pan-monastery, in which great numbers would reach a union with God, and Hecker's stress on the active virtues, insisting that obedience is really an active virtue, although not the kind of activity that he, Leclerc, claimed he found in America. Further, he defended the union of Church and State indicating that separation was the result of the Reformation, and rejected the thesis of O'Connell as expressed in the Fribourg address.

Continuing in the second part Delattre attacked the use by Klein of the notion of liberty as expressed by Saint Paul. Klein's liberty, he said, was only material and had only to do with the animal man and not the spiritual as Saint Paul had used the word liberty. Delattre then turned his attention to Klein's and Hecker's treatment of the vows. He denied that they were merely remedies for weakness and said that they add to a virtuous act. He explained the decision of the early Jesuits to take vows and indicated that the Americanists omitted the help of grace in doing good. The Paulists chose the freer way but vows were not just external bonds, for Delattre claimed that Hecker himself had different notions about vows in his earlier years as a Redemptorist. The idea of not taking vows is not new in the church. Even if the

[28] A. -J. Delattre, S.J., *Un Catholicisme Américain* (Namur, 1898).

Paulists were praised by Pius IX that does not take away the value of vows and of the contemplative life.

In the third part of the book Delattre turned upon the asceticism of Hecker and the claim that in the modern age, since the Vatican Council, a new type of asceticism is needed. History he said furnished a denial of the charge that the previous three centuries were merely an age of passive virtues. First he pointed out that contrary to O'Connell the golden age of the Church was in the first centuries when the Church was under that Roman law rejected by O'Connell. Delattre rejected Hecker's notion about not needing a director saying that this is contrary to Saint Paul, as well as to the teachings of Christ. The political freedom of Catholics in the United States he noted was not of their creation, and the Catholics in the United States do not fight for their liberties as do members of the Church in France. As to Hecker's notions about the interior direction of the Holy Ghost, what was good in his doctrine was not new. The only change Hecker added had been in the limiting of spiritual direction and that Delattre rejected.

In the fourth part of the book Delattre rejected the Hecker interpretation of the past three centuries as well as the role of the Vatican Council, using the Roman catechism which has been the guide of those teaching in the Church since the Council of Trent to show that Hecker was misinformed about the spiritual life of those three centuries. Specifically he quoted from accepted Catholic historians to show that the faithful were not rendered passive as little children. Further he pointed out that most of the heroes of the period, especially among the missionaries of America, were Latins not Anglo-Saxons. Finally he closed his account with a comparison of the growth of the Church in the United States with its growth in mission countries elsewhere, indicating that the growth in the United States was rather by immigration than by conversions.

In the meantime the conservative papers of France began to publish letters of praise from various French prelates for the book of Maignen. *La Défense de Seine et Marne* of June 11, gave a letter of the Bishop of Annecy to Maignen claiming that the *Life of Hecker* contained a new conception of the priesthood and of the religious life, even of the government of the Church. Hecker, the letter said, was not a saint and did not know how to be a reformer. Another letter of praise was from Cardinal Labouré of Rennes. On June 15, *La Vérité*, while renewing the statements in *La Croix* about the imprimatur, corrected a previous statement in its column that Gibbons had given the imprimatur of the English life. Maignen indicated that the visit of Martinelli to Ireland had really been for purposes of enquiry suggesting that there had been a change in papal policy. On June 18, *Espérance du Peuple* in an editorial on the two books claimed that the *Vie* was having serious effect on the younger clergy; and that the three chief ideas of the Americanists were the cult of the active virtues, legitimate confidence in one's self, and a robust faith in the Holy Ghost, but that "Romanus" had extended these ideas to an attack on the Scriptures and the election of Gibbons as Pope. These same ideas were repeated in *Le Nouvelliste* of Bordeaux. On June 25, there appeared two important defenses of the Americanists, the last notable defenses in the controversy. In Paris Klein published an article on "The Campaign against the Church in America" in *Le Correspondant*[29] and in *L'Opinione Liberale* in Rome there appeared an article on the discussion claiming that Hecker stood for true Catholicism.

At one time Klein[30] had written to O'Connell that he saw no use answering the articles of Maignen in *La Vérité* because he could not hope to influence the readers of that periodical or of *La Croix*. However when he returned from the trip he had taken to Scandinavia to restore his health and read the article by "Don Abbondio" (Périès in *La Croix* of June 14, repeated in *La Vérité* of June 15, he felt that he should yield to the editor of *Le Correspondant* and give some kind of answer. He had an interview with Richard. While Richard admitted that he had refused the imprimatur because of his desire not to offend the American

---

[29] Klein to O'Connell, March 20, 1898, in the Richmond Diocesan Archives.
[30] Klein to O'Connell, June 14, enclosing letter to the Editor of *La Croix*, dated June 15, and Klein to O'Connell June 25 in which he announces that he is writing an article in *Le Correspondant* without receiving a letter from Keane. All are in the Richmond Diocesan Archives.

prelates he also made it evident that he did not intend to make
any statement about his refusal. Klein then composed his article
for the June 25 *Le Correspondant*.[31] In general he charged Maignen with an attack not only on the venerated founder of the
Paulists but also on the Church in the United States and against
the persons of Cardinal Gibbons and Archbishops Ireland and
Keane. He stated that although the imprimatur had been refused
by Cardinal Richard the book had received an imprimatur from
Rome, and had been advertized by a regular campaign in *La
Croix, La Vérité, Le Courrier de Bruxelles, Les Études Religieuses*
and *La Voce della Verità*, the latter two Jesuit periodicals. Yet
he said that the granting of the imprimatur had been regretted
by Cardinal Rampolla who said he was unaware of its issuance. Klein pointed out that there were three other attacks
on the Church in America: the forced resignation of Keane
which the Pope later regretted, the attack of Monsignor Schroeder on Conaty and Keane and the efforts of Rome to protect
Schroeder when the bishops demanded his resignation, and the
rumors of the fall of 1896 that the Pope was going to demand
the resignation of Ireland and give a coadjutor to Gibbons. He
compared the campaign against the Americans to the bad diplomacy that had led to the Greek schisms in an earlier age, to the
losses of the sixteenth century, and to the recent losses to the
rationalists among the Latin peoples. On the other hand Klein said
he regarded the charges of conspiracy against the American prelates, whom he named, as fantastic. He listed the campaigns
described by Maignen, making special mention of the fourth
which he said was based mostly upon the anonymous articles of
"Tiber" and "Romanus" and had even dragged in Ireland's efforts
to prevent the Spanish-American War. In answer to these charges
Klein quoted at length from the letter of Gibbons in praise of
Hecker which appeared in the sixth edition of the *Vie*. Finally
Klein attacked the volume as the work of a party. He hoped this
fratricidal war would not go further and that the attacked
Church of the United States would be consoled by regrets to

---

[31] *Le Correspondant*, June 25, 1898, 1145-54, "Une Campagne contre l'Église
d'Amérique" signed "H. Delorme," one of Klein's regular pen names.

be expressed by the Papal Secretary of State. He signed the article H. Delorme, a pen name he had used before.

On the same day in *L'Opinione Liberale*[32] in Rome there appeared an article on the discussion with regard to Father Hecker. This article began with a brief account of Father Hecker. The author considered him as the true founder of Americanism and mentioned O'Connell's speech. Against Hecker and Americanism the writer said there had appeared the volume of Maignen which lacked the imprimatur of Cardinal Richard and this did not conform to the new rules of the Index proclaimed the previous year. Yet despite this, Monsignor Alberto Lepidi gave his imprimatur to the book. The act of Lepidi he explained by the fact that the Dominicans had allied themselves with the Jesuits to eradicate the peril of Americanism. The *Osservatore Romano* when invited to publish some disavowal of the Pope's part in the imprimatur remained silent. In summing up the doctrines of Hecker about the influence of the Holy Spirit in the new age, the decline of the Anglo-Saxons, and the proposals of reform, the writer in *L'Opinione* seemed to have relied more on the quotations from Maignen than on any knowledge of Hecker. The article ended by repeating its condemnation of Lepidi and demanding that the Vatican contradict Maignen's volume.

Les Études of May 9, carried a notice of the Maignen volume on its cover, more or less as an advertisement, and *La Voce della Verità* had carried, in addition, in its bibliography a list of the table of contents. The attack by Klein on these notices of Maignen's book was not to be allowed to go unnoticed. The July 20 issue of *Les Études* contained an article by Hippolite Martin on Americanism and also an answer to Klein's charges in another special article entitled "*Les Études et Le Correspondant*." In addition a pamphlet with an imprimatur of Lepidi written apparently by Father Brandi appeared in Rome answering the article in *L'Opinione Liberale*. Of the two articles against the Americanists in the July 20 *Les Études*, the second by Father J. Brucker, S.J.[33]

[32] *L'Opinione Liberale*, (n. 171), June 25, 1898.

[33] "Le Correspondant et les Études," *Études*, Publiés par des Pères de la Compagnie de Jésus, Tome 76, Juillet-Août-Septembre, 1898, pp. 232-35.

was in answer to the Klein articles in *Le Correspondant*. Klein in the June 25 article in *Le Correspondant* had accused Les *Études* of being a part of a campaign against the Church in the United States. In answer to this Brucker had denied the charge in a letter to the editors of *Le Correspondant*. Those editors had answered in another article entitled "Again the campaign against the Church in the United States" in which the editors of *Le Correspondant* repeated the charge against Les *Études* basing it on the advertisement that had appeared on the outer cover of Les *Études* for May 5. Brucker denied that this was a just basis for a charge against Les *Études* since they were permitted to carry ads for any book which was not against faith or morals. Before the article by Father Martin which appeared in the same issue as this, it could not be said that Les *Études* was sympathetic to Father Maignen. If the Americanists thought that the advertisement of Maignen's book was unfair they should have protested to the editors of Les *Études*. Brucker ended his article by saying that the attack in *Le Correspondant* did no good for the author of the article nor for the editors of *Le Correspondant*.

More important was the second attack written by Father Hippolite Martin[34] entitled "L'Américanisme." It was a review of Maignen's book. Martin prefaced his article with a statement that to discuss Americanism without approving it was not an attack on Americanism, and he felt that this was what Maignen had done. Americanism had always been to him something a bit ridiculous, a kind of exotism. The Americanists wanted to call the older systems of education superannuated and neglectful of muscular activity. The Americanists wanted the French clergy to imitate them by going to the people, and understanding the age, to give themselves to the spirit of the age, to have also a "Congress of Religions."

Martin said that Americanism was innocent in political and social matters but that in religion it had attempted to introduce a new apologetics. But novelty can be false and Hecker was a case in point, since while he was a good man he was not the ideal priest and the example of the priest of the future. Maignen, he said, was

[34] *Ibid.*, pp. 214-24.

correct when he saw in Americanism the old liberalism returned from overseas, but that this so-called Americanism was rejected even by the majority of American bishops and Catholics. The Americanists pretended that progress in the Church had stopped, yet they themselves had made progress among only a minority of the Church in the United States.

Martin then set forth what he considered a few characteristics of Americanism. First he said there was a want of modesty, telling of an American bishop who had explained the lack of a Lourdes apparition in America by saying that the Americans did not need such an apparition. Secondly he said the Americanists falsely implied that there was less need of the supernatural on the grounds that the supernatural depressed the natural, and had invented passive virtues which they attributed to the Church during the recent centuries. Thirdly he said they implied that the faithful had doubts concerning the knowledge about the future world in men who are so ignorant of the things of this life. He cynically added that apparently the economists would be the best persons to save souls under this supposition. If America had produced men lacking this earthly knowledge but possessed of knowledge of the world to come they would be better off. Fourthly he said the Americans accused the Church of lacking modernity (*modernism*). He said this charge was not clear. Maignen wrongly accused the Americanists of the errors of Charbonnel and "Romanus," but Martin added that these two held the same doctrines as the Americanists in so far as all three errors were based on the condemned liberalism.

Martin then examined certain charges which he said the Americanists made against the Church. The Americanists accused the Church of being opposed to science, but Martin said they offered no proof of their charge. Further, he said the Americanists had invented the modern mind, and he denied that there had been any real change in the new conditions. The Americanists wanted to unite the dissident groups by removing the customs houses. Martin said that this could be done only by removing the dogmas of the faith, placing emphasis on moral principles only, and accepting evolutionism. That he said would result in making all of them Protestants. Further, he rejected the proposal to substitute the Anglo-Saxons for the Latins, and he coyly added that the leaders of the movement were really neither, being rather Celto-Latins. Finally he claimed that the Americanists would modify the very constitution of the Church, making individualism supreme over the hierarchy. That, he said, was Hecker's Protestantism.

Martin then turned to the character of Hecker. Hecker, he maintained, was just the occasion of Maignen's attack, the real target was Americanism. Maignen was pitiless but just. Martin regretted the exorbitant praise of Hecker who he said was a good priest, a bit nervous, with personal ideas, but no theologian. Further he said Hecker was not a mystic in the real meaning of the word, but a subjectivist whose notion of devotion to the Holy Ghost was very dangerous for the Church, and contrary to the spirit of the Church and the teaching of the masters of the spiritual life. Finally Hecker's disdain for the vows and the religious life seemed to be the result of a leaven of Protestantism and was a deviation from the Catholic mind. Martin quoted the figures on the comparative growth of the Paulists and the Redemptorists to show that the majority of Americans had not followed Hecker's ideas on the religious life. Martin concluded his article with a word of praise for Maignen for taking the unpopular side of the question. He himself felt that he was of the old Faith—a Catholic without epithet and French with no desire to Americanize.

There could no longer be any doubt about the position of *Les Études* on the controversy. But if there was any further doubt it was dissipated by a further article of Father A. Delattre in the issue of August 20, "Encore L'Américanisme:[35] un planche de Salut," in answer to the pamphlet of E. Coppinger,[36] a lay paleographer of Louvain who had tried to explain away the charges against Hecker by saying that the errors were contained in a

---

[35] *Ibid.*, pp. 535-42.
[36] E. Coppinger, *La Polémique française sur la vie du P. Hecker* (Paris, 1898). Coppinger was a lay scholar who thought he could eliminate the controversy by improving the translation and adaptation. He apparently was unaware that the translation was only the occasion of the controversy and that his efforts would be so badly received.

faulty translation of the original life of Hecker. Besides making light of the differences which Coppinger had found between the two versions, Delattre claimed that he himself had used the English version to avoid such a charge and that the distinctions were without any great importance. Further he claimed that Hecker had misinterpreted the words of Saint Paul about liberty, since Saint Paul had meant liberty from the Judaic and Mosaic law and not the liberty of which Hecker spoke.

The pamphlet[37] published in Rome in answer to the article in *L'Opinione* followed similar lines. The pamphlet bore the imprimatur of Father Lepidi and in some circles it was attributed to Father Salvatore Brandi. Brandi himself attributed it to Cardinal Segna. It began with a condemnation of innovations, pointing out that the experience of the Church indicated that everything that opposed the eternally ancient and yet new teachings of the Church was usually false; even adding that the finding of modern science had not changed this situation, as can be proved from quotations from Saint Paul who warned the faithful against such novelties. The *L'Opinione* article in question claimed that the Church was divided into two camps over the question of Father Hecker. The author answered that, while there is a division between those who hold to the true doctrine and those who hold to evolutionism, the latter group is really small since it has practically no followers in Europe, Asia, Africa, Australia or in Latin America and only a minority in the United States. The author then took up the question of Father Hecker himself and indicated that the author had passed over the real circumstances of the departure of Father Hecker from the Redemptorists and the foundation of the Paulists. The expulsion of Hecker and his companions from the Redemptorists was justified. Further, Hecker, he said, proposed to found a community, the Paulists, to convert Protestants to a revitalized Catholicism. The author of the article in *L'Opini-*

---

[37] *L'Americanismo ovvero risposta ad un articolo dell' "Opinione Liberale"* (N. 171-25 Giugno 1898 sul P. Hecker) (Roma, 1898). In his letter to Archbishop Corrigan on September 3, 1898, Father Brandi in support of his claim that the Pope approved of the original imprimatur indicates that he understands this answer was prepared by Cardinal Segna. Cf. letter in the Archdiocesan Archives of New York.

one did not say what the real ideas of Hecker were: a new relation between God and the soul. The writer went on to say that he did not have time to discuss all the ideas of Hecker, but he found the mysterious interior voice that Hecker followed was not the voice of God but an hallucination. The distinction between passive and active virtues, he said, was a new discovery resulting from the change from monarchy to democracy in government. Hecker further did not discover this until he left the Redemptorists. This, he added, was the reason for Hecker's insistence on individualism, his rejection of a director, and his insistence on being guided directly by the Holy Ghost. The author found in these ideas of Hecker wrong notions about confidence in one's self, about the importance of the active and natural virtues, and on the giving of one's self to the internal direction of the Holy Ghost. The idea of subjection to the guidance of the Holy Ghost is not new in the Church, the Saints all held it but they also insisted on the guidance of a director or master of the spiritual life. This idea of individualism of Hecker, the writer claimed, was the revitalization advocated by Hecker but which had not yet claimed the majority of the Church even in America. For the rest, the author made fun of the articles in *L'Italie* of June 6 and 12 against Maignen and Father Lepidi, sarcastically praising these critics for their pretended orthodoxy but indicating that their arguments made it clear that they were evolutionists and progressivist liberals who hypocritically invoked the censorship of the press and the power of anyone who seemed to support them.

By this time the summer vacation time of 1898 had arrived and there was a comparative lull in the activity in Rome. O'Connell wrote to Ireland on July 12, 1898,[38] that he understood from his conversations with Lepidi that a new edition of Maignen was being prepared and that an English edition was also being prepared. He hoped that a distinction would now be made between political Americanism and religious Americanism. Of political Americanism there was nothing to fear. The religious American-

---

[38] O'Connell to Ireland, July 12, 1898, in the Archdiocesan Archives of Saint Paul. Also O'Connell to Father Elliott, August 22, 1898, in the Paulist Fathers Archives.

ism which they attributed to Father Hecker was, he said, really repugnant to all that Father Hecker held. O'Connell went off to Switzerland for a rest, feeling that he could not accomplish any more in Rome. Ireland was restless in Minnesota but did not go to Rome because of a letter from Rampolla,[39] in which Rampolla asked him in the name of the Pope not to take any public action and promised action on the matter by the Pope. Ireland in turn promised to remain silent.[40]

The controversy had continued unabated in France with the Abbés Democrats, Abbés Naudet, Dabry and Lemire, especially Abbé Naudet, in his *Justice Sociale*, taking up the side of the Americanists. Naudet's articles during July produced answers from *La Vérité*. Suddenly there appeared on August 15, 1898, in *La Vérité* an edited version of some notes that O'Connell had given to Lepidi, in which he was made to repudiate "religious Americanism." O'Connell wrote on August 28[41] to Ireland retelling the incident, insisting that he had given the notes for publication in the *Osservatore Romano*, and claiming that Lepidi by omitting certain portions of the statements had placed him in a false light. The only satisfaction O'Connell said he found was that a distinction was now made between the true Americanism and the false Americanism and that the travesties attributed to them by their adversaries were repudiated. Apparently O'Connell did not know then that these same statements were to be published in the appendix of the English translation of Maignen's book.

In the meantime, O'Connell[42] wrote to Ireland that Bishop Sebastian Messmer had been in Rome, and he implied that he had counseled with those who were attacking the Americanists. Archbishop Corrigan had also written in a supporting way to Father Maignen. *La Vérité* was publishing the letters of the bishops to Maignen, which were to appear in the supplement of the English

[39] Rampolla to Ireland, quoted in Soderini manuscript.

[40] Ireland to Rampolla, quoted in Soderini manuscript.

[41] O'Connell to Ireland, August 28, 1898, in the Saint Paul Archdiocesan Archives.

[42] O'Connell to Ireland, July 20, 1898, in the Saint Paul Archdiocesan Archives.

edition, including one by Satolli[43] in which he commended Maignen for his book.

Cardinal Gibbons did not send his protest against the imprimatur until August 27, but since it came from the ranking prelate of the country and was so forthright in its statements it must have carried weight with the Holy Father.[44] First he said that the book by Maignen was a combination of falsehood and violent hate in which Father Hecker and his community, the Paulists, were attacked. Then also, the book spoke of Americanism as an heretical and a schismatical doctrine, and the gravest insults were offered to certain American prelates. Gibbons said he did not write to defend the orthodoxy of the Hecker, which can be found in the biography. He was writing against that part of the book which attacks Americanism. He added:

> The impression produced by that part of the book and desired by the author is that we are scarcely Catholic, that we are lacking submission to the teachings and direction of the Holy See and that the spirit of schism is very strong among us. Truly, Your Eminence, one can hardly believe his eyes or his ears when he reads or hears such heinousness.
>
> I have been a bishop thirty years; I have already held the see of Baltimore for twenty-one years; I am a member of the Sacred College of Cardinals since 1886; I presided over the Third Plenary Council of Baltimore; I have, as a result, had many and continued relationships with the bishops of this country and I know the American clergy very well.
>
> What is meant when one speaks of Americanism in connection with our bishops and our clergy? Surely, we love our country and are ready to sacrifice our lives for it; we love its institutions because they leave us the liberty to do good and allow us to spread religion and the influence of the Church more and more. This is not a matter of theory, of system, of maxims laid down as absolute principles. It is entirely a question of application. If that were what we call Americanism, what would be the harm in so doing? But no; the word is used as a bugbear. The aim is to make others think of a perverse inclination, of a not only questionable but a largely erroneous and even heretical doctrine, one to be classified with liberalism, Gallicanism and other isms of that kind. Now I can assure Your Eminence that it is all false, unjust, slanderous. No doubt among us as everywhere else, there are differences of opinion and appreciation, but I do not hesitate to assert that nowhere

[43] *La Vérité*, June 11, 1898.
[44] The draft of the letter in French is in the handwriting of A. Magnien, S.S., in the Cathedral Archives of Baltimore.

in the universe will you find bishops, clergymen and lay people more deeply Catholic, more constant in their faith and more entirely devoted to the Holy See. Besides in that we are only following tradition. The Sovereign Pontiff Pius IX could say in all truth that from nowhere did he receive more support than from the United States, and His Holiness Leo XIII can say as much. In no other part of the Catholic world was the most firm and wise direction he gave the Church followed with more submission and respect than among us.

Gibbons pointed out that the book was a republication of essays from *La Vérité* and that Father Maignen was really a person of no importance, but that this situation had been changed in the publication of the book because of the Roman imprimatur. It is to the imprimatur that he objected.

Whatever may be the import and real value of an imprimatur for our thoroughly Catholic people who are not accustomed to subtle distinctions, for our clergymen, and especially for the Protestants and others, it is no longer the Reverend Maignen and his collaborator, but the Holy See itself, which is publicly accusing us of errors in the faith and of schismatical tendencies. Now this, Your Eminence, is very serious. It means the ruin of our influence for the good of the Church in the United States. It is the confirmation of the Protestant prejudice that the Catholic Church is of necessity opposed to the civil and political institutions and that a Catholic cannot but be a disloyal American citizen.

Just when Pope Leo XIII decided to take to himself the study of the question of Americanism is not clear from available sources, but the action had taken place at least by October, 1898.[45] O'Connell's report to Klein and to Ireland about the interviews with Lepidi, and Father Salvatore Brandi [46] in his letter to Archbishop Corrigan on July 11, make it quite clear that most of the Roman prelates were deeply influenced by the book of Maignen. Probably the American conquest of Spain had something to do with the feeling. Probably also in the background must be considered the growing Modernist movement which was to receive its condemnation in the next pontificate. O'Connell in his letters to

45 Klein to Dufresne, October 11, 1898. Klein reports that he is informed that the Pope has taken the matter out of the Congregation that was considering it.
46 Brandi to Corrigan, July 11, 1898 and October 11, 1898, in the Archdiocesan Archives of New York.

Keane and Ireland before he left Rome for the vacation and his first letters from Fribourg,[47] Switzerland, seemed to indicate a situation in Rome far more unfavorable to the Americanists than he or his friends had realized. This emphasizes a fact that must be understood to explain some of the events of the next six months. The Americanists refused to think that any one seriously believed that they held the theological heresies exposed in Maignen's book, and knowing the friendly attitude of the Holy Father towards democracy and social reform they felt that their position was secure. O'Connell's and Keane's conversations with Roman officials[48] should have convinced them that many of these Roman prelates really believed that Americanism was a well organized movement which threatened schism or at least a major heretical trend in the Church if successful. The aggressiveness of O'Connell and Ireland for what O'Connell called political Americanism was confused by many Roman prelates with the theological Americanism which was being belabored by the conservative press in France. The denials of the heresy by Keane, Ireland and O'Connell were balanced easily by the conversations of Bishop Sebastian Messmer of Green Bay,[49] and letters of Archbishop Corrigan[50] to Lepidi and Maignen, if not to Rampolla and the Pope. The Roman prelates best informed by experience in the United States, Mazzella and Satolli, likewise felt that the progressivism of the American prelates needed some condemnation. When the crisis was reached in the summer of 1898, Ireland had been prevented from going to Rome by the letter of Rampolla which indicated that the negotiations about the Church in the newly conquered

---

[47] O'Connell to Ireland, September 27, 1898, in the Archdiocesan Archives of Saint Paul, O'Connell to Father Elliott, August 8, 1898, in the Paulist Fathers Archives, and O'Connell to Klein, August 7, 1898 in the same Archives.

[48] O'Connell to Ireland, April 19, 1898, and Keane to Ireland, June 4, 1897, and June 12, 1898, in the Archdiocesan Archives of Saint Paul. This opposition to Americanism is frequently referred to in O'Connell's and Keane's letters but they kept believing that Americanism would ultimately triumph.

[49] O'Connell to Ireland, July 12, 1898 and July 20, 1898, in the Archdiocesan Archives of Saint Paul. O'Connell was convinced that Messmer was the source of Lepidi's opinion about the existence of the wrong Americanism.

[50] Maignen to Corrigan, March 31, 1899 speaks of the earlier letter. Ireland claimed that a letter of Corrigan to Lepidi was waved in his face when he tried to stop the apostolic letter, *Testem benevolentiae*. Cf. Ireland to Father Deshon, February 24, 1899 in the Paulist Fathers Archives.

islands would be upset by such a visit. Keane was in America. O'Connell had gone from Rome leaving behind a series of notes in the possession of Lepidi which seemed to indicate that he had abandoned Americanism. The Roman press had begun seriously to fight the battle, with little knowledge of the United States, but with real acrimony, bringing in the question of the Pope and the Italian state as well as the question of the separation of Church and State. Under these circumstances it is clear that later in the summer the Pope, alarmed by the bitterness, suppressed the movement to put the life of Hecker on the Index, forbade any further controversy in the curia about the heresy,[51] and appointed a commission to study the problem and make a report to him. The members of the commission were not definitely indicated in any document now available. Since they would have to read some English documents O'Connell thought it would include Satolli, Mazzella, and one of the Vannutellis. Later the committee was reported by Croke, the Roman correspondent of the *Philadelphia Standard*,[52] as consisting of Cardinals Ledochowski as President, Di Pietro, Satolli, Vincenzo Vannutelli, and Ferrata. The Roman correspondent of the *Freeman's Journal*[53] claimed the commission was headed by Satolli and Mazzella.

In France during the summer the battle continued in the press. On July 1 an article in *L'Éclair* spoke of the reappearance of the revolution under various forms, as Gallicanism, then liberalism, and now as Americanism. The Church was to be dominated in a democracy by the imposition of Protestantism and the triumph of individualism and authority reduced to the minimum. The writer summarized the controversy and indicated that the Americans did not wish to separate from the Church but to go into the Church like the *ralliés* into the Republic. This article was reprinted in many other French newspapers. Klein answered it with a letter published July 3 in *L'Éclair* and *L'Univers et le Monde*, calling the editor's attention to his article in *Le Correspondant* of

[51] O'Connell to Father Walter Elliott, Paris, December 10, 1898, in which he says that the Pope was influenced by the letter of Cardinal Gibbons and prevented the *Vie du Père Hecker* from going on the Index.

[52] Issue of December 31, 1898.

[53] Issue of December 3, 1898.

June 25 in which Rampolla was credited with saying that neither he nor the Pope knew of the imprimatur. Klein thanked the paper for coupling his name with that of Gibbons and Ireland.

On July 7 a writer in *L'Éclair* offered a refutation of the letter of Klein. The writer denied that the article in the *Correspondant* was a refutation of his previous article. Klein would unite the Americanists by appealing to the jingoism of Americans, but Maignen had pointed out that the Americanists were only a minority among American Catholics. The writer also denied that Rampolla regretted the imprimatur, claiming that Lepidi was a considerable person, and indicated that to set aside dogma and the rules of discipline was a serious matter. This he claimed ended the polemic and he would await the decision of the Index. This article was reprinted that same day in *La Vérité*. On the same day Arthur Loth complained of the speech of M. Maruejouls at a Fourth of July celebration in Paris as an act of unfriendliness to Spain in time of war, calling it an act of anti-clericalism because Spain was Catholic.

On July 9, Abbé Naudet in *La Justice Sociale* began to take the side of the Americanists in the battle, on the grounds that Maignen had placed the Abbés Democrates in the same boat as the Americanists. He regretted that Klein's preface was generally too individualistic and placed too much praise on personalism, and regretted that certain ideas were not better developed in the biography because they could be misinterpreted by persons of ill will. Yet the biography was good. He then reviewed the attack on the Americanists beginning with the November sermons, and delineated the character of Maignen and the conservative character of *La Vérité*. Maignen, he said, by piecing certain documents together had created a secret society with passwords and tactics. Outside of the small controversy between *L'Univers* and *La Vérité*, who had few readers, the articles would have had little significance had they not been published in the book.

On July 17, L. Henri Mallon, as "Honticlair" wrote an article in *La Justice Sociale* of Brussels on Klein and Hecker in which he reviewed Klein's attendance at the conference at Gand and his writings. He rejected Delattre and suggested that the latter should go back to his oriental studies. On July 19, J. Cornelys in *Le Matin* reviewed the two main books of the controversy comparing the two camps, one of which he said was devoted to Pius IX, the other to Pope Leo XIII. Some American ideas he said were good but not all American ideas were good for the French. On July 21, *La Croix* mentioned the Roman brochure in answer to *L'Opinione* and announced the appearance of E. Coppinger's *Polémique Française sur le vie du P. Hecker*. In the meantime Abbé Naudet continued his weekly articles in *La Justice Sociale* concerning the controversy over the life of Father Hecker. *La Vérité* pointed out on July 22, that while Naudet said in the first article that the life of Hecker had an imprimatur, in the second he said that as a biography it did not need one. Naudet in his fourth article repeated the charges of Klein's article in *Le Correspondant* and related the story about the attack on Keane in 1896, the attempt to prevent the resignation of Schroeder in 1897, the publication of Maignen's book, and the attempt to charge the Americanists with all the apostasies of recent years. He concluded the article with a plea for his friends to take courage and to keep their good humor, and with a sarcastic account of the destructive functions of *La Vérité* and the *réfractaires*. Périès in the meantime published his views on the controversy in *La Revue Canonique*[54] of June, 1898.

In *La Revue Bibliographique et Littéraire* for August, Ducis reviewed the life of Hecker and Maignen and Coppinger. He was definitely friendly to Maignen, adding figures from the *North American Review* on the growth of secret societies in the United States and some figures on the heavy Jewish immigration into the United States. Thus he departed from the text of Maignen to see an invasion of America by the Freemasons and Jews towards the establishment of a universal nation, and then he coupled this with the campaign against the Church as seen in Maignen. He mentioned the letter of Gibbons on Hecker added to the sixth edition. Coppinger he accused of hostility towards the translators of the life of Hecker. In *La Mercure de France* Charbonnel reviewed briefly the *Life* of Hecker claiming that the French clergy

[54] Quoted in *The Review*, August 4, 1898.

were divided, one group led by the Jesuits and the other by priests who defended the liberal tradition. He predicted that Klein would soon be a victim, and said that he awaited the new struggle. On August 6, *La Vérité* published a review of Delattre's book by Périès under the name Saint Clement. After summing up the book in a favorable way, Périès quoted the conclusion at length, adding that the Jesuit had expressed his ideas, too.

In the meantime the English edition of Maignen's book had been prepared. On its title page was inserted the name of the publisher, besides the Roman publisher Desclée, as Benziger Brothers, but when that publisher refused to receive the book and demanded that its name be removed, a small tab was pasted over the Benziger name imprinted with that of Burns and Oates of London. The book was published in Rome and had the imprimatur of Lepidi and a permission dated July 19 of the Superior General of the Brothers of Saint Vincent de Paul. Some phrases had been changed but in substance the book was the same. In the appendix however, as in the August 15 issue of *La Vérité*, were the quotations from the statements of O'Connell to Lepidi of July 12 and 14. Taken alone they deny that he holds the doctrines of religious Americanism described by Maignen, or that the Americanists hold the doctrines of "Romanus"; and they insist that his speech at Fribourg explained that he held the accepted thesis on the relations of Church and State, but that he was speaking of the actual hypothesis in the United States. Maignen and the editors simply added a caustic sentence that he should change the title of his pamphlet to "Americanism *according to Father Hecker*." The English translation also had a special preface. In this preface Maignen spoke of a twofold tendency in American Catholicism: one looking with disfavor on old methods of teaching the Church's doctrines, and the second accepting rash ideas and risky methods. He then devoted several pages to Ireland's activities in France and Klein's speech at the Conference at Gand. Also in the front of the book were the letters of the Bishop of Annecy, the praise for the French edition by Cardinal Labouré of Rennes and the Bishop of Mende which had been published in *La Vérité*. On August 20, *La Vérité* quoted an article on the book from the *Review* of Saint Louis, in which Father Meifuss called Americanism liberalism, and denied that the fight was one between races, but insisted that it was a fight about ideas. In the meantime however, Father Meifuss, apparently after a study of the articles in *La Vérité*, had been publishing a series of articles in the *Review*[55] in which he summarized the life of Hecker in the manner of Maignen and compared it with the life of Bishop John N. Neumann, the saintly Redemptorist bishop of Philadelphia. The *Review* apparently subscribed generally to the ideas expressed by Maignen and quoted at length the Roman pamphlet against the Americanists. *La Semaine Religieuse* of the diocese of Nancy, of August 19, besides announcing a book by Bishop Turinaz on the question of Americanism and Christian democracy, mentioned the letter of Cardinal Satolli praising the English translation of Maignen's book. The letter was quoted in detail in translation in the August 25 issue of the *Review* of Saint Louis. In it Satolli praised the improvements in the translation, and hoped that the good God would assist Maignen in arresting the progress of "the disastrous pest which had spread its contagion in two worlds."[56] The same issue of the *Review* defended the character of Périès from an attack in the *Hartford Transcript*, and quoted an article in the *New York Sun*[57] by "Innominato" which claimed that Klein had made a mistake in calling Hecker a type of the future priest on the continent. The *Review* and *Le Courrier de Bruxelles*[58] indicated that the Americanists were now fighting among themselves in their effort to avoid condemnation.

[55] The articles began in the May 19, 1898 issue and continued throughout the summer.

[56] Soderini in his manuscript is of the opinion that Satolli did not read the book he praised.

[57] *The Review* of August 11 quotes "Innominato" writing in the *New York Sun* from Rome on July 16 as saying that Hecker was in error in his use of the ideas of Petau, Ramière and Scheeben on the Holy Ghost, in his use of the Hegelian philosophy, and in his views on the Anglo-Saxons. "Innominato" added "Let us admire the great founder of the Paulists, but let us not make, blunderingly make, of him a symbol and an absolute model." Apparently "Innominato" had been shaken by Maignen's book, according to his articles. *New York Sun*, November 13, 1898 "Catholic Americanism." Boeglin, "Innominato," showed in his correspondence with O'Connell that he was worried about the possibilities of a condemnation.

[58] Quoted in *La Vérité* of August 26, 1898.

The Brussels editor quoted from Keane's article in the *Catholic World* and from O'Connell's Fribourg speech to show that they held up Hecker as a model and a type of Americanism. He warned the French Americanists and the editors of *Le Correspondant* that the Americans were trying to save Americanism in the United States and perhaps Elliott and Hecker at the expense of French Americanists.

On August 29, Auguste Roussel published a friendly review of Delattre's answer to Coppinger, and indicated that these textual differences could not explain the fervor of Archbishop Ireland, Abbé Klein and the other people who had praised Hecker. This article was reprinted the next day in *Le Courrier de Bruxelles*. On August 31, Pierre Veuillot published an article "Americanists" in *L'Univers et le Monde*. He complained about the use of the name. He said that if Hecker had not lived it would have been necessary for the anti-Americanists to invent another qualification but since Hecker lived and died and had a biographer there was a new epithet—Americanists. He added that it was not possible to open one's mouth and offer any proposition without being called an Americanist. By extension the name had been applied to anyone who wished to progress, to attempt reform, or who even broached any idea from the New World. Instead of conducting a discussion the opponents now merely threw an epithet. Monsignor Baunard, for suggesting a friendly attitude towards science, had been called an Americanist; Mère Marie du Sacré Coeur had suggested improvement in the teaching in the Catholic schools, and she was called an Americanist. A congress of priests and workers to improve the condition of the workers had been called Americanist. Veuillot warned that one cannot stop these people by an epithet.

In the September issue of *La Revue Générale*, edited by the Jesuits in Brussels, Father J. B. Paquet, S.J. devoted a noteworthy three page article to the subject "Ascétisme Américain." Because of the publicity given to these matters Father Paquet said that some clarification of this phrase was necessary lest it be used against the generally zealous episcopate of the United States. He reviewed the various articles and books, especially the life of

Hecker, which had appeared on the subject, pointing out that Professor Hermann Schell in his *Die Neue Zeit und der Alte Glaube* had indicated that the movement was responsible for the apostasy of several French clergy. Paquet said that such an idea was exaggerated but the problem was one that could not be ignored. He discussed the question indicating that while it was the traditional doctrine of the Church that inspiration came from the Holy Ghost, Hecker and Klein had added to this the immediate obedience to inspirations of the Holy Ghost and the independence of external guidance. As to Hecker himself Paquet implied that his special doctrines were the result of hallucinations, implying that Hecker's background as a Protestant, a Kantian, and a Methodist were the source of these ideas. The particular doctrines of the Americanists about the inspirations of the Holy Ghost, he claimed, were based on a false notion of the ability of the soul to go naturally to the Holy Ghost. There have been saints who had such special gifts but that was not the ordinary way, and external guidance was necessary according to the traditional teachings of the Church. In insisting that this external guidance was the ordinary way of the soul, Paquet agreed with Delattre that Hecker had given the wrong meaning to liberty as used by Saint Paul. As to the distinction between active and passive virtues he insisted that there were no passive virtues and hinted that for Anglo-Saxons respect for tradition was a weakness. He indicated some of the accomplishments of the Celto-Latins, paying considerable respect to Father Peter De Smet, but he repeated the idea that what was good in Americanism was not new and what was new was not good.

On September 1, *La Vérité* published a letter of Bishop Turinaz of Nancy dated August 28, and addressed to Maignen. He explained his delay in entering the discussion by saying he was waiting the opportune moment. He denied that Maignen had been excessive in his charges. Even Maignen's suggestion that Hecker was a saint was too honorable for Hecker. He agreed with Father Monsabre who had said in a letter in *La Vérité* of June 17, that he would have been less sweet than Maignen had he written the book. He quoted also Satolli's praise of the book, and O'Connell's quotations in the Appendix of the English translation which had been published in *La Vérité*. Turinaz recalled that Lepidi had not been reprimanded but had given the imprimatur to the pamphlet answering the article in *L'Opinione*. He answered Klein's article in the June 25 *Le Correspondant* by quoting Klein's article in *La Revue Française d'Édimbourg*. He quoted favorably also Delattre's answer to Coppinger and indicated that some day he might himself give an opinion of Americanism and other perils of the Church.

On July 16, 1898, in *La Semaine Religieuse de Cambrai* there appeared the first of a series of articles, "Un Catholicisme Américain," from the pen of Canon Henri Delassus. In the first of these articles Delassus indicated that he had already mentioned this subject in reviews of certain books and that he wanted it understood that this heresy was not the Church in the United States, since most Americans did not hold it and since it was also held outside the United States. He said that there was a doctrinal tendency whose teachers intended to take over the direction of the formation of the clergy. He indicated that this school had been active for six years and indicated that he would have to offend some persons by name in his effort to expose this threat. By attack and counter-attack in the press Americanism as a definite doctrine had been evolved. Its existence was being presumed by its attackers and even by some who tried to be impartial. The defenders of the Americanists did not seem to know how to answer this presumption of fact.

In the meantime Abbé Périès, as "Saint Clement," felt impelled to answer the various defenders of the Americanists. On September 19, he began by criticizing the article by "Innominato" in the *New York Sun* which had implied that the Americanists had erred in praising too strongly the character of Hecker, and which had indicated that Americanism was free from this excess. Quoting the article in the *Review* of Saint Louis of August 25, Périès proceeded to show that this defense like that of Coppinger could not evade the basic truth of Maignen's charges. On September 22, Périès answered an article by Abbé Bricout, the editor of the *Revue du Clergé Français*, who had denied that the Pope was a party to the Lepidi imprimatur and had gone on to defend the Americanists from the charges of Maignen. Périès cited the second imprimatur to the translation and pointed out that Bricout seemed to be ignorant of the various articles in *Revue Canonique* by Périès, of the answer to the article in *L'Opinione*, of the articles of Delattre and the like. He made fun of Bricout's charge that Maignen lacked charity in his attack in the face of such a serious danger. He pointed out that Bricout admitted that the Americanists were too enthusiastic both in their efforts to make Hecker a type of the future priests and in their insistence that France copy the American relations between Church and State. Périès added that the same thing could be said of O'Connell's distinction between thesis and hypothesis, and he suggested that it was best for the faithful to stick to the traditional doctrines and to avoid these innovators who do not say what they mean.

On September 21, *Le Temps* of Paris took notice of the controversy, saying that Americanism was decidedly the order of the day, not merely in the political order on account of the war between Spain and the United States, but also in the religious world where the battle of great intensity had been going on for some months. Americanism it called a kind of Catholicism formed in the United States with its leaders being Bishops Ireland and Keane, Father Hecker and Cardinal Gibbons, whose key words were the "Church and the age." The new tendency encouraged the study of science and democracy. These ideas, the article said, are not new having been held by Montalembert and Lacordaire. But the tendency had been attacked by Maignen as a dangerous heresy. The article by Père Martin in *Les Études* stressed the evidence that the Americanists were preferring the Anglo-Saxons to the Latins. The author of the article in *Le Temps* wondered if this argument from nationalities would not have some effect in the results of the defeat of Spain. In answer, the September 23 issue of *Le Temps* quoted an article of A. Roussel of *La Vérité* pointing out that Ireland had imbibed the milk of liberalism at the seminary of Meximieux where some of the professors were disciples of Lamennais.

On September 2, 1898, the *London Catholic Times* published

a strongly worded defense of the Americanists in which it insisted that the Americanists merely wanted to free the Church from some of its European slavery and praised the advances made in the Church in the United States as compared with the Church in France. The *Civiltà Cattolica*, however, in the meantime had published a favorable notice of the pamphlet answering *L'Opinione*.

L'Ami du Clergé, a journal a little more conservative than the *Revue du Clergé Français* finally felt compelled in its issue of October 13 to discuss the controversy in an article "L'Américanisme et Mystique Américaine." The article began with a review of the controversy indicating that insofar as it was a revival of the old condemned liberalism Americanism was not desirable, but that insofar as it was a movement to improve the condition of the Church it was desirable. The author related the events of the controversy, how the life of Hecker had not attracted much attention until it had been translated and adapted by the *ralliés* in France, and of the publication of Maignen's articles and book which were partisan but theologically quite correct. Hecker, the subject of the attack, had been successful in America but this, he said, did not mean that he should be as successful in France. As to Maignen's book the writer in *L'Ami* said that it was Americanism rather than Hecker that was the object of the attack. The quality of Maignen's book was affected by the fact that it was printed first in a daily newspaper. The author then took up the question of Americanism. Americans, he said, were a young people with much energy, but like children inclined to be noisy and impulsive. They loved their liberty, but it must be remembered that left to themselves men abuse liberty and there is no other check on this abuse of liberty than law. The tendency to develop personal initiative is good and also the practice of liberty and self-expression; but a too great confidence in oneself, a disdain for custom, and a too great confidence in natural virtue is bad, especially if the development of natural powers is carried out until the supernatural appears only as a complement of the natural. But in America, a country dominantly Protestant, there was too much concern about material welfare. Likewise the constitutional republican government in the United States suited very well the condition of that nation. He admired the inventions, machines, and high buildings of the United States but said their literature was poor, their philosophy poor, their theology even poorer—almost reduced to natural thought. Then the author turned to the "Mystique Américaine."

The author distinguished between American Catholicism and American "mystique." This latter was the idea of a few: that one must seek the human and natural perfection and liberty and thus emancipate the individual in all his orders, in politics by democracy and in religion by the active virtues with as little intervention as possible of dogmatic authority, external ritual practices, the vows, etc. The ideals of the past, before the Vatican Council, served their purpose, so also the old ways of religious living, but now the new must be adopted. Do not destroy nature, there is no contradiction between nature and grace. Do away with the customs houses between religions, and facilitate the approach of non-Catholics to the Church. The Americanist said perfection consists in action—that is external action which leaves no place for contemplatives. The author rejected this doctrine saying that to think and to love liberty itself is internal and of the highest activity of man. It is true that not all men are called to this interior perfection, but the tradition of the Church shows that it is the better part. The theory of the majority does not work here, universal monachism would be an absurdity. But monachism will be the life of a minority. The evangelical virtues will be the flower of the Christian life. It is permissible to appeal to the passing thing, to use the language of opportunity, but when Americanism would make the language of occasion and of opportunity the language of permanent life, that cannot be accepted. Providence will take care of the future. The ideal of the Church living a life of natural ease and splendor here below is false. Further, the writer said, there are no passive virtues, all virtues are active. The Americans deceived themselves by such pleasantries. Humility is not a passive virtue but an heroic act. So also for obedience. Likewise the Paulists had made a false exegesis of the words of Saint Paul about liberty. Further, the author said, that while it is laudable to escape from extreme obedience to civil law, that idea is not correct applied to the law of religious obedience to the Church. It is true that the Americanists indicated that they submitted to all teachings of the Church, yet they did not want to have these teachings mentioned any more than is necessary—a practice which is certainly dangerous.

The source of the problem the writer found in the question of original sin. In the United States and in France there were some who talk about theological things without sufficient knowledge. The doctrine of the effects of original sin is one of these theological facts which must be recognized. That is the reason why Christ undertook to reform our human nature and why the Church insists on asceticism and its supernatural mystique. If Americanism sought to ignore this truth it was erroneous, especially, he continued, if it does not see a contradiction between the perfect development of this natural life and the supernatural. To avoid this error there is needed authority and law, and man must be formed to obedience, to supernatural obedience, guaranteed from abuse by the authority of the Church.

Finally the author took up the question of democracy and the Holy Ghost. Insofar as it is true that the great preoccupation of the faithful is to cooperate with the Holy Ghost, the Americanists argued that now the soul would be best disposed if it received the widest development of its natural active virtues. This, the writer said, was new and false. This doctrine was not modern but what was modern was the opposition now discovered between the monarchic and the democratic world. In the old order the Americanist claimed the passive virtues were necessary for the submission to order, but now the Holy Spirit must act, as it were, democratically inspiring each one. The writer said that one must distinguish between the individual and private life and the social life. The action of the Holy Ghost on the individual is not new but is found in the lives of all the saints. But eternally the Holy Ghost, at the command of Christ, calls for obedience to proper authority. That condition has not changed. Only the Protestants held that there was individual private guidance in this sphere.

As to democracy, one can hold that it is the best form of political life without any contradiction from his faith, but in religion he must hold that the constitution of the Church is never democratic either in its form or in its exercise. Here the author found Americans in error when, enamored with the love of democracy in government, they want to bring this idea into the Church and have the Holy Ghost work democratically among the faithful, to enlarge the individual autonomy, and to add the sanctifying action of the Holy Ghost to the greatest possible happiness here below. They are seduced by an ideal that is unattainable. Americans have fallen into this, which is the old condemned liberalism, by an ignorance of theological language.

In conclusion the author pointed out that this is the old conflict between liberty and authority. Not all liberty is equally acceptable to God, there are limitations by law. So also the limits of social life are willed by God. To refuse obedience to these laws would be to suffer shipwreck and failure to attain one's purpose in life. This is not to destroy independence, because the purpose of law is to preserve the proper independence of the individual to attain his goal. The author admitted the human love of liberty and foresaw that within the limits there must be a growth of liberty. Perhaps this will come about by the spread of a republican political regime. But the Church will not change in any way its monarchic constitution. If the new freedom means anything else it will lead to the fatal subjection of man to the animal. If Americanism held to this essential idea that the Church has nothing to fear from liberty, in so far as this liberty will be Christian it will bring the largest measure of individual liberty possible. The rest was to be condemned, said the author. More than ever there must be the practice of passive virtues, of the internal virtues of love and faith. The Americanists have endeavored to make their message more audible to those outside the Church and to the ultra-liberals, but they will find that opposed to any new dogma stand the entire doctrines of the Church which have passed through the centuries. Maignen when he read this article attacked it in *La Vérité*[59] as too friendly to democracy.

In the meantime while these articles appeared in newspapers

[59] *La Vérité*, October 22 and 31, 1898.

and magazines throughout France the ex-Abbé Victor Charbonnel also contributed an article on the controversy in the *Revue
Chrétienne* of October 1. In this he made Hecker out to be a
Methodist who was introducing a neo-Protestantism into the
Church, and said that nothing was more contrary to Catholicism
than Americanism. He claimed that this doctrine was brought
into the Church by Hecker and that his leaving the Church followed logically from his Americanism. He listed by names the
members of the Americanists in France and the United States
and their chief opponents.[60] In the Americanist camp he listed
Gibbons, Ireland, Elliott and all the Paulists, Keane and O'Connell in Rome, Conaty, Hogan, and Corrigan by his imprimatur; in France Félix Klein, Abbé Naudet of *La Justice Sociale*,
L'Abbé Lemire, deputé du Nord, M. Captier, Superior of St.
Sulpice, Abbé Quiévreux, Abbé Dufresne of Geneva, M. Gondal
of St. Sulpice, M. Georges Fonsegrive of *La Quinzaine*, M.
Georges Goyau, M. Comte de Chabrol, M. Vicomte de Meaux,
and the writers on the *Correspondant*, *La Quinzaine*, *La Revue du
Clergé Français* and *L'Univers*. As anti-Americanists he listed
the Jesuits, the anonymous writers of *La Vérité* and *La Croix*,
Études religieuses, *Voce della Verità*, *Courrier de Bruxelles*, Abbé
Périès (Saint Clement) and Charles Maignen (Martel).

Whether the action of the pope in taking the problem to himself had any immediate effect is not clear, but there does seem to
have been a cessation of official or quasi-official action in the controversy after the beginning of October, 1898. This was not true
among the lesser controversialists. Not knowing exactly what to
do, Klein restrained himself from taking any action. Some had
suggested that he withdraw the preface. Count de Chabrol[61] felt
that the only possible move would be to get an imprimatur in
Rome for the *Life*. He thought that Archbishop Ireland, being
needed in Rome, would be able to get this for them. There was no
deep theological controversy over this essay in the United States,

---

[60] Victor Charbonnel, "L'Américanisme, les Dangers d'un Néo-Protestant-
isme dans l'église Catholique," *Revue Chrétienne*, (Paris) 3rd series, VIII, 241-68.
This list is given on pages 254-5.

[61] Chabrol to Klein, September 24, 1898, Klein papers in the Archives of the
University of Notre Dame.

although the *Northwestern Chronicle*, the *Western Watchman* and the like kept up a running controversy over liberalism in minor matters with the *Review* and certain German Catholic papers; and in the meantime the Roman correspondents of the various Catholic papers tried to keep their readers informed on the progress of the Roman controversy. It was clear now that the center of the controversy was in Rome and that everything now depended upon the action to be taken by the Pope or those about him. It was rumored that the life of Hecker had been submitted to the Index and had been condemned, but the decree was not to be published because of a protest by Cardinal Gibbons. Nevertheless Father Brandi wrote to Archbishop Corrigan on October 12,[62] that Americanism would soon receive a blow in the shape of a pontifical document to the bishops of the United States. Gibbons himself received a notice of an impending letter from Cardinal Rampolla in answer to his protest on the imprimatur.[63]

The maze of newspaper and magazine discussions of the controversy that persisted after the Holy Father had taken over the study of the question is very difficult to classify.[64] The most important fact in all the available printed materials is the absence of any further defense of Americanism or the ideas of Hecker by the main exponents of Americanism. Klein and O'Connell were not well, nor did they seem to see any way to answer the flood of criticisms that were being heaped on them. Keane did not return to Rome until November. Ireland was busy in America. Neither Keane nor Ireland seemed aware of the possibility of condemnation at this time. On the fringe of the debate were the articles of Delassus in the *Semaine Religieuse de Cambrai* during September and October. Taking for granted the existence of a plot of the Jews to destroy the Church, he found in the accusations of liberalizing and minimizing made against the Americanists by Maignen

---

[62] Brandi to Corrigan, October 12, 1898 in the New York Archdiocesan Archives.

[63] Rampolla to Gibbons, September 23, 1898, in the Baltimore Archdiocesan Archives.

[64] The clippings saved by Abbé Klein are very numerous and represent many shades of opinion. They are saved for the most part in the Klein papers in the Archives of the University of Notre Dame and in the Paulist Fathers Archives.

and Périès a further plot by which Catholicism would be watered down and betrayed to the plotters. In such a scheme, the Congress of Religions, the actions of Bishop Scanlan at the monument of Brigham Young, and the attempt of Abbé Charbonnel to hold another Congress of Religions were related with copious quotations from other sources to show the existence of this secret conspiracy against the Church. The charges of Maignen were merely presumed in these articles and fitted into his charge of a conspiracy of the Jews and the Freemasons to overthrow the Church. Only the extreme followers of *La Vérité* seemed to give any credence to these writings which were published in book form after the papal letter of the following January.[65]

On October 11, a dispatch from Rome to the Paris newspapers announced that the Pope had taken over the question himself to stop the bitter discussion. However, the sniping continued. In *La Vérité* of October 16, Maignen showed that the apostate Charbonnel was, as he himself had maintained, an Americanist. Articles on the controversy continued to appear throughout Europe, and speculations were rife about the decision of Rome. On October 29, *La Vérité* quoted the *Osservatore Cattolico* of Milan to the effect that the life of Hecker had been condemned by the Sacred Congregation of the Index but that the announcement of the condemnation had been delayed. The next day *La Vérité* announced Satolli was among the members of the papal commission which had been appointed to examine the question. Further, on October 3, Maignen listed the chief articles against the Americanists and pointed out that answering articles defending them, except those of Coppinger and Bricout which he disregarded, had not appeared. He made fun of their silence.

On November 1, although proofs of the article were available to some editors before, Ferdinand Brunetière published an article in the *Revue des Deux Mondes* entitled "Le Catholicisme aux États-Unis." Since Brunetière had announced the bankruptcy of science and had visited the Holy Father, his article

[65] M. L'Abbé Henri Delassus, *L'Américanisme et la conjuration anti-chrétienne* (Lille, 1899). Not the least interesting part of this strange book are the appendices and explanations.

in such an important journal signalized strong support for the Americanists. The major part of the controversy was already over and it is doubtful if the article had any great importance in Rome, but in the popular press and in the press controversy it aroused much resentment among the opponents of Americanism, and was attacked in French-Canadian and German-American papers. Brunetière based his article on what he had learned in a visit to the United States. The first part of the article outlined the growth of the Church in the United States, showing that in this growth the Church had overcome not only opposition but even persecution. Further, in the acceptance of the dogmas of the Immaculate Conception and Papal Infallibility, the Church had to insist on two dogmas very much opposed by American Protestantism. Discussing the insistence on individualism in the American Church, Brunetière pointed out that this must be understood in the sense in which it was used in America, and that these and some other terms had a different meaning in the United States than they had in Europe. In the acceptance of Infallibility as pointed out by Father Hecker, the dogmas of the Church were not subject to further controversy and, in case of doubt, appeal could be made to the infallible pontiff, just as in the United States appeals were made to the Supreme Court for an interpretation of the Constitution. Here again the American insistence on individual action must be understood. The individual action must be in conformity with the external authority of the Church, because the internal inspiration would come from the Holy Ghost who was likewise the guide of the external Church.

Brunetière pointed out that the Europeans were mistaken in holding that the United States was not a nation. Thus, the actions of Ireland and Keane in opposing the petition of Abbelen and in opposing Cahenslyism were in his opinion justified. Further, he agreed with Ireland and Keane that the age was not evil or Voltairean or anti-Christian. He did admit that for America which was new, the proper motto is "onward," although this is not necessarily that of the old world. In discussing Cardinal Gibbons' activity regarding the Knights of Labor he found something good in the fact that Catholics in the new world were of the lower classes.

Brunetière admitted that activities could take place in America that would not be proper in Europe—listing among these the activities at the Chicago Congress of Religions—but he pointed out that the American bishops did not place the Catholic doctrines before the meeting for discussion but merely gave information about the Church's teaching. He praised Archbishop Ireland's speeches and insisted that Catholicism had nothing to fear from liberty or liberty from the Church. Catholics in America belong to no party. He listed the growth of the Church in immigration as well as from converts. Explaining this growth he claimed that Americans were drawn to the Church first by the unity of the Church as compared to the divisions among Protestants, also by the security of the Church's doctrines on marriage in preserving the family, and finally by the attractiveness of the Church and its doctrines to human nature in a condition of freedom. He concluded his article by calling the growth of the Church in the United States something of great importance to France, showing what could be accomplished in France in a democracy.

One could say that Brunetière and Delassus represented two extremes of the controversy. At the same time on the Americanist side in France were the Abbés Democrates, and their periodicals *La Vie Catholique* and *La Justice Sociale*. *L'Univers et le Monde* also supported Klein. In *La Vérité*, Maignen continued to gather what support he could from *L'Éclair* and *La Croix*, and from other publications. In England the Catholic papers generally supported the Americanists and insisted that European customs should not be fastened on American Catholicism. In America, Preuss in the *Review* became the chief organ of those who were opposed to Ireland and the Americanists. In the November 3, 1898 issue an article by Tilley described the "elements" of Americanism as, 1, "hyperpatriotism," 2, "Americanizing" foreign groups, and 3, "inordinate desire to please Protestants." Opposing the *Review* were the *Western Watchman*, the *Northwestern Chronicle* and the *Freeman's Journal*. All the American papers having a Roman correspondent carried brief notes on the struggle. Thus Croke in the *Philadelphia Standard* announced the members of the papal commission, and the impending encyclical. St. Kilian More in the

Freeman's Journal indicated that the controversies among the Roman newspapers were really harmful to the cause of American Catholicism because even the friends of the Americanists were misinformed. Such was the article of November 19, in the *Roman World*, entitled "Studies in Americanism" by J.E.H. The author of this article called himself an American Catholic layman, but wrote like a Protestant attacking Roman ecclesiastics and religious orders as well as Maignen. *L'Italie* on the other hand, while praising Brunetière's article, hoped that the Pope would separate the true from the false in these accounts of American Catholicism. *Le Figaro* of Paris claimed that Brunetière had closed the controversy by showing the silliness of the charges against Americanists. *L'Univers et le Monde* in articles by Lucens pointed out that Brunetière had proved that the Americanists were misunderstood. The Americanists did not want to change the Church. The American tool of expansion was liberty and its own relations between Church and State, and this situation could not be transferred to France. The liberty of the Church in the United States was not a philosophy but a fact which could not be transported overseas. *Le Patriot de Bruxelles* praised Gibbons' *Ambassador of Christ* and suggested that Catholicism was the remedy for American defects. It further said that the Americans were not deceived by the danger of trying to naturalize the supernatural. In answer *La Vérité* quoted the articles of Preuss in the *Review* which attacked the *Ave Maria* for supporting Benziger's refusal to handle Maignen's book. Preuss indicated that the book was doing a service by pointing out a danger to the Church in the United States.

On December 3, 1898, the New York *Freeman's Journal* published an interview of an unnamed ecclesiastic in Rome by St. Kilian More, the regular correspondent. The statement seemed to be an impartial summary of the controversy at that time. He indicated that the press controversy had been quite bitter. The word Americanism he felt was unfortunate since there had been many kinds of isms discussed, and many who were using the word Americanism knew little or nothing about the United States. His informant insisted that there were at least four kinds of Americanism. The first was Italian which he said was merely Italian liberalism "decked out in the Stars and Stripes." The proponents were the Italian liberal press, *Populo Romano, Italie, Opinione* and *Fanfulla,* and its chief tenets were opposition to the temporal power of the Pope, opposition to religious orders, and opposition to the union of Church and State. They claimed as adherents, Cardinal Gibbons and Archbishop Ireland. Their opponents were chiefly *Osservatore, Voce della Verità,* and *Vera Roma,* although these papers seldom mentioned Americanism as such. This type of Americanism had existed only a few months. Even younger was German Americanism or Reform Catholicism which was intent on reforming the Church and had attacked the inspiration of the Sacred Scriptures. More did not mention Joseph Müller, Hermann Schell or Franz X. Kraus, although these were the names connected with a German movement which had at best only accidental connections with the Americanist movement. Speaking of the French Americanism, More noted that this was better known in the United States, and it involved the effort of a Catholic country like France to imitate the practices that American Catholics had worked out in Protestant United States. This French Americanism, the interviewer said, represented an attempt to explain the progress of the Church in the United States by these practices. He did not believe these practices had anything to do with either the gains or losses of the Church in the United States. He likewise made light of the "Americanism" as defined by Monsignor O'Connell, as simply a statement of loyalty to the American government which had nothing to do with the French Americanism. He claimed that the recent published letter of O'Connell to Lepidi proved that O'Connell was not interested in the religious French "Americanism." As to American "Americanism" the ecclesiastic interviewed admitted that in the United States some things had happened in an effort not to offend Protestants but they were not approved by Church authorities. In all these matters, especially that concerning the relations between Church and State, the Pope had admitted that the American condition could be tolerated but had insisted that such was not the ideal state. The one interviewed indicated that the Pope probably, if he gave out any statement on the question at all, would not discuss any one of these four forms of Americanism in the forthcoming document but the general principles that govern the situation.

On December 17, in the *Freeman's Journal*, St. Kilian More announced in a letter dated Rome, December 3, that amidst all the newspaper controversy on Americanism a papal document had been prepared, that originally it was to have been an encyclical but that now it had been changed to a letter of the Pope to Cardinal Gibbons. "It strongly recommends moderation in controversial methods, and it touches upon a number of points of dogma and discipline which were in danger of misconstruction." He claimed that it would deal a heavy blow to false Americanisms everywhere.

In the United States the Catholic papers followed at a distance the news from Rome with *The Review* unrelentingly following the line of *La Vérité*. The conservative *Church Progress* of Saint Louis announced on December 17, that liberalism—alias Americanism—was about to be put into a "cul de sac," and on December 28, Father Meifuss stated in *The Review* that Americanism was losing the controversy. The *Freeman's Journal* quoted on December 31, from the New York *Herald* of December 28, that Archbishop Corrigan had denied through his secretary, Father Connolly, that he had sent a congratulatory letter to Father Lepidi. However, the Archbishop added that Lepidi had given a second imprimatur without reprimand. On the same day *Church Progress* contained an editorial in which the editor, Condé B. Pallen, distinguished between Heckerism which was the theological liberalism and Americanism which he said was social and political.

> The controversy in regard to "The Life of Father Hecker" written by Father Elliott and Dr. Maignen's criticism thereof in his book entitled "Is Father Hecker a Saint?" has to do with questions of theology and doctrine. Americanism, that is to say what is politically and socially understood by that term in this country, has no more to do with the subject than the question of the rotundity of the earth. It is a confusion and misleading to speak of the dispute as a controversy between Americanism and something not American. . . .

The same paper on January 28, 1899, insisted that "Heckerism" was not "Americanism." On February 4, there appeared in Rome,

the *True American Catholic*, written in Italianized English with
the aim of protecting the real Americanism from the Jews and
Masons and international Protestants. It also attacked Archbishop
Ireland. It was repudiated by all Americans. The news of the im-
minent papal letter was now generally known and the stage was
set for its reception.

CHAPTER 5 ❦ *The Condemnation*

UNFORTUNATELY, the more the story of Americanism turned to Rome, the less available are the documents which will permit us to relate the full story, partly because the Roman discussion between officials was oral and partly because some of the documents are still secret. In the United States with the exception chiefly of *The Review*, the Catholic newspapers settled down to watch the events at Rome. The ordinary American Catholic layman was almost unaware of the bitter controversy that was filling the Catholic press in Europe.

Indeed the feelings of the American Catholics about the controversy are well pictured in a letter of Father Elliott to Abbé Klein on October 20, 1898.

> As to our going into print to show soundness of views in reference to obedience, or anything else, what is the good of it? It is good, I doubt not for you and your friends to do so in France. You know your ground. But in America not a soul has ever questioned our soundness as Catholics in any respect. America is absolutely mute in the whole controversy, with the exception of *The Review*, edited by Arthur Preuss of Saint Louis, Mo. That is a small paper, with a very limited subscription, mostly among German priests. *The Review* has taken sides against F. Hecker. Now, we are glad that the Jesuits of America have been silent, especially they, though we are pleased though not surprised that almost the entire Catholic press here—all with the exception of *The Review* are favorable. Perhaps some German Catholic papers may have talked against us, though I have not heard of any. Well so long as the anti-Heckerists in Europe find no echo in America, Hecker's own country, it is a standing argument in our favor of the highest value in Rome. Well in case we undertook action in the press we could not help adverting directly or indirectly to the Jesuits in Europe who are against us. And then would come a mandamus from the Father General of the American Jesuits to open fire. The American Jesuits are very strong. They are fine men, full of peace and good will. Their leading men are among our warmest friends. They have about 30 colleges in the States, and no less than 1,000 priests, nearly all Americans. God guide them in the ways of peace. We must keep

them silent in this controversy. If we do so first and last, Rome will hesitate before striking Hecker.[1]

In Germany the controversy was signaled by a series of articles in the *Stimmen aus Maria-Laach* by Father Otto Pfülf,[2] but while these articles summarized the biography and the controversy, they gave no strong opinion on Americanism or Heckerism other than to indicate that Hecker had been praised inordinately. In France after the editors of *L'Univers et Le Monde* had refused to print a reply of Maignen to their article of June 24,[3] he went into the courts and eventually obtained a legal order demanding that they print his reply. As the controversy became bitter a bulletin to *L'Univers* from Rome dated October 11[4] stated that Cardinal Rampolla had announced the Pope had asked the cessation of the controversy and had taken the problem to himself. The Roman correspondents of the American newspapers, however, told nearly every week of the progress of the controversy and the latest rumors of papal action. But the official decision of the commission appointed by the Pope or any written documents describing the actions of Cardinal Rampolla, if they exist, are not yet available.

One thing seems fairly clear now. Archbishop Ireland had been kept away from Rome by the reply of Rampolla, Keane had gone to the United States to collect money for the University, O'Connell after his interviews with Lepidi had retired to Switzerland for a vacation. The publication of portions of O'Connell's letters to Lepidi in *La Vérité*, with the implication that he had repudiated the doctrines of "religious Americanism," was resented by O'Connell, but he apparently felt that he had no way of securing redress. He insisted that he had intended merely to repudiate the charge of religious Americanism which he said was held neither by the American bishops nor by Hecker.

To Elliott he wrote on August 22, 1898, another long explana-

[1] Walter Elliott to Abbé Félix Klein, October 20, 1898, in Paulist Fathers Archives, New York.
[2] *Stimmen aus Maria-Laach*, XXXX, LIV (1898), 388-406, 469-86.
[3] Maignen wanted *L'Univers et le Monde* to print his reply to their article of June 24, 1898. They refused, Maignen sued and the case was decided in his favor. Cf. *Gazette de France*, Dec. 2, 1898 and *Le Vérité*, Dec. 2, 1898.
[4] *L'Univers et le Monde*, Oct. 12, 1898.

tion of the notes he gave Lepidi. He claimed that he meant merely
to reject the travesties which were being called "Americanism"
and "Heckerism" by their enemies. Then he added:

> Imagine my surprise on receiving a copy of the *Vérité* the other
> day to find there that Maignen without my knowledge or consent had
> published the "substance" of all my different notes taking out pieces
> here and there and leaving out everything that could put them in their
> true light as a protest against himself and his hand. I imagined I was
> drawing up an official note for the Vatican official to appear in the
> "Osservatore Romano" or the "Voce," and never dreamed I was being
> fooled to furnish an appendix for the man I was protesting against. I
> don't call that "fides punica." These men are not honest, and it is an
> illusion to treat them so.
> Anyhow great good can come out of the evil. The distinction is
> now made between the true & false Americanism; the true & the false
> teachings of Father Hecker. False Americanism is the intention of
> making a new religion in the Church, new dogmas, & c. and that natur-
> ally we all despise and oppose. The rest is true Americanism. The sub-
> jectivism supplanting the Church to which Maignen gave the name
> Heckerism is false and repugnant to everything that Father Hecker
> and his followers ever held. It is a calumny upon him and upon us.
> That excluded, the true teaching of Father Hecker is simply Catholi-
> cism. This distinction was always in my mind and this purpose, viz. to
> reject heartedly the travesties of our adversaries and protest against
> their attempt to attach them to us. That done, the ground is taken
> from under their feet.[5]

Ireland and Gibbons had both protested by letter. The Gibbons
protest was sufficient, it seemed, to nullify the decision of the Sacred Congregation of the Index to place the life of Hecker on the
Index of Prohibited Books. Rampolla in answering Gibbons' protest had even felt obliged to assure Gibbons that the imprimatur
did not really give approval to the Maignen book. In the same letter of September 23, Cardinal Rampolla assured Gibbons that the
Holy Father would soon write him on the controversy. From that
time on the speculation increased about the nature of the papal
statement that could be expected.

In the meantime other Americans were actually faring badly
in Rome. When O'Connell returned to Rome one of the first
problems he met was the prohibition of the book *Evolution and
Dogma* by his friend, Father John A. Zahm, C.S.C., newly ap-

[5] O'Connell to Elliott, August 22, 1898, in the Paulist Fathers Archives.

pointed American Provincial Superior of the Congregation of
Holy Cross. The Sacred Congregation of the Index had decided
on September 10,[6] that the book should be prohibited in all languages. The proviso that the Superior General of the Congrega-
ãon of Holy Cross should be consulted before the publication of
the decree allowed room for an appeal. Father Gilbert Français,
the Superior General, immediately went to Rome and sought the
aid of Monsignor O'Connell. Zahm prepared to submit, but was
prevented by his friends who maintained that his public submission or the publication of the decree would be a blow to the
Church in the United States. O'Connell succeeded in getting Cardinal Serafino Vannutelli[7] to go personally to the Pope and ask
for the suppression of the decree. To this the Pope agreed, although a subsequent warning from officials of the Sacred Congregation forced the withdrawal of the translations of the book
which were still being sold. The book of Father George Zurcher
of Buffalo, *Monks and Their Decline*, was placed on the Index on
September 1, 1898. The life of Hecker seems to have been recommended to be placed on the Index by the Sacred Congregation but
the decree was suppressed by the Pope when he received the letter of protest of Cardinal Gibbons. O'Connell was not well and
did not remain much in Rome during these first critical months
of the fall of 1898. His information about the trend seems to have
come from Keane who in turn obtained it from the Vannutellis.

When Keane returned from the United States to Rome in the
first week of November he went first to see Cardinal Rampolla.[8]
Rampolla acknowledged receiving the letter of Cardinal Gibbons
and indicated that the whole problem was in the hands of the
Holy Father. Rampolla spoke of a special commission appointed
by the Holy Father to discuss the question. Whether this is the
commission reported earlier in letters from Rome or not is not

[6] Letter to Father Gilbert Français, Superior General, C.S.C., from Father
John A. Zahm, C.S.C., September 16, 1898, containing a copy of the Roman
letter reporting the action of the Sacred Congregation, dated September 10, 1898.

[7] O'Connell to Zahm, November 7, 1898 and Archbishop Keane to Zahm,
Nov. 9, 1898, in the Archives of the Provincial of the Priests of Holy Cross,
South Bend, Indiana.

[8] Keane to Gibbons, November 9, 1898 in the Cathedral Archives, Baltimore.

clear. The membership seems about the same. Keane then learned from Cardinal Serafino Vannutelli that the Holy Father had admitted to him that some persons had been urging him to be severe with the Americans, but that he thought more good could be obtained by gentle means. Then the Pope told the Cardinal the points of the encyclical which he was preparing: chiefly on the relations between Church and State—the American situation being all right for the United States but not to be copied indiscriminately in Europe; secondly on the question of individualism and the need of a spiritual director; and thirdly on the proper attitude towards the vows—that the vows were not a sign of weakness but an act of heroism. In general, the encyclical was to show that, while these American practices might be acceptable in certain circumstances, they are not to be represented as ideal. Later rumors were spread that even this mild form of rebuke to the Americanists was to be suppressed.

The *Journal de Genève* of October 23, compared the current controversy to that between Veuillot and Dupanloup, although it said the talents of the present contenders were not the equal of the former controversialists. The Catholicism of Dupanloup was not dead but had emigrated to the United States. The Chicago Congress was its great manifestation and its return to France was "Américanisme," preached by Archbishop Ireland. Its three characteristics were that it was "*moderne, démocratique et individualiste,*" fully under the direction of the papacy. This Americanism was, it continued, friendly to science, to the age, and to the country. However the counter-attack by Maignen would win out and the Americanists would give in or get out of the Church.[9]

Conservative papers in the meantime brought out rumors that a severe condemnation of Americanism was being prepared.[10] Some had heard that the original decree which the commission had

[9] *La Journal de Genéve*, October 23, 1898, in the Klein clippings, University of Notre Dame Archives.

[10] *The Review*, Nov. 17, quoted the *Osservatore Cattolico* of Milan, that the biography had been condemned by the Congregation of the Index but that the decree had been held up. There was indication that a condemnation would soon be forthcoming.

prepared was very severe but that the Pope had taken the matter under advisement and was to soften the measure.

Ireland in the meantime had felt some reassurance when Cardinal Rampolla acknowledged his letter and assured him that there was no necessity for him to go to Rome. He did object to the English translation of Maignen's book with its new imprimatur and the letter of praise for it from Satolli.[11] When the archbishops held their annual meeting in Washington on October 12, he did not attend but remained in Chicago to give a speech.[12] Both he and Keane had hoped that the archbishops would prepare a stern protest against the Maignen book. For this purpose Father George Deshon, C.S.P., the Superior General of the Paulists, had prepared a rather strong statement in defense of the community and Father Hecker, and gave it to Archbishop Corrigan to present to the assembled archbishops.

The Paulist defense read as follows:

October, 1898

To the Archbishops Assembled in Annual Meeting:

Your Graces:

It is known to you that under the title "Études sur l'Américanisme. Le Père Hecker, Est-il Un Saint" there has been published a book in both French and English by the Rev. Charles Maignen, in which some of the Archbishops of the American hierarchy by name have been attacked and Father Hecker and the Paulist Community in particular have been assailed and charged with teaching opinions that are, if not contra fidem, at least in opposition to the spirit and teachings of the best theologians of the Church.

It might not be the part of wisdom to notice these accusations just now, except for the fact that many of the learned and devoted Prelates of the Church in Europe have been impressed by these accusations.

The Life of Father Hecker, around which the controversy particularly rages, was published ten years ago, carefully scrutinized by Very Rev. A. F. Hewit as Censor Deputatus, and published under the Imprimatur of the Most Rev. Archbishop of New York. During these ten years while the book has been extensively circulated both in this country and in England, not a word of accusation was made against it; and only since its translation into French has any difficulty arisen. It was written in English for English readers, and expresses an adapta-

---

[11] Rampolla to Ireland, August 6, 1898, quoted in Soderini's manuscript (see n. 27, ch. II). Also Ireland to Rampolla, Aug. 29, 1898, quoted by Soderini.

[12] Ireland to O'Connell, Oct. 27, 1898, Richmond Diocesan Archives. He also told O'Connell that he intended to come to Rome.

tion of the conservative truths of Holy Church to the new political and social conditions especially in America. The French translation was published somewhat over a year ago with some omissions and inaccuracies. Appearing at a time when a bitter controversy raged among Catholics in France, mainly inspired by political antagonisms, this translation has been attacked and defended by the parties to that controversy with incredible violence. Abbé Maignen's book is the bitterest and most prominent of the assailants. His calumnies against American Prelates and American Catholics generally, can be considered by you without suggestion from us.

But we are in duty bound to protest emphatically against his attacks on the Paulists, which are utterly untruthful, and, seemingly, malicious.

It may be said in all truth that the Paulists are known to their Archbishop as men who are faithful in duty, submissive to discipline, obedient to ecclesiastical authority and zealous in the prosecution of apostolic labors.

The accusations of heterodoxy against Father Hecker may be gathered under three heads. The first concerns the devotion to the Holy Spirit. In this matter we beg to submit that Father Hecker's teachings are identical with the teachings of the Fathers and theologians of the Church as well as the doctors of mystical theology. An explicit statement of his spiritual doctrine on this point may be found in Chap. XXVII of his Life.

Second, as to spiritual direction. It is a mistake to say that Father Hecker was opposed to all spiritual direction. He firmly believed in the necessity of direction, and in practice himself always consulted men of experience and piety.

Third, as to the question of vows, the teachings of Father Hecker are in accord with the teachings of St. Philip Neri, Père Lallemant, S.J., and other respected authorities on this subject. As is stated by Father Elliott in the Life, p. 299 "It never entered into the minds of the Fathers to question the doctrine and practice of the Church concerning vows." Father Hecker's test of a true Paulist was that he should be fit and ready to take the solemn vows at any moment.

The separation of the Paulists from the Redemptorists is also made a peg on which are hung many misstatements of facts, perverse views of the difficulty which led to the separation, and baseless recriminations which serve only to wound charity and set against each other zealous missionary priests. A relationship of extreme cordiality and warm mutual friendship exists between the Paulists and the Redemptorists of this country.

Abbé Maignen's book is calculated to breed discord and strife. Moreover the public reopening of this question, long since thoroughly investigated and finally settled by the Holy See itself, is a constructive insult to the decisions of Rome.

In regard to certain dangerous movements among the French clergy resulting in some apostasies, and other evil signs of the times which Abbé Maignen attributes to views like Father Hecker's, no one, as is well known to you, could be more sensitive to evil-bearing movements, more vigilant in guarding the treasures of truth, or more courageous in antagonising enemies of the Church than Father Hecker himself and his community. Abbé Maignen seems to have conjured up an evil spectre of his own imagination which he calls "Americanism," and to the pernicious influence of this baneful spirit he attributes some notorious apostasies which have recently happened in France. While we are not without some evils to lament in this country, still it is well known that there is no portion of the Universal Church where the faith is so strong and where its expansion is so remarkable and where it bears such fruit in devout and practical Catholics as in these United States. Father Hecker and the Paulists have always been welcome and at home among all classes of Catholics in this country. The Catholics of America can truthfully affirm that their devotion to the Holy See is as strong, and their love for the Holy Father as warm and as earnest as that which may be found in any other part of the Lord's Vineyard.

Another alleged fault of "Americanism" is that individuality is extolled by Father Hecker, and that religious humility and obedience are thereby injured. With a little honesty, not to mention charity, it would be impossible to form such an opinion. Father Hecker was a man of high mental gifts and of great activity, completely occupied in promoting the glory of God, but he was entirely humble. He thought the individual should use all his mental endowments for God's glory, and that superiors and subjects, clergy and laity should be active, and make the most of their talents and opportunities. He saw no opposition between individuality and obedience. Abbé Maignen does his best to pander to the idea that prevails in many in Europe that Americans are all inclined to be rebels, and he interprets individuality as nothing better than rebellion against lawful authority.

In view of the foregoing statements it is earnestly hoped that some action will be taken in reference to this book. Such a bitter and calumnious attack on American Catholics deserves to be officially resented and the eminent Prelates and persons of Europe who already half believe that there is some truth in Abbé Maignen's affirmations should be disabused of any such delusions.

In order to avoid strife the Paulists have hitherto abstained from taking any notice of this book.

For the Paulist Fathers.
(SIGNED): George Deshon
Sup'r. [13]
ARCHBISHOP'S HOUSE
452 Madison Avenue.
New York, Oct. 14th, 1898.

[13] From the Paulist Fathers Archives. Attached to the copy is the following letter of Archbishop Corrigan and a note by Father Walter Elliott.
Very Rev. Dear Sir:
I return to you the document you entrusted to my charge. It was presented at the meeting of the Archbishops, but as the Cardinal had a very satisfactory

However, Corrigan did not press the matter since Rampolla's letter to Gibbons had promised a papal letter on the matter, and Ireland being absent no one really suggested that a strong statement be issued. As a result no action was taken.

Writing to Father Elliott on November 6, Ireland said:

> It was not possible for me to be at the meeting of the Archbishops. I regretted very much that I was not to be there—as I was anxious to break a lance against all comers in defense of Heckerism. You no doubt have heard how your cause was treated at the meeting. The Archbishop of New York timidly & as acting under protest, offered a paper from the Paulists—& added at once his own opinion, which was that the hierarchy of America should lie low in this war. No voice bellowed out in the name of justice—& all was over. . . .

He added as a postscript "Tell Mr. Chabrol that I have not been & am not idle: that I have spoken to the Vatican in warlike tones—that I am going to the Vatican."[14]

In the meantime Ireland had decided that he must go to Rome and see what could be done. He hoped to be there by Christmas but being delayed he finally sailed on January 12.

The Klein correspondence during the last months of 1898 show

letter from the Cardinal Secretary of State, and is expecting one from the Holy Father in the premises, it was thought best not to act on the matter.

I am,
Very faithfully yours,
M. A. Corrigan, Abp.

Very Rev. G. Deshon, C.S.P.

(The following note, written with pen and ink by Father Elliott is at the bottom of the above letter.)

The Archp. presented our memorial. As soon as he had read it to the Archps. he immediately moved that inasmuch as the Cardinal had received a "very satisfactory letter," as above, the Am. Archps. had no need to interfere. And so it was agreed to do nothing. Archp. Ireland was not present at the meeting. Card'l Gibbons read Card'l Rampolla's letter to me sometime before this meeting, or after it, I forget which. It was so framed as to allay forebodings, yet said nothing really reassuring. All this time Archp. Corrigan had been working by letters of his agents in Rome in favor of Maignen's book, and knew far better than Card'l Gibbons, (or perhaps even Card. Rampolla) or any of our friends, the real purposes of the Holy See—to wait an opportune moment to strike a blow at us.

(signed) W. Elliott.

[14] Ireland to Elliott, Nov. 6, 1898, in the Paulist Fathers Archives.

that Klein and his friends were aware that they were in danger of an adverse Roman decision but yet they seemed to think that some action might save them. Klein himself offered if necessary to withdraw his preface, although he indicated to Ireland and O'Connell that this did not mean that he had changed his ideas. His friend, Count de Chabrol, felt that the only answer was to get a Roman imprimatur on the French translation.[15] This he felt Archbishop Ireland could obtain because of his position in Rome, since his aid was needed in connection with the negotiations about the Philippines and Cuba. Father Dufresne[16] had become anxious not to involve his community, the Society of the Priests of Saint Francis de Sales, in any condemnation. On November 3, he suggested to Klein that Klein publish a letter in *L'Univers* in which Klein would deny that he held the ideas on Hecker attributed to him in Maignen's publications and would speak of the necessity of humility and obedience and of the necessity of grace. Klein, he suggested, should also explain the references to Anglo-Saxons and to individualism. Father Elliott should make a similar statement. Chabrol on November 26[17] wrote to Klein that he had heard from Rome that the Pope would write a friendly letter but advised caution in any expression of satisfaction if such should take place.

When O'Connell finally returned to Rome he wrote to his friend Klein[18] that while they had been in the greatest danger at one time, the danger was now passed and victory was near, and that their enemies were wild and were watching for some acts of imprudence on their part to destroy them. He advised Klein to keep silent. Father David Fleming, the English Franciscan who had been friendly at times with the American group, wrote on November 16[19] to Klein advocating the suppression of Klein's

[15] Chabrol to Klein, Oct. 17, 1898. In the Klein papers, University of Notre Dame Archives.

[16] Dufresne to Klein, Nov. 3, 1898 and Nov. 16, 1898, in the Klein papers in the University of Notre Dame Archives.

[17] Chabrol to Klein, Nov. 26, 1898, in the Klein papers, University of Notre Dame Archives.

[18] O'Connell to Klein, Oct. 31, 1898, in the Paulist Fathers Archives.

[19] Fleming to Klein, Nov. 16, 1898, in the Klein papers, University of Notre Dame Archives.

preface. He compared the attempt to introduce American ways into Europe to the attempt by Lamennais to introduce the ideas of Daniel O'Connell into France in the earlier period. Further, he maintained that even in America the Americanists had obtained only limited following. Keane, he did not consider a brilliant theologian.

Writing on December 1, O'Connell summed up the situation in Rome for Klein on information apparently obtained by Keane from the Cardinals Vannutelli.

> Here is the situation at the present moment,
> 1° There is to be no condemnation nor even examination either of Hecker's life, nor of your preface.
> 2° The treatment of the entire question will be reduced to the publication of an encyclical or letter to Cardinal Gibbons.
> 3° At the present moment, it is the intention to treat in that encyclical principally of three points, (a) The relations existing between Church & State in America are very good in America but they do not represent the type for the entire Church (b) We cannot wholly dispense with an external director since v.g. his agency is necessary for the Sacrament of Penance. (c) On vows, the doctrine of St. Thomas— a solemn vow, made to God is an act of dignity & heroism.
> It may not represent all we would wish, and it may not even appear necessary to publish an encyclical to make those things known; but on the other hand, how far it falls short of what the enemy desired & expected! In the 'stylo curiae' it gives the movement a certain "droit de cité" and canonical recognition. And it will ever be a movement onward and in the direction and never backward. . . . .[20]

Available sources do not make clear the story of the composition and publication of the papal letter. The account that seems most nearly true was published in the New York *Freeman's Journal*,[21] by the correspondent who signed his name as St. Kilian More. He claimed to know the whole story of the Roman action but to be bound to secrecy as to the details. The information of

[20] O'Connell to Klein, Dec. 1, 1898, Paulist Fathers Archives.
[21] Among the most important of these articles by St. Kilian More are those of November 26, Dec. 3, 10, 17, 24, 1898, and Feb. 4, 1899. The eccentric William Henry Thorne, whose *Globe* "a Quarterly Review of Literature, Society, Religion, Art, and Politics" was as erratic as its editor, devoted several of his "Globe Notes" to attacking the Paulists, Father Hecker, and to explaining the purpose of Archbishop Ireland's trips to Rome, but no one took Thorne seriously. Cf. *The Globe*, VIII (1898), 459-62, IX (1898), 104-9.

Keane and O'Connell seems to have come from Cardinal Serafino Vannutelli. Father Salvatore Brandi undoubtedly had his information from Cardinal Mazzella.[22] The available sources indicate that there was a definite decision to condemn the life of Hecker reached by the Sacred Congregation of the Index. At about this time the Pope received the strong protests of Cardinal Gibbons and Archbishop Ireland. O'Connell and Keane were apparently out of Rome at this time. The attitude of the Roman prelates generally was perhaps best expressed by O'Connell in his summary of the views of Father Lepidi in which Lepidi distinguished between political "Americanism" and "religious Americanism" and described the latter as a regular movement which was spreading in Europe. This "religious Americanism" threatened a schismatical and heretical movement, and subscribed to the doctrines summed up in the books of Maignen and Delattre, and in the answer to the article in *L'Opinione Liberale* published with the approval of Lepidi and written by a Cardinal or with the approval of one. Apparently the Holy Father decided that something must be done to stop the controversy which was manifest not only in France and Germany but even in Rome. He suppressed the decree of the Sacred Congregation of the Index and appointed a commission of Cardinals to study the matter. This action had taken place early in October if not before. One rumor said that the Pope had intended to write an encyclical on the subject and Rampolla had written to Cardinal Gibbons in October promising a papal letter on the matter. Later a story was told by Ireland[23] of a special document prepared by Cardinal Mazzella and Lepidi which formed the basis of the papal letter. No one had ever made available the original document submitted to the Pope, but the final letter sent to Cardinal Gibbons does not say that anyone held the condemned propositions, and definitely exempts American political opinions from disapproval. These omissions were to be the basis of a new controversy after the appearance of the document.

[22] Letters of Brandi to Archbishop Corrigan, Oct. 12, 1898. January 2, February 8, 1899, in the New York Archdiocesan Archives.

[23] Ireland to Father Deshon, February 24, 1899, in the Paulist Fathers Archives.

A very interesting summary of the situation in official Roman circles before the Christmas holy-days was supplied by Monsignor O'Connell to Father Elliott. Although he and Keane had interpreted the papal interference too optimistically, he was fairly well informed.

Paris, Dec. 10, 1898

My Dear Father Elliott:

I arrived here this morning and had not time to write you the news before leaving Rome. You may know by this time that during the vacation everything was prepared for the condemnation of Hecker, and the decree was placed before the H. Father on his table for his signature. Just at that time however a letter came from Cardinal Gibbons that "shook him." When they pressed him to sign he replied. "No, I can do no more against those Americans. Moreover, I reserve now the entire affair to myself and I permit no more examinations of book or anything else. I will arrange all myself with an encyclical." That encyclical at first conception was to have been composed on three points. 1. The relations existing in America between Church & State are very good there but they are not to be put forward as the model for other nations not to be elevated to the dignity of a principle. 2. As regards "individuality" and the dispensing with the services of a Director, he would have said that a director cannot be entirely dispensed with, as v.g. in the Sacrament of Penance. 3. As to vows the doctrine of St. Thomas "that vows are not an act of weakness but of heroism." [sic] That was the substance. Our enemies were angry not to have had more, tho some of us thought these three concessions were not necessary.

Now it appears, and appears certain that there will be no encyclical at all. It was in the mind of the Holy Father, in the last development to "do something pleasing to the Americans and say things they would like," and then he agreed himself what would Spain think of him if at this moment of her humiliation he were to pay compliments to her conqueror. So he decided not to publish the letter at all.

I think it is better. The situation is improving with every minute that passes. The charges heaped together by the Maignen combination are melting like clouds before the light of truth. "Americano religioso" is regarded as another Diana Vaughan and the other figment of "subjective Heckerism" has gone with it. This is the result of continued & courageous knocking from without. It seems the report of the Cardinals was favorable only very partially. The Cardinals on the Committee were: Pres. Ledochowski, Vannutelli vieux, Satolli, DiPietro & Ferrata. The strongest argument adduced in favor of the calumnies of Maignen were the congratulations sent by Abp. Corrigan on his publication, Pere Hecker est-il un Saint? but he desired that his congratulations be kept secret.

The tide has turned at last and is now running the other way.

These gentlemen here in Paris have invited me to come & confer with them on these and kindred matters for a few days.

In a letter now in the hands of Cardinal Rampolla, Brunetière wrote Abp. Keane, "any measure of severity, taken in Rome now against Hecker or Americanism, will be considered in France as an evidence of the consolidarity of Catholicism & Jesuitism." . . . And will render it extremely difficult for us to continue any longer the defense of the good cause.

Wilfrid Ward has just left Rome. He told Rampolla on the part of the Duke of Norfolk that severe measures against Hecker or Americanism in Rome would hurt Catholicity in England.

All the continent is now palpitating with these two ideas. The newest effort of the enemy to push it to [sic] assert that the whole movement is towards Protestantism and that we intend founding a paper in Paris to be called "The New Era" for the purpose of preparing a "Reformer's Catholicity" after the manner of Prof. Müller's last pamphlet, and that *the plan has won the favor of the Pope*. These last words were put in simply to frighten the poor old Pontiff the more and to insinuate that his mercy to Americans was interpreted in that sense by the public.

But let us hope & pray & work.

And so I trust—the new year will bring peace and confidence to you all,

> Always,
> Sincerely yrs.
> D. J. O'Connell[24]

When Ireland arrived in Rome he had an interview with Cardinal Rampolla on January 27, and with the Pope on February 1.[25] The letter sending the document to Cardinal Gibbons is dated January 31, and that to Archbishop Martinelli, the Apostolic Delegate, is dated February 1. Thus Ireland arrived too late to prevent the publication of the document. Gibbons hearing that the letter was about to be published cabled to Rome on February 7 asking for a delay, but received an answer from Cardinal Rampolla dated February 9,[26] that his message arrived too late because the letter had already been sent to some American bishops. Rampolla added the rather strange statement that the letter would not be unsatisfactory to Gibbons when he received it.

[24] O'Connell to Elliott, Dec. 10, 1898, in the Paulist Fathers Archives.

[25] *Freeman's Journal*, Feb. 4, 1898. *La Vie Catholique*, February 24, 1899, Clipping in the Klein papers in the University of Notre Dame Archives.

[26] Rampolla to Gibbons, Feb. 9, 1899, in the Cathedral Archives of Baltimore.

The apostolic letter, entitled *Testem Benevolentiae*,[27] the Pope declared was a testimony of his affection for the American episcopate and the American people, as he had previously testified of his admiration for the increase in the Church and for their work. This letter although written "to point out certain things which are to be avoided and corrected" was to be regarded as a proof of his affection, especially since it was written "to put an end to certain contentions which have arisen lately among you, and which disturbed the minds, if not of all, at least of many, to the no slight detriment of peace." The Pope further said that Gibbons was aware that the *Life of Father Hecker*, especially through the works of those who have translated and interpreted it in foreign languages, had excited considerable controversy "on account of certain opinions which are introduced concerning the manner of leading a Christian life." The Pope consequently, by reason of his apostolic office, wished to write on this subject.

The new ideas, he said, are based on the principle that in order to bring to the Church those who dissent from her the Church should adapt herself somewhat to the advanced civilization and, relaxing her ancient rigor, show some indulgence to modern theories and methods, not only in matters of discipline but also in the doctrines which are contained in the Deposit of Faith. These ideas maintain that it is opportune to draw the wills of those disposed towards the Church, that the Church should pass over or soften certain points of doctrine as if of lesser moment or to soften them so that they may not have the same meaning invariably held by the Church. On these ideas, the Pope said he did not have to say much since these matters had been defined in the Council of the Vatican (*Constitutio De Fide Catholica*, C. IV), in which it declared that the Catholic faith is not a theory of philosophy which can be elaborated by the human understanding, but a divine deposit given by God to be faithfully guarded and infallibly de-

[27] The Apostolic letter *Testem Benevolentiae* appeared in translation in most of the American Catholic papers. However when there was some objection to the translation issued by Cardinal Gibbons, another translation was published in New York by the Apostleship of Prayer with the signature of approval of Archbishop Corrigan. It contains the Latin and English in parallel columns. The English version is in the appendix of this volume.

clared and once declared "not to be departed from under the specious pretext of a more profound understanding." This likewise applied to any attempt to omit certain Catholic principles or to bury them as it were in oblivion; and he quoted the Scriptures and the Council of the Vatican again in support of this position. The Pope desired all to return to the Church but only by the one way that Christ had pointed out.

The Pope then went on to say that while the Catholic discipline is such that it can be modified to suit different times and places, the Church always teaches the same doctrine in the same sense and in the same mind. Yet the Church has always modified that rule of life and has not disregarded the manner and customs of the various nations which it embraces. However, these modifications are not to be determined by the individual, but must be determined by the judgment of the Church. The contrary opinion was condemned by Pope Pius VI in rejecting the 18th Proposition of the Synod of Pistoia which would subject the discipline of the Church to scrutiny, as if the Church would impose a discipline that would be too heavy to bear. In the present case those who are advocating these new doctrines advocate the introduction into the Church of the liberty which has of late been introduced into the foundations of nearly all civil communities. Pope Leo said here that he has distinguished very clearly, in his encyclical on the Constitution of States, the difference between the Church which is of Divine right and all other associations which exist by the free will of men. This new argument claims that since the declaration of Infallibility there is no further need of solicitude or worry about the infallible teachings, and that now a wider field of thought and action is open to the individuals. Pope Leo said such a doctrine is preposterous, since there is even greater need to be submissive and to be guided by this infallible authority in order to be preserved from private error. In the present day license is confused with liberty, and the habits of saying and printing everything have cast such shadows upon men's minds that there is greater utility and need of the Church's office than before. The Pope does not mean to repudiate the genius of the day, but the present search for truth will have greater efficacy if it accept the authority and wisdom of the Church.

Pope Leo then took up certain conclusions which have been derived from these false premises which, he says, even though they are not wrong, at least they are not free from suspicion. The first of the conclusions is the rejection of all external guidance as superfluous and as even disadvantageous to those who are seeking Christian perfection because the Holy Ghost now pours forth his gifts in greater abundance than in times past and by a certain hidden instinct teaches them without any intermediary. The Pope questioned whether the history of the martyrs and saints of the past indicate any less outpourings of the gifts of the Holy Ghost in times past. The Pope quoted the Second Council of Orange to the effect that no one man can accept the saving teachings of the Gospel without the prior aid of the Holy Ghost, but he points out that the inspirations and promptings of the Holy Ghost are for the most part not discerned without the guidance and aid of an external guide. It is also true that the common way of God is to save men by men as has been pointed out by St. Augustine and Saint John Chrysostom. Even Saint Paul was directed to Ananias at Damascus. And those who are entering upon a more perfect way are that much more in need of guidance. This is the ordinary way of acting in the Church and those who would depart from it "do so rashly and at their peril."

The second doctrine that has been deduced from those false premises listed in the beginning of the letter is that these teachers "extol beyond measure the natural virtues as more in accordance with the ways and requirements of the present day, and consider it an advantage to be richly endowed with them, because they make a man more ready and more strenuous in action." The Pope asked if nature is then weaker because of the added grace. He said that even if we admire acts of natural virtues, the men who possess them are rare who are not assailed by passions so violent that they need grace to overcome them. But even these men who seem to have these natural virtues in abundance would strive in vain if they did not also have supernatural grace, because they would not thereby earn supernatural beatitude or become more solid and more enduring in virtue.

Thirdly, in connection with this praise of natural virtues, these false teachers divide virtues into passive and active, and say that while the passive virtues were better for former times, the active virtues are to be preferred for the present day. Pope Leo quotes St. Thomas Aquinas to show that all virtues are active. Christ is the model of all virtues and he was meek and humble of heart—obedient unto death. And Saint Paul says "And they that are Christ's have crucified their flesh with their vices and concupiscences."

Among these passive virtues these teachers place the evangelical virtues, the religious life, and the vows pronounced by religious orders, which they regard as out of keeping with the new age, as limiting human liberty, and as better adapted to weak minds and availing little for human perfection. These teachings the Pope rejected as contrary to the usage and doctrine of the Church. Such an opinion, the Pope said, will not be accepted by any one acquainted with the history of the religious orders in the United States, recalling that a statue to one—apparently that of Father Marquette in the National Capitol—was now being erected publicly. He pointed to the continuance of the work of the religious orders in the propagation of the Faith, and added that no distinction should be made here regarding the utility of the contemplative religious or the active religious orders. Further, if some wish to devote themselves to a society without vows they may do so, for such a practice is not new in the Church, but they should beware of putting themselves above religious orders.

Lastly, the Pope took up the question of whether new ways of bringing converts to the Church are to be adopted. He said it was not prudent to cast aside what the Church had long approved. It is the duty of each one to try to aid in the salvation of his neighbor according to his station in life: the faithful by their integrity of life, charity, and prayer; and the clergy by the wise preaching of the Gospel, by the decorum and splendor of the sacred ceremonies, and especially by showing in their lives the teachings of the doctrines of the Apostles. In this matter of new methods, if in the teaching of the Gospel it is felt that those who dissent should be spoken to, not in the church, but in private place, not in disputation but in friendly conference, this is not to be reprehended, provided that these men who do this work have the approval of their bishop who should choose men for this who have given proof of their knowledge and virtue.

From what he had said, the Pope said it was clear that he could not approve of the opinions which some call "Americanism." If the term is used to designate the characteristics of the American people just as other nations have qualities proper to themselves, or if the name implied the condition of the commonwealth or the laws and customs which prevail in it, the Pope sees no reason why it should be repudiated. But if the term is used to designate the doctrines he has discussed above, he is sure that the bishops of the United States would be the first to repudiate and condemn this Americanism as unjust to them and their nation. For such a doctrine raises the suspicion that there are those among the Americans who desire to have a church different from that which is in the rest of the world, which is one in unity with the Church of Peter—the Roman Church.

The Pontiff concluded with the desire that Gibbons convey his love for the rest of the bishops in America, and for the nation which has done great good in the past and which promises to do still more in the future. The letter was dated January 22, 1899.

Taken as a whole the document is such that it is difficult to understand why Cardinal Rampolla would think, as he said in his letter of February 9, that it would not offend Cardinal Gibbons. It is true that the life of Hecker was saved from the Roman Index, and the Pope did not say that any American held the doctrines he condemned, but the document did refer to certain things "to be corrected" and did condemn Americanism as defined in the letter. The doctrines as summarized were taken not so much from the writings of the Americanists as from those who were their opponents and who were interested not so much in the doctrines as in the political and social Americanizations which the Pope exempted from his reprobation. It is true that the Pope and Cardinal Rampolla had received support in this action from Bishop Mess-

mer and from Archbishop Corrigan, if not from a direct letter
at least through his letter of approval to Abbé Maignen, and it is
also true that there had been a lack of writings by the "Americanists" from which their real teachings could be drawn. This lack
of publications by those charged with "Americanism" can be explained first by their feeling that the Pope would not take action
against them, and secondly because the Americanists felt that the
charges against them were so outrageous—especially charges of
schism and heresy, that they thought no one could seriously believe they held them. A third factor undoubtedly, in this lack of
defense of Americanism, was the hesitancy on the part of the
Americanists to attack the life of Hecker whom they respected,
but whose memory they felt would suffer if they backed down
from the exaggerated praises of his biographers. Above all, there
is no evidence that the Americanists ever thought of themselves
as propagators of a new doctrine at all. They were advocating, in
their minds at least, a new approach to the modern era in matters
that were not of really essential doctrine or practice, and were
merely opposing certain traditions which they thought were out
of step with the modern scientific and democratic world. Insofar
as they had wandered into the field of dogma or morals the Pope
felt it necessary to reprove them without saying explicitly that
they had so wandered in any instance. The reaction of the contestants in the controversy is evidently based upon their opinions
whether the Americanists had or had not proposed the errors condemned by the Pope. Of great importance in the subsequent discussion is the fact that none of the Americanists defended in any
way the doctrines condemned by the Pope. Heretical Americanism was dead and apparently was not mourned by anyone except
Charbonnel and his modernistic friends. The blow to the non-
heretical Americanism became the subject of a debate which is
not yet complete.

The most interesting document of the immediate reaction is
the letter of Archbishop Ireland to Father George Deshon, the
Superior General of the Paulists, dated from Hotel Bristol, February 24, 1899.

My Dear Fr. Deshon:

So the letter is published. I cannot now go into details—but all that giant will could do was done by me to prevent the publication—It had been signed, sealed & printed before my arrival. And in what I did I can [*sic*] the strong cooperation of Card. Gibbons by cablegram. But the forces against us were enormous—Jesuits, Dominicans, & Redemptorists fought for very life—& again & again Abp. Corrigan's letter to Lepidi was flung in my face. It was said—But the American episcopate is divided—& when at last I called for proofs, a cardinal, whose name is not to be written, said: "Corrigan has written to Lepidi a letter of approval & congratulation—& I read the letter!"

Your celebration on Jan. 25—in view of what was happening in Rome was the veriest of comedies—& the Paulists of N. York accepted the comedy as a reality.

Rampolla gave me to understand that after the letter had been signed & printed, he in deference to my words had it softened—"in the beginning & in the end." [*sic*] I believe a second printed edition was made—Rampolla says—that the words of the letter allow us to say that the things condemned were never said or written in America not even by Hecker—but were set afloat in France—as "Americanism" at the occasion of the Life, & especially of its translation, & of interpretations given in foreign languages, & he added, that I should do my best to spread this view. Small comfort—but we must make the most of it. In my letter to the Pope—I accepted the letter, swore against all the opinions condemned in it, which I said had never been heard of in America, & declared it an insult to America to have covered such extravagances with the name of Americanism.

Read the letter carefully—& you will see that the Americanism condemned is Maignen's Nightmare, v.g.,—who ever "preferred" natural to supernatural virtues? Who ever taught that the practice of natural virtues was not to be vitalized & supernaturalized by divine grace? Who ever taught that in hearkening to the H. Ghost the Christian was not to be constantly guided by the visible magisterium of the Church! etc.

Fanatics conjured up an "Americanism"—& put such before the Pope. Lepidi & Mazzella wrote the body of the letter—I cannot pray that God forgive them.

My love to all my friends.

Sincerely Xt.

(Signed) John Ireland

V. Rev. Fr. Deshon.[28]

To the Pope himself Ireland wrote the answer which, more than that later sent by Cardinal Gibbons, represented the feeling

[28] Ireland to Deshon, February 24, 1899, in the Paulist Fathers Archives.

of the Americanists. It was published on February 24 in the *Osservatore Romano*.

Most Holy Father,

Immediately on finishing reading the letter Your Holiness has just addressed to his Eminence Cardinal Gibbons and the other members of the episcopate of America, I hasten to thank your holiness for this act of esteem and love for the Catholics of the United States and for the whole American people.

To-day the light has been shed abroad and misunderstandings cease. Now we can scotch the error which some have wished to cloak under the name of Americanism, and we can define the truth which alone Americans call Americanism. Moreover, so clearly and precisely are distinctions drawn and explanations made in the letter Apostolic that the peril which was not understood by everybody in the United States —a peril which I must confess I thought was to be feared—can no longer present itself.

In view of the extraordinary confusion of ideas and the bitter controversies which have arisen in France over the book *The Life of Father Hecker*—the extent of which the Apostolic letter permits me to measure—it was, I cannot but now see, necessary for the Supreme Pastor to make his voice heard to enlighten and tranquillize people's minds.

Verily, with all the energy of my soul, I repudiate and I condemn all the opinions which the Apostolic Letter repudiates and condemns— all those false and dangerous opinions to which, as the letter points out, certain persons have given the name of "Americanism." I repudiate and condemn these opinions without exception as literally as your Holiness repudiates and condemns them, and I repudiate and condemn them with all the more alacrity and heartfelt joy because never for a moment have my Catholic faith and my knowledge of the teaching and practices of the Holy Church permitted me to entertain such extravagances. The whole Episcopate of the United States in their own name and in the name of their flocks are ready to repudiate and condemn these errors. We cannot but be indignant that such a wrong should have been done us—our Bishops, our faithful people, and our whole nature—as to designate as some have come to do, by the word "Americanism" errors and extravagances of this sort.

Most Holy Father, those men are enemies of the Church of America and false interpreters of the faith, who "imagine" that there is, or who wish to establish in the United States, a church which differs one iota from the Universal Church which other nations acknowledged, which Rome herself recognizes, and cannot but recognize, as the infallible guardian of the revelation of Jesus Christ.

Begging your Holiness benevolently to accept my assurances of love and devotion, and to grant me the favour of the Apostolic Benediction, I have the honor to be,

Your Holiness's devoted Son,
John Ireland, Archbishop of St. Paul.

February 22, 1899.[29]

Archbishop Keane submitted in the following terms:[30]

> I declare that I fully and without any reserve accept and profess anything that your Holiness teaches in this letter. I declare that I reject and condemn that which your Holiness condemns. And I declare to your Holiness in the presence of God that never in my life have I thought or accepted any of the ideas Your Holiness reproved in this letter.

But this letter was not published. Nor has there ever been published any statement of Monsignor O'Connell except the declarations which he gave to Father Lepidi in the interviews of July 11 and 14, 1898.

Abbé Klein felt an obligation to assure Cardinal Richard of Paris of his submission to the papal letter. He wrote to him on February 24,[31]

> Permit me without delay to assure you with all my heart that I adhere to the letter written by the Sovereign Pontiff on January 22, to Cardinal Gibbons the text of which I find this very day in *L'Univers*, I have indeed the filial confidence that Your Eminence has not for one instant doubted my sentiments of absolute and perfectly sincere submission to the authority of the Church; but I hasten to seize the present occasion to affirm those sentiments again unreservedly.

He then gave the Cardinal permission to use this letter as he wished. The Cardinal answered on February 26, saying that he was not at all surprised by Klein's promptness. His friends, however, urged him that he should also write a letter of submission to the Pope, since Archbishops Keane and Ireland had already done so. Klein was much disturbed by this, particularly since he did not know what the archbishops had written. However he decided to

---

[29] Many translations of this letter appeared in the papers in this country. Cf. *Freeman's Journal*, March 4, 1899, and *Northwestern Chronicle*, March 3, 1899.

[30] This quotation is from Soderini's manuscript but he does not give his source.

[31] Klein's own story is told in his *Souvenirs*, (Paris, 1949) IV, Ch. XXI, and in the translation of the volume.

withdraw the French *Vie* from sale and send a letter of submission to the Pope with a phrase that would indicate his own sense of not holding the erroneous opinions. His letter read as follows:

> Holy Father:
> Will your holiness allow me as the most humble and most obedient of your children to declare to you in all loyalty that I adhere unreservedly to the letter which you wrote on January 22, to Cardinal Gibbons, and to affirm that I am withdrawing from sale the French edition of *La Vie Du Pere Hecker,* occasion of the heated controversies which your letter has now ended.
> If ever, unknowingly and unwillingly, I have fallen into the errors condemned by Your Holiness, I readily and gratefully take advantage of the present occasion to repudiate them all; and I do this now with all my heart without any reservation or subtlety, completely and literally as condemned by Your Holiness—most happy that I am thus able to avert harmful suspicions and to profess once again my absolute submission to the divine authority of the Church and its visible head.

Cardinal Richard sent this letter to the Holy Father and received an acknowledgment from Cardinal Rampolla on March 6.

The Paulists felt likewise constrained to make an act of submission and the Superior General wrote as follows:

> New York, February 28, 1899
>
> Holy Father:
> As soon as we read the letter of your Holiness regarding the errors to which the name of "Americanism" is given and addressed to his Eminence James Cardinal Gibbons, Archbishop of Baltimore, as this letter was given in English in the New York daily papers we immediately, fully, and willingly embraced the doctrine laid down in this Pontifical document; and we signified this without delay by telegraph to your Holiness. And for this letter we cordially thank your Holiness, because, in the discharge of your office of supreme Doctor and infallible Teacher, you lead us in the way of truth and keep far from us the darkness of error; and in the same spirit Father Hecker, if he were still living, would with filial veneration have received the Pontifical decree.
> But the reading of the letter of your Holiness gave us no little comfort, because therein it is stated that the errors reproved by the Holy See are rather to be ascribed to the interpretations of the opinions of Father Hecker than to those opinions themselves. But if there be anything, either in the doctrine or the 'Life' of this Father, which is ordered by the wise judgment of your Holiness to be corrected, we willingly acquiesce in the sentence of the Holy See, both because the Roman

Church is the pillar and ground of truth and because it is commanded as follows in the Rule of our Institute: "Let a prompt and cheerful religious submission to the Holy Church, and to every lawfully constituted authority in it, and to all the ordinances established by its authority, be a principal and evident characteristic of our society and of all its associates. First of all, let this obedience be shown to the Vicar of Jesus Christ, and to the Holy Roman Church, and to all the decrees and instructions of the Holy See, whether relating to doctrine or discipline." This manner of obedience is deeply imprinted in our hearts, so that we have never thought of departing from the integrity and strictness of Catholic doctrine. But if, according to the judgment of your Holiness, we have either had this tendency, or have appeared to have it, or by our way of acting have given any favor in any way to such a tendency, we gratefully receive the paternal correction of your Holiness.

The Constitutions of our Institute strictly require us to aim at perfect orthodoxy, and to have as our standard not only the definitions of the Church, but also its institutions, and the writings of approved authors of the spiritual life, and to promote the devotions which the Church fosters and recommends. And in these Constitutions the following declaration is to be found: "To all, including the priests, it is prescribed to use spiritual direction, according to the principles laid down by approved writers." In these and in all matters we declare that we shall follow the instructions laid down in the letter of your Holiness, and we likewise profess full obedience and faithful adherence to your Holiness and to the Holy Roman See.

> George Deshon
> Superior General.[32]

Writing to Father Deshon, Archbishop Ireland objected to Deshon's promise to withdraw the biography from sale.

No one has asked you to withdraw the book from circulation, no one expected this of you and by so doing you give rise to the belief that the book itself is somewhat condemnable. Otherwise the letter is all right, especially that part in which you say that the interpretations of the book are more to blame than the statement of the book itself. . . .

As a matter of fact the body of the letter was prepared by Mazzella and was intended to hit hard. The beginning and the end of the letter were dictated by the Pope and let us all out. Things here are very quiet and the general opinions that "Praeter intentionem Mazzellae" the letter passed over heads and hits only Maignen's figment. What you will have to do is to have a new "Life of Father Hecker" published.[33]

Ireland, Keane, Klein, O'Connell, the Paulists, these were the

[32] This letter is given in Klein's account and the translation.
[33] Ireland to Father Deshon, March 16, 1899, in the Paulist Fathers Archives.

chief Americanists and the submission was quite complete, although in none was there any admission that they held the condemned doctrines. The letter was addressed to the Cardinal of Baltimore and many waited for his answer to appear, but that answer was not published. Over forty years later the first draft of this answer in the Archives of Baltimore was printed.[34] The effect of its publication at the time might have been serious since it did not admit the existence of the error. The draft in French, in the handwriting of Father Alphonse Magnien, is as follows:

March 17, 1899

Very Holy Father,

The letter in which your Holiness condemns the errors described by certain persons as Americanism reached me about the middle of February. I had an English translation made of it which I published at the same time as the Latin text.

My sentiments are too well known to your Holiness for me to have to tell you that I thank you with all my heart for having shed light on all these questions which certain people outside the United States for the past year have taken pleasure in confusing, but with which public opinion here is not concerned.

This extravagant and absurd doctrine as I would willingly call it, this Americanism as they have chosen to call it, has nothing in common with the views, the aspirations, the doctrines and the conduct of Americans. I do not think that in the whole country could be found a single bishop or priest or even a well instructed layman, who has ever put forward such extravagances. No, this is not, never has been and will never be our Americanism. I am deeply grateful to your Holiness for having yourself made this distinction in your Apostolic letter.

My first impulse was to write at once to your Holiness to thank you for this further act of kindness toward us; but I have waited in order to see the effect produced by the papal document on public opinion and on American Catholics in particular.

I am happy to be able to tell your Holiness that the sentiments which were manifested—mixed with a certain astonishment that such doctrines should have been attributed to American Catholics—were those of profound respect for the papal pronouncement, of great gratitude for the kindness that you have shown us, and of sincere appreciation of the distinction that your Holiness made so justly between the doctrines which we reprobate as you do, and those feelings of love for our country and its institutions that we share with our fellow citizens, and which are to us so powerful a help in the work that we have to accomplish for the glory of God and the honor of Holy Church.

It is with deep respect, etc.

James Card. Gibbons.

[34] Published in the *American Catholic Historical Review*, XXX (October, 1944) 346-48.

It is worth noting that Cardinal Gibbons arranged the release of the Pope's letter only to the *Baltimore Sun*[35] so that it would appear only in Baltimore. This killed its news value for the New York papers and there was only a mild discussion in the American press and most American comments were not favorable to the letter. Whether this was necessary to limit its news value or not is not clear. While the controversies between the American bishops had been front page items during the preceding months it is doubtful that a great percentage of the American newspapers were aware of the controversy, and the claims of the American prelates that the heresy was generally unknown in the country and that the letter created little excitement in the United States were undoubtedly true.

The *New York Sun* of February 26 stated that:

> The Allies of Americanism in its true form also contend that instead of sweeping victory for their enemies, the Pope's letter is a point in their favor. They say it has cleared the air and forever buried all the lies and vituperations hurled upon the cause by the royalists of Europe. They say that it has made a new foundation for greatly extended operations and for progress in liberal thought.[36]

Abbé John Hogan, S.S., of the Boston archdiocesan seminary, who was considered by his contemporaries as a friend of the progressives, gave an interview to the *Boston Herald* of March 6, in which he traced the story of the controversy, a brief account of Father Hecker, the biography, and Maignen's book. Summing up the effects of the letter Father Hogan said:

> I do not believe that in the form objected to by His Holiness they are held by any enlightened Catholics in this country, and those whom I found most enthusiastic over the life of Father Hecker in France are entire strangers to them. . . . From the tone of his letter, it will be seen that the Pope speaks principally in view of the discussion that has risen in regard to the matter in France, and that his strictures bear in no manner or measure on the present society of the Paulists, who are as remote as any other body of men from what the Pope objects to.[37]

[35] Rooker to O'Connell, February 24, 1899.
[36] *New York Sun*, February 26, 1899.
[37] *Boston Herald*, March 6, 1899. Commented on by Father Meifuss in *The Review* of March 30, 1899.

Since the publication of the French *Vie* was the work in the first place of Count Guillaume de Chabrol, it is interesting to read his reaction in a letter to his friend, the Vicomte de Meaux, less than a month after the publication of the papal letter, apparently after the Vicomte had written him a letter of sympathy. The letter reads as follows:

Riom, March 17, 1899

My Dear Friend:

I thank you for your friendly sympathy and anxiety. To tell the truth, I do not feel that I have been hit by the pontifical letter, for in all conscience the book never contained the propositions condemned: I have been urged to keep silent: the translation being anonymous and Abbé Klein having taken the responsibility for the work: I would have very easily given my total acceptance of the censures of the Holy Father, just as I would have rejected any plot for stealing the dome off Saint Peter's. But two things are hard to bear: 1° that calumny is so readily believed in Rome, 2° that the work of the Paulists can be hampered by the solemn declaration which results from this calumny. It is important to notice two things: 1° that Spirit of infallibility in spite of men has softened this solemn proclamation to such a degree as to cause only a small amount of wounds; 2° and above all, the precedent, recently created in the Church by this letter, of a warning that is not a condemnation and of pre-supposing good faith and even admitting it in some one whose ideas are condemned. A real progress is shown by a pontifical letter minus the usual noisy display of excommunications, if we have accomplished nothing but this innovation, we have not been useless.

I hope that the Americans will take the matter in a free and easy manner just as we ourselves no longer take it tragically. We have passed the time of great hearts bleeding generously from a deep wound, like the Montalemberts and the Lacordaires of other days. Ultramontanism would make Italians out of us all by taking away from us our liturgy, our tradition, our national Christian life: That's just what we are [Italians] and instead of Knights [illegible word] we have all become Monsignors: We ward off the blow cleverly, and we conceal our suffering with a smile: obedience to be sure gains thereby: But I hope to God that the power of resistance and moral greatness may not be the loser and that the papacy itself be not the first to notice it.

A strong current of individual initiative in religious matters would have been the only way of raising up the Latin races and of giving them a decisive part in the Church: obviously that isn't in God's plans! The races which derive this initiative from their own political setup and their own peculiar temperament will therefore remain the strongest. They will be the ones who, when they come to the Church, will reinvigorate it. When God wishes to sink the royal power, He brings into this world a Count de Chambord, when He desires the end of the temporal power, He gets Pius IX elected; when He wishes the destruction of the Latin races He gives the tiara to Leo XIII. That is to say His will is done by the very men who think they are going most directly against the current of the facts.

We must raise ourselves on high, look far ahead, love the definitive Truth for itself and not be anxious to see with our mortal eyes the outcome—and in union with the great men now dead, accept the sufferings we are judged worthy to undergo, less than they of course, and with less glory, but let's hope at least with some profit to our souls and with a humility which it is good to have at the end of our life.

A hearty handshake to you and my respects to Madame de Meaux.

G. De Chabrol.

Send me what news you get from America.[38]

There is a remarkable similarity in ideas to the letter the Count de Meaux[39] himself received from his friend Abbé Klein a couple of weeks later.

Bellevue (S. de O.) 18, r. de Velizy
April 8, 1899

My dear Count:

Having returned last night from a trip in Normandy and having been restored for good this time, I hope, to life, to confidence, to action, I hasten to send to you first of all the alleluia of one risen from the grave. Your very kind and consoling letter would have deserved a more prompt "thank you": But there are certain states of mind where the only thing we can do is to be silent, keeping our eyes focused on Him who was also judged a culprit and who fortunately judges everything without appeal. It is the memory of Him which sustains us in our trial, in the terrible trial where one doesn't even have the right to explain: *Jesus autem tacebat.*

I have used above the word "risen from the grave." I do not mean my dear sir, that I am not still shattered by the sacrifice and particularly oh! particularly aghast at the injustice and lack of understanding on the part of the ones you know what! in a time like ours, to use all the powers of the Church to combat Cardinal Gibbons, Archbishops Ireland and Keane, those holy religious the Paulists, and poor miserable me, too!—to accuse us in a word of misunderstanding the divine authority of the Church and the power of the Gospel! Do they think then that we keep silent just for the honor of obeying certain ones among them and for the joy of being treated this way?

But the thing that strengthens me and gives me courage is the thought that the battle in which we have received so many wounds marks a date and an advance in the history of the Church. It serves like

---

[38] Chabrol to De Meaux, March 17, 1899, in the Archives Chateau d'Ecotay.
[39] Klein to De Meaux, April 8, 1899, in the Archives Chateau d'Ecotay.

so many other acts to make better known the frontier beyond which the Supreme authority can no longer count on God's infallible assistance, and also it helps the modern world to become aware of the two elements (aside from points of faith) which are dividing the Church. The words are poorly chosen, but let's take them such as they are and let's accept their symbolism: Americanism or Italianism (essential Catholicism, does not enter into the question). We will see all right which one will win out over the other definitively. You have seen, dear sir, other defeats of the same army representing the union of faith and progress; There was a revival after Montalembert and he became a great man: There will be a revival after Father Hecker and who knows if some day he will be beatified like Savonarola was.

If you are in Paris be so kind as to get in touch with me so that I can go to see you and renew my courage.

Respectfully yours,
Felix Klein.

After the publication of the letter Archbishop Ireland went to the seaside to rest and to prepare for his speech on the anniversary of Jeanne d'Arc at Orleans. To his friends he spoke of things that would happen after Orleans. But in general one could say that the silence of Klein represented the reaction of the Americanists to the blow.

Cardinal Gibbons wrote on March 2, to O'Connell of the American reaction.

It has excited scarcely any comment in the secular papers or the Catholic papers as far as received have little to say about it except that they don't see the application to our country. . . .

But it is very discouraging to us that the American church is not understood abroad and that its enemies are listened to and that they can lie with impunity. I do not see that any of the questions discussed was a living question here. But I suppose the Holy Father had to act.[40]

Some of the American archbishops had taken little part in the controversy before the condemnation and they could be expected to have little to say afterwards. As Bishop O'Gorman was to point out later there were fourteen archbishops in the country at the time. They usually spoke for the bishops in their respective provinces, although not always for all of them as can be easily understood. The archbishop of Chicago, Feehan, Dubuque's John Hennessey, and Santa Fe's Bourgade kept silent and did not publish

40 Gibbons to O'Connell, March 2, 1899, in the Richmond Diocesan Archives.

any opinion on the controversy. Four, Cincinnati's Elder, New Orlean's Chapelle, Portland's newly appointed Christie, and Philadelphia's Patrick Ryan acknowledged the letter and thanked the Holy Father but did not admit the existence of the heresy in this country. Four, Riordan of San Francisco, Kain of Saint Louis, Williams of Boston joined with Gibbons in denying that the heresy existed in the country. Holding up the opposition were Archbishops Corrigan of New York and Katzer of Milwaukee. Undoubtedly the most important recognition of the existence of the heresy was contained in the letter of Archbishop Corrigan, although that of Milwaukee coming later was not without its effect among the German opponents of Archbishop Ireland. Probably the clearest statement of the neutral bishops is that of the letter of May 18, 1899, to the Pope from the Province of Cincinnati, and signed by Archbishop William H. Elder of Cincinnati and the bishops of Louisville, Grand Rapids, Covington, Detroit, and Cleveland. While not admitting of the existence of the heresy in this country the letter does say:

> The errors you therein condemn were calculated to work great harm to souls. Your Apostolic letter, with its lucid explanation of Catholic truth will, we feel confident, end all future misunderstanding. "Roma locuta est; causa finita est." Our good people are strong in the faith and ever loyal to the Holy See. In our own name, and that of our clergy and flocks, we give you the hearty assurance that we all approve of what Your Holiness approves, we condemn what you condemn.[41]

The Apostolic Letter was not addressed to those who had carried on the attack on the Americanists, but these were not slow to acknowledge its acceptance and to give their own interpretations to the letter itself. Probably the first to accept the papal document and to thank the Holy Father for it was Bishop Louis Isoard of Annecy whose letter of February 22 was published in the *Osservatore Romano* with that of Ireland. He said that if anything could add to the veneration and gratitude of the bishops of France to His Holiness it would be this letter to Cardinal Gibbons, and added: "I know sufficiently the sentiments and the anxieties of many of my colleagues in the episcopate to dare to address to Your

41 Quoted in *The Review* of August 24, 1899.

Holiness our common thanksgiving on the occasion of this new and signal benefit."

But as one might expect the most significant letter from the United States came from the man whose letter to Lepidi and to Maignen was credited with being most important in defeating the efforts of Archbishop Ireland to prevent the sending of the letter. The original was in Italian but an English translation was released in New York by the Archbishop's secretary. Archbishop Corrigan signed it in his name and in the name of his suffragans, although there were some questions raised later about his right to sign the names of some of his suffragans to the letter. It was addressed to the Holy Father and dated March 10, 1899.

March 10, 1899

Most Holy Father:

We cannot express in words the feeling of admiration, of joy, and of gratitude with which our hearts have been penetrated towards your Holiness in reading the masterly and admirable letter which you have deigned to issue on what, for some time past, has been designated under the name of "Americanism."

With what wisdom has your Holiness known how to write in one whole the multiplicity of fallacies and errors which it has been sought to pass as good and Catholic doctrines under the specious title of "Americanism." But at the same time with what prudence, discretion and gentleness, in union with force and clearness, has your Holiness fulfilled the office of supreme and infallible teacher. In truth the last document of your Holiness' wisdom is in no way inferior to so many others which in the course of your glorious pontificate have excited the universal admiration of the nations.

For us, whom the Holy Ghost has placed as Bishops to rule the Church of God, under the infallible guidance of your Holiness, we hasten to offer and to make known to you our sentiments of admiring and unqualified adhesion. We receive, then, and we accept in the most absolute manner, for ourselves and our clergy, for the religious orders and congregations which labour with us for the salvation of souls, and for all our flocks, the doctrinal letter of your Holiness, Testem Benevolentiae. We accept it and we make it wholly ours, word by word, sentence by sentence, in that very same sense in which your Holiness, according to the tradition and wisdom of all Christian antiquity, understood and understands it, and desires that it should be understood by all.

In its regard we shall never make, nor shall we ever permit that others depending from us, either directly or indirectly, should make any reservation or tergiversation. Your Holiness has spoken. The question is, therefore, ended. This thought has given us great satisfaction, and it is this which we wish to say when, in our first words, we manifested the joy of our hearts. We can say also that the monster which, in order to obtain a lasting abode, to acquire the rights of citizenship among us, assumed to itself the fair name of "Americanism," has almost on its first appearance been struck down dead. But it is to you that the glory of this happy result is due.

If your Holiness had not opportunely come to our aid with your admirable letter, how numerous might have been those who, through ignorance rather than malice, would have been taken in the snare. The Bishops and clergy would have had a heavy task to keep the people far from error. Error would have been able, little by little, always to take a greater hold, and we should soon be marked out by the thoughtless as not being Americans.

Meanwhile this false Americanism understood like other similar titles which, to the great injury of souls, lasted for ages among our nation, would have taken tranquil possession in our midst, ever increasing its conquests in enormous proportions of time and place. It is therefore that we rejoice greatly; by reason of your infallible teaching we will not have to transmit to our successors the ungrateful task of having to struggle with an enemy which perhaps would never die.

And now we can with heads erect repeat that we also are Americans as much as any one else. Yes, we are, and we glory in it. We glory in it because our nation is great in its institutions and in its undertakings, great in its development and in its activity; but in the matter of religion, doctrine, discipline, morals and Christian perfection, we glory in thoroughly following the Holy See.

For these reasons we are, and shall ever be most grateful to your Holiness, who, by your imperishable letter, *Testem Benevolentiae*, has conferred on us and all the Catholics of America a signal benefit. Yes, by the testimony of kindness, your Holiness roots out on its very appearance this cockle from the field of wheat.

May Almighty God preserve the health of your Holiness for many years to come, so that you may see with your own eyes the perfect fruit of your apostolic vigilance. Prostrate at the feet of your Holiness, we implore for ourselves, our clergy and our flocks, the apostolic benediction. For the Right Reverend Bishops of this Ecclesiastical Province.

> Your most obedient servant,
> Michael Augustine,
> Archbishop of New York.[42]

Some French bishops soon joined in the chorus of approval of the papal action. The Bishop of Beauvais, Msgr. Fuzet,[43] wrote a long letter to his flock in which while acknowledging that the letter was not addressed to the Church of France he said it had its application to their times and their country. He quoted at

---

[42] There were many printings of this letter. This copy is from the *London Tablet* of May 20, 1899, XXIII, 779-80.

[43] *La Vérité*, March 7, 1899.

length passages of the Apostolic Letter adding comments of approval. He added a plea that the Church in France remain faithful to its old and cherished traditions. "Let us not borrow foreign models of piety, of devotion, of ecclesiastical zeal. The Church of France is sufficiently rich in its own source and its own genius."

The letter of Cardinal Archbishop Richard of Paris to his priests dated March 7,[44] is a very interesting document. He told how when he visited Pope Leo, the Pontiff had promised this letter to the American bishops on the question of Americanism but indicated that he would not publish it until the American bishops had received it. Now that it had been published Richard felt that he could send a copy to his priests. He noted that in the last lines of the letter the Pope had indicated that the American bishops would be the first to repudiate Americanism if it meant the doctrines that he condemned in the letter. He said the doctrines the Pope condemned are not new in the Church. Richard himself had spoken along similar lines in his pastoral of the previous year. In times of struggle there are always some who are led astray by new opinions, who yet, while trying to remain faithful to the teachings of the Church, try to reach out to those outside the Church weakening the teachings and discipline of the Church. Richard recommended that his flock avoid novelties, adhere to the virtues of humility, meekness and mortification, and insist on the evangelical counsels. He added that he was not surprised that those who had been seduced by these errors were quick to declare their adherence to the papal admonitions.

In Rome where the liberal papers were already implying that the real Americanism was not condemned, the *Civiltà Cattolica*[45] felt an obligation to insist on the reality of the condemnation. Sarcastically stating that those who were so strongly teaching those doctrines a few weeks or months ago now seemed to have forgotten the word Americanism, the article claimed that the condemned doctrines had their origin in America. Then it added a rather bitter note.

[44] Quoted in *La Vérité*, March 15, 1899 and *La Semaine Religieuse de Cambrai* of March 18, 1899.

[45] *La Civiltà Cattolica* (March 6, 1899) Series XVII, V, 641-53. Translated in *The Review* of April 6, 1899 which dates the *Civiltà* as March 18.

Just so the Jansenists were unable to discover in the *Augustinus* of Jansenius, the propositions condemned in the celebrated bull "Unigenitus," and the Rosminianists read nothing in the works of Rosmini except what was in the Summa of Saint Thomas.

However this may be, it is a historical fact that the word "Americanism" was not coined in France or Germany, nor anywhere else in Europe by the enemies of the United States. It originated in America, and there was first used to designate, in general, the "new idea," which was to rejuvenate the Church, and, in particular, the "new crusade," which was to be undertaken against the intransigence of the Catholics of the ancient faith.

The article then proceeded to give the actual religious statistics of the United States showing that Catholics were outnumbered by Protestants, and that besides about 40 millions who do not belong to these groups there are about 5 to 10 millions who could be classed as infidels. The word Americanism cannot be attributed to this whole group and above all it must not be attributed to the majority of the Catholics of the country. However, it is not a phantasm. The author, with his tongue in his cheek no doubt, added: that while not wishing to name persons for whom he professes the highest respect, he did not think that anyone acquainted with the facts had any doubt about the existence of the condemned Americanism, especially if he was aware of the Americanists' "printed discourses, the introductions they have written to the works of others, the applause they have given to certain books, the articles they have written for certain periodicals, the memoranda they have presented right and left." He will know that Americanism is not "a puffed up windbag, nor an invention of the enemies of the United States, but a sad reality."

The author added the closing sentences of the Holy Father in which he excludes from the condemnations of the letter the political and social qualities of the country designated under the name Americanism, and he added that the Church does not fear either democracy or monarchy; but pointed out that Pope Leo in his previous letter had said that the peculiar situation of the Church in the United States was not necessarily to be recommended for all people. These words were not spoken of religious Americanism which is specifically described in the Pope's letter. The author then pointed out how from the translation of the life of Hecker there grew up the representation of Hecker as the ideal priest and the model for the new Paul, and how this brought about the criticisms of Maignen and Delattre and others. Now the writer said the Americanists, who have been praising Hecker in this way, disfavor Hecker and openly repudiate his opinions in much the same way that the sailors in the scriptural story threw Jonas overboard for their own safety. He likewise rejected the claim of Coppinger that only the French translation of the life of Hecker was at fault.

Some French periodicals were quick to catch on to the suggestion that the Archbishop of Saint Paul and other Americanists who were denying that the heresy existed were using a Jansenistic mental reservation. But this charge was given an official character when the bishops of the Province of Milwaukee in their letter to the Pope dated Pentecost Sunday, 1899, not only accepted the letter and thanked the Pope for it but added:

> While congratulating Your Holiness with all our hearts upon the fatherly and kind indulgence wherewith, while condemning the errors, you have recalled the erring to the way of right thinking, we cannot, however, help expressing our pain and just indignation over the fact that not a few have been found among our countrymen, and so many especially among the Catholic newspaper editors, who indeed affirmed that they reprobated and rejected the aforesaid errors, but did not hesitate to proclaim again and again, in Jansenistic fashion, that there was hardly any American who had held them and that the Holy See, deceived by false reports, had beaten the air and chased after a shadow, to use a popular expression.
>
> It can escape no loyal Catholic how injurious to the Infallible See and how alien to the orthodox faith such conduct is, since those erroneous opinions have been most assuredly and evidently been proclaimed among us orally and in writing, though perhaps not always so openly; and no true Catholic can deny that the magisterium of the Church extends not only to the revealed truths, but also to the facts connected with dogma, and that it appertains to this teaching office to judge infallibly of the objective sense of any doctrine and the existence of false opinions.
>
> We moreover deplore vehemently the mode of speaking and writing of some, even Catholics, by which they traduce those who have admitted the existence of the errors of Americanism among us and signified to Your Holiness their assent and gratitude for your Apostolic Letter—as rather unfriendly to their country and its institutions; although it must be manifest to every sane and truth-loving man that the

Apostolic Letter contains not a word of censure for the American
Republic, nor for any of our laws and institutions, nor finally for
peculiar customs and national endowments, but solely for the opinions
brought to it and uttered by some—by the condemnation of which
most assuredly no disgrace or injury nor brand has been stamped either
upon the American republic and its citizens or upon the Catholics of
America.[46]

It is doubtful if the comment of the Milwaukee prelates' letter
on the Catholic editors properly represented the American reaction. In the first place there was no great reaction in the secular
press. Catholicism was an issue of a minority, and while the leading
prelates had been front page characters in their controversies, the
American people were not much concerned about the theological
aspects of their disagreements. Further, by timing its release,
Cardinal Gibbons prevented any American newspapers from
making a scarehead article on the letter. The discussion was rather
in the weekly Catholic press.[47] In general the Catholic press,
although not always close to the local chancery, followed the lead
of the local prelate in most cases. The major exception was the
Review of Saint Louis which had been called to task at least
once on some statements about the local ordinary, Archbishop
John J. Kain. The other Saint Louis Catholic paper, *Church Progress*, which had been attacking Ireland, had been making a distinction for some weeks before the appearance of the letter between
Heckerism and Americanism. By Heckerism, the editor, Condé
B. Pallen, had indicated was meant liberalism and he announced
in late December 1898, that this liberalism was about to be put
into a *cul de sac*. When the letter appeared the *Church Progress*
of February 25 said:

> *The Church Progress* long ago pointed out and insisted upon the dis-
> tinction between Heckerism and Americanism. . . . The consequences
> will be an effective blow at Liberalism, which has all along virulently
> espoused the cause of Heckerism under the assumption that it was one

[46] A copy of this letter with commentaries by the *Catholic Citizen* of August
5, *The Northwestern Chronicle* by H. M. (Archbishop Ireland) and the *Catholic Columbian* is in the Archives of the Archdiocese of Saint Paul.
[47] Beginning with the issue of March 4, 1899, *The Review* gathered for its
readers the comments of the various Catholic papers, and some secular papers
on the papal letter.

and the same with Americanism, the particular shibboleth of Liberals in this country. But the Holy Father's letter does away with this subterfuge and Heckerism stands exposed upon its own merits or demerits.

In the April 1 issue the editor, Pallen, insisted that the letter was a slam at Ireland, Keane and the Paulists, and in the May 25 issue, in an article on "Archbishop Ireland's Preface," the editor insisted that the condemned Heckerism was in Ireland's preface and added a few brief editorials making fun of the charge that the Pope had condemned an imaginary heresy.

Father David Phelan of the *Western Watchman* had no brief for Father Hecker or for Archbishop Keane whom he had attacked and accused of Pelagianism on previous occasions. His editorials are the usual strange arguments of this strong personality. He claimed first that the *Western Watchman*[48] was the first to condemn the teachings reprimanded by the Holy Father. He maintained that Ireland had written his introduction without reading the book, that he was not a real admirer of Hecker, and that Elliott had known Hecker only in his later life when he was ill. These defects of Hecker were tied together by writers and attributed to Ireland and the other American prelates. Phelan insisted that a more severe letter had been written but that the Pope had substituted for it this condemnation of a so-called Americanism. In the issue of March 9, Phelan attacked "That Sudden Outburst of Orthodoxy" and blamed the controversy on the German newspapers. He pointed out that when the book first appeared there was no opposition by the German newspapers but that the real controversy was brought about by Professor Schroeder. "This storm in the American Church has been brought about by this Professional Jonah and should have ceased when he was thrown overboard."

Der Wanderer[49] of Saint Paul naturally regarded the papal letter as a victory for the opponents of Archbishop Ireland and

[48] *The Western Watchman*, February 23, 1899. Phelan claimed that Archbishop Ireland had once claimed that Father Hecker was crazy, but this is hardly supported by the other statements of Ireland that we have. Phelan in his desire to save his hero, Archbishop Ireland, was willing to condemn almost everyone else.

[49] Excerpts of these articles are in the March 16, and March 23, 1899, *Review*.

did not conceal either its pleasure or its interpretation of the letter. Some of the other papers such as the *Northwestern Catholic* of Sioux City seemed to believe the condemnation necessary, but for the most part the Catholic papers generally held to the line that the letter might have been necessary in France but that the doctrines condemned had no real acceptance among educated Catholics in the country. Thus the *Pittsburgh Catholic* spoke of a "bugaboo rather than a reality," the *Catholic Standard and Times* of Philadelphia seemed to blame the controversy on a faulty translation of the life of Father Hecker. The *Providence Visitor* took a similar stand to that of *Church Progress* without any evident hostility to Archbishop Ireland, making the distinction between Heckerism and real Americanism. The *Cleveland Universe* felt that the American people had been done an injustice in being held responsible for the vagaries of Americanism. The *Ave Maria* of March 11, expressed the same ideas as Gibbons, that no one educated in his religion held the condemned doctrines. The editor added "What is to be avoided is perfectly plain, but it is not so clear what stands in need of correction. On this point there are differences of opinion." The *Colorado Catholic*, whose editor ranked in frankness of opinion with that of the *Western Watchman*, took a strong stand almost disrespectful towards the Holy See indicating that he did not know what the letter was about. "What Leo XIII directed his letter against was not the spirit and teaching in the life of Father Hecker, the true Father Hecker, but the man of straw, the imaginary Father Hecker, who was built up by the enemies of real Catholicity in the hope that truly apostolic men might be humiliated at the hands of the Holy Father."

One of the sanest comments on the controversy from an editor who nevertheless showed his sympathy for Archbishop Ireland and the Americanists was expressed in the San Francisco *Monitor* of March 4, 1899. The editorial said:

> . . . It was a plain and simple letter dealing principally with the matters of doctrine which nobody ever had the least intention of disputing. The questions of discipline touched upon are not of general importance and concern only a few persons in America. . . .

It would be comparatively easy to deal with the question of "Americanism" if anybody would tell us what the thing really is. In France and England they think they know all about it, and maybe they do. Some of the European ecclesiastics are very learned men so far as books go. But since nobody has as yet written an authorized book on "Americanism," there is nothing very tangible on which our European brethren may build an indestructible argument. They have endeavored to theorize from insufficient data, to argue from false premises, and if their conclusions are smilingly denied in this country they have no right to feel hurt over the matter.

The cause of the trouble was that the opponents of this so-called "Americanism" were flying at higher game than Father Hecker and his disciples. Archbishop Ireland and his friends were the ones really attacked. Their policy has always been denounced by a strong party in the Church in the United States. Long before the publication of the "Life of Father Hecker" this denunciation had gone on in season and out of season. Archbishop Keane was removed from the rectorship of the Catholic University at Washington through the intrigues of this party. The controversy was still continued and everything that could possibly be done was done to show the Archbishop of St. Paul in a false light at the Vatican. No very great progress was made for a time. Monsignor Schroeder lost his position at the Catholic University. All looked black. Then the "Life of Father Hecker" with a preface by Archbishop Ireland, came out. Here was a chance that should not be neglected and was not. Prove Father Hecker a heretic and you prove Archbishop Ireland an abettor of heretics. Rome could not countenance a man whose opinions must share the ignominy of Father Hecker's condemnation. This was victory and the paean was accordingly loud and long. "Heckerism" and "Americanism" were inseparably united for evermore. Both were false and to be condemned.

We cannot see that the letter of the Holy Father at all closely touches the question of "Americanism" as the vast majority of the Catholics of this country understand the word. Some sort of reproof is certainly implied for those who believe in European "Americanism," but it scarcely concerns American Catholics. . . .

. . . Every people have their own characteristics, every nation its own laws and customs. The American people are Americans, not German, or French, or Anglo-Saxons or Irish. The genius of a people will necessarily show itself in religion as well as political affairs. The Church in France and Italy and Ireland while it is the same church essentially is yet not altogether the same. But the difference is not a matter of faith or morals, and arises from the different dispositions and traditions and customs of the different races. That difference shows itself distinctly among the Catholic people of foreign birth in this country and this is the cause of the whole difficulty. To erase this difference as far as possible, and to make the Catholics in America one homogenous body in touch with the institutions of the country and partaking of the genius of the American people—this is the "Americanism" that Archbishop Ireland and his friends and supporters stand for. This the Pope has not condemned and never will condemn, because to do so would be an important attempt to stop the natural progress of things which cannot be effected. It is a pity that such a question as "Americanism" should ever have been raised. . . .

But if there were doubts in the minds of so many American Catholic editors about the existence of the condemned doctrines in this country, there were no doubts in the minds of the editors of *La Vérité* and especially in the mind of the chief prosecutor of Americanism, Abbé Charles Maignen. In an article of March 11 in *La Vérité*, Maignen tried to give theological values to the various parts of the letter. In the first place he raised the question whether an apostolic letter addressed to only one bishop or one group can be *ex cathedra*. He answered in the affirmative since Pope Innocent so condemned the Pelagians and this had happened in other cases recognized by theologians. He claimed that the Pope speaks 1) in virtue of his supreme charge of his apostolate, 2) to safeguard the integrity of the faith, and 3) to see to the salvation of the faithful. Again in an article of March 6, he drew up a little syllabus of the errors of Americanism as condemned in the Apostolic letter—this was translated in the *Review* of April 6. In the first place he quoted the sentence of a letter condemning the efforts to attract dissidents into the Church by silence on certain doctrines of the Church. This he said is "reprehensible" and is a restatement of Proposition 80 of the *Syllabus of Errors*. And this silence is not exempt from sin. The second proposition in the Pope's statement is that a certain liberty must be introduced into the Church so that each one can develop his initiative and his activity; the third, that there must be a change following the changes in modern liberties, and the fourth, that after the Vatican council greater liberty is now granted the individual. These propositions Maignen said were dangerous and opposed to the doctrines of the Church like the 18th proposition of the condemned Synod of Pistoia which Pius VI said was injurious to the Church. The fifth proposition of the little syllabus was that external direction was superfluous and even less useful. This proposition Maignen said was very temerarious. The sixth proposition was that the natural virtues were better suited to the modern times. This, Maignen said, was inconceivable in a man of faith. The seventh proposition stated that the Christian virtues were divided into passive and active, and that the passive were suited for times past but the active virtues for the present times. This he characterized as false and contrary to divine revelation. Proposition eight was that religious vows are opposed to the genius of the times because they restrain human liberty. They are suitable for weak souls. The ninth states that the religious life is of little use to the Church. These two he characterized as false and offensive. The tenth proposition he stated was calling for the abandonment of procedures and methods of other times to lead dissidents into the Church. This he characterized as imprudent.

Whether one looks to these exultations of Maignen, the letters of the Archbishop of New York, or of the Archbishop of Milwaukee or on the other hand examines the statements of Archbishop Ireland, Cardinal Gibbons, Archbishop Keane or the more liberal Catholic press of the United States, one is definitely sure that the question of Americanism had entered into a new phase. The careful reader of all the available documents of the time can agree with the verdict of the editor of the San Francisco *Monitor* that there was no dispute about the correctness of the papal doctrines. Nowhere except in the columns written by the apostate Victor Charbonnel do we find any tendency to hold that the condemned doctrines were not worthy of condemnation. Nowhere does one find any real resentment against the aged Pontiff who had written the letter. But since there was more at stake than the spiritual ideals of Father Hecker and even more at stake than any theological principles of Americanism, the subsequent controversy about the value and importance of the heresy and the condemnation must be studied if one is to obtain a useful perspective on the controversy over Americanism. The new controversy was begun almost as soon as the papal letter appeared. We have already seen the makings of a real difference of opinion. But there were new and various manifestations of the new dispute.

THERE WERE TWO neutral observers of the controversy whose opinions are of special interest. Abbé Alfred Loisy,[1] the leading modernist writer of the day, was a friend of Klein and an acquaintance of O'Connell and Ireland. To him of course the controversy was of no essential interest since it did not really concern his biblical problems. He claimed that Duchesne was making too much of the condemnations of the Americanists and of Schell. He added in a letter to Von Hügel:

> The Condemnation is beside the point, since it is formulated according to the indictment of Maignen who does not present the Americanism of the Americans which is the true Americanism nor even the literary Americanism of Abbé Klein which had never been anything existing *in rerum natura*, as St. Thomas says. All the noise that has been made, and which was entirely artificial—for the French Catholic opinion has been much less moved by the Americanist peril than by the revelations of Leo Taxil—all this noise, I say, tended to obtain a censure disagreeable for certain individuals whom the Jesuits do not love and who do not love the Jesuits, Gibbons, Ireland etc. The situation of American Catholicism is changed in nothing by that letter and Catholic Americans remain Catholic Americans.

Ex-Abbé Victor Charbonnel was another interested observer since he had been classed as an Americanist both by himself and by the critics of the Americanists—although he was disowned by the Americanists, particularly by Klein. He made fun of Klein, calling him "Poor Klein" and adding: "What naïveté, in effect to have even thought that the Church would make any concession to the human spirit." He made fun also of Abbé Naudet, closing

[1] Alfred Loisy, *Memoirs pour servir à l'histoire religieuse de notre temps.* 3 vols., (Paris, 1930) I, 514-17.

his article with the words: "Let us go, Naudet makes his genu-flexion which Tartuffe counsels. Poor Abbé Klein."[2]

Loisy, having no great interest in the controversy itself, chiefly regretted the manifestations of reaction among the Roman pre-lates. But Charbonnel felt some personal satisfaction in seeing Klein suffer because Klein and the Americanists had generally dis-owned him when he announced his departure from the Church after the papal letter against the Paris Congress of Religions.

In the meantime, the *Gazette de Lausanne* of February 28, representing a Protestant observer on the controversy, noted that the letter ended the period in which there were stories that the Pope's letter would be either for or against Americanism. Its cor-respondent noted also that the letter was not an absolute condem-nation of Americanism; that it distinguished between political and religious Americanism. Political Americanism in the sense of the Church's adaptation to democratic life was not condemned. The paper said significantly that this was not the condemnation that the anti-Americanists expected although it predicted that even this would be exploited by them. Further, the paper pre-dicted that the Americans would submit.

On March 10 there appeared in the same journal an interview with Archbishop Ireland dated Rome, March 6. It is not clear why Ireland gave this interview since he seemed to have determined to wait until after his speech at Orleans before returning to the battle. However, the correspondent indicated that the interview was intended to appear in an English publication, the *Daily Chronicle* of London, perhaps at some later time. If the reporter is correct one can see that Ireland himself was preparing his de-fense. In the interview Ireland said the papal letter was good and not what the opponents of Americanism wanted and that, while he did not want it published, he now applauded it because it did not hit him. What the Pope condemned was not Americanism but a caricature of Americanism. These ideas were not what Hecker taught but what his enemies attributed to him. Ireland said that there were three points in the letter: 1, individual inspiration of the Holy Ghost; 2, the question of natural virtues; and 3, that of religious orders. As to the first he said he was never quite clear

[2] *Le Signal*, (Paris) February 26-27, 1899.

what Hecker held since Hecker seemed to hold that certain strong inspirations came from on High, from the Holy Ghost, but that such ideas were peculiar to Hecker and to no one else in America. As to the second, Americans were accused of accentuating the importance of the natural virtues but that was a misunderstanding. Americans merely insisted on a substratum of natural virtues, for the same reason Americans never ceased to preach loyalty and veracity. In contrast he rejected the mental restriction taught so much in Latin countries. So also in the United States they insisted on the civic virtues. Unfortunately Hecker had left himself open to attack by his distinction between the active and passive virtues, but Ireland said he had personally reproved Hecker for this. As to the religious orders, some Americans think they are too numerous but no one wishes to diminish the merits of the religious vows. He did not deny the value of religious orders but if in Japan there had been a regular hierarchy he thought religion might have survived better. He admitted under questioning that he acted somewhat like Manning regarding the admission of certain religious orders but insisted that Manning went farther than he. He admitted also that he opposed the turning over of the Catholic University to the Jesuits unless the Pope so instructed.

On March 18, in one of several essays in *Le Signal* of Paris—also a Protestant paper—on the subject, Raoul Allier insisted that the condemnation was a victory for the Jesuits. He listed the succession of attacks by Jesuits beginning with that of Père Coube, the articles in *Les Études,* and Delattre, and those of the Fathers of the Assumption and of the Dominican, Monsabré. He claimed that the Jesuits did not want to admit their victory. He listed those who had submitted and indicated that liberalism was weaker at each successive appearance. Also, on May 18 Ch.P. in *Le Signal* made fun of the claims of Maignen and expressed the hopes that the Paulists would continue to feel satisfied with their mental reservation.

On March 15[3] Alcide Ebray commenting on the controversy

[3] Quoted in *Le Signal* of March 16, 1899. Unless otherwise noted these articles are contained in the clippings of the Klein papers in the Archives of the University of Notre Dame.

in *Le Journal des Débats*, which could be considered neutral, indicated that the Americanists had submitted as had Schell and added the comment that as in the time of Lamennais the Holy See had taken action in the presence of a liberal Catholic movement. Now silence reigned anew in the Church and discussion had been silenced, but he asked the question whether the Church should praise herself for this. To that question time alone could answer.

But the French publishers and editors who had been strong partisans of Americanism in the *Life* of Hecker and, above all of the democratic ideas which they had endeavored to propagate through the *Life*, at first seemed stunned, because they had regarded Pope Leo XIII as their friend. Gradually they began to see this friendship even in the letter. Richeville—apparently Msgr. Boeglin—in *La Vie Catholique* on February 24 called the letter a grand piece of liberation which recognized Americanism before and after Heckerism and distinguished between Hecker and Heckerism. Real Americanism, he said, was integral Catholicism. On February 28 in a brief note in the same paper he praised the answer of Archbishop Ireland, adding that the philosophical and religious Americanism never existed across the Atlantic—the Americanism across the Atlantic was only political and social and that the Pope blessed. But Richeville must have had his tongue in his cheek when he added that Ireland experienced one of the great joys of his life in seeing these words of ratification come down from the Vatican.

By March 7 the defense of the *Abbés Démocrates* began to take on a more formal character. Abbé Pierre Dabry published an extensive treatment of the papal letter in *La Vie Catholique*. The editors had not intended to discuss the papal letter because they did not feel that the doctrines discussed by the Pope concerned them, since the condemned doctrines were not held by anyone they knew. In Dabry's opinion the Pope in this letter was a liberator; he wrote the letter to put the faithful on their guard against certain errors, particularly concerning the magistrature of the Church. Certainly he and his fellow Democrats had not been the ones who had objected to this authority of the Holy

Father. For years they had been fighting those who objected to the commands of the Holy Father. Neither did the Pope's words about the separation between the natural and the supernatural have any bearing against the Christian Democrats who had always insisted on a supernatural basis for their teachings. On the distinction between active and passive virtues Dabry said there was no real trouble here since there was no real theological distinction between them; but the passivity of those who had not followed the papal directives in the political world had caused a transfer of these theological words into the political world. Dabry then went on to maintain that the Pope did not say who had started these discussions but the Democrats knew they were raised by the Pope's enemies to cause confusion. Like Abbé Klein, the Christian Democrats readily submitted to the papal directives and did not resist, as their opponents had resisted the Pope for ten years.

Again on March 14, Abbé Dabry published in the same journal an article entitled "La Démocratie Chrétienne et L'Américanisme." He said that while the letter to Cardinal Gibbons was not addressed to the French it did concern them. The *Life* of Hecker was the occasion, yet this *Life* was ardently accepted by the Christian Democrats and attacked by the French liberals and the Gallicans. He called this a curious phenomena because Christian democracy was interested in social laws and was opposed to that individualism which was so prominent in America. Americanism should really have made friends with European liberalism. In the condemnation, the doctrines condemned by the Pope should have been those sustained by the adversaries of Christian democracy. In the papal letter he found the exaltation of authority, the recognition of individual weakness, the rejection of those who have no faith in external direction and were enemies of all interference with individual interests. Thus he maintained that Christian democracy was not at all affected by the papal letter. The fact that American individualism was considered the friend of the European Christian democrats, he held to be the result of historical events. The fact was that Americanism had been at the same time progressive, apostolic, and republican—which were qualities also of the Christian Democrats. The idea of progress had been the common interest; for the Americans by material conquests through the development of personal powers and individual abilities, for the Christian democrats by social laws. This also explained the repercussions of the papal letter on the French quarrels. Thus Dabry maintained that the doctrines condemned were really those of the *réfractaires*. The instrument of this treacherous operation was the *Life of Hecker* in which the *réfractaires*, by cutting off passages and accenting certain parts of the book, misrepresented the ideas of both Hecker and of the translator. The Pope was not deceived and would not let the *Life of Hecker* be put on the Index. In his admirable letter, said Dabry, the Pope showed good will to the propagators of his own ideas, stating that he knew well that the American bishops rejected the doctrines which he reproved. There were indeed, added Dabry, certain errors to which the Americans and the Christian Democrats could be led if they were not careful and these the Holy Father felt it necessary to point out. But the Pope did not say that either Hecker or his followers held these theories. Even Saint Augustine could not be held responsible for the interpretations made of his writings by the reformers of the seventeenth century. Thus the idea of admitting only natural virtues and sole guidance by the Holy Spirit, two ideas reproved by the Pope in the letter, were in themselves contradictory and not held by Hecker, Klein, the American bishops, or the Christian Democrats. Further Dabry noted that the Holy Father was so sure about this in those to whom he addressed the letter that he seemed to have in mind others. Some had misunderstood the law of progress and some sheep had left the fold, and to prevent further defections the Holy Father felt it necessary to put on guard those who marched ahead on the road of progress. For ten years some Catholics had refused to listen to the Holy Father. Now they said they had heard the Holy Father's words. Those who were now addressed by the Holy Father could imitate these *réfractaires*, but Dabry told them to keep calm. Those who were with the Holy Father then were still with him and those opposed to him were still opposed. The Christian Democrats were not compromised by the theological formulas given out by some writers and attributed to them or by the extravagances attributed to men who denied that they held them. The Heckers, the Gibbonses, the Irelands with Leo XIII at their head were continuing to mark the way ahead. Far from being disturbed, like alpine climbers, they were pleased to be sheltered from error by the advice of their guide.

However, on April 11, *La Vie Catholique* summarized the speech of Leon Harmel at Blois in which he had indicated that the condemnation of Americanism, and the rejection by the Sacred Congregation of bishops and regulars, of Mère Marie du Sacré Coeur's plan for a Normal school for teaching sisters had given rise to an opinion that the Holy Father had changed his attitude and his program. To this Abbé Dabry added an editorial in which he admitted that the confusion existed and suggested that some clarification was needed. Again on April 18, Abbé Dabry published in the same paper a full page letter to Bishop Isoard on the bishop's actions, referring to Isoard's letter of February 22 on Americanism and to his letter of April 6 felicitating Canon Delassus. Dabry demanded that Isoard bring forth his proofs and the names of his witnesses in answer to the charge that the members of the Congress of Rheims and the Christian Democrats had been disloyal to the Church. He cited with some detail the refusal of the *réfractaires* to submit to the Pope in the matter of the Republic and then demanded that Isoard bring out his proof for his charges.

On April 21 Richeville in *La Vie Catholique* published an imaginary dialogue between a "*réfractaire*" and a "pontifical" in which the *réfractaire* made fun of the Progressives who had earned only censure for their zeal. The whole dialogue made fun of the victories of the conservatives. In one passage the *réfractaire* said: "In the Catholic Church, the advance guard, whatever their intentions, are always sacrificed. It is to the laggard and the lazy ones that the happy role belongs." The pontifical answered that the *réfractaires* deceived themselves; that Pope Leo had not condemned but sanctioned the social, political, and religious action of the Americans.

On March 11, Abbé Naudet, the editor of *La Justice Sociale* of Paris, a member of the Assembly and also one of the leaders of the *Abbés Démocrates*, published an article "A propos de L'Américanisme" in his journal. Naudet praised the letter of the Pope and the answer of Archbishop Ireland and then asked, "What is Americanism? Is it a state of mind? Is it a doctrine?" If it was a state of mind, one did not need to go across the ocean to study it because Lacordaire and Montalembert had said all that could be found in the speeches of Archbishop Ireland, and it was what the Pope had been advising the Catholics of the French Republic. If it was a body of doctrine it was found only in the writings of Abbé Maignen, and not elsewhere, even in the French *Life* of Father Hecker. He admitted that the adaptation of this biography, and the preface of Klein, was not free of criticism, but the charges of attacking discipline and dogma had been drawn up by men of bad faith. Naudet did not feel that he had to defend either Hecker or Klein. Hecker appeared to him to have been an excellent religious with originalities perhaps a bit strong, but such as one finds in the lives of saints. As to Klein, he was capable of defending himself. Naudet did not intend to enter into the battle except to fulfill his duties as a journalist, leaving it to *La Vérité* to make him an Americanist—an individualist—although individualism and the Christian Democrats were at opposite poles. Naudet admitted that he did not agree with Hecker about the superiority of the Anglo-Saxons. He did admire the members of the Church in America for their great accomplishments and their audacious spirit. Perhaps it was well to distinguish between this audacious Americanism and Heckerism. Abbé Klein failed perhaps first, to distinguish between these two and then to depart clearly from the second. His adversaries were quick to take advantage of this and pretended to take action to prevent the growth of a pernicious heresy in the Church. They knew that the system did not exist. The Pope after admitting that these doctrines were not in the writings of Hecker, Gibbons, Ireland, Keane or other American theologians and philosophers, designated them as Americanism and was careful not to attribute to the Americans the child of the imagination of the editors of *La Vérité*, who had endeavored by tricks to make suspect the methods of Americans. The chief tool for this was Maignen's book. Now these attackers were beside themselves because the Pope had addressed a letter of praise to Cardinal Gibbons in which he had not condemned the methods of the American bishops nor accused them of approving the methods which he has condemned. This ought to have ended the campaign, but the *réfractaires* would not disarm. As a postscript Naudet noted that *La Croix* had announced that Ireland had submitted completely. Naudet said Ireland had not admitted that he held the condemned teachings but added he had never held them and suggested that *La Croix* owed him an apology.

Likewise in *La Justice Sociale* of August 15, Abbé Naudet again took up the question of the position of the *Abbés Démocrates* following the decisions on Americanism and Mère Marie du Sacré Coeur. He maintained that only those in bad faith can see in these decisions any change in the Pope's attitude towards democracy and the Christian Democrats. For ten years they had always followed the Pope's decrees and had fought the *réfractaires* and *La Vérité* who had opposed the Pope's wishes. Naudet spoke of the bad faith of the *réfractaires* in their attacks on him, their unjust imputation that he had attacked the *Imitation of Christ*, the character of Saint Francis of Assisi, and that of Saint Ignatius and others. Everyone knew, said Naudet, that the Church was divided into two camps: one which sought to bring out the new means already in reserve in the eternal wisdom of the Church to enable the Church to meet new problems, and the other which included those who were closed to all new ideas and were content to see everyone perish in order to save the status quo. Continuing along these lines he defended the action of the progressives, especially their belief in democracy. Others, he said, place their faith in a Caesar or a king. The former march on, and advance knowledge, not only in the scientific field but also where it touches on exegesis and history. The latter close their eyes even at midday and charge with heresy others who do try to go ahead. Conflict, he claimed, is inevitable between the two groups. He added that the Christian Democrats were in union with their bishops and that they had not received any official blame. Naudet admitted that in their efforts to renew and to give new forms to old truths they sometimes went too fast or too far—something the conservatives never did—but that they then listened to the advice of the Church. He begged his fellow Christian Democrats not to be discouraged. The great founders, Saint Benedict, Saint Bruno, Saint Francis and Saint Dominic were regarded as innovators.

On February 25 *L'Univers et le Monde*, also friendly to the Americanists, pointed out that the Pope exempted from the condemnation American customs and usages. The paper claimed that it had previously made some exceptions to the translation of the *Life* of Hecker; if there is any Americanism in the sense reproved it must be rejected. On the same day *Le Patriot* of Brussels pointed out that the Pope did not say in his letter that the heresy existed in America.

In the meantime there appeared on March 1 in *La Quinzaine*, the organ of Georges Fonsegrive, an article entitled "A Propos de l'Américanisme" by Saint Roman. The editors, who had also favored the Americanists, admitted that they had received a copy of the papal letter but that the article was written before the letter and would show that there was a distinction between the real Americanism and that which was being discussed by certain theologians and now condemned by the Pope. The article had for its purpose to prove that Americanism was a tactic not a doctrine. The author showed how Europe had admired the growth of Catholicism in the United States. Leo XIII had realized that the future belonged with the democracies. The Americans, he said, accept democracy as the best formula of government, but this idea had been fought by the enemies of the Pope and by the reactionaries. In American Catholicism the Church is not in politics: Catholics belong to both parties; American Catholicism is like that of the second century. In France by the union of the throne and the altar, Catholics had become the enemies of the democratic state. Further he pointed out, contrary to the writer in *Le Temps*, American democracy is not the old condemned liberalism. American Catholics are liberal Catholics insofar as they belong to the groups who uphold the flag of political liberties, of the common law, and the scientific renaissance. But for the rest they stand for the social doctrines of the Gospel as set forth in the *Rerum Novarum*. Contrary to the continental liberals the Americans are social, democratic, and respectful of a constitution. With the foundation of the Catholic University a new era had begun for the Catholic Church in the United States. The leaders of this new era were John Lancaster Spalding, John A. Zahm, Gibbons, Ireland, Keane, and O'Gorman who took an active part in public affairs, as church leaders once did in France in the time of Bossuet and Fenelon. In the United States the sacristy is behind the Church, in France the Church is behind the sacristy. Unfortunately in its attention to other labors the American Church had not yet built its intellectual edifice, but this had now begun with the creation of the Catholic University.

Saint Roman argued that it was the absence of tradition and integral comprehension that explained certain opinions of Father Hecker which had been the subject of controversy. If Hecker had been better acquainted with certain continental notions he would not have given such occasions for attacks by his critics. These critics had been unjust to him in making his ideas into a philosophy. Saint Roman rejected Hecker's opinions about the Holy Ghost as being, like those of Manning and other converts from Protestantism, based on a too Hebraic interpretation of the Scripture. Saint Roman also rejected Hecker's opinions about the comparison between the Anglo-Saxon and Latin races, especially when Hecker attributed to the Anglo-Saxons a greater interior life. Hecker's critics were unfair to him to draw from this book a system of philosophy for which the whole Catholic Church in the United States would be held responsible.

At last on April 1, *La Quinzaine* published a more definitive article by Georges Fonsegrive entitled "Américanisme et Américains." Fonsegrive recalled that in an article of November 1, 1898 *La Quinzaine* had expressed its views on Americanism which were similar to those of *L'Ami du Clergé* and those of the pontifical letter. The editor therefore had thought that the best conduct was one of silence and submission to the words of the Pontiff, which they accepted. But because of the letter in *Le Temps* of March 17, 1899 and *L'Univers et le Monde*, which seemed to say that certain doctrines condemned by the Pope existed in the United States, Fonsegrive thought it best to speak out. In the first place he pointed out that Archbishops Keane and Ireland did not renounce their errors but insisted that they had never held these extravagances. The question remained then, did the Pope condemn a heresy that did not exist on the advice of some visionary, which fact would be injurious to the Divine Magisterium of the Pontiff, or did the prelates by a doubtful maneuver deny they held the doctrines to escape the condemnation of doctrines which they had really held. Fonsegrive pointed out that writings can be misinterpreted in such a way that erroneous ideas can arise and be held which were not in the mind of the author of the writings. So also, teachings of one country or environment when transferred to another have a meaning which they did not have in their original environment. Thus the infallible Magisterium might feel itself obliged to condemn such a transposed doctrine lest it cause evil in its new setting. Fonsegrive thought that this could easily be proved to be the case with the errors listed under the name of Americanism by the Holy Father, which he implied were derived from statements and practices actually existing in America but which had acquired a different meaning in Europe because of the exaggerated enthusiasm of those who had introduced them there. In this he did not wish to blame the translators of these writings but rather those who misinterpreted their translations.

As an example, Fonsegrive pointed out that the American mind was essentially practical and concrete while the French mind was above all theoretical and a lover of abstractions. One thinks of things, the other of ideas. Thus on the matter of omitting and slighting certain dogmas for the sake of making converts which the Pope condemned, the Americans simply would not begin proving the existence of hell or infallibility because such doctrines were not under discussion in America, but not because the Americans would not accept these dogmas; in France such a tactic would imply that these dogmas had been abandoned in fact, something that the Americans would not think of. He claimed that the attackers had formed this interpretation of American practices merely as a means of assailing American democracy. Further, regarding the *Life* of Father Hecker, the Pope did not say the doctrines were in the *Life*, as was said about the errors of Jansenius, but that the book was the occasion of the rise of the errors. So also on the role of authority in the Church, the Americans, seeing the lack of initiative of Catholics because of the fear of falling into Protestant individualism, suggested that the role of authority in the Church had been exaggerated. To the French this was heretical but to the Americans it merely meant that Catholics had been too timid. And the declaration of infallibility, according to the Americans, should aid in overcoming this timidity. So also in speaking of greater activity of the Holy Spirit in our times Father Hecker would be speaking rashly if he implied increased activity of the eternal Holy Spirit, but he was speaking only of the temporal manifestations of the Holy Spirit.

On the question of the division between the active and passive virtues Fonsegrive admitted that the Heckerians had used this distinction—which is false—and had spoken lightly of the *Imitation of Christ*, but what they wished to indicate was that certain virtues, such as obedience and humility, do not require the kind of activity that is required in an act of courage and initiative, for example. Fonsegrive said this was just picturesque language among the Americans because one must have humility and obedience to have courage and initiative. The Americans, moreover, were speaking in concrete instances and not of the theoretical comparison of the virtues. Again, when Archbishop Ireland said that the natural virtues should not be neglected for the supernatural, he did not imply the superiority of the natural over the supernatural but he wanted Catholics not to neglect their natural obligations, such as voting and performing their social duties, to go on pilgrimages. Fonsegrive here took particular issue with the writer in *Le Temps* of March 17, who implied that this notion of Ireland was against interests of the religious orders, who saw to it that Ireland was condemned. *Le Temps*, like some of the other critics of Ireland, wrongly implied that Ireland was attacking the doctrine of the superiority of the supernatural over the natural virtues. The real doctrine is that one who does not have natural virtue does not have grace, and therefore does not have the grace to perform supernatural acts. What Ireland really meant was that, in certain circumstances, the natural virtues were just as important as the strictly supernatural, but it must be understood that even these natural virtues are supernaturalized under the circumstances by grace. This, he explained, is the teaching of Saint Francis de Sales and of Bishop Isoard.

Fonsegrive added that it was the same in the matter of the religious vows. No one denied that the evangelical vows are superior to none, and that the contemplative are superior to the active orders, but in practice the American bishop would prefer an active community to a contemplative to care for his missions. So also Father Hecker felt that for the particular circumstances of his community it would be best for them not to have vows. As in all these cases, the Americans were thinking in concrete circumstances not in the theoretical or abstract way of the French thinkers, and so must be understood.

In this way Fonsegrive said that the American bishops could say that they have never held the doctrines reproved by the Holy Father because they have not held them. At the same time the supreme magisterium of the Holy Father was not deceived because the principles drawn out of these concrete circumstances in the French writings were deserving of reprobation. Fonsegrive went on to suggest that the activities of the Church in the United States, as that of the Church in all countries, should be studied for their good examples. But for doctrine all should do as the Americans themselves have done, go only to the supreme magisterium of the Church. There were to be other answers but this article attracted the most attention. Others discussed other points.

Answering *La Flandre Libérale* of March 1, which had made fun of the liberal newspapers, especially *La Justice Sociale*, and claimed that they were condemned, *La Justice Sociale* of Brussels on March 5 denied this, quoting Archbishop Ireland that the Americanism condemned was not held by any educated Catholic. The reactionaries, the article said, were trying to pin the heretical doctrines on Ireland, Klein, and Gibbons without success. Nor had any American bishop nor did Father Hecker hold the Protestant doctrines attributed to them by *La Flandre Libérale*.

Likewise on March 11, *La Justice Sociale* of Brussels, again answering *La Flandre Libérale*, denied that Ireland, Hecker or Klein ever held the doctrines condemned by the Pope and said that, if they had, they would have submitted because of their love of the truth, because the Church is infallible and not *La Flandre Libérale*.

The conservative papers, as was to be expected, were quick to claim victory. On February 26, E. Delfico in *Le Mémorial Diplomatique* maintained that he had predicted the letter of condemnation and insisted that the condemned theories were the vague liberal ideas of the Americanists. On March 5, Delfico continued his analysis of the papal letter discussing the distinction between the natural and supernatural virtues, the active and passive virtues, and the attitude towards the religious life and the vows. He also examined Ireland's letter, praising Ireland's submission but rejecting Ireland's statement that no one held the condemned doctrines. He did not understand the charge that the enemies of the Church had created this confusion.

On February 27 a writer in *Le Nouvelliste* of Lyons claimed that the ideas called Americanism had been formulated and spread throughout the United States and then introduced into France. The letter of the Pope was more absolute in its condemnation than would be the placing of the *Life* of Hecker on the Index. The writer stressed those parts of the papal letter which dealt with the natural and supernatural virtues, the active and passive virtues, and with religious orders. He added that it was hard to imagine a consecration more glorious of the criticisms which M. Maignen and the newspaper *La Vérité* had made the history of Father Hecker. Further, the writer said, the condemnation fell very hard on the Christian Democrats, who with Abbé Klein had been so hard on the critics of Americanism. He signaled for special condemnation Abbé Naudet, who, he claimed, had spoken strongly about the action of the Holy Ghost, of religious evolution, of the active and passive virtues, and of the new era. He placed in the same category Mère Marie du Sacré Coeur, whose plan for a Normal school for nuns had been condemned. He linked Brunetière and the *néo-chrétiens* to the condemnation and said that even at the risk of losing Brunetière and the *néo-chrétiens* the Pope had spoken out against these errors. He demanded absolute submission.

On March 7, however, *La Flandre Libérale* again returned to the attack against *La Justice Sociale* claiming that Clericals are never embarrassed and insisting that in its July 10, 1898 number *La Justice Sociale* and the Social Democrats had embraced the ideas of Hecker. Now that the Pope had spoken they denied that anyone ever held these doctrines. *La Flandre Libérale* called this monumental impudence, and asked why Klein had withdrawn his book if the ideas were not condemnable. Keane had been removed, the writer said, because of his Americanism. Ireland had attacked religious orders. But now the Pope had touched an electric button and the machines had responded.

The more persistent conservative viewpoint was expressed in *La Vérité*, which had published the Pope's letter with great satisfaction. On March 7 it published the letter of Bishop Fuzet of Beauvais, in which the Bishop found that the great problem in the discussion lay in the distinction between what was changeable and unchangeable in the Church, and found the great threat to the Church in a "spirit of independence" which would limit the power of the external magisterium of the Church. Fuzet expressed his desire to retain what was old and French.

On March 28 *La Vérité* reprinted in large part the article of the *Civiltà Cattolica* on "Pope Leo XIII and Americanism," adding also a quotation from the *Courrier* of Brussels. On March 29, the editors copied from the *Semaine Religieuse* of Cambrai the announcement of the publication of the book of Canon Henri Delassus, giving the lengthy titles of each chapter. The book was based upon the articles previously published in the *Semaine* of Cambrai with additional notes. The author of the *La Vérité* article, Maignen, called attention to Delassus' reference to the influence of the Jews and the effect on the young clergy, as worthy of special notice. Maignen admitted that the book would arouse anger but insisted that it would also do good.

Again on April 24, Maignen published in *La Vérité* a long article of "Warning to the Democrats" in which, besides identifying

Richeville as Monsignor Eugene Boeglin, he quoted from the writings of Naudet and Dabry and other Democrats to show their alarm about the condemnation. He said they were correctly alarmed because the condemnation of Americanism was the commencement of a campaign against the Christian Democrats and that they surely would be condemned also. The article was preceded by a long list of quotations from letters of praise sent to Canon Delassus[4] on his book. Delassus claimed he had received letters from nine cardinals and many other bishops and priests.

In another notable article, *L'Éclair* of March 14, noted the growing controversy on the application of the Apostolic letter and, supported with quotations from Klein, Ireland and the French *Life*, proved that they held the doctrines condemned by the Pope. Ireland's letter, the writer claimed, lacked contrition. He compared the Americanists in their denial that they held the condemned doctrines to the Old Catholics, and spoke of the new importation as "the Catholic faith of Chicago." On March 18, *Le Journal* of Caen insisted that the Pope had reinstated the *Syllabus* and made fun of the dreams of the young clergymen that a renewal of the Church was possible. *La Semaine Religieuse* of Cambrai, on the same day attacked the article of Abbé Dabry and insisted that Abbé Naudet had not made his submission. Charles Dupuy in *La Gazette de France* in the issue of March 25 gave an account of Bishop Turinaz's visit to the Pope and Turinaz's statement in which he thanked the Pope for the condemnation, and took to task the Americanists Ireland, Klein, and Naudet for denying that they held the condemned doctrines.

As if to add to the confusion, Bishop Turinaz of Nancy wrote in his weekly publication about his visit to Rome in which he presented Father Maignen's superior, General of the Brothers of Saint Vincent De Paul, Father Leclerc, to the Holy Father. He claimed that Pope Leo said that Father Maignen should be satisfied with his letter on Americanism and added that they must be vigilant. And on April 1, the indefatigable Bishop of Nancy, besides repeating the Pope's words about Abbé Maignen in his *Semaine Religieuse*, challenged the statement of Father Deshon and

[4] Letter of Bishop Isoard to Canon Delassus is printed in *La Croix*, April 18, 1899.

of the American Catholic press that the heresy was not contained in the *Life of Father Hecker*. Besides repeating the charges of a Jansenistic mental reservation he quoted at great length the article in the March 15 *Civiltà Cattolica*. He rejected the supposition that the fact that the Pope did not permit the book to go on the Index meant that the condemnation was less severe. As he had previously said in *La Semaine* of March 4, Bishop Turinaz insisted that the letter was rather a more solemn condemnation than a mild one.

In the meantime, Archbishop Ireland had gone to Naples and the seashore to work on his speech on Joan of Arc. He was really discouraged and did not hesitate to admit this to O'Connell. But for the public he merely kept quiet assuring O'Connell in the meantime that he would speak out after his speech on Joan at Orleans.[5] In France in the meantime some of his critics were beginning to protest against his giving the oration in honor of Joan of Arc. Charles Dupuy in *La Gazette de France* of May 2 wrote a whole column against him under the title "What a Great Pity!" in which he surveyed Ireland's activity from the first speech of 1892.

Of all the articles defending the Americanists and explaining the attitude of Ireland, Keane and Deshon on the papal letter, the one that attracted the strongest reaction was that of Fonsegrive in *La Quinzaine* of April 1, 1899. To Bishop Turinaz of Nancy, who was probably the strongest opponent of the Americanists in the French hierarchy, the article was particularly dangerous and in his *Semaine Religieuse* of Nancy of April 19 he formally condemned the article, forbidding his flock to read it. Bishop Isoard of Annecy joined Turinaz in a letter of the same date, April 19, condemning not only the article but the whole magazine. Other French bishops felt otherwise, and Fonsegrive himself was welcomed in Rome affectionately by Pope Leo XIII a few months later.[6] On May 2 *L'Univers et le Monde* gave recognition to the action of the two bishops but added a note from the *Semaine Reli-*

[5] Ireland to O'Connell, April 23, 1899, in the Richmond Diocesan Archives. O'Connell to Countess Sabina di Parravicino di Revel, May 13, 1899.

[6] Edouard Lecanuet, *La Vie de l'Église sous Léon XIII* (Paris, 1930), pp. 594-96.

gieuse of Chalons which claimed that the Pope had indeed spoken of some of the best sons of the Church in his letter, but that he had spoken to them as sons, and that it was proper for the members of the Church to speak of these men in the same fraternal spirit. On May 6 Auguste Roussel in *La Vérité* quoted the article of *L'Univers et le Monde* but claimed that *L'Univers et le Monde* had not shown any fraternal feelings in its attack on *La Vérité*. In *L'Éclair* of May 6, Jean de Bonnefon made another attack on the choice of Ireland for the Joan of Arc speech quoting the French Canadian journals of the United States and other publications to show that he was not really a friend of the French. The same writer penned a bitter criticism of Ireland and his speech in *Le Journal* of May 9. But on the same day Julien de Narfon wrote in *Le Figaro* a rather eloquent and certainly a friendly account of Ireland's speech, quoting him at great length. Abbé Dabry praised the discourse in *La Vie Catholique* of May 12.

From Orleans Ireland proceeded to Paris where he spoke in the Church of Saint Clotilde on May 15. *L'Univers et le Monde* of May 16 said that he spoke three times, once from the pulpit in the morning, at one o'clock at the distribution of prizes, and at vespers on Saint Clotilde. At the first the basilica was filled and there were many noted friends including Abbé Klein in attendance. He touched on his usual themes of praise for France, a plea for activity by Catholics. On the next day he went to Plaisance where he spoke to the workers. With him was M. Brunetière, Abbés Lemire and Gayraud, and in the audience was Archbishop Mathieu of Toulouse. This time Ireland improvised his talk, which was mostly about the eighth anniversary of the *Rerum Novarum*, on the dignity of human labor, and the first rights of the laboring man to the fruits of his toil. The speech was reported by Pierre Veuillot in *L'Univers et le Monde* of May 17. Other papers mentioned the speech, paying particular attention to the hearty reception given him by the people. But the controversy over the papal letter continued.

On May 15, *La Vérité* republished a letter of Frederic Boudin from *Le Signal* in which he announced that he had resigned his presidency in the Progressive Union of Catholic Youth, saying that he no longer could retain his position in the face of the trend in the recent papal decrees. He claimed that the libertarian age which began with the earlier encyclicals of Pope Leo was now closed. In his pamphlet published that year he had come to understand the impossibility of founding a third party—neither clerical nor Jacobin—uniting in the same thought and in the same love, the Church and democracy.[7] The *La Vérité* article was signed by Maignen who said that these brilliant laymen had no right to speak in matters of religion. Maignen denied that the Church was dying either in France or America. In America those who held the true doctrines live on as was shown by the letters of the bishops of New York and New Orleans in their answer to Pope Leo. The same issue quoted the Milwaukee *Catholic Citizen* and the Philadelphia *Presbyterian* as saying that the *Life* of Hecker was having a wider sale since the Pope's letter, and asked if Father Deshon was really carrying out his promise to withdraw the book.

On May 18, the Pastoral of Cardinal Richard, calling the priests of the Archdiocese of Paris[8] to their annual retreat, contained a passage referring to the Pope's letter against Americanism, saying that the Pope had warned them against trying to win souls to the Church by lessening or softening the truths of the Church, and insisting on firmness in holding to the old doctrines and not being seduced by the pretext of making the doctrines of the Church answer the need and aspiration of the day.

From Paris Archbishop Ireland went on to Brussels where he renewed his contacts with the Bellamy Storers at the American embassy. Mrs. Storer was a strong partisan of Archbishop Ireland, trying not only directly to defend him at the papal court by letters to Cardinal Rampolla but also indirectly by trying to persuade officials in Washington to intercede in Rome to secure a cardinal's hat for him. Under their patronage Ireland was entertained at dinner by King Leopold, preached in the Cathedral of Saint Gudule, and on May 24 addressed a large audience at the Palais

[7] Frederic Boudin, *Le Mouvement Néo-Chrétien* (*étude rétrospective*) (Paris, 1899) p. 15.

[8] *Lettre Pastorale de son Éminence le Cardinal Richard Archevêque de Paris aux Prêtres de son Diocèse relativement à la Retraite Ecclésiastique*, no. 184, (Paris, 1899).

des Académies. Again he went back to France, visiting his old schools at Meximieux, Belley, Montluel and returned to Paris before going to England and Ireland. In all this he was much the same Americanist he had been before the papal letter, to the amazement and chagrin of those who had hoped to see him crushed by the impact of that letter. From Brussels he wrote to his friend O'Connell describing the round of banquets, speeches and receptions. "To judge from welcomes and acclaim Americanism is the one thing that is triumphant today." But he adds, "Mon Dieu, what a sad visit mine was to Rome. I wish that those three months were blotted out of my life's story. However, they revealed to me realities heretofore hidden."[9] He added that he would not attack because the mass of the people were with him. He later wrote that he could not go to Germany on this trip because of the international feeling and because of the grand welcome he had received in France. But on June 3 he wrote to O'Connell the warning note: "My letter on Americanism will appear on the eve of my departure from Paris. I will take high grounds—avoiding allusions to persons whom we must despise."

On May 25 *La Vérité* announced the publication of Abbé Georges Périès'[10] pamphlet on the condemnation of Americanism. Writing under the name of Saint Clement, Périès had published the essays in his *Revue Canonique* and now reprinted them in book form. He was much disturbed by the denials of Ireland, Keane, and the American Catholic press. He explained that Americans do not think before they speak and therefore can change opinions and deny what they have previously said. He made sarcastic remarks about the editors of the *Catholic Citizen* of Milwaukee and the *Western Watchman*. In answer he quoted Charbonnel's charges against Klein, Klein's statements in *La Revue Française d' Edimbourg*, the letter of Corrigan, and an editorial in *Church Progress*. These errors he claimed were not new. Cardinal Richard, he said, preferred the old virtues and praised the religious

[9] Ireland to O'Connell, Brussels, May 18, 1899 in the Richmond Diocesan Archives.

[10] Saint Clement, *Cuique Suum—Liquidation du "Consortium" Américaniste* (Paris, 1899).

life. In general Périès rejected the suggestion that the Pope had attacked an imaginary heresy.

On May 29 Abbé Maignen published in *La Vérité* a long criticism of Fonsegrive's article in the April *Quinzaine* on Americanism. He accused Fonsegrive of misinterpreting what Father Hecker taught concerning the Holy Ghost and insisted that Hecker's teachings were those condemned in the Pope's letter as temerarious. He rejected Fonsegrive's explanation for the distinction between the active and passive virtues. He likewise found holes in Fonsegrive's explanation about the relations between the natural and supernatural virtues. Finally Maignen claimed that Fonsegrive was confused on the nature of the vows of religious. Maignen admitted that Fonsegrive knew many things that he did not but suggested that Fonsegrive was not a theologian. Likewise he added a few lines of criticism of the praise bestowed on Fonsegrive's article by Abbé Naudet and Abbé Dabry.

During this period there arose in the Catholic press of France and Belgium another rather bitter controversy based in part on the wild claims of Canon Henri Delassus that the Americanist heresy was part of a campaign of Jews and Freemasons to undermine the Church. Particularly Delassus had attacked the Christian Democrats and their congresses of workers, implying that they too were under papal disapproval. Against him Abbé Naudet and Abbé Dabry produced the telegrams of approval from Rome for the congresses. Eventually all these attempts to make the condemnation of Americanism, and the other restrictive papal documents, imply a change in papal policy about political, economic and social reform, received a rebuke in the form of a papal letter dated May 25.

In the midst of the controversy about the meaning of the papal letter and the attempts to interpret it as a condemnation of the Christian Democrats, Archbishop Pierre Servonnet of Bourges had written to the Holy Father for a clear statement of the effect of the recent decrees on the papal policy. The papal answer began with a direct denial of any change in the papal policy in France regarding political and social matters.

"The truth is," said the Pontiff, "these documents which we

have recently published are related uniquely either to dogma or the Christian discipline and do not concern in any way the prescriptions which we have given concerning the Catholics of your country and are clearly contained in our letter to the French of the month of February, 1892 and in the encyclical *Rerum Novarum*."[11] The Pope went on to say that in these matters nothing had been changed, as such a change would be unworthy of the Apostolic See. The Holy See wished to renew those exhortations and his hopes for a compact nation in carrying them out. In *La Vie Catholique* of June 6, Abbé Dabry quoted the whole letter with a fervent commentary. Pope Leo XIII, he said, had rehabilitated the traditional policies of the Church in a country extraordinarily blinded by passions. Those policies he claimed were the political and social reform demanded by the Pope. In the same issue Richeville in his column could not suppress his satisfaction at what he considered a papal justification of their stand. Of course it can be added that the papal letter did not undo anything said in the earlier papal letter, but it did deny the right of the opponents to use it as a condemnation for all progressive ideas in politics and social reform. On June 13, *La Vie Catholique* quoted an appeal from *La Croix de Provence* asking that *La Croix de Paris* accept and announce the papal letter to Servonnet, and chided *La Vérité* for its silence on the letter, an the failure of the *Semaine Religieuse* of Rennes, Beauvais and Nancy to publish it. This chiding was echoed in *L'Univers et le Monde* of June 15 in an article signed by Eugene Veuillot. In answer, *La Vérité* published a letter of Cardinal Cascajares of Valladolid praising Delassus' book, challenged the liberal publications about their assertion that *La Vérité* had misrepresented the papal doctrines, and added the letter of Bishop Ignatius Horstmann of May 24, published in the Cleveland *Universe*, in which Horstmann asserted that it was wrong to say that the errors condemned did not exist in the *Life* of Father Hecker. Horstmann had stated that to say that the Pope

---

[11] The papal letter was first published in *La Semaine Religieuse* of Bourges. Abbé Dabry reprinted it in *La Vie Catholique*, June 6, 1899 with the comment that the Pope had intervened to cut off the false interpretations of the letter to Cardinal Gibbons. Charles Maignen reprinted the letter in his book, *Nouveau Catholicisme et Nouveau Clergé* (Paris, 1902) pp. 234-36.

wrote the letter without full knowledge of the affair was simply absurd and that it was worse to say that the letter did not apply to the United States. The *La Vérité* article was signed by Maignen. Against this article and Bishop Horstmann, *La Vie Catholique* of June 20 pointed out that the Pope did not say what Horstmann had said. The arguments about the meaning of the papal letter were not checked by this letter to Archbishop Servonnet.

On June 20, in an article which probably was prepared before the appearance of the papal letter to Servonnet, Father Gabriel Desjardins, S.J., discussed the *Testem* in "La Lettre au Cardinal Gibbons."[12] After giving a brief account of how the controversy had eventually reached Rome, Desjardins said that, while addressing the letter to one bishop the Pope was really speaking *ex cathedra*, and that the application of the letter was shown in the answer by Archbishop Corrigan, which he quoted. Thus, he said it was unheard of that a Pope speaking *ex cathedra* should condemn a heresy that did not exist. Those who maintain this were using a Jansenistic distinction. He then took up the points of the letter. On the question of discipline Desjardins said that a young country always resists authority and insists on liberty. This, he said, explained Father Hecker's insistence that during the past three centuries the exterior submission to authority had been insisted on but that now in the modern age there was insistence on interior direction by the Holy Ghost with a kind of self-government. Desjardins said the Pope had rejected the ideas of Father Hecker about external direction. Desjardins gave examples of the saints of the so-called centuries of passive submission who had been very active but who had insisted on external direction. Further Desjardins repeated the papal insistence on the superiority of the supernatural and the non-existence of the distinction between the active and passive virtues, giving the Thomistic doctrine on virtues. He said that America seemed to be the land offering the greatest opportunities for members of religious communities and it was strange that Hecker should attack the value of the religious life. Finally, said Desjardins, the Pope praised the activity for the conversion of those outside the Church but disapproved the giving up of old and approved methods. What Desjardins did

[12] *Les Études Religieuses*, LXX, XIX (1899) 760-77.

not mention was the last paragraph of the papal letter in which the Pope said that he was sure that the American Bishops would be the first to denounce this so-called Americanism and that the letter in no way concerned the political and social matters of the American people.

By this time Ireland was in England and at last began his promised defense of the Americanists. The organ for the attack was the *New Era* of June 17, a Catholic weekly published in London by Burns and Oates.

The first defense was an article in the June 17, 1899 issue of the *New Era* entitled "The Real Author of Americanism"[13] in which Ireland was asked his opinion of Canon Delassus and of Saint Clement. Of Saint Clement he said that he was Father Georges Périès, a priest of the Church of the Holy Trinity in Paris who had been discharged from his professorship of Canon Law at the Catholic University of Washington in 1896, and who had instigated the attacks upon the American Church. Ireland submitted to the reporters copies of the official correspondence between Périès and the bishops at the time of his dismissal, particularly his letter to Bishop Horstmann in which he threatened to attack the University if he was not cleared by the bishops. The interview then pointed out how Périès returned to France and immediately began to attack the University and its friends by forceful arguments to the strong and by stories of scandal to the weak. The ultimate result of this attack begun by Périès was the letter of Pope Leo to which the loyal American bishops had given their full adherence. This *New Era* article was reprinted at great length in *La Vie Catholique* of June 23, by Abbé Dabry who seconded the hope of the editor of the *New Era* that the article would end the false stories about Americanism. Dabry, however, expressed his doubt that such a good result would follow. On June 23 and 24, 1899[14] many other French papers translated passages from Ireland's statements to the editor of the *New Era*.

In general, Ireland had told the reporters that if by American-

---

[13] *La Vie Catholique*, June 23, quotes the June 17 article in the *New Era*. Cf. also *The Review*, July 13, 1899 on Preuss's opinion of this article.

[14] The French newspapers quoted the *New York Herald*, for this statement to the *New Era* editor. Cf. *Le Temps*, *Le Peuple Français*, June 24, *Le Petit Universel*, June 25, 1899.

ism one understands the logical errors condemned by the Pope there was nothing like it in the United States. The only thing about this whole affair which had created a little disturbance among American Catholics was the gratuitous insult to the American Catholics by the people in France who had designated these errors as Americanism. He had told the Pope this in his own letter and the Pope had been so pleased with his letter that he had immediately ordered it published in the *Osservatore Romano*. If, on the other hand, said the Archbishop, one understood by Americanism the loyal adherence by American Catholics to the political conditions of their country, to its Constitution, and to its laws then Americanism does exist among them. And if by Americanism is meant a desire to turn to the profit of the Church the circumstances which modern times and the special conditions of America have created, then Americanism can be charged to the American Catholics. In America they do not worry about the past but do the things before them. Further, if by Americanism is meant the activity in religious works, indefatigable personal initiative in seeking success but under the direction of the Pope and the bishops, then Americanism exists among American Catholics. They do not cross their arms and say that they will do nothing nor do they recoil and retreat before powerful anti-Catholic attacks. Ireland was given a grand reception wherever he went in England, and in Ireland, taking time occasionally to repeat his story of the origin of Americanism.

The interviews had their repercussions in the French press. In *Le Figaro* of June 25, Julien de Narfon quoted an interview of Ireland in which, while the statements on the subject of the true and false Americanism are about the same, he quoted at length Ireland's opinion of Delassus. Delassus, Ireland had said, was a pathological case sufficiently rare on the American side of the Atlantic but more common on the European side. It was that mental state which permitted some French Catholics to believe the story of Diana Vaughn as told by Leo Taxil. Asked if they had such people in America, Ireland said that they send such men as Delassus to the hospital in America. *La Justice Sociale* further published an article entitled "Saint Clement, Is he a saint?" and followed it with an editorial demanding that Périès use his own name in future articles in *La Vérité* and the *Revue Canonique*. The *Univers et le Monde* demanded from *La Vérité* if the charges were true. Finally on July 3 Auguste Roussel answered for Périès explaining his departure from the Catholic University. He claimed that his teachings were fully orthodox and quoted the letter of Satolli to Cardinal Richard at the time of the dismissal asking for a place for him in Paris. *La Vie Catholique* of July 4 answered that the best proof of Périès' integrity would have been to have remained at the Catholic University and to have there served the Church.

Having made his answer Archbishop Ireland, as he had planned,[15] sailed for the United States. He was received publicly in New York and continued his public statements to the effect that only the false Americanism had been condemned. Against Archbishop Katzer he felt it necessary to write to the *Catholic Tribune* of Dubuque to deny a statement that he had been among those who had written to the Pope stating that the error did not exist, but this apparently was before the Milwaukee provincial letter came to his attention.

In the United States Ireland again faced the argument over the meaning of the papal letter. Bishop McQuaid,[16] who had not been very prominent in the later stages of the controversy, rose to the occasion of the denial of the heresy and on June 25 in his Cathedral attacked those who said the condemned doctrines did not exist. His examples of Americanism in the sense of the papal letter were; first, the Congress of Religions; second, the attempt to adopt the state system of public schools for Catholics; third, the attempt to prevent the ban on Catholics joining secret societies; fourth, the appearance of Bishop Keane in his pontifical robes in the halls of a non-Catholic university. This address was in answer to the story in the London *New Era* which had been published in the

---

[15] Ireland to O'Connell, June 3, 1899. "My letter on Americanism will appear on the eve of my departure from Paris. I will take high grounds avoiding allusions to persons we must despise." The disclosure of the Périès documents hardly fits in with the latter part of this statement.

[16] *Rochester Union and Advertiser* of June 26, 1899. Quoted and discussed in *The Review* of July 13, 1899.

New York *Herald* under the date of June 22. On July 13 the *Review* summarized the June 17 article in the *New Era* and contradicted it over the name of the editor, Arthur Preuss, with a postscript by J. F. Meifuss supporting Périès and his recent publications. To the exasperation of the conservatives, Father William Barry contributed an article to the July *North American Review* under the title "Americanism, True and False," which in general supported the story of Archbishop Ireland in his battles with the Germans and the conservatives, and attributed the apostolic letter, among other things, to the Spanish influence suffering from the Spanish-American War. The real Americanism he claimed was not affected by the *Testem Benevolentiae*. "It will then, we trust, be clear that there is a noble and necessary use of the word 'Americanism,' against which Pope Leo does not in any way set his face: while there is another, not necessary, and far from noble, for which those are responsible who employ it in a sense entirely foreign to the American people. . . ."[17] In general, however, the controversy was simmering down in the Catholic press.

Writing to his friend O'Connell from Saint Paul on July 24, 1899, Ireland indicated that he was meditating on the events of his European trip.

> I ask myself—what the cause, What the meaning? One thing is sure— & the *Civilta* & its adherents make no impression on the world—save the Archbishop of Paris and the Jesuits of Paris & London all of whom I scorned. Orders were sent from the General in Rome, to the Jesuits of Paris & Rome to shun me—I have this from most reliable inner source— Hence the Parisian Jesuits animosity—which has recoiled upon the society in the anger of young men.
>
> You were wise in counselling me not to return home at once: I now go back triumphant, with the American people satisfied that Americanism is all right.
>
> The movement was never so widespread, so genuine, so strong. C'è l'av[v]enire—senza dubbio—all we need is courage, work and patience. I will do my part. I will keep in touch with friends in Europe as never before.[18]

The rest of the letter reprimanded O'Connell for talking too much. Apparently O'Connell did speak strongly against the Curia,

[17] Rev. William Barry, "Americanism, True and False," *North American Review*, CLXIX (July, 1899), 33-49.

[18] Ireland to O'Connell, July 24, 1899, in the Richmond Diocesan Archives.

but this talking was in direct contrast to O'Connell's own letter to Klein in November in which he said that not feeling well and being much upset he had said nothing for four months.

Ireland in the meantime under the pen name H. M. refuted the letter of the bishops of Wisconsin in the diocesan paper *The Northwestern Chronicle*,[19] of August 25, 1899. The *Chronicle* had already protested the statement of the bishops of Wisconsin in its August 11 issue, but this was a more detailed criticism in which Ireland added the criticism of the *Catholic Weekly Register* of London, that the American hierarchy was badly confused on its notion of infallibility. Ireland said that the bishops of the Wisconsin province were guilty of two errors, one of fact in charging the Catholic editors with disloyalty to the Holy See, and the second in theology in affixing the seal of infallibility on the papal letter. On the first point Ireland insisted that the American Catholics did not learn of the existence of the errors until the arrival of the papal letter and the charge that the Americanism was spurious came from every corner of the land. The Catholic writers merely repudiated a false charge. Further he pointed out that the Holy Father nowhere indicated who held these heresies and therefore the Wisconsin bishops were making stronger charges than the Holy See.

On the second point Ireland quoted Cardinal Hergenröther on the general teachings of the Church that when the Pope makes an infallible decision that must be manifested by the Pope, usually by such words as "we declare" or "we define." He said he was slow to believe that the Wisconsin bishops held that every time the Pope writes a letter or makes a statement he is making an infallible decision. Finally Ireland took up the question of the Jansenistic reservation charged against the Catholic editors and Ireland by the Wisconsin bishops. The Jansenistic error, he pointed out, consisted in denying certain propositions which were dogmatic facts definitely contained in a book. In the papal letter the Pope did not say that these errors are in any document or book, and secondly he did not attribute it to any person. Ireland suggested that the Milwaukee bishops had cast, by their letter,

19 Ireland to Abbé Klein, Sept. 15, 1899, in the Paulist Fathers Archives.

foul aspersions on Cardinal Gibbons and the American Catholic editors.

When the archbishops met in Washington in October, the matter of these charges was brought up. Among other matters discussed in the meeting of October 12, at the Catholic University, was the question of the letter of the Milwaukee prelates and their charge that the heresy of Americanism existed and that those who denied this were Jansenistic. Archbishop Katzer was not present.

> Then Archbishop Riordan, having called attention to the letter of our Holy Father, *Testem Benevolentiae*, which we all accept with gratitude, referred to the letter of the Archbishop and Bishops of the Province of Milwaukee, in which the existence in this country of the condemned errors was admitted, and in such manner that those who deny their existence are now branded as Jansenists. This he considered a matter of grave importance, being a direct charge of heresy against some of ourselves.
>
> Archbishop Kain spoke on the same lines and expressed his opinion that some action would be taken by us in protest against the charge implied in that letter.
>
> Archbishop Ireland followed and, tracing the development of the charge of erroneous teaching in the Church of America and deprecating the letter of the Milwaukee prelates, he moved that the Most Rev. Secretary be instructed to write to all the Bishops of America and ask from them an expression of their opinion on these two questions:
>
> First—"Whether these errors do exist in their diocese or in other parts of America," and
>
> Second—"If they do, then to specify *where* they exist and by *whom* they are held."
>
> The Archbishop of New York strongly deprecated the adoption of the above resolution, because he thought that it would be disrespectful to the Holy Father.
>
> Archbishop Ryan also objected to the resolution and offered the following substitute:
>
> "That the Prelates here present do all they can to induce all the Bishops, who have not written to the Holy Father, in response to his letter to Cardinal Gibbons, to write to him."
>
> The substitute was lost by a tie vote.
>
> The original resolution was then put and defeated by a vote of four ayes to five nays—His eminence casting his vote against it.[20]

Shortly after the meeting, on October 21, Ireland wrote on the matter to O'Connell.

[20] Printed minutes in the Cathedral Archives, Baltimore.

I have been very happy since my return—working hard and knowing of no country outside of America. I have totally forgotten Rome—never again to think of it. Never again to see it and terrible experience—that of last winter. No, never again—never.

Americanism! The country never thinks of it. I do, however: I am angry with the two men who belied America. Corrigan and Katzer. Two Archbishops admitted the existence of erroneous opinions. Six—Saint Paul, Baltimore, Boston, Saint Louis, San Francisco, and Philadelphia, denied—Four Balt. Santa Fe. Saint Louis and Boston denying it so strongly that [sic] does not publish their letters—Three—Chicago, Dubuque and Santa Fe as far as I can learn did not write at all. Three Cincinnati, Portland, N. Orleans wrote neutral letters.

We had a strong meeting at Washington. San Francisco, Saint Louis, Portland, Saint Paul tried to get a joint protest against the idea of existence of errors. Philadelphia almost joined in but Baltimore cried "peace, peace—death for the sake of peace," And nothing was effected.

Corrigan said, My Roman correspondence [sic] tells me that all the articles on Americanism in the *Civilta* were ordered to be written by the Pope, personally, that the non-publication of certain letters from American Archbishops was the direct act of the Pope. I challenged him to give us the names of his correspondents. He refused and I called him a coward, and bade him cite no Roman correspondence. The chasm between him and me is most wide.[21]

On December 23, 1899, Ireland wrote again to O'Connell and said among other observations: "Nothing is heard here of 'Americanism'—No one seems to know that the Pope ever wrote—outside of Corrigan and the Jesuits—who gloat over their supposed triumph. Corrigan imagines he is forever 'cock of the walk'. Can you with any kind of stick haul him down? Try."[22]

There was one other important exchange in this controversy. The calm of which Ireland and his friends wrote was a bit disturbed when in the March, 1900, *North American Review*, there appeared an article by Monsignor P. L. Péchenard, the rector of the Catholic University of Paris, entitled "The End of 'Americanism' in France."[23] It began with a comparison of the controversy to a violent storm that suddenly abates. He claimed that Americanism had had a long period of incubation in America but that it had suddenly passed over to France with the translation of the life of Father Hecker. When the minds of the controversialists

---

[21] Ireland to O'Connell, Oct. 21, 1899, in the Richmond Diocesan Archives.
[22] Ireland to O'Connell, Dec. 23, 1899, Richmond Diocesan Archives.
[23] *North American Review*, CLXX, (March, 1900), 420-32.

had become excited the Pope had ended the discussion by his Apostolic Letter. While from a distance it might have appeared that Americanism had made great progress in France it had really affected only a few priests, writers, and journalists. Péchenard indicated that the chief errors pointed out in the papal letter were that while American conditions might have permitted some minimizing of the Church's doctrines such a situation did not exist in France where there was no controversy between Catholics and Protestants. So also the question of independence and insubordination did not bother France since the end of the Gallican and Jansenistic heresies. Likewise he said there was no question of France's accepting the value of the vows and religious life and of the direction of the Holy Ghost. The errors of the Americanists were quickly pointed out by French writers. Only two aspects of Americanism appealed to the French, the first its democratic and social ideals which were gaining ground in France and the second the glitter of natural activity which the French admired in the Anglo-Saxons even though the French had not been deficient in these qualities.

Péchenard claimed that the controversy aroused considerable feeling but that the French Bishops were not disturbed but awaited the Papal letter of January 23 [sic] 1899. As soon as the Pope sent his letter the French submitted, including Abbé Klein. Cardinal Richard and Bishop Fuzet of Beauvais were moved to write a few words in support of the papal letter. The controversy was conducted for awhile by L'Univers and La Vérité, and Canon Delassus and Périès published pamphlets against the errors. The only untoward incident was the article by Fonsegrive in the April 1, 1899 Quinzaine which tried to say that the error did not exist but that some American ideas had acquired a wrong meaning when interpreted in France. But Fonsegrive was handled by the condemnation of Bishop Turinaz of Nancy. Péchenard quoted the letters of Corrigan and Katzer and their suffragans to show that the errors did exist in America. Further proof of the end of the controversy was the fact that in all his travels through France on the occasion of his speech in honor of Joan of Arc Archbishop Ireland never touched upon the question of Americanism. "The disavowal, moreover, which he had made of it in his letter to the Pope dispensed him from any explanation."

One has only to read the article to understand the feelings of Ireland and his friends. In the French press, for it was translated and published in pamphlet form in France, the reactions of the friends of Archbishop Ireland were very strong. The answer was not long in coming. In the May issue, 1900, of the same *North American Review* there appeared an article entitled "The Genesis of 'Americanism' "[24] by J. St. Clair Etheridge. Some have claimed that it is written in the style of Archbishop Ireland, but that would be hard to prove. Certainly it is known that his secretary, Monsignor Humphrey Moynihan, wrote to O'Connell for detailed information. Father James Burns, C.S.C.[25] in his diary of those days at the University of Notre Dame says that Father Zahm knew of the article before it appeared and seemed to have had some share in its preparation. When it appeared Ireland sent some copies to Abbé Klein[26] asking that it be translated and adapted for some French periodical, adding that Klein should keep his "secret." Klein in an interview on May 25, 1951 said the "secret" was Ireland's authorship. The only doubt about this is a letter May 7, 1900[27] from Ireland to O'Connell in which he sent some copies of the article to O'Connell adding, after pointing out the expert knowledge of the writer, especially about Father David Fleming, O.F.M., "If you know the writer, give him my most sincere compliments." There are two reasons which might be advanced for Ireland's writing in this way to O'Connell if he were the author. In the first place this is a letter of introduction for Mr. W. B. Dean. If it were sent by him Ireland would not dare indicate the real author of the reprints. The second is the fact that Ireland had complained that O'Connell[28] was talking too much and he may have felt that he should not admit his authorship

[24] *North American Review*, CLXX, (May, 1899), 679-93.

[25] This diary was kept in shorthand, Provincial Archives of the Priests Province of Holy Cross, South Bend, Indiana.

[26] Ireland to Klein, May 9, 1899, in the Klein papers in the Archives of the University of Notre Dame.

[27] Ireland to O'Connell, May 7, 1900 in the Richmond Diocesan Archives.

[28] Ireland to O'Connell, July 24, 1899 in the Richmond Diocesan Archives.

to his Roman correspondent who had been so badly fooled in his dealings with Lepidi. Certain it is, that Ireland had some hand in the composition, and it is highly probable that he either wrote it or supervised its composition.

The article began with a reference to what it calls the funeral oration on Americanism published in the March issue of the *North American*, and proposed to give the history and the origins of the heresy. "The literature of Americanism is almost entirely in a foreign language, and Americanism itself was unheard of in the United States until the moment when the news of its condemnation was cabled from Rome." Etheridge then proceeded to distinguish between political and religious Americanism, attributing the prominence of political Americanism to the writings of Father Hecker forty years before. This Americanism was just good citizenship and was approved and blessed in this sense by Pope Leo XIII. The religious Americanism was derived by Father Charles Maignen from the *Life* of Father Hecker as adapted in French and that story Etheridge intended to relate. Maybe G. Périès, he said, was the "Coryphaeus of Americanism." The account of Périès' resignation was quoted from *The New Era* of June 17, 1899. Périès had returned to Paris after his dismissal from the Catholic University and was joined by Maignen. Etheridge pointed out the crude passages in the original attack on Hecker which were omitted from the English translation, especially that about America not yet being born as a nation. Etheridge proceeded to show how Maignen by clever use of quotations and borrowings from other writers had built up his charges. He accused Maignen of dishonesty in denying the devotion of Father Hecker to Christ. Etheridge claimed that it was no wonder that the Archbishop of Paris refused his imprimatur to Maignen's book. Etheridge then quoted from contemporary sources to show that the charges against the character of Father Hecker were false. He next referred to some of the errors of fact in the book of Canon Delassus, then he attacked the *Civiltà Cattolica* pointing out how the editors of that publication had been fooled by Leo Taxil and his fake revelations of Diana Vaughn. The next opponent examined was Jules Tardivel, the French-Canadian author of the just published *La Situation religieuse aux États Unis*.[29] He had been a bitter opponent of the Americanists in his *La Vérité* of Quebec and was likewise fooled by Taxil. Etheridge showed him to be an intemperate critic of America.

Etheridge classified Péchenard as the next in line of these critics and added the names of Cardinal Mazzella and Cardinal Satolli who had been opposed to the Americanists, and Father David Fleming who was formerly friendly but had become "reactionary." These are the men Etheridge claimed engineered the condemnation of Americanism. These men, he said, hate America as standing before the world for democracy and had charged Father Hecker with heresy so as to condemn all that he stood for, especially his love for democracy.

But the condemnation which they sought from the Holy Father, Etheridge said, was "in reality the only bright page in the history of Americanism." The Pope not only did not impute these heresies to Americans but implied that they would be the first to reject them. Of the fourteen archbishops Etheridge accounted for each one and only two, New York and Milwaukee, professed to believe that the heresy existed in America. But the Wisconsin bishops who admitted that they had not read the *Life of Father Hecker* were the bishops from the pet preserve of Cahenslyism, and Archbishop Corrigan of New York was opposed to Archbishop Ireland and Cardinal Gibbons, and did not see these heresies when he gave his imprimatur to the original *Life of Father Hecker*.

Etheridge attacked the *Civiltà Cattolica* for publishing only those letters of the American prelates which seem to admit the existence of the heresy and particularly for not publishing the

[29] Jules Tardivel, *La Situation Religieuse aux États Unis—Illusions et Realité* (Montreal, 1900). The book is preceded by a letter of Canon Delassus and the imprimatur of Archbishop M.-A. Sonnois, Archbishop of Cambrai, where the book was actually printed. The book is a refutation of the article of Brunetière in the *Revue des Deux Mondes* of November, 1898. First it lists the claims of Brunetière about the growth of the Church in the United States, gives a brief survey of the obstacles, and a survey of the recent controversies. It concludes that the regime of separation of Church and State as it exists in the United States is unfavorable for the growth of the Church. Tardivel was the editor of *La Vérité* of Quebec, which continually attacked the Americanizing prelates of the United States in the interest of the French Canadians.

letter of Cardinal Gibbons. This he called a kind of Jansenistic reservation that the Wisconsin prelates attributed to those who had denied the existence of the heresy. As to Péchenard, Etheridge points out that he had furnished no proof that the three charges against the Americanists—of "bending in dogmatic matters," of a separatist tendency "with respect to the central ecclesiastical authority" or "minimizing in the practices of the Christian and especially the religious life"—were true. Péchenard had said that Americanism was dead. Etheridge said that in France it was born and there it was dead, and it was well that the French bishops had taken care to see that it was dead in their dioceses. Archbishop Ireland did not speak of Americanism in his visit to France because he regarded it as a dead thing and because the Pope and the Cardinals had praised him before he left Rome for correctly interpreting the papal document.

There were to be a few other echoes of the controversy after this date. Ireland made sure through Klein[30] that the Etheridge article was translated, published in the *Spectateur Catholique* of July, 1900 and published also in pamphlet form.[31] The sniping between the chief surviving contestants continued for several years. It might be said that no one changed sides because of the papal document and the silence that settled on the controversy for a generation was an armed silence so long as the contestants lived.

Monsignor Joseph Schroeder wrote his opinion of the controversy. It was first published in a special historical issue of the *Herold des Glaubens* of Saint Louis September 26, 1900. In the introduction to his article Schroeder stated that he did not intend to treat of individuals nor to give an historical survey of the controversy. He regarded it as an insult to a Catholic reader to prove that the Pope did not condemn a phantom. Schroeder pointed out that the condemnation was not in solemn form nor addressed to the whole church nor were the censures stated in technical form. He admitted that it was not *ex cathedra*. He analyzed the papal

---

30 Ireland to Klein, May 9, 1900 in the Klein papers in the University of Notre Dame Archives.

31 J. St.-Clair Etheridge, Trad. Georges Grappe, *La Genèse de "l'Américanisme," Histoire d'une hérésie-fantôme* (Brussels, 1900).

letter, giving each part its meaning. He called the fundamental principle of the error minimism—a term he had used while teaching at the Catholic University. After stating the principles of the Pope, he discussed certain conclusions which could be drawn from the erroneous principles—those about the Holy Ghost, which he called temerarious, about natural virtues, monastic life, etc.

Schroeder then added his interpretation of the letter. In the first place, he said, the Pope had assured the Americans of his affection and that he did not speak of a political or civil Americanism. Here Schroeder made a distinction implying that the erroneous religious Americanism had some connection with American political patriotism. He cited the various errors that were tainted with nationalism and implied that their preference for American political theories was based on "almost a cult of democracy and of the republican constitution." Hecker, he said, thought Americans were of a higher race which he claimed was the product of American liberties. Hecker even insisted that Catholics had to defend this republican faith. But Hecker went further and set himself up as a teacher who would change the whole Christian life, and teach the new order accommodated to modern man. Further Hecker would adapt the Church to moderns, and then open the doors to those of other creeds. Hecker, he claimed, did not recognize the essential nature and supernatural character of the Catholic Church. The followers of Hecker eulogized him and while deliberately avoiding a definition of their doctrines still did not abandon any of his teachings before the condemnation. Later his sickness had been used to explain his extravagances.

But in all this Schroeder did not find the greatest error of the theories of Hecker. The greatest error in his opinion was Hecker's theory about the reconciliation of the Church with the age, the same liberalism which had been taught by Lamennais and Doellinger and condemned by Pope Pius IX in his *Mirari Vos* and the *Syllabus*. Not only Hecker but his followers also were guilty of this in their claims that the Constitution of the United States is the ideal of political wisdom and that it corresponds with the spirit and principles of the Catholic Church more than any other constitution, especially in its principles of religious liberty and separation of Church and State. Pope Leo XIII had warned that this was not ideal in his encyclical *Longinqua*. To support this charge Schroeder quoted Bishop McQuaid and Father Brandi in the *Civiltà*, especially the *Civiltà's* charge of Pelagianism. He claimed that the *Catholic World* was guilty of teaching the condemned errors, as had been pointed out by Arthur Preuss.

In making this charge of liberalism Schroeder was expressing the older accusations against the Americanists by the Germans and by Corrigan, Preston and "Tharseus." This "liberalism" was a major problem in Europe where the battle between the antireligious liberalism and the Church had been joined by the *Quanta Cura* and the *Syllabus of Errors* of Pius IX. But there is very little evidence that Ireland, Keane, O'Connell, Gibbons or any of the other Americanizers were ever much disturbed by the *Quanta Cura* or the *Syllabus of Errors*. They showed little concern even to accept the liberal interpretations of Bishop Dupanloup. The American prelates were practical men, in the American fashion, and they were interested in the practical problems of spreading Catholicism in the United States. They saw in the charges of liberalism made by Schroeder and the conservatives merely attempts to draw a theological red herring across their American opposition to foreign influences. The condemned Americanism was an ascetical and a strategical error, not a dogmatic heresy in the strict sense. And it is very significant that even Schroeder could not find any real statements of the condemned liberalism in the public utterances of Ireland, Keane, and the other Americanists.

Schroeder must have been aware of this difficulty of finding in the American prelates a coherent definition of liberalism because he added: "The Liberal Catholic does not deny a dogma and is therefore prepared to meet any criticism, but basically he makes all dogmas shallow and insipid." He complained that no one can beat the liberal in his praise of the Pope but only because the liberal felt exempt from his obligation to base his political religious system on the decisions of the Holy See. The lengthy conclusion of Schroeder's article was a condemnation of any attempt to reconcile the Church with the spirit of the age which he regarded as condemned by Pope Pius IX and the *Syllabus*. He quoted the best definition of this liberalism as that of the *Freeman's Journal* "that American Catholicism is nothing else than the enlightened progress of the Church as it is appropriate for our age and our country." That definition was in itself sufficient for Schroeder since it included an idea of accommodations and liberalism.

> Americanism mixes up the order of nature and grace when it tries to limit the bounds of the supernatural order, to withdraw society, state and public life in general from the influence of supernatural religion, and in so doing actually degrades the Church to a merely natural and human association that has to keep pace with the "Zeitgeist" from which it is even supposed to get instruction and enlightenment.

Schroeder's article was not reprinted in translation in this country and remained almost unknown in the United States, and without any real influence.

There appeared in Paris in 1900 another pamphlet which apparently did not receive wide circulation, which shows that the nationalistic prejudices were still alive. It was entitled *L'Américanisme jugé par un Prêtre Américain*. Printed in French and English with few capitals, the style indicates that the author of, at least the English version, was probably an American, who probably knew that he would not receive an American imprimatur. He likewise seemed upset by the praise of American Catholicism by Brunetière, although he did not mention him by name. He seemed little impressed with the current controversy, but sought to find the real evils in the character of the clergy governing the Church in the United States. He asked why the Catholic Church which had grown in numbers and wealth had so little influence upon the "thinking and daily life of the American people." He explained this by the character of the bishops who were chiefly Irish and too powerful, and by what he called the charity education of the American clergy. His conclusion was noteworthy because it represented a viewpoint that was not that of either party in the controversy, but was probably that of a disgruntled Catholic clergyman.

. . . The Roman Catholic church is in the midst of the American people, but she is not of them, or in sympathy with them. Why?

Because the Roman Catholic Church in the United States, forgetting that she represents, the universal church, has become in a great measure, at least in church government and feeling, a national Irish church, a much more pronounced national church, than the branches of the churches of England, Scotland, and Germany upon our shores.

Because her rulers, forgetting the poverty in which they were born, and the God of Bethlehem and of Calvary whom they serve, are as eager in their mad chase after wealth as other clerical and lay worshippers of Plutus in the land. Because instead of the simplicity, which is suitable to a republic as it is to christianity, they seek to establish an aristocracy of Irish peasants, with high sounding titles, large revenues, and all the characteristics of men whose ancestors for twenty generations had only to command in order to be obeyed. They surround themselves with an atmosphere that breathes: "I say to my servant do this and he doeth it." Lastly because some of the leading prelates, in their great desire to distinguish themselves by their exaggerated Americanism, fall down and worship the national God of America, the incarnate greatness and wealth of the land, the God set up by politicians for the worship of the American people, and for the envy and wonder of the world. The root however of all these evils is the system of ecclesiastical education, which attracts unfit subjects to the priesthood, at the same time that it repells desirable ones. . . .[32]

But even this critic did not find that the condemned Americanism existed in the United States. Later, Americanism seemed to receive belated approval in the appointment of Archbishop Keane to the archdiocese of Dubuque on July 24, 1900, and the election of Monsignor O'Connell to the rectorship of the Catholic University on January 5, 1903. But the glory of the first was dimmed when the Pope wrote a personal letter dated August 18, 1900, to Archbishop Keane[33] at the time of his appointment urging him to make sure that his flock avoided the errors of Americanism. Gibbons and Ireland were hurt by this as much as Keane, and were unable to understand why the Pope, while assuring Ireland that the letter was intended only for some French dioceses, could apply it to the United States. On the second appointment Ireland

[32] The French printer was apparently unacquainted with the English rules of capitalization or punctuation. Only one copy of this has been found, in the Bibliothèque Nationale.

[33] Keane to Ireland, October 29, 1900 in which Keane tells Ireland of this letter. Cf. Patrick Henry Ahern, *The Life of John J. Keane, Educator and Archbishop, 1839-1918* (Milwaukee, 1954) pp. 285-89. Father Ahern was unable to find any copy of this letter.

felt that there was justification and wrote exultingly to O'Connell on January, 1903[34] "Viva L'Americanismo! Viva Sempre." But the controversy was really dead. Actually the appointment of O'Connell seems to have been the result of a friendship with Satolli that O'Connell had revived at Ireland's suggestion[35] in order to find out why Satolli had changed sides in America, and the fact that in the unsettled state of the Catholic University, this friend of Cardinal Gibbons was perhaps the best available man. Certainly by that time the controversy of Americanism was dead. Of the meaning of this appointment, there will probably be no definite answer for many generations, if at all.

[34] Ireland to O'Connell, January 14, 1903, in the Richmond Diocesan Archives.
[35] Ireland to O'Connell, January 15, 1898, Richmond Diocesan Archives. Later letters show that Satolli responded to O'Connell's approach.

CHAPTER 7 ❧ *Conclusion*

FOR THE CATHOLICS in the United States the question of Americanism was a silenced issue. It was not a dead issue, nor were the issues of Cahenslyism, or the schools, although the questions of the Parliament of Religions and the secret societies seemed to have lost interest for the American Catholics who were never really interested in joining their Protestant neighbors in religious services. But for nearly a generation there was a kind of armed truce about the question of Americanism, from the beginning of the century until the participants in the controversy had passed from the scene. It was a question "too hot to handle." A further reason for the discontinuance of the discussion was another issue that arose almost as soon as the Americanism controversy had been silenced, the question of the heresy called modernism—the condemnation of which brought about a theological silence to the infant schools of theology in the United States.

There were also sentimental reasons for this silence on Americanism. No American Catholic was very happy about the use of the word "Americanism" to designate a condemned teaching. Had any other name been given to the doctrines perhaps those opposed to the Americanists would have been more ready to examine the papal letter and to make proper applications to the American scene. In addition, there was the fact that the great leaders of the Americanists were still on the scene, very active and very important for nearly two decades in the relations between the Catholic minority and the non-Catholic majority in the country. Their best and most active years were past, but they were for the most part front-page characters, well known to the general public. Further, they seemed to be acceptable to the new pontiff, Pius X.

There were other facts that led to the forgetting of this controversy and the obscuring of its importance in the history of the Church in the United States and in Europe. In the United States outside of a burst of newspaper and epistolary discussion immediately after the issuance of the *Testem Benevolentiae*, there was no great popular excitement, even among fervent Catholics, about the heresy. There was no one who defended the doctrines reproved by the Holy Father and for many of the faithful there was no real connection between their practices and the condemned doctrines. American Catholics have always lived a practical religious life; until recently there have not been any real theological centers or any speculative journals in which even the important theologians could discuss the theological implications of the heresy and its condemnation. The *Catholic World* certainly was not inclined to continue to talk about an incident in which the name of the Paulists and their founder had suffered. The *American Ecclesiastical Review*, more of a pastoral than a theological review and also very conservative by tradition, was not inclined to talk about the disputed questions or to arouse the suppressed but truly hard personal feelings of the chief participants in the controversy. The newspapers did continue to show prejudice between the Irish and the Germans, the French Canadians, and the newer immigrants. The new controversy over the doctrines of modernism was not very strong in the country before the issuance of the *Pascendi Gregis*, and that really put the quietus on controversy in the Catholic press until after the First World War. Even then, the activity was in the field of reconstruction and social reform, not dogma or even morals, strictly so-called.

In Europe even before the condemnation of Americanism there was a definite movement concerned with the higher biblical criticism, absolute evolutionism, and religious and philosophical subjectivism which soon absorbed the attention of theologians and theological journals and brought on the condemnation of modernism.[1] Some of the liberal leaders in these new tendencies

---

[1] J. Brugerette, *Le Prêtre Français et Société Contemporaine*, 3 vols. (Paris, 1938) has a good treatment of the modernistic controversy in France in volume III, 125-345.

were friends of the Americanists. Alfred Loisy lived near Abbé Klein and followed with sympathy the reaction against the publication of the *Life* of Father Hecker. Franz X. Kraus of Freiburg im Breisgau[2] had been, with Schell, very friendly with the Americanists and had defended the Americanists against the reactionary Schroeder. But although there was general regret among these theological revolutionaries at the condemnation of Americanism there was no very great concern among them for the doctrines condemned in the *Testem Benevolentiae*. After a few years, outside of the actual defenders of Americanism before the turn of the century, there was no great recollection of Americanism in France, Germany or Italy. Americanism, then, meant the doctrines condemned by the papal letter, something which had flourished in the new world and been introduced into France where it had been condemned by the Holy Father after the error had been exposed by some French writers. As a matter of fact, the *Dictionnaire de Théologie* in 1902 summarized the account of Americanism under the headings of the *Testem Benevolentiae* with a short preface showing how Americanism was the natural outcome of American naturalistic and liberalistic tendencies, which in turn were the result of the great natural richness and frontier freedom of the new country. The concluding sentences said that the author of the article, F. Deshayes, had not mentioned any other name than that of Father Hecker. "For what good would he do otherwise? Rome had spoken, the debate is closed; it pertains, for the rest, only to history."

Unfortunately history has not been content to let the matter drop, but under the impact of the condemnation of modernism historians have endeavored to consider Americanism as the practical preface of the modernistic controversy. Undoubtedly the first definitely to give this interpretation to the controversy was Albert Houtin,[3] who wrote the best documented account of the

---

[2] Dr. Hubert Schiel, *Im Spannungsfeld von Kirche und Politik-Franz Xaver Kraus* (Trier, 1951).

[3] Albert Houtin, *L'Américanisme* (Paris, 1904). This is the chief source of most of the incidental treatments of Americanism in European histories because the book is so well documented in newspaper clippings. Houtin, of course, did not have access to the papers of the participants in the controversy.

controversy and was the chief source of most of the writing on it during the first decades of the twentieth century. Houtin was a modernist and consequently had no sympathy with the condemnation of liberal tendencies in the Church which culminated in the *Pascendi Gregis*, during what he calls the crisis of the faith. Like Maignen and Turinaz and other critics of the Americanists he attributed most of the apostasies in France during the last decade of the nineteenth century to Americanism, placing the controversy and the subsequent condemnation among the other—to him—oppressive and condemnatory actions of the Church as though they were all of one piece. His book, however, was really part of the modernistic controversy and merited being put on the Index for his apparent sympathy with the religious radicalism which was condemned under the name of modernism. More important in propagating the charge that Americanism was a direct cause or at least a part of the tendency towards modernism was the book of Professor, later Bishop, Dr. Anton Gisler, *Der Modernismus, Dargestellt und Gewürdigt*[4] in which he traced a direct lineage from Americanism and Reform Catholicism in Germany to modernism. Gisler had no real knowledge of the Catholics in the United States except through European publications and was apparently deeply affected by the fact that the Americanizers were also severely critical of the conservative Germans in the United States. In the minimism charged by Schroeder and his fellow Germans, in the Parliament of Religions, in the exaggerated democracy of the Americanists and in particular in the apologetics of Hecker which had been introduced into Europe by Klein, etc., and especially as seen in the writings of Maignen and which he associated with that of Schell in Germany, and Blondel and Brunetière, Gisler found the beginnings of modernism in Europe.

Jean Rivière in his *Le Modernisme dans l'Église. Étude d'histoire Religieuse Contemporaine*[5] lists the "Controverse Amér-

---

[4] (Einsiedeln, 1912). Gisler shows too much uncritical dependence on Maignen's *Père Hecker, Est-il un Saint?*.

[5] (Paris, 1909). Rivière gives the impression that the relationship between modernism and Americanism was a proven fact instead of a descriptive assumption by de la Taille.

icaniste" among the "Incidents précurseurs" to the crisis of modernism, applying the terms of other writers and calling it a kind of "practical preface" of modernism. This characterization was likewise given to Americanism in a longer but inaccurate account of the controversy by J. Brugerette in the third volume of his *Le Prêtre Français et la Société Contemporaine*.[6] Both of these authors base their charge that Americanism was a practical preface to modernism on an article on "Modernism" published in *L'Ami du Clergé*,[7] in December 6, 1907, shortly after the condemnation. But De la Taille's paragraph summary of Americanism in that article characterizes it as the kind of subjectivism charged against the Americanists by Abbé Maignen, and cites no actual reference to any Americanists, writings or publications. Cardinal Suhard in his famous pastoral *Growth or Decline*[8] makes a similar unfortunate reference to Americanism. The Americanists were anything but subjectivists and even their modernist friends knew that they were not teaching any modernistic doctrines in the strict sense. However, the tradition based upon De la Taille's sentences has been too often repeated. It can be said in justification of this opinion that the authors based their opinions chiefly on the doctrines condemned in the *Testem Benevolentiae* and perhaps on Maignen and not on American writings. Thus, when Abbé Klein published his autobiography in 1949 and named his volume IV *Une Hérésie fantômie—L'Américanisme*, the controversy over the existence of the heresy was not entirely dead.

Given the absence of American Catholic historical writings on later Catholic history until very recent years, and the tendency to underestimate religious factors in the history of the United

[6] III, 164-93, Brugerette shows no real connection between Americanism and Modernism.

[7] The passage on Americanism on page 872 is very superficial and offers no proof of any real understanding by the author of the Americanist controversy. Strangely this has been the chief source for the later writings indicating that Americanism was a practical preface of modernism. The author called Americanism "une sorte de préface, pratique et d'épisode avant la lettre." M. de la Taille in his study of Modernism in *Les Études* (1907) CXIII, 649 gives one sentence to Americanism calling it a preface to modernism, but without proof.

[8] Emanuel Cardinal Suhard, *Growth or Decline? The Church today*, translated by James A. Corbett, (South Bend, 1948) p. 47.

States, it is not surprising that most American historians show no real consciousness of the controversy. The present writer in his investigations of the history of the Catholic minority in the United States during the 1930's felt quite free to study the controversy independently of the strong feelings of the previous generation. The question in his mind was whether the real Americanism actually existed and whether it was really anything peculiarly American. Taking for granted that there must be some reality behind the controversy he used the term frontier to cover those changes in European civilization which had been effected in the new and rich land this side of the Atlantic, and attempted to find in that term or those forces an explanation for the changes in Roman Catholicism once it had become established in the new world, without fully defining what those changes were. These changes he thought were the material out of which European notions of Americanism had been formed. Thus, he distinguished three Americanisms.[9] The first is that political Americanism which is a byword in the United States for patriotism and devotion to the political and social ideals of this country under the Constitution, and which the Pope expressly exempted from his condemnation. The second was the Americanistic heresy as condemned by the papal letter, and the third was the American Catholicism in fact, which was the source of those doctrines condemned in the papal letter. A more complete investigation of the controversy with all the evidence that has as yet come to light has not essentially changed this preliminary notion, although it has modified his concepts of each of these tendencies.

In the first place it is quite clear that not all the participants in the controversy exempted from condemnation with Pope Leo those political customs and social traditions which are ordinarily accepted as Americanism. The question of Americanism was proposed in France and in western Europe generally as a democratic form of government in which there was wide social reform. The conservatives in politics and in the Church had no great affection for the democratic form of government, which was in their minds

[9] Thomas T. McAvoy, C.S.C., "Americanism and Frontier Catholicism," *Review of Politics*, V (July, 1943), 275-301.

associated sometimes with the excesses of the French Revolution and sometimes with the anti-Christian policies of the French Republic and with the extreme socialism advocated by the radical reformers in western Europe. Further, most of these conservative writers did not accept the United States as a nation. In the words of Abbé Maignen as a nation the United States was not yet born but was just a conglomeration of peoples of other nationalities, occupying a new country and not yet formed into a nation and possessing none of the characteristics of a European "fatherland." Some even thought that with the continuing immigration there would never be a nation in the new country.

Likewise in this country, this same lack of respect for the traditions of the new country was shown by many of the immigrants from Europe and from French Canada who were attached to their own language and looked back on the national traditions of their former countries with a kind of worship that was not easily transferred to the crudities and bustle of the United States. For the immigrants from Catholic communities of the Rhineland, or French Canada, Americanism also meant Protestantism, easy divorce, and the ignorance and materialism that seemed such a prominent feature of the country enjoying such remarkable material resources. The immigrants and their pastors felt that their children would lose their respect for them, for their traditional culture, and for their religion if they made a too hasty transition into American life. The Irish had felt the same way when they faced the antagonistic Yankee in the first part of the nineteenth century,[10] although there was no difference of language between the Irish and the Yankee. Regarding American Catholicism the later non-Irish immigrants not only had no great respect for the materialistic Yankee but they had less for the Irish whom they regarded as without culture or tradition and as not any more American than themselves. As the writer of one of these pamphlets[11] summed up the dominance of Irish or Irish descendents in the American Cath-

---

[10] Thomas T. McAvoy, C.S.C., "The Formation of the Catholic Minority in the United States, 1820-1860," *Review of Politics*, X (January, 1948), 13-34 and "The Catholic Minority in the United States 1789-1821," *Historical Records and Studies of the U.S. Catholic Historical Society*, XXXIX-XLX (1952), 33-50.

[11] *L'Américanisme jugé par un Prêtre Américain* (Lagny, 1900) p. 12.

olic hierarchy, the American Church was the only noted Catholic national church in which the hierarchy was not of the nation. The resentment towards Irish members of the hierarchy has remained in some slight measure where the recent immigration had congregated in large numbers and where the chief pastorates and curial offices are held by Irish clergy. For the most part under the recent Roman appointment of bishops where less attention has been paid to ancestral origins and more to fitness for the local problems, there has been less and less feeling that the American hierarchy is Irish and the hierarchy and their clergy throughout the country have ceased to think of themselves as apart from the American civilization. No American Catholic feels any longer that there is a problem about being a good American and being a good Catholic. American Catholics enter into most of the political and social controversies of the nation to defend their own peculiar economic and social status with the feeling that anything that is good American can be Catholic. Recent European Catholic immigrants and visitors are not so sure that the American way can be Catholic.

On the question of the Americanism condemned by Pope Leo XIII in the *Testem Benevolentiae* there can be little controversy. In the letters of submission of the Paulists, of Abbé Klein, of Archbishops Ireland and Keane and of Cardinal Gibbons not one word is said that would imply that they felt any inclination to defend the propositions reprobated by the Holy Father. In this connection it is important to bear in mind that the Holy Father did not say in the letter that anyone held the doctrines he mentioned.[12] As a matter of fact, he said simply that these doctrines have arisen in

[12] Joseph Clifford Fenton "The Teaching of the *Testem Benevolentiae*," *American Ecclesiastical Review*, CXXIX (August, 1953), 124-33, objects to the author's saying that the Holy Father condemned the teachings of the Americanists as heretical because the Holy Father did not use the designation of heresy, but the author was using the term as it was applied to the Apostolic letter at that time. Dr. Fenton objects to the use of the words "phantom heresy" without showing that the letter of the Holy Father in any way said that anyone held the doctrines he disapproved. The author does not think it is any less disrespectful to use the Pope's statements beyond their actual meaning to condemn another than it is to limit their meaning to their actual statement to escape condemnation. The author's attention has also been called to the condemnation of Nestorianism. The claim that Nestorius did not hold the condemned heresy does not imply any disrespect towards the ecclesiastics who condemned Nestorianism.

connection with the publication of the translation of the *Life of Father Hecker* and that if by Americanism these doctrines were to be understood he was sure that the American hierarchy would be the first to repudiate it. Neither do the Americanists deny the statement of the Holy Father that the doctrines have arisen as a result of the French translation of the *Life of Father Hecker*. But they do say in their private correspondence and in some of their public statements that these doctrines which have acquired the name of Americanism are caricatures of the real American Catholicism and of the real ideas of Father Hecker. On this point the statement of Americanism as found in the Fribourg speech of Monsignor Denis O'Connell and in the speeches of Archbishop Ireland is chiefly a political and social approach to religion which these prelates were hoping to see adopted generally throughout European Catholicism. Ireland had proclaimed them in Paris several years before the publication of the translation of the *Life* of Hecker in France. Even after the publication O'Connell had indicated that Americanism was political and that even in that sphere it was a practical solution which did not fulfill the absolute thesis about the relations between Church and State. The particular error of the Americanists—which in the mind of their opponents attached to them the errors of theological Americanism—was their tacit acceptance of the adapted and translated *Life* of Father Hecker, and the campaign in the French press which portrayed Hecker as a saint and a reformer, exaggerating his ascetical principles and apologetical practices. When the attacks of Maignen and Périès appeared, these Americanists could think of no answer except to prepare a new version of the life of Father Hecker, which would repudiate these exaggerations, but they never did accomplish this act of defense. The Americanists had chosen to side with the whirlwind of a press campaign organized by Count de Chabrol, Klein and their friends to sell the book. When the counter-campaign organized by Périès and Maignen came back upon them they were without a defense. Both campaigns were exaggerated. Hecker was not known as the apostle of American Catholicism in the United States, and his life had hardly been known by the majority of American Catholics. Likewise the exaggerated doctrines attributed to Hecker and the Americanists by the writers of *La Vérité* not only went beyond the statements of Hecker, Keane and Ireland but were filled out with the statements of the unknown "Romanus" in the *Contemporary Review* who definitely was not an American or an Americanist.

The question then arises as to whether the Pope condemned an imaginary heresy. That of course depends on what is implied by the imaginary or phantom heresy. The Pope himself allowed this charge by not asserting that anyone held the doctrines which he thought worthy of reprobation. He says that if they were held they were to be condemned. Whether or not he really believed anyone actually held the reprobated doctrines can be proved only if or when his papers and those of Cardinal Rampolla are made available. It is possible that even then no solution will be found, because their discussions may have been oral. Certainly the Pope must have felt that there was a danger that these false doctrines would be advocated or he would not have condemned them. Even if he felt that they were not really in existence among the Americanists his action would be justifiable for the purpose of stopping a controversy which had gotten out of hand, and that purpose is definitely expressed in the letter. In that sense the heresy was not a phantom heresy and there is no reflection on the Apostolic action in saying that the Americanists actually did not hold the doctrines. In this it must be borne in mind that none of the Americanists defended the condemned doctrines, and that Cardinal Rampolla wrote to Gibbons, after sending the letter, that he felt that Gibbons would find the letter acceptable. The only reasonable explanation of that letter of Rampolla is that he felt that the Apostolic letter would clear the air of false doctrines and enable the Americanists to pursue more intelligently their advocacy of the real Americanism. This of course was the interpretation of the actual letter by the *Abbés Démocrates* and of Ireland himself in his interviews with reporters.

Against such an interpretation, the Wisconsin bishops, Archbishop Corrigan and Bishop McQuaid in this country, and the *La Vérité* writers in France, insisted that the denial of Ireland and the action of the Catholic papers in his support were based upon a

Jansenistic mental reservation. For the most part the statements of Ireland and Gibbons—that they knew no intelligent Catholic, instructed in his religion, who held the condemned doctrines— must be accepted at face value. Nevertheless, the expressed statement of Archbishop Ireland against religious priests and Hecker's explanation for not giving vows to his community, as well as the slighting remarks of Ireland and the Americanists about pilgrimages and some penitential practices, and their opposition to the condemnation of certain secret societies, could be interpreted as implying a kind of asceticism and apologetics much like that condemned in the letter. Ireland undoubtedly would explain his attitude towards religious priests by his difficulties with the Jesuits; Hecker had the right of any founder to defend the special rules of his community; and any pastor has a right to try to get an exemption from action by a superior which he regards as harmful to the welfare of his flock. Whether these explanations fully justify their statements that they never held any of the condemned doctrines was and can be a matter of controversy. Nevertheless the second type of Americanism—that described by the Holy Father, can be distinguished from the first and from the American Catholicism in the United States.

There was an American Catholicism, whether it was that described by Abbé Klein in his article in the *Revue Française d'Edimbourg*, by Delattre in his book, or by Monsignor Denis O'Connell, or by any other writer during the controversy. That American Catholicism has been always essentially the same as any European, Asiatic, or African Catholicism, but at the same time it has almost always had some qualities brought about by circumstances of time and place which make it American. Even in colonial America under the Calverts one might find some peculiarities of American Catholicism in the controversy between Lord Calvert and the Jesuits. Again in the controversy over the choice of the first bishop, John Carroll, the peculiar position of the Catholic minority in the English colonies tended to dictate special customs and practices. Likewise the privileges of nomination accorded to America in the appointment of bishops during the nineteenth century was a recognition of a peculiar problem. The ultimate decision eliminating lay power over church property—in the controversy over trusteeism—while not perhaps unique, represents a solution of a problem special to the United States. In most of these particular trends in American Catholicism the dominant tone was supplied by the English Catholic minority in the New World and was in many respects similar to the privileges and peculiarities of the Catholic minority in England. But during the course of the nineteenth century American Catholicism became quite different from Catholicism in England. The very nature of the new country made that inevitable. Likewise the social classification of the Catholics in the New World was quite different from the Catholic remnant in England. The American Catholic immigrants were for the most part disinherited peasants, or small farmers. Only in some of the earlier Catholic families and in a few immigrants who "struck it rich" was there any upper class—but still bourgeois—members. Among these poorer immigrants who soon overwhelmed the existing cultural and social institutions of the Catholic minority the chief were the Irish, who came in floods of tens of thousands during the years of famine in Ireland. Almost at the same time there were thousands of German immigrants who settled for the most part in the Middle West or around the Great Lakes. They were slightly better off than the famishing Irish, but they were really peasants and farmers who sought good farmland and peace and did not at first affect the dominant English traditions, but kept their own familiar traditions and language. The great need of this suddenly multiplied Catholic population in increasing importance was the multiplication of bishops, priests, religious, hospitals, orphanages, schools, colleges. Some priests came with them and aided in the establishment of seminaries for training others, but there were never really enough priests for the scattered Catholic population that extended from ocean to ocean. Rome multiplied dioceses and bishops whenever the existing hierarchy asked for the subdivision. The bishops went to Europe begging for priests, for religious communities, and for funds. They could scarcely meet their needs either in supplying sacramental administration or instruction in the elements of the Faith. But their flocks were poor and frequently ignorant, and the burdens of poverty, sickness, and ignorance were as much the problems of the American bishops and priests as the administration of the sacraments or the preaching of the gospel.

The result of this situation was that while the number of Catholics in the United States grew and the number of priests, churches, missions and even elementary schools was multiplied, there could be no corresponding cultural growth and certainly no large growth of cultural institutions. In the United States of the earlier decades of the nineteenth century this was not so noticeable because the country generally devoted itself chiefly to the conquering of the almost untouched natural resources, carving out farms, building canals, and later railroads, to carry the exchange between the older settlements of the east and the newer settlements of the west. But the proportion of wealthy among the older majority was far greater than among these newly arrived immigrants. Furthermore, the majority being Protestant and mostly English speaking were part also of the established tradition and easily fitted into the cultural tradition of Protestant-English America. From the old centers of American education in New England and the Middle Atlantic states the new colleges and Protestant seminaries of the Middle West carried on the education of the dominant majority. There were indeed converts to Catholicism from this educated majority and there were heroic French and German missionaries from Europe who came to devote themselves to the establishment of seminaries and colleges here and there among the Catholics, but the bishops of the Second and Third Plenary Councils were well aware that if the Catholics were to retain what they had and make any headway in the United States, there must be established a system of Catholic schools and colleges and universities. But in communities in which the political leaders, the educated professional people, the school teachers, and the chief landowners or merchants were Protestants and educated in a Protestant tradition, the problem of maintaining Catholicism in its European Catholic tradition was very hard. Coupled with this handicap was the fact that in this new country the Catholic people who were settling the land were not the best educated, or the richest; they were freed peasants and other émigrés who were enjoying the advantages of material and intellectual freedom for the first time. Americans were not looked upon as cultural equals of the educated peoples of Europe by the Europeans, although after Emerson the Americans had begun to claim a cultural maturity, but the situation of the Catholic minority was regarded as even lower than the general American cultural level, partly because they were not of the dominant cultural tradition and partly because so many of them were of lower social and economic strata.

Taken together, these factors in the New World which crowded in upon the rapidly growing American Catholic group did have some effect, although no one has yet pointed to any essential difference between European and American Catholicism. Certainly these peasants and workers were enjoying for the first time economic independence. Popular elementary education was a great boon and one that Archbishop Ireland, Father Hecker, and the other Americanists were to credit to democracy. But in trying to generalize their new situation Father Isaac Hecker and Archbishop John Ireland, and the French observers such as Vicomte De Meaux, Brunetière and Klein did tend to overlook the defects which were bound to accompany this rapid expansion and hasty promotion to positions of some wealth and independence. These Catholic Americans, with the exceptions of those who lived in compact communities—especially the Germans, and French Canadians at that time—were outside the traditional atmosphere of a Catholic country. They lived, worked, and associated with non-Catholics, some of whom were antagonistic but the majority of whom were simply ignorant of the origins of their Protestant faith and just different from Catholics. To the newly arrived foreign groups within the country, and to the unfriendly European observer, the compromises that these American Catholics were willing to make in order to obtain harmony were wrong. The willingness to compromise on the school in order to get some Catholic instruction to the whole Catholic group, the unwillingness to express a condemnation of the social organizations in which American rural communities found their social pleasures in the later decades of the nineteenth century, the close participation of the American worker in labor organizations which did not take their instruction from the parish priest—all these things were called minimizing by the foreign critics and, when coupled with domestic notions of government and programs of social reform, were condemned as the false liberalism of early nineteenth century France by some more conservative priests and bishops. Some of these American tendencies had been dramatized by the Parliament of Religions in Chicago, in the Faribault–Stillwater School controversy, in the friendly actions of Archbishop Kain in welcoming the Salvation Army in Saint Louis, in Bishop Scanlan's participation in a public ceremony with Mormons, in Bishop Keane's appearance in the Harvard College Chapel. This special quality of American Catholicism is not the kind of Catholicism expressed in the reproved doctrines of the *Testem Benevolentiae*. Taken together and considered apart from the circumstances they could be said to constitute tendencies which the critics of American Catholicism had generalized into the condemned Americanism. In that sense also it can be said that the Pope and the European critics of American Catholicism were not talking about phantom heresies, or imaginary doctrines and practices. But certain elements in this picture must be distinguished. In the first place the critics both in Europe and America were for the most part harsh critics of modern democracy, who were too ready perhaps to attribute to democracy the errors of the French Revolution and of many radical departures towards democracy in the nineteenth century. They were people who felt that there must be classes and that for inferior people to rise and to claim equality could result only in anarchy. They regarded any form of social reform as against the existing order. Further they were unable to understand the situation in the New World in which the Church could use for its glory this new environment, these new situations, just as she had used the environment of the old regime and of the old national fatherlands. Abbé Maignen was quite bitter in his criticism of Bishop Keane's suggestion that in the United States these old national lines would be overcome and forgotten. Nor were the Latin writers willing to accept a notion of Anglo-Saxon superiority which was written into the political action of the late nineteenth century—and one might add a fur-

ther opposition to Irish ecclesiastical dominance within that Anglo-Saxon dominance. American Catholicism was, then, to these
observers something different from old European Catholicism,
and some errors, which were the product of new surroundings
and perhaps ignorance, were magnified because of a prejudice in
favor of the old order of the European fatherlands.

We have thus entered unwittingly into trying to define what
it was that the American critics of the Americanists and their
European counterparts were talking about. What then were the
characteristics of American Catholicism? Abbé Bricout indicated
at least two rather important qualities of American Catholicism:
love of science[13] and love of democracy. These he said were not
new but they were not the badge of European Catholicism of the
nineteenth century. But he more particularly pointed out that the
characteristics of American Catholicism were expressed in the
title of two important documents of American Catholicism which
were published as a kind of preface and introduction to the controversy—Father Isaac Hecker's *Church and the Age* and Archbishop Ireland's sermon at the jubilee of Cardinal Gibbons on
"The Church and the Age." American Catholicism can hardly be
said to have taken the lead in scientific discoveries, although the
activities of Father John A. Zahm and the work of the Catholic
summer schools were along that line. Perhaps, a better sign of the
attempt on the part of American Catholicism to enter into the
spirit of the times was its advocacy of the beginnings of social reform. Dr. Aaron Abell had pointed out that the bishops in the
Knights of Labor and the Henry George cases were not acti-
vated so much by love of social justice[14] as by the desire to keep
the flock within the Church—yet the elements of social justice
are found in the activities of Gibbons, Ireland and Keane, and
they were in the vanguard in the advocacy of what is now called
social justice in twentieth century social problems. To the efforts
of these three might be added the efforts of Bishop John Lancaster Spalding to solve the threat of socialism, although his theo-

[13] J. Bricout, "Américanisme" in *Revue du Clergé Français*, XV (June-July-
August, 1898) 416-35.
[14] Aaron Abell, "Origin of Catholic Social Reform in the United States:
Ideological Aspects," *Review of Politics*, XI, 294-309, especially p. 309.

logical utterances were not so clearly orthodox as those of Ireland, Gibbons and Keane. On the question of democracy the stand of all these bishops was without equivocation, and while they may have been a bit hasty in their efforts to Americanize the newly arrived immigrant, they felt that they were asking these immigrants to give up nothing Catholic in making the transition. But were there any theological or ascetical doctrines involved in these changes? Had there been an American theological school in which American problems were being solved, this question might be anwered. Hecker was not a theologian, nor was Gibbons, Ireland or Keane. But since they were speaking of religious matters and of the advancement of the Church, they felt that the Church would develop to meet these new situations just as the Church had developed institutions to meet older situations. It was the implications, not the statements, of these arguments that were attacked by the anti-Americanists.

The followers of Hecker felt that Hecker had been misinterpreted, and felt also that Hecker would have found the principles of the *Testem Benevolentiae* easy to accept. Ireland knew that some of his statements were under attack but he felt that he too had not held the doctrines drawn from the *Life* of Hecker by the anti-Americanists. Strangely—probably because of this condemnation—there has never developed a really strong American Catholic theological tradition in which the applications of Catholic dogmas to American problems have been made. Of course in this result, the effect of the condemnation of modernism in the next decade must also be reckoned with. But the absence of an American theological school has added to the tradition in Europe of a practical American Catholicism which is activist, and a bit crude, even when the majority of American Catholic theologians are trained in Europe. The recent American publications in theology and canon law probably will soon change this opinion.

The recognition that the condemnation of modernism has complicated any evaluation of the results of the condemnation of Americanism also calls attention to the fact that dogmatic historians have tended of late to classify the Americanist controversy as a "practical preface" to the heresy of modernism. In the first place the sequence in time lends a certain justification for this evaluation of the description. More important in such an interpretation is the fact that some of the more prominent modernists of the times were friends of the Americanists. Loisy was a friend of Klein and a correspondent of O'Connell, Kraus was a correspondent of O'Connell and Ireland and had gone to their defense with Schell in the attack of Schroeder. Henri Berenger, the leader of the néo-chrétien school had also shown some sympathy, as did the apostate Charbonnel. Bishop John Lancaster Spalding, who was not really an Americanist although a defender of American traditions, was quite immanentist in his writings, although himself not a theologian. But it is important here to note that none of these modernist friends felt that the condemnation of Americanism was a condemnation of their ideas, but just a signal of the reactionary trends in the Church which they knew would eventually reach them. Certainly the Americanist movement in France with the glorification of democracy, social reform, and a new life for the clergy was part of the movement which was endeavoring to return religion to the life of France and to create a Christian intellectual and social movement. But the heresy of modernism was neither a social nor a political movement, whereas Americanism as it was advocated by Ireland, Keane, O'Connell and Klein was an effort to promote a close alliance between the spirit of the new democracy and the Church. Had Klein, Ireland, Keane, or the Paulists in any way admitted that they held any of the condemned doctrines then there would have been a just basis for the charges of the anti-Americanists. In the three chief points where the papal letter did really touch the participants in the controversy—the opposition to religious orders, the active virtues, and the personal direction of the Holy Spirit, as well as in the friendliness to those outside the Church—there is no necessary heresy. It is important to note that Loisy did not claim that Ireland was at all sympathetic to his own doctrines, and that O'Connell while urging Ireland to cultivate Schell and Kraus did at the same time warn Ireland not to align himself too closely to these men because he had doubts about their orthodoxy. O'Connell wanted merely to use these men to show that the opposition of Schroeder was not on nationalistic grounds but on questions of progressiveness.

Only in the Parliament of Religions and in the arguments about an evolution of religions could there be any charge that would make Americanism a precursor or preface to modernism. But even in this it is worth noting that Maignen found it necessary to use the arguments of the mysterious "Romanus" of *The Contemporary Review* to make the statements of Keane at the Brussels Congress or the writings of Hecker imply any real change. Throughout all the arguments of Ireland and Hecker was the notion that in essentials the Church had not changed and would not change. The adaptation of the externals of the Church to new surroundings was very far from the evolutionism of the modernists. Neither can there be proved any connection between the devotion to the Holy Ghost which Hecker had derived from Lallemant and Scheeben and the immanentism of the modernists. On the question of the Scriptures and the higher criticism there were really no special notions among the Americanists. Likewise in their attitude towards science the Americanists were really anxious to show that nothing in science could contradict religion; the evolutionism of Zahm was not the creative evolution of the modernists. Finally, there is the major question of the doing away with the barriers and the customs houses of the Church which played such an important part in the writings of Ireland and Hecker. For the European this might imply a rejection of some dogmas but for the Americans it meant choosing the points of contact between themselves and their non-believing neighbors. The optimism of the Americanists may not have been justified but at no time in their writings was there any suggestion that the non-Catholic would be converted to anything but traditional Catholicism.

It can be maintained that the Holy Father and the Cardinals who formulated the condemnation of the Americanists' doctrines did have in mind the growing liberal theological tendency in western Europe and thought that through the condemnation of Americanism they were checking the tendency towards what was later called modernism. The doctrines condemned considered in the abstract and out of the context of the writings of Hecker, Ireland, Keane, and Klein could be understood as part of a trend that was definitely evident in the critical writers of the day on scriptures and philosophy in France. It is evident that Loisy and Kraus did definitely so understand the action of the Roman court, but the implication that Americanism was part of the modernistic movement, if understood in the sense that there was any essential or integral connection between the two movements, is not justified by the facts. Houtin probably can be credited with the creation of this idea, but no one has denied that Houtin was an interested observer who wanted to make all those condemned by Rome to be part of the progressive movement of which he was in many ways a member. But Houtin, despite his fulsome documentation on the actual events of the controversy, does not show any connection between the apostasies of Charbonnel and the other French Modernists and the Americanist movement.

The final question to be answered concerns the results of the controversy and the condemnation. In Europe it is apparent that the Americanist movement was killed by the papal letter. Ireland came storming across France with his usual gusto but he no longer talked about the advantages of training the French clergy after the American model. Neither did he advocate any further the cooperation with the French government. It is true that before he left Europe he had exposed his charges that the attack on Americanism had been inspired and engineered by Périès, and had insisted that he had not been touched by the papal reprobation. Keane likewise was soon to have fulfilled his ardent desire to leave Rome. Even O'Connell through his renewed friendship with Cardinal Satolli obtained a return to the United States as rector of the Catholic University. The student of French religious history soon lost sight of the incidents of the controversy as having no real bearing on the internal religious crisis of France brought on by the Dreyfus affair and the breaking of the concordat. If the condemnation had any permanent effect it strengthened the general European Catholic notion of superiority to the peasant and lower class Catholicism of the United States. In contrast to the tradition created by Gibbons in the United States that the American hierarchy was the friend of the laboring man and greatly democratic, the French hierarchy and clergy generally retained the tradition of being very conservative for another generation, particularly in social and political matters. Any possible understanding and cooperation between the Catholics of Europe and the United States was checked; even the cooperation of French and American clergy during the First World War did little to create an exchange of useful ideas between the clergy and lay groups of France, Germany, and the United States.

In this country, the suppression of open conflict did not end the bruised feelings and attitudes of hostility between the groups that had carried on the American phases of the controversy. After the condemnation there was a persistent attempt on the part of the conservatives and some Germans to make out that the Americanists had really been guilty of teaching the reprobated doctrines. Had there been no papal action, and if there had been no real charge of heresy, the issue might have been openly discussed and solved. Instead, there came a great silence in public discussion which was deepened by the condemnation of modernism.

The history of the modernist controversy in this country has not been written and the destruction of pertinent records will make such a study very difficult. Certainly the conflict between the foreign professors and the Americans—if one includes Shahan and other Irish among the Americans—had a paralyzing effect on the growth of the Catholic University, which was heightened by the inept financing of the succeeding administrations. One other sad effect of the controversy was a continuation of the nationalistic differences between the Irish and nativists and the Germans and later non-English immigrants. This was manifest in antagonisms which persisted until the inevitable Americanization—and the lack of interest in an Ireland that had been freed and in a Germany that had turned against the United States in war—destroyed the popular appeal of the aroused groups.

To look for any change in the religious life of the American people as a result of the condemnation is a waste of time because

at no time did the American Catholic body have any definite notions of American Catholicism. The quality which Ireland, Gibbons and the French Democrats had admired in the American
Catholic body was a spirit of freedom that arose from the freedom
of Americans and had little to do with religious concepts. When
the European Catholic immigrant enjoyed the freedom from governmental persuasion in religious matters, he may have given up
the Faith that he did not really have, but for the millions who did
not give up their Faith but who saw in the freedom of the United
States a chance to live their Faith to the fullest, American Catholicism became something distinct. It was practical, and this prac-
ticality became sacramental after the revival of frequent Communion. It was not dogmatic or even too liturgical because these
freed peasants did not have the education or the means to aspire
to the finer things. As before the *Testem Benevolentiae* they took
their dogmas and moral code on the authority of their pastors and
particularly from the infallible Pope and did not quarrel with
their teachers. They continued to associate with their non-Catholic neighbors in all the things that were not essentially religious
—in labor unions, in chambers of commerce, in business firms, and
in sports. One element that seemed so noticeable in the writing
and speeches of Archbishop Ireland did more or less fade from the
scene—the hope that America would become Catholic. In place
of that hope of mass conversions the American Catholic assured
himself that his rights to practice his religion were secure under
the law and that as he progressed in the social and economic
world, he would be better received and accepted by his non-
believing neighbors. The American Catholics remained proud of
the close association between Catholics and the leaders of the
government, and were quick to go into the armed services in
time of war. Likewise the bishops, as Gibbons declined in age,
turned each one to his own diocese and concentrated on that
practical Catholicism which is the badge of American Catholics
generally—on the establishment of parochial schools, seminaries,
a local Catholic press, and local and diocesan church organizations.

To have hoped that the conservative and more traditional—as

some might say sacristarian—Catholicism of western Europe would accept the practical, rough, and democratic notions of American Catholicism in the closing decades of the nineteenth century, probably was too much. It was unfortunate that there was not a better exchange of ideas between these two Catholic peoples. Only after fifty years, despite the continuing agreement on essentials, have European Catholics been urging the social and practical reforms which Americans have always found rather easy. And American Catholicism is growing in theological awareness, in liturgical splendor, and in the appreciation of the high cultural inheritance of the older Catholic communities of western Europe. The exchange has only begun even in this day. May this study of past failures do away with a few obstacles which had little to do with the essentials of religion and promote a union of western Christendom in the present battle against the great atheistic heresy of the age.

Crisis within the Church

As America entered the twentieth century, a difficult question confronted the rapidly-growing Catholic Church: To what degree, if any, should religious practices be adapted to the American milieu?

The Catholic hierarchy of the United States in these years was sharply divided between conservatives and "Americanists." The former group believed that republican governments were, per se, opposed to religion. The "Americanists," on the other hand, not only saw democracy as the best possible government for a pluralistic society such as obtained in this nation, but were convinced that a pragmatic approach to cultural problems was an absolute necessity.

The controversy and its resolution, as here unfolded by Reverend Thomas T. McAvoy, C.S.C., provide rich material for a fascinating and hitherto little-studied piece of history. Father McAvoy, formerly Head of the Department of History at the University of Notre Dame, now functions as University Archivist while continuing on the History faculty.